Microsoft® C

Advanced Programming Techniques

FOR MS® OS/2 AND MS-DOS®
OPERATING SYSTEMS

MICROSOFT CORPORATION

Document No. LN06514-1189 OEMO711-6Z
10 9 8 7 6 5 4 3

Contents

PART 1   *Improving Program Performance*

Chapter 2   Managing Memory 31

PART 2   *Improving Programmer Productivity*

Chapter 5   Compiling and Linking Quickly   97

Chapter 6   Managing Development Projects with NMAKE 103

PART 3 Special Environments

Chapter 11 Creating Charts and Graphs 245

Chapter 12 Programming with Mixed Languages 275

PART 4   OS/2 Support

Chapter 14   Building OS/2 Applications 347

Chapter 15   Creating Multithread OS/2 Applications 367

Appendixes

Introduction

Advanced Programming Techniques describes how to get the most out of the Microsoft® C Professional Development System with its new integrated development environment—the Microsoft Programmer's WorkBench—and source-level debugging tool—the CodeView® debugger.

In this manual, you will see how all the components of the Microsoft C Professional Development System work together to provide you with the most powerful development environment available. A key element in the power of the Professional Development System is your ability to customize it to suit your individual needs as a programmer.

Because this book is arranged by topic, it answers questions about using Microsoft C version 6.0, rather than providing lists of options. If you have specific questions about menu items in the CodeView debugger, the Programmer's WorkBench, or any of the command-line utilities included in the Professional Development System, you can use the Microsoft C Advisor (on-line help) or the *C Reference* manual.

Advanced Programming Techniques shows you how tools and utilities all fit together.

Scope of This Book

Advanced Programming Techniques is divided into four parts. Part 1, "Improving Program Performance," helps you write more efficient programs. It provides specific information about optimizing—when and why to use various optimizing options. It also explains new memory management options and when to use them. For example, Chapter 3 describes the in-line assembler, a new feature that lets you mix assembly language with your C source code.

Part 2, "Improving Programmer Productivity," will help you perform programming tasks more quickly and efficiently. Chapter 8 explains the different ways you can customize the new Programmer's WorkBench (PWB)—an editor and integrated development environment that allows you to

- Create new programs

- Modify existing programs

- Browse source files

- Obtain help about PWB, the C language, and the C run-time libraries

- Set program build lists

- Build programs

- Debug programs with the CodeView debugger

Chapter 8 also describes how to change PWB behavior to suit your programming style by making keyboard assignments, recording or writing macros, and writing C extensions.

Also in Part 2 is a chapter about the Microsoft Program Maintenance Utility, NMAKE. NMAKE is a new program maintenance facility that allows you to use program lists as input, which provides extra flexibility in your program build process. It is a superset of the Microsoft XENIX® MAKE utility and is substantially more powerful than previous versions of MAKE.

Chapter 9 in Part 2 describes the CodeView debugger, which is even more powerful than in previous releases. With CodeView version 3.0, you get many new features, including the ability to record a debugging session, then play it back (history and dynamic replay).

Part 3, "Special Environments," describes new graphics capabilities. It also shows how to program in mixed languages and offers tips to make your programs more portable. Microsoft C helps you create graphics applications easily. The Microsoft C run-time libraries contain graphics functions for low-level graphics operations, such as drawing lines, rectangles, and circles. The libraries also contain functions for creating presentation graphics, such as pie charts and bar charts.

Part 4, "OS/2 Support," describes how the Professional Development System helps you build OS/2 applications. The three chapters in Part 4 provide information about dual-mode applications, creating multithread applications, and creating dynamic-link libraries.

A postage-paid documentation feedback card is at the end of this manual. After you have had a chance to become familiar with Microsoft C 6.0 and its documentation, please give us your opinion. Your ideas will help us as we develop future documentation. Also at the end of this book is a Product Assistance Request form. If you need to call Microsoft for assistance, use this form first to compile and organize pertinent information.

Document Conventions

NOTE *The pages that follow use the term "OS/2" to refer to the OS/2 systems—Microsoft Operating System/2 (MS® OS/2) and IBM® OS/2. Similarly, the term "DOS" refers to both the MS-DOS® and IBM Personal Computer DOS operating systems. The name of a specific operating system is used when it is necessary to note features that are unique to the system.*

Example	Description
STDIO.H	Uppercase letters indicate file names, segment names, registers, and terms used at the DOS- or OS/2-command level.
_cdecl	Boldface letters indicate C keywords, operators, language-specific characters, and library functions, as well as OS/2 functions. Within discussions of syntax, bold type indicates that the text must be entered exactly as shown.
expression	Words in italics indicate placeholders for information you must supply, such as a file name. Italics are also occasionally used for emphasis in the text.
[[*option*]]	Items inside double square brackets are optional.
#pragma pack {1|2}	Braces and a vertical bar indicate a choice among two or more items. You must choose one of these items unless double square brackets surround the braces.
`CL A.C B.C C.OBJ`	This font is used for examples, user input, program output, and error messages in text.
CL *options* [[*files...*]]	A horizontal ellipsis following an item indicates that more items having the same form may follow.

```
while( )
{
    .
    .
    .
}
```
A vertical ellipsis tells you that part of the example program has been intentionally omitted.

CTRL+ENTER

Small capital letters are used for the names of keys on the keyboard. When you see a plus sign (+) between two key names, you should hold down the first key while pressing the second.

The carriage-return key (sometimes appearing as a bent arrow on the keyboard) is called ENTER.

The cursor-movement keys (sometimes called direction keys) are called the ARROW keys. Individual keys are referred to by their direction (LEFT, UP) or by the name on the key (PGUP).

"argument"

Quotation marks enclose a new term the first time it is defined in text.

Enhanced Graphics Adapter (EGA)

The first time an acronym is used, it is often spelled out.

PART 1

Improving Program Performance

CHAPTERS

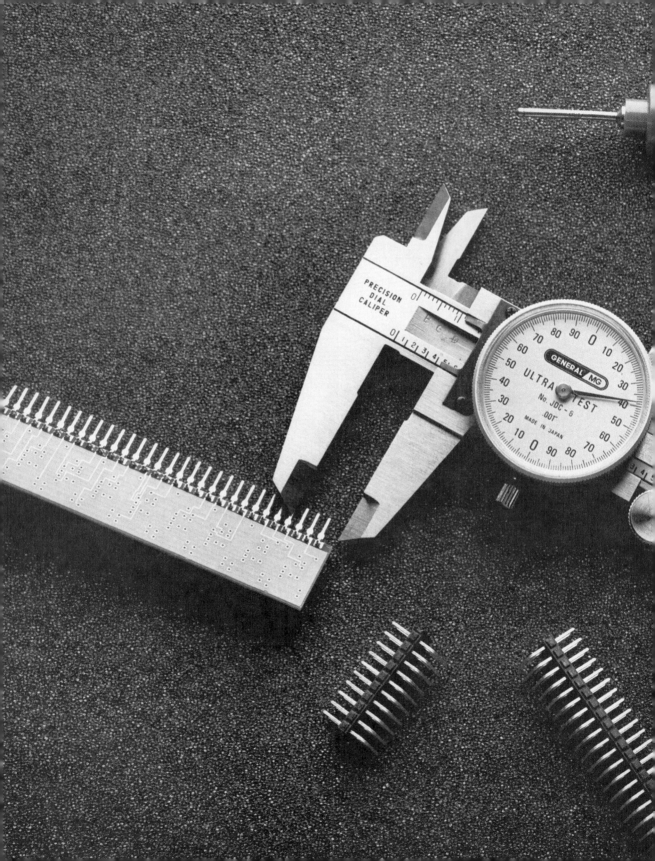

Improving Program Performance

The Microsoft C Professional Development System helps you create the fastest, smallest applications using its sophisticated optimizer and enhanced memory management capabilities.

Chapter 1 tells when to use certain optimizations and describes how Microsoft C generates code that is efficient in execution speed and size. Chapter 2 explains the sophisticated tools Microsoft C gives you to allocate and manage program memory, including the new **_based** type. For cases where your program requires localized optimization, you can use the in-line assembler, described in Chapter 3, to introduce the tightest possible code. If your application requires floating-point math computations, you will find Chapter 4 helpful in explaining the options in the Microsoft C math packages; it explains which floating-point options yield the fastest, smallest, and most flexible code.

Optimizing C Programs

The Microsoft C compiler translates C source statements into machine-executable instructions. In addition, the compiler rewrites or "optimizes" parts of your program to make it more efficient in ways that are not apparent at the source level.

The compiler performs three general types of optimization:

1. It modifies or moves sections of code so that fewer instructions are used, or so that the instructions used make more efficient use of the processor.

2. It moves code and combines operations to maximize use of registers because operations on data stored in processor registers are far faster than the same operations on data stored in memory.

3. It eliminates sections of code that are redundant or unused.

This chapter explains the various ways you can control how the Microsoft C compiler optimizes your code.

1.1 Controlling Optimization from the Programmer's WorkBench

The Programmer's WorkBench (PWB) is an integrated development environment for editing, building, and debugging applications written in Microsoft C. For more information on the PWB, see *Installing and Using the Microsoft C Professional Development System*.

There are two ways to compile from inside the Programmer's WorkBench:

1. Debug compile. In a default debug compile, the compiler performs no optimizations at all.

2. Release compile. In a default release compile, the compiler performs most optimizations.

By modifying the settings in C Global Build Options, C Debug Build Options, and C Release Build Options (on the Options menu), you can fine-tune optimization by individually enabling or disabling any of the optimizations the compiler performs.

The optimizations in each of the Build Options dialog boxes correspond to a command-line option to CL. (In fact, the PWB constructs a command line from your input and passes it to CL.)

NOTE   *In this chapter, optimization options are discussed in terms of the effect of the optimization, the command-line option to invoke the optimization, and pragmas that control the optimization. All of these optimizations can be controlled at the compilation-unit (file) level using the Build Options dialog boxes.*

1.2 Controlling Optimization from the Command Line

Controlling optimization from the command line requires that you determine which optimizations you need for your application. You then specify those optimizations using command-line options that begin with /O (and in some cases /G).

If there is any conflict between options, the compiler uses the last option specified on the command line. The command line

```
CL /Oa /Ol /Ot TEST.C
```

compiles the program TEST.C. It specifies that the compiler can

- Optimize on the assumption that you are doing no aliasing (/Oa)

- Perform loop optimization (/Ol)

- Perform other general speed-enhancing optimizations (/Ot)

The preceding command line can also be written

```
CL /Oalt TEST.C
```

1.3 Controlling Optimization with Pragmas

Occasionally you will need to exercise a fine level of control over compiler optimizations. Command-line options allow you to control optimization over an entire compilation unit (file). In addition, Microsoft C supports several pragmas that allow you to exercise such control on a per-function basis.

The pragmas that control optimization are described in this chapter under the type of optimization they affect.

The optimize pragma is new to version 6.0.
In version 6.0, you can control each of the following optimization parameters on a function-by-function basis using the **optimize** pragma:

- Behavior of code with respect to aliasing (**a** and **w**)

- Reduction of local common subexpressions (**c**)

- Reduction of global common subexpressions (**g**)

- Global register allocation (**e**)

- Loop optimization (**l**)

- Aggressiveness of optimizations (**z**)

- Disabling of unsafe optimizations (**n**)

- Achieving consistent floating-point results (**p**)

- Optimizing for smaller code size or for faster execution speed (**t**)

Any optimization or combination of options can be enabled or disabled using the **optimize** pragma. For example, if you have one function that uses aliases heavily, you need to inhibit optimizations that could cause problems with aliases. You do not, however, want to inhibit these optimizations for code that does not do aliasing. To do this, use the **optimize** pragma as follows:

```
/* Function(s) that do not do aliasing. */
   .
   .
   .
#pragma optimize( "a", off )
/* Function(s) that do aliasing. */
   .
   .
   .
#pragma optimize( "a", on )
/* More function(s) that do not do aliasing. */
```

The parameters to the **optimize** pragma can be combined in a string to enable or disable multiple options at once. For example,

```
#pragma optimize( "lge", off )
```

disables loop optimization, global common subexpression optimization, and global register allocation.

1.4 Default Optimization

Many optimizations are not explicitly disabled by any command-line option except /Od (disable optimizations). These optimizations are small in scope and are almost always helpful. They include

- Short range common subexpression elimination

- Dead-store elimination

- Constant propagation

1.4.1 Common Subexpression Elimination

In common subexpression elimination, the compiler finds code containing repeated subexpressions and produces modified code in which the subexpressions are evaluated only once. Subexpression elimination is usually done with temporary variables as shown in the following example:

```
a = b + c * d;
x = c * d / y;
```

The preceding two lines contain the common subexpression c * d. This code can be modified to evaluate c * d only once; the result is placed in a temporary variable (usually a register):

```
tmp = c * d;
a = b + tmp;
x = tmp / y;
```

1.4.2 Dead-Store Elimination

Dead-store elimination is an extension of common subexpression elimination. Variables that contain the same value in a short piece of code can be combined into a single temporary variable.

In the following code fragment, the compiler detects that the expression `func( x )` is equivalent to `func( a + b )`:

```
x = a + b;
x = func( x );
```

Thus, the compiler can rewrite the code as follows:

```
x = func( a + b );
```

1.4.3 Constant Propagation

When doing constant propagation, the compiler analyzes variable assignments and determines if they can be changed to constant assignments. In the following example, the variable `i` must have a value of `7` when it is assigned to `j`:

```
i = 7;
j = i;
```

Instead of assigning `i` to `j`, the constant `7` can be assigned to `j`:

```
i = 7;
j = 7;
```

While you could make any of these changes in the source file, doing so might reduce the readability of the program. In many cases, optimizations not only increase the efficiency of the program but allow you to write more readable code without any actual efficiency loss.

Remove optimization before using a symbolic debugger.

In some cases, you might want to disable even the default optimizations. Because optimizations may rearrange code in the object file, it can become difficult to recognize parts of your code during debugging. It is usually best to remove all optimization before using a symbolic debugger. You can remove all optimization with the /Od (disable optimizations) option.

You can disable all optimizations for a function by including the statement `#pragma optimize( "", off )`. To restore optimization to its former state, use the statement `#pragma optimize( "", on )`.

1.5 *Customizing Your Optimizations*

The default optimizations are sufficient for many applications, but you may want to tune your programs according to criteria not known to the compiler. The optimization options offer you a way of providing the compiler specific goals for optimizing your code.

1.5.1 *Choosing Speed or Size (/Ot and /Os)*

In addition to the default optimizations, the Microsoft C compiler also automatically uses the /Ot option, which optimizes for speed. The /Ot option enables optimizations that increase speed but may also increase size. If you would rather optimize for program size, use the /Os option. The /Os option enables optimizations that decrease program size but may also decrease program speed.

To optimize for speed or size on a per-function basis, use the **optimize** pragma with the **t** option. The on setting instructs the compiler to optimize for speed; the off setting instructs the compiler to optimize for compactness of code. For example,

```
#pragma optimize( "t", off )    /* Optimize for smallest
                                    code. */
    .
    .
    .
#pragma optimize( "t", on )     /* Optimize for fastest
                                    code. */
```

1.5.2 *Generating Intrinsic Functions (/Oi)*

In place of some normal function calls, the C compiler can insert "intrinsic functions," which operate more quickly. Every time a function is called, a set of instructions must be executed to store parameters and to create space for local variables. When the function returns, more code must be executed to release space used by local variables and parameters and to return values to the calling routine. These instructions take time to execute. In the context of an average-sized function, the additional code is minimal, but if the function is only a line or two, the additional code can comprise almost half of the function's compiled code.

One way to avoid this type of code expansion is to avoid such short functions, especially in often-used sections of code where speed is critical. But many library functions contain only a line or two of code. The compiler provides two forms of certain library functions. One form is a standard C function, which requires the overhead of a function call. The other form is a set of instructions that performs the same action as the function without issuing a function call. This second form is called an intrinsic function. Intrinsic functions are always faster than their function-call equivalents and can provide significant optimizations at the object-code level.

For example, the function **strcpy** might be written as follows:

```
int strcpy(char * dest, char * source)
{
    while( *dest++ = *source++ );
}
```

The compiler contains an intrinsic form of **strcpy**. If you instruct the compiler to generate intrinsic functions, any call to **strcpy** will be replaced with this intrinsic form.

NOTE   *While the example above is written in C for clarity, most of the library functions use assembly language to take full advantage of the 80x86 instruction set. Intrinsic functions are not simply library functions defined as macros.*

Compiling with the /Oi option causes the compiler to use the intrinsic forms of the following functions:

abs	labs	outp	strcpy
_disable	lrotl	outpw	strlen
_enable	lrotr	rotl	strset
fabs	memcmp	rotr	
inp	memcpy	strcat	
inpw	memset	strcmp	

While the following floating-point functions do not have true intrinsic forms, they do have versions that pass arguments directly to the floating-point chip instead of pushing them on the normal argument stack:

acos	fmod	acosl	fmodl
asin	log	asinl	logl
atan	log10	atanl	log10l
atan2	pow	atan2l	powl
ceil	sin	ceill	sinl
cos	sinh	cosl	sinhl
cosh	sqrt	coshl	sqrtl
exp	tan	expl	tanl
floor	tanh	floorl	tanhl

WARNING *The compiler performs optimizations assuming math intrinsics have no side effects. This assumption is true except if you have written your own **matherr** function and that function alters global variables. If you have written a **matherr** function to handle floating-point errors, and your function has side effects, use the **function** pragma to instruct the compiler not to generate intrinsic code for math functions.*

If you want the compiler to generate intrinsic functions for only a subset of the functions listed above, use the **intrinsic** pragma rather than the /Oi option. The **intrinsic** pragma has the following format:

#pragma intrinsic(*function1*, ... **)**

If you want to have intrinsic functions generated for most of the functions above and function calls for only a few, compile with the /Oi option and force function use with the **function** pragma. The **function** pragma has the following format:

#pragma function(*function1*, ... **)**

The following code illustrates the use of the **intrinsic** pragma:

```
#pragma intrinsic(abs)

void main( void )
{
    int i, j;

    i = big_routine_1();
    j = abs( i );
    big_routine_2( j );
}
```

Generating intrinsic functions for this program causes the call to **abs** to be replaced with assembly-language code that takes the absolute value of a number. The program will execute more quickly because the function-calling overhead is no longer required when **abs** is called.

In the previous example, the overall speed increase is small because there is only a single call to **abs**. In the following example, where the call to **abs** is in a loop and there are many calls, you can save a significant amount of execution time by generating intrinsic functions.

```
#pragma intrinsic( abs )
void main( void )
{
int i, j, x;
```

```
for( j = 0; j < 1000; j++ )
{
    for( i = 0; i < 1000; i++)
    {
        x += abs( i - j );
    }
}
printf( "The value of x is %d\n", x );
}
```

The following is a list of restrictions on using the intrinsic forms of function calls:

- Do not use the intrinsic forms of the floating-point math functions with the alternate math libraries (*m*LIBCA*y*.LIB).

- Do not use the intrinsic forms of the floating-point math functions in OS/2 dynamic-link libraries (DLLs) because you must use the alternate math library with LLIBCDLL.LIB.

- If you use the /Ox (maximum optimization) option, you are enabling the /Oi (generate intrinsic functions) option. Be careful that your use of /Ox does not conflict with the points listed previously.

NOTE *Intrinsic versions of* **_enable**, **_disable**, **inp**, **outp**, **inpw**, *and* **outpw** *do not work under OS/2. You must use the library versions. You can use the* **function** *pragma to force these functions to become library calls.*

1.5.3 Assuming No Aliasing (/Oa and /Ow)

An "alias" is a name used to refer to a memory location already referred to by a different name. Because a memory access takes more time than it takes to access the CPU's registers, the compiler tries to store frequently used variables in registers. However, the aliasing reduces the extent to which a compiler can keep variables in registers.

A pointer is a reference to a memory location. Because the value of a pointer is not determined until the program is run, the compiler has no way of knowing which memory location will be modified when the program executes; it could be a reference to a variable. Therefore, the compiler must assume that any time the value pointed to by any pointer changes, the value of any variable might also change. This limits the extent to which the compiler can move values from memory to registers.

The /Oa option tells the compiler to ignore the possibility of multiple aliases for a memory location. In the list that follows, the term "reference" means read or write; that is, whether a variable is on the left-hand side of an assignment statement or the right-hand side, you are still referring to it. In addition, any function calls that use a variable as a parameter are references to that variable. When you tell the compiler to assume that you are not doing aliasing, it expects that the following rules are being followed for any variable not declared as **volatile**:

■ If a variable is used directly, no pointers are used to reference that variable.

■ If a pointer is used to refer to a variable, that variable is not referred to directly.

■ If a pointer is used to modify a memory location, no other pointers are used to access the same memory location.

To clarify how these rules affect your code, consider the following example:

```
char    p;
char    *ptr_p;

ptr_p = &p;    /* Take the address of p. */
```

You can now refer either to `*ptr_p` or to `p`, but not to both within the same function. If you must refer to the variable by both names, you are using aliases.

Code referring to the same location with two pointers uses aliases. For example,

```
char    *p_buf;
char    *p_alias;

if( (p_alias = p_buf = malloc( 5000 )) == NULL )
    return;
else
{
    .
    .
    .
}
```

The code in the example above is common. It demonstrates dynamically allocating a block of memory from the heap, and preserving the original address in `p_buf`. The program then performs all pointer arithmetic on the alias `p_alias`. When the function finishes with the block of memory, `p_buf` is a valid argument for the **free** function because it still contains the original address.

The /Oa and /Ow options tell the compiler that you have not used aliases in your code.

The difference between the /Oa and the /Ow option is that when you use /Oa you specify that you will not be doing aliasing (which allows the compiler to perform significant optimizations that might not otherwise have been possible), and that function calls are safe. The /Ow option is similar to the /Oa option, except that after a function call, pointer variables must be reloaded from memory.

Here is an example of a program that would be a poor candidate for the /Oa or /Ow optimization option:

```
int g;

void main( void )
{
    add_em( &g );
}

int add_em( int *p )
{
    *p = 2;            /* Assign a value to an alias for g. */
    g = 3;             /* Assign a value directly to g. */
    return( *p + g );
}
```

In the function `add_em`, both `g` and `*p` refer to the same memory location. This location is first assigned `2`, then `3`. The value pointed to by `*p` (the alias for `g`) is then added to `g`, and the result is returned to the main program. If you do not use the /Oa command-line option, the compiler assumes that the reference to `*p` could refer to the same memory location as does `g` and makes no attempt to use a register to store the value of either. If, however, you do specify the /Oa option, the compiler assumes that `g` and `*p` refer to different memory locations and stores each in a different register. At the return statement, `g` will have a different value than `*p`, even though both aliases should actually contain the same value.

Note that the compiler keeps values in registers for only a limited time. If different aliases to a memory location occur in different functions, for example, they will not cause unexpected results. When in doubt, avoid aliasing.

Bugs involving aliasing are difficult to spot. Aliasing bugs most frequently show up as corruption of data. If you find that global or local variables are being assigned seemingly random values, take the following steps to determine if you have a problem with optimization and aliasing:

- Compile the program with /Od (disable optimizations).

- If the program works when compiled with the /Od option, check your normal compile options for the /Oa option (assume no aliasing).

- If you were using the /Oa option, fix your compile options so that /Oa is not specified.

NOTE *You can instruct the compiler to disable optimizations that are unsafe with code that does aliasing by using the* **optimize** *pragma with the* **a** *or* **w** *option.*

1.5.4 Performing Loop Optimizations (/Ol)

The /Ol option enables a set of optimizations involving loops. Because loops involve sections of code that are executed repeatedly, they are targets for optimization. These optimizations all involve moving code or rewriting code so that it executes faster.

Loop optimization can be turned on with the /Ol option or with the **loop_opt** pragma. The following line enables loop optimization for all subsequent functions:

```
#pragma loop_opt( on )
```

The following line turns it off:

```
#pragma loop_opt( off )
```

The /Ol option removes invariant code.

An optimal loop contains only expressions whose values change through each execution of the loop. Any subexpression whose value is constant should be evaluated before the body of the loop is executed. Unfortunately, these subexpressions are not always readily apparent. The optimizer can remove many of these expressions from the body of a loop at compile time. This example illustrates invariant code in a loop:

```
i = -100;
while( i < 0 )
{
    i += x + y;
}
```

In the preceding example, the expression x + y does not change in the loop body. Loop optimization removes this subexpression from the body of the loop so that it is only executed once, not every time the loop body is executed. The optimizer will change the code to the following fragment:

```
i = -100;
t = x + y;
while( i < 0 )
{
    i += t;
}
```

Loop optimization is much more effective when the compiler can assume no aliasing. While you can use loop optimization without the /Oa or /Ow option, use /Oa to ensure that the most options possible are used.

Here is a code fragment that could have an aliasing problem:

```
i = -100;
while( i < 0 )
{
    i += x + y;
    *p = i;
}
```

If you do not specify the /Oa option, the compiler must assume that either x or y could be modified by the assignment to *p. Therefore, the compiler cannot assume the subexpression x + y is constant for each loop iteration. If you specify that you are not doing any aliasing (with the /Oa option), the compiler assumes that modifying *p cannot affect either x or y, and that the subexpression is indeed constant and can be removed from the loop, as in the previous example.

NOTE   *All loop optimizations specified by the /Ol option or the* **loop_opt** *pragma are safe optimizations. To enable aggressive loop optimizations, you must use the enable aggressive optimizations (/Oz) option. While the optimizations enabled by the combination of /Ol and /Oz are not safe for all cases, they will work properly for most programs.*

1.5.5 *Disabling Unsafe Loop Optimizations (/On)*

The disable unsafe loop optimizations (/On) option is an obsolescent option and is only retained for compatibility with existing makefiles. Loop optimizations are, by default, safe optimizations. The /On option is the default and has the opposite effect of the /Oz (enable aggressive optimizations) option.

1.5.6 *Enabling Aggressive Optimizations (/Oz)*

The compiler can perform extremely aggressive optimizations. These optimizations produce high code quality both in terms of speed and size. Certain programs, however, cannot be optimized with the technologies enabled by the /Oz option. For these programs, you should not specify this option; you can still use all other optimization options.

Because the optimization strategies enabled by the /Oz option are so aggressive, they are not part of the maximum optimization (/Ox) option.

Examples of the effects of the /Oz option are

■   Loop optimization (/Ol). Loop optimization enables a technology that antici-
    pates program flow and tries to remove invariant expressions from loops.
    When you specify the enable aggressive optimizations option (/Oz), the com-
    piler removes invariant expressions even when it might cause an error. Errors
    with the enable aggressive optimizations option occur most often when an in-
    variant expression that can cause an exception is protected by an **if** statement.
    The invariant expression is hoisted out of the loop body, causing it to be eval-
    uated prior to the evaluation of the **if** statement that was designed to protect it.
    Here are two examples that illustrate this problem:

```
for( i = 0; i  100; ++i )
    if( float_val != 0.0F )
    /* Protect against divide-by-zero. */
        float_result = pi / float_val;

while( condition )
    if( ptr_val != NULL )
      /* Protect pointer dereference. */
        char_var = *ptr_val;
```

■   Global register allocation (/Oe). The enable aggressive optimizations option
    enables some register allocation strategies that can cause invalid segment
    selectors to be placed in registers. Although this problem is benign in DOS, it
    causes protection faults in OS/2.

NOTE   *You can instruct the compiler to enable aggressive optimizations on a function-by-
function basis by using the* **optimize** *pragma with the* **z** *option.*

1.5.7 Removing Stack Probes (/Gs)

Every time a function is called, the stack provides space for all parameters and
local variables declared in that function. A short assembly function that checks
for a stack overflow condition is then called. Stack overflows are usually caused
either by infinite loops or by runaway recursive routines. Such errors can also be
caused by extremely large parameters or local variables.

Stack probes can be important during program development. Stack-overflow
errors alert you to problems in your code. When the program has been tested,
however, stack checking often becomes unnecessary. The compiler allows you
to remove stack-checking code with either the /Gs option or the **check_stack**
pragma. Eliminating stack probes produces programs that are smaller and that
run more quickly.

1.5.8 *Enabling Global Register Allocation (/Oe)*

The global register allocation option (/Oe) instructs the compiler to analyze your program and allocate CPU registers as efficiently as possible. Without the global register allocation option, the compiler uses the CPU's registers for several purposes:

- Holding temporary copies of variables

- Holding variables declared with the **register** keyword

- Passing parameters to functions declared with the **_fastcall** keyword (or functions in programs compiled with the /Gr command-line option)

When you enable global register allocation, the compiler ignores the **register** keyword and allocates register storage to variables (and possibly to common subexpressions). The compiler allocates register storage to variables or subexpressions according to frequency of use. Because of the limited number of physical registers, variables held in registers are sometimes placed back in memory to free the register for another use. Here is a C program example that demonstrates how the compiler might rewrite your code to accomplish this:

```c
/* Original program */

func()
{
    int i, j;
    char *pc;

    for( i = 0; i < 1000; ++i )
    {
        j = i / 3;
        *pc++ = (char)i;
    }

    for( j = 0, --pc; j < 1000;
        ++j, --pc )
        *pc--;
}
```

```
/* Example of how the compiler might optimize the
 * code to move i and j in and out of registers */

func()
{
    int i, j;
    char *pc;

    {
    register int i; /* i is in a register for this block. */
        for( i = 0; i < 1000; ++i )
        {
            j = i / 3;
            *pc++ = (char)i;
        }
    }

    {
    register int j; /* j is in a register for this block. */
        for( j = 0, --pc; j < 1000;
            ++j, --pc )
            *pc--;
    }
}
```

In the preceding example, there are blocks (enclosed in curly braces) whose only purpose is to delimit the span of code across which variables should remain in registers.

NOTE *You can enable or disable global register allocation on a function-by-function basis using the **optimize** pragma with the **e** option.*

1.5.9 Enabling Common Subexpression Optimization (/Oc and /Og)

When you use option /Og (enable global common subexpression optimizations), the compiler searches entire functions for common subexpressions. Option /Oc (default common subexpression optimization) examines only short sections of code for common subexpressions. You can disable default common subexpression optimization with the /Od option. For more information about common subexpression optimization, see Section 1.4, "Default Optimization."

NOTE *You can enable or disable block-scope common subexpression optimization on a function-by-function basis using the **optimize** pragma with the **c** option. You can enable or disable global common subexpression optimization on a function-by-function basis using the **optimize** pragma with the **g** option.*

1.5.10 Achieving Consistent Floating-Point Results (/Op)

Floating-point numbers stored in memory use either 32, 64, or 80 bits, depending on whether they are of type **float**, type **double**, or type **long double**. The 80x87 family of coprocessors uses 80-bit registers for all operations. If a value of type **float** or type **double** is kept in these registers through a number of operations, it will be more accurate than if that value is moved to and from memory between operations.

Because of the difference in precision between memory and register representation of a floating-point number, a value stored in memory is not always equal to the same value in the 80x87 register.

The difference in precision primarily affects strict equality or strict inequality tests (== and !=); however, relational tests of magnitude (>, >=, <=, and <) can behave erroneously if the coprocessor is able to maintain significant digits that memory variables cannot.

You can avoid the difference in precision by using the /Op option. This option forces floating-point values to be written to memory between floating-point operations. While storing these values to memory reduces the precision of floating-point expressions, it also ensures that these expressions will produce consistent results regardless of the rest of the code.

You can change the handling of floating-point results on a function-by-function basis using the **optimize** pragma with the **p** option.

NOTE   *Using the /Op option suppresses other optimizations because the floating-point registers are not available for storage of intermediate results. Because you suppress these optimizations, code compiled with the /Op option executes more slowly than code compiled without this option. Careful coding practices, especially in tests of strict equality and inequality, can alleviate the need for this option.*

1.5.11 Using the 80186, 80188, or 80286 Processor (/G0, /G1, /G2)

The compiler generates 8086 object code (/G0) unless you take special steps. Because the newer processors (the 80186, 80188, and 80286) are backward-compatible with the 8086 instruction set, using this instruction set ensures compatibility with all 80x86-based computers. While you gain compatibility across the entire family of 80x86 processors, you lose the advantage of some of the more powerful instructions in the newer processors.

If you know your program will only be running on an 80186, 80188, or 80286 processor, you can cause the compiler to generate instructions specific to these processors. These instructions increase the speed of your program, but you lose compatibility with machines that use older processors in the 80x86 family. Table 1.1 lists the options for processor-specific code generation:

Table 1.1   Processor Compatibility

Command-Line Option	Compatible Processors
/G0	8088, 8086, 80188, 80186, 80286, 80388, 80486
/G1	80188, 80186, 80286, 80386, 80486
/G2	80286, 80386, 80486

NOTE *When developing only for OS/2, always use the /G2 option, because OS/2 does not run on the 8086, 8088, 80186, or 80188. Do not use /G2 for Family Applications because they might be run on machines with 8088, 8086, 80188, or 80186 processors.*

1.5.12 *Optimizing for Maximum Efficiency (/Ox)*

The /Ox option combines a number of different optimizations:

- Enable global register allocation (/Oe)

- Enable global common subexpression optimization (/Og)

- Enable block-scoped common subexpression optimization (/Oc)

- Generate intrinsic functions (/Oi)

- Perform loop optimizations (/Ol)

- Optimize for speed (/Ot)

- Remove stack probes (/Gs)

Use /Ozax /Gr to get the fastest program.

The /Ox option does not include several optimizations that can improve code efficiency: /Oa (assume no aliasing), /Oz (enable aggressive optimizations), and /Gr (use fastcall calling convention). Before enabling these optimizations, you should read the sections that describe the /Oa and /Oz options and the fastcall calling convention to determine if they are appropriate for your application.

Use the optimize pragma to reduce code size.

If you are more concerned with executable file size than execution time, use the /Ox and /Gs options, then issue the **optimize** pragma as follows:

```
#pragma optimize( "t", off )
```

This set of options produces the smallest possible code, while also performing some speed optimizations.

1.6 Linker (LINK) Options that Control Optimization

Most code optimization is performed before the object file is produced. There are four optimizations that the linker can perform to speed program execution and reduce the disk space used by an executable file.

1.6.1 Enabling Far Call Optimization (/FARCALLTRANSLATION)

You can call a function two ways. In a far call, the function is called using both the segment and the offset of the function. This allows a program to call a routine outside a 64K segment. In a near call, both the calling statement and the function must be located in the same segment. Only the offset is used to access the function; the segment address is implicit. You can only use near calls to routines located in the same segment.

Because of the architecture of the processor, near function calls execute faster than far calls. The decision to declare functions as near or far is often made when selecting a memory model. As it is difficult to determine where the linker will place a given function in memory, it is impractical for the programmer to choose the way a function is called.

Use /FARCALLTRANSLATION with medium, large, and huge model programs.

The /FARCALLTRANSLATION option enables far call optimization. When you use this option, any function calls within the same segment as the function being called are converted to near calls. This optimization has no effect if you have selected the tiny, small, or compact model, because all calls are already near calls.

The abbreviation for the /FARCALLTRANSLATION option is /F.

How /FARCALLTRANSLATION Affects Your Code

The linker can perform a form of post-optimization (an optimization that occurs after most of the actual code generation is complete) that translates far calls into near calls when possible. This optimization allows a given function to be called with both near and far calls in the same program. To perform this translation, the linker takes a section of object code such as

```
CALL    FAR    _func
```

where `func` is defined in the current segment, and replaces it with the following code:

```
PUSH    CS
CALL    NEAR    _func
NOP
```

This substitution works because the linker has inserted `PUSH CS` to place a far return address on the stack.

Use /FARCALLTRANSLATION with /PACKCODE. The /FARCALLTRANSLATION option is most effective when used in conjunction with the /PACKCODE option discussed in Section 1.6.2. Using the /PACKCODE option causes far calls that were intersegment to become intrasegment calls. The /FARCALLTRANSLATION feature can then take advantage of the new grouping to translate all intrasegment far calls into near calls.

Benefits of /FARCALLTRANSLATION

The /FARCALLTRANSLATION option is of significant benefit to protected-mode programs. Table 1.2 illustrates why.

Table 1.2   Processor Clock Cycles for Calling Sequence

Instructions	Cycles (Real Mode)		Cycles (Protected Mode)	
	286	**386**	**286**	**386**
Far Function Call				
CALL FAR PTR _func	13	17	26	34
Total	13	17	26	34
Near Function Call				
PUSH CS	3	2	3	2
CALL NEAR PTR _func	7	7	7	7
NOP	3	3	3	3
Total	13	12	13	12
Savings	0	5	13	22

1.6.2 Packing Code (/PACKCODE)

The /PACKCODE linker option groups neighboring code segments together. When used with the /F option, the /PACKCODE option greatly increases the number of near calls that can be made to a function. This option can be followed with a limit (expressed in bytes) at which to stop packing and to begin a new group. Here is the syntax for the /PACKCODE option:

/PACKCODE:*number*

where *number* is an optional hexadecimal, octal, or decimal number that specifies the limit for packing. The radix (octal, decimal, or hexadecimal) is specified just as you would specify it to a C program.

Radix	Rules for Specification
Octal	Specify the octal number with a leading 0. You can only use the digits 0 through 7 in an octal number. For example, 07777.
Decimal	Specify the decimal number without a leading 0. For example, 65530.
Hexadecimal	Specify the hexadecimal number with a leading 0x. For example, 0x3FFF.

If you omit the packing limit, the linker supplies a default value of 65, 530.

The abbreviation for the /PACKCODE option is /PACKC.

1.6.3 Packing Data (/PACKDATA)

The /PACKDATA option is analogous to the /PACKCODE option, except that it groups together neighboring data segments instead of code segments. This option is most useful when you have a large-model program that exceeds the OS/2 limitation of 255 segments. By using /PACKDATA, you can group segments, thereby reducing the total number OS/2 has to manage. Here is the syntax for the /PACKDATA option:

/PACKDATA:*number*

where *number* is an optional hexadecimal, octal, or decimal number that specifies the limit for packing. The radix (hexadecimal, octal, or decimal) is specified just as you would specify it to a C program. For more information on specifying hexadecimal, octal, or decimal numbers, see Section 1.6.2 above.

If the packing limit is omitted, the linker supplies a default value of 65,535 (0xFFFF).

The abbreviation for the /PACKDATA option is /PACKD.

1.6.4 Packing the Executable File (/EXEPACK)

The executable file created by the compiler often contains sequences of re-peated bytes. You can remove these repeated sequences with the /EXEPACK op-tion. This decreases the size of the resulting executable file as well as program load time.

WARNING   *Because the /EXEPACK option removes debug information from the execu-table file, you should not use it with the /CODEVIEW option.*

1.7 Optimizing in Different Environments

The environment in which you plan to use a program can have a bearing on the types of optimizations that you should use.

1.7.1 Optimizing in DOS

You need not take special precautions for programs written under DOS unless you are writing a terminate-and-stay-resident (TSR) program. If an interrupt-driven routine could modify a memory location in a program, you should declare that variable **volatile**.

1.7.2 Optimizing in OS/2

Many of the rules for interrupt routines apply to OS/2. If one thread can modify variables in another thread, declare these variables as **volatile**.

1.7.3 Optimizing in Microsoft Windows ™

Microsoft Windows™ can move segments dynamically. As a result of dynamic heap compaction, pointers maintained in registers can be invalidated. The /Ow option instructs the compiler that you will not be using aliases, but that Windows might cause certain optimizations to be unsafe across function calls.

If you are not using any aliases you must still use the /Ow option with Windows programs. See Section 1.5.3, "Assuming No Aliasing (/Oa and /Ow)," for more information.

1.8 Choosing Function-Calling Conventions

In Microsoft C, version 6.0, functions can call other functions using three different conventions. Note that, while no calling convention has been defined as
"standard," most C compilers use conventions similar to those described here.
The C calling convention requires the most object code to set up, but it is the
only calling convention that supports functions with variable-length argument
lists. The FORTRAN/Pascal calling convention is more compact, but does not
allow for variable-length argument lists. The **_fastcall**, or register calling convention is the fastest of the three calling conventions, but it does not support
variable-length argument lists or mixed-language program interfaces.

1.8.1 The C Calling Convention (/Gd)

Because C allows functions to have a variable number of parameters, parameters
must be pushed onto the stack from right to left. (If parameters were pushed from
left to right, it would be difficult for the compiler to determine which parameter
was first.) If you do not specify command-line options that modify the function-
calling convention, the C calling convention is used; otherwise, the **_cdecl** keyword must be used before any function using the C calling convention.

If, for example, you use the /Gr (register calling convention) option when you
compile, and the function `add_two` must have the C calling convention, declare `add_two` as follows:

```
int _cdecl add_two( int x, int y );
```

1.8.2 The FORTRAN/Pascal Calling Convention (/Gc)

Use the FORTRAN/Pascal calling convention for any functions declared with
either the **_fortran** or **_pascal** keywords. (The two keywords currently produce
identical results.) Parameters to these functions are always pushed on the stack
from left to right. While any function can be declared with the FORTRAN/
Pascal convention, it is used primarily for prototypes to Pascal or FORTRAN
routines called from within C programs. This calling convention can also produce smaller, faster programs.

The /Gc option (generate Pascal-style function calls) can be used to make all
functions in a file observe the FORTRAN/Pascal calling convention.

Note that C run-time library routines must still be called using C calling conventions. Because these routines are declared using the **_cdecl** keyword header files,
you must include the appropriate header files in any program using run-time library routines.

Functions with variable-length parameter lists (such as **printf**) cannot use the FORTRAN/Pascal calling convention.

NOTE *The /ML, /MD, and /MT options cause all floating-point functions to be declared as FORTRAN/Pascal. See Chapter 16, "Dynamic Linking with OS/2," for more information.*

1.8.3 The Register Calling Convention (/Gr)

You can decrease execution time if parameters to functions are passed in registers rather than on the stack. Compiling with the /Gr command-line option enables the register calling convention for an entire file. The **_fastcall** keyword enables the register calling convention on a function-by-function basis.

Because the 80x86 processor has a limited number of registers, only the first three parameters are allocated to registers; the rest are passed using the FORTRAN/Pascal calling convention. The register calling convention can increase the speed of a program.

NOTE *The compiler allocates different registers for variables declared as **register** and for passing arguments using the register calling convention. This calling convention will not conflict with any register variables that you may have declared.*

Exercise caution when using the register calling convention for any function written in in-line assembly language. Your use of registers in assembly-language could conflict with the compiler's use of registers for storing parameters.

1.8.4 The _fastcall Calling Convention

This section describes the details of the **_fastcall** calling convention. The information is for the use of assembly-language programmers who are interested in using either the in-line assembler or the Microsoft Macro Assembler (MASM) to write functions declared as **_fastcall**. Functions declared as **_fastcall** accept arguments in registers rather than on the stack; functions declared as **_cdecl** or **_pascal** accept parameters only on the stack.

WARNING *The register usage documented here applies only to Microsoft C, version 6.0. It may change in future releases of the compiler.*

Argument-Passing Convention

The **_fastcall** calling convention is a "strongly typed" register calling convention. This typing allows the compiler to generate better code by passing arguments in registers that correspond to the data type you are passing. Because the compiler chooses registers depending on the type of the argument and not in a strict linear order, the calling program and called function must agree on the types of the arguments in order to communicate data correctly.

For each type of argument there is a list of register candidates. The arguments are allocated to registers or, if no suitable register remains unused, are pushed onto the stack left-to-right. Each argument is put in the first register candidate that does not already contain an argument. Table 1.3 shows the basic types and the register candidate list for each.

Table 1.3   Register Candidates

Type	Register Candidates
character	AL, DL, BL
unsigned character	AL, DL, BL
integer	AX, DX, BX
unsigned integer	AX, DX, BX
long integer	DX:AX
unsigned long integer	DX:AX
near pointer	BX, AX, DX
far or huge pointer	passed on the stack

All far and huge pointers are pushed on the stack, as are all structures, unions, and floating-point types.

Return Value Convention

The **_fastcall** return value convention is based on the size of the return value, except with floating-point types. All floating point types are returned on the top of the NDP stack. For more information about the NDP stack and returning floating-point values, see Chapter 4, "Controlling Floating-Point Math Operations." The following list shows how values 4 bytes or smaller, including unions and structures, are returned from a **_fastcall** function.

Size	Return Convention
1 Byte	AL Register
2 Bytes	AX Register
4 Bytes	DX, AX Registers (for pointers, the segment is returned in DX, the offset in AX; for long integers, the most-significant byte is returned in DX, least-significant byte in AX)

Note that the protocol for returning values 4 bytes or smaller is the same as for functions declared as **_cdecl.** To return structures and unions larger than 4 bytes, the calling program passes a hidden parameter as the last item pushed. This parameter is a near pointer, implicitly SS-relative, to a buffer in which the value is to be returned. A far pointer to SS:*hidden-param* must be returned in DX:AX. This is the same convention for returning structures as **_pascal.**

Stack Adjustment Convention

Unlike functions declared as **_cdecl,** functions declared as **_fastcall** must pop the arguments off the stack. The calling program does not adjust the stack after function return.

Register Preservation Requirement

All functions must preserve the DS, BP, SI, and DI registers. Your **_fastcall** function can modify the values in AX, BX, CX, DX, and ES.

Function-Naming Convention

The public name put into the object file for a function declared as **_fastcall** is the name given by the user with a leading "at sign" (@). No case translation is performed on the function name. The function declaration

```
int _fastcall FCFunc( void );
```

causes the compiler to place the public symbol @FCFunc in your object file at every location FCFunc is referenced in your program.

If you do not declare the function as **_fastcall** in your C program, the compiler assumes the default calling convention. The default is usually the C calling convention but can be changed by the /Gc (Pascal Calling Convention), /Gr (Register Calling Convention), or /Gd (C Calling Convention) options. If the linker gives you an unresolved external reference, you may have failed to declare an external **_fastcall** function properly. For more information about calling conventions, see Chapter 12, "Programming with Mixed Languages."

Managing Memory

When you develop advanced applications in Microsoft C, you must pay attention to memory management—that is, how data and code are stored and accessed in memory. A well-thought-out memory strategy will make your programs run faster and occupy less memory.

You can follow one or more of these memory management strategies:

- Choose a standard memory model.

- Create a mixed-model program with the **_near**, **_far**, **_huge**, and **_based** keywords.

- Create your own customized memory model.

- Allocate memory as you need it with the **malloc** family of functions.

This chapter explains pointers, memory models (including the new tiny model), variations such as custom memory models and mixed models, and based pointers.

2.1 Pointer Sizes

One of the strengths of the C language is that it allows you to use pointers to directly access memory locations.

Every Microsoft C program has at least two parts: the code (function definitions) and the data (variables and constants). As a program runs, it refers to elements of the code or the data by their addresses. These addresses can be stored in pointer variables.

Pointer variables can fit into 16 bits or 32 bits, depending on the distance of the object to which they refer.

2.1.1 Pointers and 64K Segments

IBM personal computers and compatibles use the Intel® 8086, 80186, 80286, or 80386 processors (collectively called the 80x86 family). These processors have a "segmented" architecture, which means they all have a mode that treats memory as a series of segments, each of which occupies up to 64K of memory. An offset from the base of the segment allows you to access information within a given segment. Moving to a new segment requires additional machine code.

A 16-bit pointer can address up to 65,536 locations. The 64K limit is necessary because the 80x86 registers are 16 bits (2 bytes) wide. A single register can address only 65,536 (64K) unique memory locations.

A pointer variable that fully specifies a memory address needs 16 bits for the segment location and another 16 bits for the offset within the segment, a total of 32 bits. However, if you have several variables in the same general area, your program can set the segment register once and treat the pointers as smaller 16-bit quantities.

The 80x86 register CS holds the base for the code segment; the register DS holds the base for the data segment. Two other segment registers are available: the stack segment register (SS) and the extra segment register (ES). (The 80386 has additional segment registers: FS and GS.)

2.1.2 Near Pointers

If you don't explicitly specify a memory model, Microsoft C defaults to the small model, which allots up to 64K for the code and another 64K for the data (see Figure 2.1).

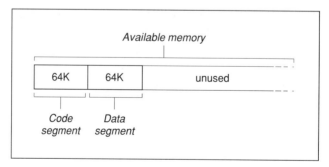

Figure 2.1 Anatomy of a Small-Model Program

When a small-model program runs, the CS and DS segment registers never change. All code pointers and all data pointers contain 16 bits because they remain within the 64K range.

These 16-bit pointers to objects within a single 64K segment are called "near pointers." Accessing a near object is called "near addressing."

2.1.3 Far Pointers

If your program needs more than 64K for code or data, at least some of the pointers must specify the memory segment, which means these pointers occupy 32 bits instead of 16 bits.

These larger 32-bit pointers that can point anywhere in memory are called "far pointers." Accessing a far object is called "far addressing."

Far pointers can address any location, but they are bigger and slower.

Far addressing has the advantage that your program can address any available memory location—up to 640K in DOS or several megabytes in OS/2. The disadvantages of the larger far pointers is that they take up more memory (four bytes instead of two) and that any use of the pointers (assigning, modifying, or otherwise accessing values) takes more time.

Allowing either code or data to expand beyond 64K makes your programs larger and slower.

2.1.4 Huge Pointers

A third type of pointer in Microsoft C is the "huge" pointer, which applies only to data pointers. Code pointers cannot be declared as huge.

A huge address is similar to a far address in that both contain 32 bits, made up of a segment value and an offset value. They differ only in the way pointer arithmetic is performed.

For far pointers, Microsoft C assumes that code and data objects lie completely within the segment in which they start, so pointer arithmetic operates only on the offset portion of the address. Limiting the size of any single item to 64K makes pointer arithmetic faster.

Huge pointers overcome this size limitation; pointer arithmetic is performed on all 32 bits of the data item's address, thus allowing data items referenced by huge pointers to span more than one segment. In this code fragment,

```
int _huge *hp;
int _far *fp;
    .
    .
    .
hp++;
fp++;
```

both `hp` and `fp` are incremented. The huge pointer is incremented as a 32-bit value that represents the combined segment and offset. Only the offset part of the far pointer (a 16-bit value) is incremented.

Extending the size of pointer arithmetic from 16 to 32 bits causes such arithmetic to execute more slowly. You gain the use of larger arrays by paying a price in execution speed.

2.1.5 Based Addressing

When you declare near, far, and huge variables, the Microsoft C compiler and linker automatically manage details such as allocating memory and keeping track of segments.

A "based pointer" is a fourth kind of pointer that operates as a 16-bit offset from a base that you specify. In this respect, based addressing differs from near, far, or huge addressing; you're responsible for naming the base, instead of letting the compiler decide.

Based pointers are new to version 6.0 of Microsoft C. They are explained in more detail in Section 2.5, "Using Based Variables."

2.2 Selecting a Standard Memory Model

If you want to choose one size for all pointers, there's no need to declare each variable as near or far. Instead, you select a standard memory model and your choice applies to all variables in the program.

One advantage of using standard memory models is simplicity. You specify the way the compiler allocates storage for code and data only once.

A standard memory model assumes all pointers are the same size.

Another advantage is that the standard memory models do not require the use of Microsoft-specific keywords such as _near and _far, so they are best for writing code that is portable to other (non-DOS) systems.

The disadvantage of standard memory models is that, because they make global assumptions about the environment, they do not always produce the most efficient code.

2.2.1 The Six Standard Memory Models

The six Microsoft C memory models are shown in Table 2.1.

Table 2.1   Memory Models

	Maximum Total Memory		
Model	**Code**	**Data**	**Data Arrays**
Tiny	<64K	<64K	<64K
Small	64K	64K	64K
Medium	No limit	64K	64K
Compact	64K	No limit	64K
Large	No limit	No limit	64K
Huge	No limit	No limit	No limit

The SETUP program creates the libraries that support the six standard memory models.

When you choose one of the standard memory models, the compiler inserts the name of the corresponding C run-time library in the object file so the linker chooses it automatically. Each memory model has its own library, except for the huge memory model (which uses the large-model library) and the tiny model (which uses the small-model library).

2.2.2 Limitations on Code Size and Data Size

When writing a program in Microsoft C, keep in mind two limitations that apply to all six memory models:

- No single source module can generate 64K or more of code. You must break large programs into modules and link their individual .OBJ files to create the .EXE file.

- No single data item can exceed 64K unless it appears in a huge-model program or it has been declared with the **_huge** keyword.

2.2.3 The Tiny Memory Model

The tiny memory model is new to Microsoft C. It resembles the small model with three exceptions:

- The tiny model cannot exceed 64K per program (including both code and data). A small-model program, on the other hand, can occupy up to 128K: 64K for code and 64K for data.

- The tiny model produces .COM, rather than .EXE, files. To produce .COM files, compile with the /AT option. Then link with the /TINY option and link in CRTCOM.OBJ.

- The tiny model applies to DOS only; it is not available in OS/2.

Although the tiny model imposes the most severe limits on code and data size, it produces the smallest programs. The tiny memory model only offers a load-time speed advantage over the small model; they both produce the fastest programs.

2.2.4 The Huge Memory Model

The huge memory model is nearly identical to the large model. The only difference is that the huge model permits individual arrays to exceed 64K in size. For example, an **int** uses two bytes, so an array of 40,000 integers, occupying 80,000 bytes of memory, would be permitted in the huge model. All other models limit each array, structure, or other data object to no more than 64K.

NOTE *Automatic arrays cannot be declared huge. Only static arrays and arrays occupying memory allocated by the **halloc** function can be huge.*

The huge model lifts the limits on arrays. Although the huge model lifts the limits on arrays, some size restrictions do apply. To maintain efficient addressing, no individual array element is allowed to cross a segment boundary. This has the following implications:

- No single element of an array can be larger than 64K. An array can be larger than 64K, but its individual elements cannot.

- For any array larger than 128K, all elements must have a size in bytes equal to a power of 2: 2 bytes, 4 bytes, 8 bytes, 16 bytes, and so on. If the array is 128K or smaller, its elements can be any size, up to and including 64K.

Pointer arithmetic changes within the huge model, as well. In particular, the **sizeof** operator may return an incorrect value. The ANSI draft standard for C defines the value returned by **sizeof** to be of type **size_t** (which, in Microsoft C, is an **unsigned int**). The size in bytes of a huge array is an **unsigned long** value, however. To find the correct value, you must use a type cast:

```
(unsigned long)sizeof(monster_array)
```

Similarly, the C language defines the result of subtracting two pointers as **ptrdiff_t** (a **signed int** in Microsoft C). Subtracting two huge pointers will yield a **long** value. Microsoft C gives the correct result with the following type cast:

```
(long)(ptr1_huge - ptr2_huge)
```

When you select huge model, all **extern** arrays are treated as **_huge**. Operations on data declared as **_huge** can be less efficient than the same operations on data declared as **_far**.

2.2.5 Null Pointers

Within the medium and compact models, code pointers and data pointers differ in size: one is 16 bits wide and the other is 32 bits wide. When using these memory models, you should be careful in your use of the manifest constant **NULL**.

NULL represents a null data pointer. The C include files define it as

```
#define NULL ((void *) 0)
```

There can be problems in models with different sizes of code and data pointers.

In memory models where data pointers have the same size as code pointers, the actual size of a null pointer doesn't matter. In memory models where code and data pointers are different sizes, problems can occur. Consider this example:

```
void main()
{
    func1( NULL );
    func2( NULL );
}

func1( char *dp )
{
    .
    .
    .
}

func2( char (*fp)( void ) )
{
    .
    .
    .
}
```

In the absence of function prototypes for `func1` and `func2`, the compiler always assumes that **NULL** refers to data and not code.

The example above works correctly in tiny, small, large, and huge models because, in those models, a data pointer is the same size as a code pointer. Under medium or compact model, however, `main` passes **NULL** to `func2` as a null data pointer rather than as a null code pointer (a pointer to a function), which means the pointer is the wrong size.

To ensure that your code works properly in all models, declare each function with a prototype. For example, before `main`, include these two lines:

```
int func1( char *dp );
int func2( char (*fp)( void ));
```

If you add these prototypes to the example, the code works properly in all memory models. Prototypes force the compiler to coerce code pointers to the correct size. Prototypes also enable strong type-checking of parameters.

2.2.6 Specifying a Memory Model

If you do not specify a memory model, Microsoft C defaults to the small model, which is adequate for many small to mid-sized programs.

You can select a memory model from the Programmer's WorkBench or from the command line.

Selecting from within PWB

If you're compiling from the Programmer's WorkBench, open the Options menu and choose C Global Build Options. The available memory models appear in the upper left corner. Choose one of the six standard models or choose Customized and type in the options for a customized model.

Selecting from the Command Line

You can choose a memory model by including an option on the command line. For example, to compile CLICK.C as a compact-model program, type this:

```
CL /AC CLICK.C
```

The /AC option selects the compact memory model. The six options and four libraries are listed below:

Option	Memory Model: Library
/AT	Tiny Model: SLIBC*xx*.LIB (plus CRTCOM.OBJ)
/AS	Small Model: SLIBC*xx*.LIB

/AM	Medium Model: MLIBC*xx*.LIB
/AC	Compact Model: CLIBC*xx*.LIB
/AL	Large Model: LLIBC*xx*.LIB
/AH	Huge Model: LLIBC*xx*.LIB

2.3 Mixing Memory Models

In standard memory models, explained above, all data pointers are the same size and all code pointers are the same size.

A mixed memory model selectively combines different types of pointers within the same program. A mixed model extends the limits of a given memory model while retaining its benefits.

A mixed memory model lets you mix near and far pointers.

For example, imagine a programming situation where you add an array to a small-model program, pushing the data segment past the 64K limit.

You could solve the problem by moving up from the small to the compact memory model. Doing so would bump all data pointers from two to four bytes. The .EXE file would grow accordingly. Execution time would slow.

A second and perhaps better solution is to stay within the standard small memory model, which uses near pointers, but to declare the new array as far. You mix near pointers and far pointers, creating a mixed model.

Microsoft C lets you override the standard addressing convention for a given memory model by specifying that certain items are **_near**, **_far**, **_huge**, or **_based**. These keywords are not a standard part of the C language; they are Microsoft extensions, meaningful only on systems that use 80*x*86 microprocessors. Using these keywords may affect the portability of your code.

NOTE *Previous versions of the Microsoft C Compiler accepted the keywords **near**, **far**, and **huge** without an initial underscore. Since the ANSI draft standard for C permits compiler implementors to reserve identifiers that begin with underscores, an underscore was added to these keywords to mark them as Microsoft-specific. To maintain compatibility with existing source code, the compiler still recognizes the obsolescent versions of these keywords.*

You can compile a program in the small model, for example, but declare a certain array to be **_far**. At run time, the address of that array occupies four bytes. The program may slow slightly when accessing items in that particular far array, but throughout the rest of the program, all addressing would be near. Note that all pointers to elements of an array declared as **_far** must also be declared as **_far**.

Table 2.2 lists the effects of these keywords on data pointers, code pointers, and pointer arithmetic.

Table 2.2   Addressing Declared with Microsoft Keywords

Keyword	Data	Code	Arithmetic
_near	Data reside in default data segment; 16-bit addresses	Functions reside in current code segment; 16-bit addresses	16 bits
_far	Data can be anywhere in memory, not necessarily in the default data segment; 32-bit addresses	Functions can be called from anywhere in memory; 32-bit addresses	16 bits
_huge	Data can be anywhere in memory, not necessarily in the default data segment. Individual data items (arrays) can exceed 64K in size; 32-bit addresses	Not applicable; code cannot be declared _huge	32 bits (data only)
_based	Data can be anywhere in memory, not necessarily in the default data segment; 16-bit addresses plus a known base provide the range of 32-bit addresses	Not applicable; code cannot be declared _based	16 bits (data only)

2.3.1 Pointer Problems

When you declare items to be **_near**, **_far**, **_huge**, or **_based**, you can link with a standard run-time library. Be aware, however, that in some cases, the modified pointers will be incompatible with standard library functions. Watch for these problems that affect pointers:

- A library function that expects a 16-bit pointer as an argument will not function properly with modified variables that occupy 32 bits. In other words, you can cast a near pointer to a far pointer, because it adds the segment value and maintains the integrity of the address. If you cast a far pointer to near, however, the compiler generates a warning message because the offset may not lie within the default data segment, in which case the original far address is irretrievably lost.

- A library function that returns a pointer will return a pointer of the default size for the memory model. This is only a problem if you are assigning the return value to a pointer of a smaller size. For example, there may be difficulties if you compile with a model that selects far data pointers, but you have explicitly declared the variable to receive the return value **_near**.

  This warning does not apply to all functions. See Section B.2.8 in Appendix B for a list of model-independent string and memory functions such as **_fstrcat**, the far version of **strcat**.

- Based pointers pose a special problem. Based pointers are passed to other functions as is (without normalization). Certain functions expect to receive based pointers, but most do not. Therefore, in most cases, you must either explicitly cast a based pointer to a far pointer or make sure that all functions that receive based pointers are prototyped.

Some run-time library functions support near, far, huge, and based variables. For example, **halloc** allocates memory for a huge data array.

You can always pass the value (but not the address) of a far item to a small-model library routine. For example,

```
/* Compile in small model */
#include <stdio.h>
long _far time_val;

void main()
{
    time( &time_val );                  /* Illegal far address */
    printf( "%ld\n", time_val );        /* Legal value */
}
```

When you use a mixed memory model, you should include function prototypes with argument-type lists to ensure that all pointer arguments are passed to functions correctly.

2.3.2 Declaring Near, Far, Huge, and Based Variables

The **_near**, **_far**, **_huge**, and **_based** keywords modify either objects or pointers to objects. When using them to declare variables, keep these rules in mind:

- The keyword always modifies the object or pointer immediately to its right. In complex declarations, think of the **_far** keyword and the item to its right as being a single unit. For example, in the case of the declaration

  ```
  char _far * _near *p;
  ```

  p is a near pointer to a far pointer to **char**, which resides in the default data segment for the memory model being used.

  By contrast, the declaration

  ```
  char _far * _near p;
  ```

  is a far pointer to **char** that will always be stored in DGROUP, regardless of the memory model being used.

- If the item immediately to the right of the keyword is an identifier, the keyword determines whether the item will be allocated in the default data segment (**_near**) or a separate data segment (**_far**, **_huge**, or **_based**). For example,

  ```
  char _far a;
  ```

  allocates a as an item of type **char** with a **_far** address.

- If the item immediately to the right of the keyword is a pointer, the keyword determines whether the pointer will hold a near address (16 bits), a based address (16 bits), a far address (32 bits), or a huge address (also 32 bits). For example,

  ```
  char _huge *p;
  ```

  allocates p as a huge pointer (32 bits) to an item of type **char**. Any arithmetic performed on the huge pointer p will affect all 32 bits. That is, the instruction p++ increments the pointer as a 32-bit entity.

2.3.3 Declaring Near and Far Functions

You cannot declare functions as **_huge** or **_based**. The rules for using the **_near** and **_far** keywords for functions are similar to those for using them with data:

- The keyword always modifies the function or pointer immediately to its right.

- If the item immediately to the right of the keyword is a function, the keyword determines whether the function will be allocated as near or far. For example,

```
char _far fun();
```

defines `fun` as a function with a 32-bit address that returns a **char**. The function may be located in near memory or far memory, but it is called with the full 32-bit address. The **_far** keyword applies to the function, not to the return type.

- If the item immediately to the right of the keyword is a pointer to a function, the keyword determines whether the function will be called using a near (16-bit) or far (32-bit) address. For example,

```
char (_far *pfun)( );
```

defines `pfun` as a far pointer (32 bits) to a function returning type **char**.

- Function declarations must match function definitions.

- The **_huge** and **_based** keywords do not apply to functions. That is, a function cannot be huge (larger than 64K) or based. A function can return a huge data pointer to the calling function. A function can return a based pointer unless it is a pointer based on **_self** (see Section 2.5.2, "Declaring Based Variables").

The example below declares `fun1` as a far function returning type **char**:

```
char _far fun1(void);                    /* small model */
char _far fun(void)
{
    .
    .
    .
}
```

Here, the `fun2` function is a near function that returns a far pointer to type **char**:

```
char _far * _near fun2( );        /* large model */
char _far * _near fun( )
{
      .
      .
      .

}
```

The example below declares `pfun` as a far pointer to a function that has an **int** return type, assigns the address of **printf** to `pfun`, and prints "Hello world." twice.

```
/* Compile in medium, large, or huge model */

#include <stdio.h>
int (_far *pfun)( char *, ... );

void main()
{
    pfun = printf;
    pfun( "Hello world.\n" );
    (*pfun)( "Hello world.\n" );
}
```

2.3.4 *Pointer Conversions*

Passing near or far pointers as arguments to functions can cause automatic conversions in the size of the pointer argument. Passing a pointer to an unprototyped function forces the pointer size to the larger of the following two sizes:

- The default pointer size for that type, as defined by the memory model selected during compilation.

  For example, in medium-model programs, data pointer arguments are near by default, and code pointer arguments are far by default.

- The size of the type of the argument.

Note that if you supply a based pointer as an argument to a function and do not specifically cast it to a far pointer type, a 16-bit offset from the base segment is passed.

Function prototypes prevent problems that may occur in mixed memory models.

If you provide a function prototype with complete argument types, the compiler performs type-checking and enforces the conversion of actual arguments to the declared type of the corresponding formal argument. However, if no declaration is present or the argument-type list is empty, the compiler will convert nonbased pointer arguments automatically to the default type or the type of the argument, whichever is larger. To avoid mismatched arguments, always use a prototype with the argument types.

For example, the following program produces unexpected results in compact-model, large-model, or huge-model programs.

```
void main( )
{
    int _near *x;
    char _far *y;
    int z = 1;

    test_fun( x, y, z );      /* x is coerced to far
                                 pointer in compact,
                                 large, or huge model */
}

int test_fun( int _near *ptr1, char _far *ptr2, int a)
{
    printf("Value of a = %d\n", a);
}
```

If the preceding example is compiled as a tiny, small, or medium program, the size of x is 16 bits, the size of y is 32 bits, and the value printed for a is 1.

However, if the example is compiled in compact, large, or huge model, both x and y are automatically converted to far pointers when they are passed to test_fun. Since ptr1, the first parameter of test_fun, is defined as a near pointer argument, it takes only 16 bits of the 32 bits passed to it. The next parameter, ptr2, takes the remaining 16 bits passed to ptr1, plus 16 bits of the 32 bits passed to it. Finally, the third parameter, a, takes the leftover 16 bits from ptr2, instead of the value of z in the **main** function.

This shifting process does not generate an error message, because both the function call and the function definition are legal. In this case the program does not work as intended, however, since the value assigned to a is not the value intended.

To pass `ptr1` as a near pointer, you should include a function prototype that specifically declares this argument for `test_fun` as a near pointer, as shown below:

```
/* First, prototype test_fun so the compiler
 * knows in advance about the near pointer argument:
 */
int test_fun (int _near*, char _far *, int);

main ( )
{
    int _near *x;
    char _far *y;
    int z = 1;

    test_fun ( x, y, z );    /* now, x is not coerced
                              * to a far pointer; it is
                              * passed as a near pointer,
                              * no matter which memory
                              * model is used
                              */
}

int test_fun ( int _near *ptr1, char _far *ptr2, int a)
{
    printf ( "Value of a = %d\n", a );
}
```

2.4 Customizing Memory Models

A third way to manage memory is to combine different features from standard memory models to create your own customized memory model. You should have a thorough understanding of C memory models and the architecture of 80*x*86 processors before creating your own nonstandard memory models.

In a customized model, you select the size of code pointers and data pointers.

The /A*string* option lets you change the attributes of the standard memory models to create your own memory models. The three letters in *string* correspond to the code pointer size, the data pointer size, and the stack and data segment setup, respectively. Because the letter allowed in each field is unique to that field, you can give the letters in any order after /A. All three letters must be present.

The standard memory-model options (/AT, /AS, /AM, /AC, /AL, and /AH) can be specified in the /A*string* form. As an example of how to construct memory models, the standard memory-model options are listed below with their /A*string* equivalents:

Standard	Custom Equivalent
/AT	/Asnd
/AS	/Asnd
/AM	/Alnd
/AC	/Asfd
/AL	/Alfd
/AH	/Alhd

For example, you might want to create a huge-compact model. This model would allow huge data items but only one code segment. The option for specifying this model would be /Ashd.

NOTE *Tiny model is identical to small model except that it causes the linker to search for CRTCOM.LIB. The executable file generated when you specify tiny model is a .COM file rather than a .EXE.*

2.4.1 Setting a Size for Code Pointers

Within a custom memory model, you choose whether code pointers are short or long:

Option	Size
/As*xx*	Short (near) code pointers
/Al*xx*	Long (far) code pointers

The /As (short) option tells the compiler to generate near 16-bit pointers and addresses for all functions. This is the default for tiny-, small-, and compact-model programs.

The /Al (long) option means that far 32-bit pointers and addresses are used to address all functions. Far pointers are the default for medium-, large-, and huge-model programs.

2.4.2 Setting a Size for Data Pointers

Data pointers can be near, far, or huge:

Option	Size
/A*n*x	Near data pointers
/A*f*x	Far data pointers
/A*h*x	Huge data pointers

The /An (near) option tells the compiler to use 16-bit pointers and addresses for all data. This is the default for tiny-, small-, and medium-model programs.

The /Af (far) option specifies that all data pointers and addresses are 32 bits. This is the default for compact- and large-model programs.

The /Ah (huge) option specifies that all data pointers and addresses are far (32-bit) and that arrays are permitted to extend beyond a 64K segment. This is the default for huge-model programs.

With far data pointers, no single data item can be larger than a segment (64K) because address arithmetic is performed only on 16 bits (the offset portion) of the address. When huge data pointers are used, individual data items can be larger than a segment (64K) because address arithmetic is performed on both the segment and the offset.

2.4.3 Setting Up Segments

Within a customized model, you can choose to make the stack segment (SS) equal the data segment (DS), in which case they overlap:

Option	Effect
/A*xx*d	SS == DS
/A[[*xx*]]u	SS != DS; DS reloaded on function entry
/A[[*xx*]]w	SS != DS; DS not reloaded on function entry

Segment Setup Option /Ad

The option /Ad tells the compiler that the segment addresses stored in the SS and DS registers are equal. The stack segment and the default data segment are combined into a single segment. This is the default for all standard-model programs. In small- and medium-model programs, the stack plus all data must occupy less than 64K; thus, any data item is accessed with only a 16-bit offset from the segment address in the SS and DS registers.

In compact-, large-, and huge-model programs, initialized global and static data are placed in the default data segment up to a certain threshold. The address of this segment is stored in the DS and SS registers. All pointers to data, including pointers to local data (the stack), are full 32-bit addresses. This is important to remember when passing pointers as arguments in multiple-segment programs. Although you may have more than 64K of total data in these models, no more than 64K of data can occupy the default segment. The /Gt and /ND options control allocation of items in the default data segment if a program exceeds this limit.

Segment Setup Option /Au

The option /Au tells the compiler that the stack segment does not necessarily coincide with the data segment. In addition, it adds the **_loadds** attribute to all functions within a module, forcing the compiler to generate code to load the DS register with the correct value prior to entering the function body. Combine the /ND option with /Au to name data segments other than the default. When /Au is combined with /ND, the address in the DS register is saved upon entry to each function, and the new DS value for the module in which the function was defined is loaded into the register. The previous DS value is restored on exit from the function. Therefore, only one data segment is accessible at any given time. The /ND option lets you combine these segments into a single segment.

If a standard memory-model option precedes it on the command line, the /Au option can be specified without any letters indicating data pointer or code pointer sizes. The program uses a standard memory model, but different segments are set up for the stack and data segments.

The /Au option is useful for OS/2 or Microsoft Windows dynamic-link libraries (DLLs), since it forces DS to be loaded on entry to each function. It is also useful for writing extensions to the Programmer's WorkBench. This is a costly operation, however, so consider using the /Aw option.

Segment Setup Option /Aw

The option /Aw, like /Au, causes the compiler to assume that the stack segment is separate from the data segment. The compiler does not automatically load the DS register at each function entry point. The /Aw option is useful in creating applications that interface with an operating system or with a program running at the operating-system level. The operating system or the program running under the operating system actually receives the data intended for the application program and places that data in a segment; then the operating system or program must load the DS register with the segment address for the application program.

As with the /Au option, the /Aw option can be specified without data pointer and code pointer letters if a standard memory-model option precedes it on the command line. In such a case, the program uses the specified memory model just as with /Au, but the DS register is not reloaded at each function entry point.

Even though /Au and /Aw indicate that the stack may be in a separate segment, the stack's size is still fixed at the default size unless this is overridden with the /F compiler option or the /STACK linker option.

The /Aw option is useful for writing OS/2 and Microsoft Windows dynamic-link libraries (DLLs), but care must be taken when it is used. Declare all entry points to the dynamic-link library as **_loadds** to force DS to be loaded on entry to the function (exactly like the /Au option). The other functions will then be more efficient, though, because they will not have to perform redundant loads of the DS register. For example,

```
_export _loadds _far pascal LibFunc( void )
{
    .
    .
    .
    HelperFunc(); }

HelperFunc( void )
{
    .
    .
    .
}
```

The library entry point, LibFunc, is declared as **_loadds** to force the DS register to be loaded on entry. The function HelperFunc, which is private to the dynamic-link library, is declared as a normal C function. Since it cannot be called from outside of the module, HelperFunc does not need to reload DS.

If you choose one of the options that specifies that the stack segment is not equal to the data segment (SS != DS), you cannot pass the address of frame variables as arguments to functions that take near pointers. That is, in tiny, small, and medium models, you cannot pass the address of a local variable (which is allocated on the stack) as an argument, because the receiving function will assume the pointer is relative to the data segment. However, the receiving function could solve this problem by declaring the pointer to be the following:

```
based(_segname("_STACK"))
```

Another solution would be to cast the pointer to a far pointer in both locations as follows:

```
/* Call func with an explicit cast to far */
func( (char far *)frame_var );
    .
    .
    .
void func( char far *formal_var )
```

2.4.4 Library Support for Customized Memory Models

Most C programs make function calls to the routines in the C run-time library. When you write mixed-model programs, you are responsible for determining which library (if any) is suitable for your program and for ensuring that the appropriate library is linked. Table 2.3 shows the libraries from which to extract the start-up routine for each customized memory model.

Table 2.3   **Start-Up Routines for Customized Memory Models**

Memory-Model Option	From Library
/Asn$x$; /AS plus /Ax	SLIBCf.LIB
/Asf$x$; /Ash$x$; /AC plus /Ax	CLIBCf.LIB
/Aln$x$; /AM plus /Ax	MLIBCf.LIB
/Alf$x$; /Alh$x$; /AL plus /Ax; /AH plus /Ax	LLIBCf.LIB

The /Ax option represents either /Au or /Aw. In the library names, f is either E (emulator library), 7 (8087/80287 library), or A (alternate math library).

2.4.5 Setting the Data Threshold

Option	Effect
/Gt[[*number*]]	Sets the threshold

The /Gt option causes all data items whose size is greater than to *number* bytes to be allocated to a new data segment. When *number* is specified, it must follow the /Gt option immediately, with no intervening spaces. When *number* is omitted, the default threshold value is 256. When the /Gt option is omitted, the default threshold value is 32,767.

The /Gt option applies only to compact-, large-, and huge-model programs, since small- and medium-model programs have only one data segment. The option is particularly useful with programs that have more than 64K of initialized static and global data in small data items, because otherwise you run out of memory in the default data segment and can't link the program. The /Gt option has no effect on uninitialized global data.

2.4.6 Naming Modules and Segments

Option	Effect
/NM *modulename*	Names the module
/NT *textsegment*	Names the code segment
/ND *datasegment*	Names the data segment

"Module" is another name for an object file created by the C compiler from a single source file. Every module has a name. The compiler uses this name in error messages if problems are encountered during processing. The module name is usually the same as the source-file name. You can change this name using the /NM (name module) option. The new *modulename* can include any combination of letters and digits. The space between /NM and *modulename* is optional.

Every module has at least two segments: a code segment (sometimes called the text segment) containing the program instructions, and a data segment containing the program data.

The compiler normally creates the code and data segment names. The default names depend on the memory model chosen for the program. For example, in small-model programs the code segment is named **_TEXT** and the data segment is named **_DATA**.

Table 2.4 summarizes the naming conventions for code and data segments.

Table 2.4   Segment-Naming Conventions

Model	Code	Data	Module
Tiny	**_TEXT**	**_DATA**	---
Small	**_TEXT**	**_DATA**	---
Medium	*module*_**TEXT**	**_DATA**	*filename*
Compact	**_TEXT**	**_DATA**	*filename*
Large	*module*_**TEXT**	**_DATA**	*filename*
Huge	*module*_**TEXT**	**_DATA**	*filename*

In memory models that contain multiple data segments (compact, large, and huge), **_DATA** is the name of the default data segment. Other data segments have unique private names. You can override the default names with the options /NT (name text) and /ND (name data).

The /ND option is commonly used to create and compile modules that contain data only. Such modules can be accessed from other parts of the program by declaring their variables as external.

If you change the name of the default data segment with /ND, your program must load the DS register with the segment selector of your named data segment before it accesses it. You must therefore compile your program either with the /A*string* form of the memory-model option and the /Au option for the segment setup, or with the /A option for a standard memory model followed by /Au. For example,

```
CL /AS /Au /ND DATA1 PROG1.C
```

The /Au option forces the compiler to generate code to load DS with the correct data-segment value on entry to the code.

All modules whose data segments have the same name have these segments combined into a single segment named `DATA1` at link time.

The functions in the small data model run-time libraries that rely on the default data segment being named "_DATA" will fail if you use the /ND option to rename the default data segment. This restriction affects tiny-, small-, and medium-model programs.

2.4.7 *Specifying Code and Data Segments*

The following pragmas give you more control over the distribution of functions and data:

■ **#pragma alloc_text** (*textsegment, function1* [[*, function2*]]*...*)

■ **#pragma same_seg** (*variable1* [[*, variable2*]]*...*)

The **alloc_text** pragma lets you name the segment in which particular functions are allocated. The **same_seg** pragma provides information the compiler can use to generate better code by assuming that the specified variables are in the same segment.

If you use overlays or swapping techniques to handle large programs, **alloc_text** allows you to tune the contents of their code (text) segments for maximum efficiency. The **alloc_text** pragma must appear before the definitions of any of the specified functions and after the declarations of these functions. Functions referenced in an **alloc_text** pragma should be defined in the same module as the pragma. If this is not done, and an undefined function is later compiled into a different code segment, the error may not be caught.

The **same_seg** pragma tells the compiler to assume that the specified external variables are allocated in the same data segment. You are responsible for making sure that these variables are put in the same data segment; one way to do this is to specify the /ND option when you compile the program.

The **same_seg** pragma must appear before a specified variable appears in the executable code but after the variable is declared. Variables specified in a **same_seg** pragma must be explicitly declared with **extern** storage class, and they must either be explicitly declared with the **_far** keyword or assumed to be far because the memory model is compact, large, or huge.

2.5 Using Based Variables

Whenever you declare a near, far, or huge data variable, the compiler handles the details of where the pointer is stored and how memory is allocated.

With based variables, however, you name a base that specifies where in memory the data resides. This section explains how and why to include based variables in your programs.

2.5.1 New Keywords

The following keywords are new to version 6.0 of Microsoft C:

Keyword	Use
_based(*base-expression*)	Qualifies a declaration to indicate that a variable is based. In the same class as **_near**, **_far**, and **_huge**. It is always followed by a base expression in parentheses.
_segment	New data type that holds a memory segment address. In the same class as **char**, **int**, and **float**.
_segname("*segmentname*")	The name of the segment.
_self	A base expression that names itself as a base.
:>	The base operator that combines a segment and an offset to produce an effective address.

2.5.2 Declaring Based Variables

The **_based** keyword is similar in most respects to the related keywords **_near** and **_far**. You can use it anywhere that **_near** or **_far** might appear.

The **_based** keyword is always followed by a base in parentheses. For example,

```
char _based(seg1) *bp
```

means that `bp` is a based pointer to **char**. In this example, the base is the variable `seg1`.

There are several types of base expressions, which are explained below.

Variables and Pointers Based on a Segment Constant

One way to declare a based variable is to give it a segment constant as a base. Four segments are predefined in Microsoft C:

Segment	Definition
_CODE	The default code segment
_CONST	The constant segment for strings such as "This is a constant string."
_DATA	The default data segment
_STACK	The stack segment

The **_segname** keyword marks the name of a segment. It is always followed by parentheses and a string, as in the example below:

```
/* Compile in Small Model */
#include <stdio.h>
#include <malloc.h>

char _based(_segname("_CODE")) mystring[] = "A code-based string.\n";
int _based(_segname("_CODE")) ib = 12345;
void main()
{
   printf( "%Fs %d", (char _far *)mystring, ib );

}
```

The variable `mystring` is declared as an array of characters based in the code segment. The variable `ib` is an integer (not a pointer) that is also based in the code segment.

Note that the small-model version of **printf** would treat `mystring` as a near pointer. The **F** in the format specifier **%Fs** forces the function to treat it as a far pointer and the cast to **char _far∗** coerces the address to four bytes.

You can also name your own segments. The declaration of `mystring` might look like this:

```
char _based(_segname("MYSEGMENT")) mystring[] = "Another based string.\n";
```

In the example above, the compiler creates a new segment called `MYSEGMENT` and places the string there.

Pointers Based on a Segment Variable

The **_segment** keyword is a new primitive type that can contain the base value of a segment. You can declare variables as type **_segment**, or you can coerce variables of other types to type **_segment** using standard C cast syntax. The key feature of variables of type **_segment** is that you can use them in the declaration of other **_based** variables. The following examples illustrate how **_segment** works:

```
/* a_segment can contain a segment value */
_segment a_segment;

/* The pointer based_on_segvar will always be dereferenced relative
 * to a segment base of a_segment.
 */
char _based( a_segment ) *based_on_segvar;

char near *near_ptr;
/* The pointer based_on_segvar will be dereferenced relative to the
 * segment base of near_ptr (which is the current value of DS).
 */
char _based( (_segment)near_ptr ) *based_on_segvar;

char far *far_ptr;
/* A pointer based_on_segvar will be dereferenced relative to the
 * segment base of far_ptr.
 */
char _based( (_segment)far_ptr ) *based_on_segvar;
```

Declaring variables as based on a segment variable allows you to group based data in the same segment.

In the example below, `segvar` is a variable of type **_segment**. The program requests memory from the heap and bases a variable there.

```
/* Compile in Small Model */
#include <malloc.h>
#include <stdio.h>
#include <string.h>
```

```
_segment segvar;
char _based(segvar) *b_string;

void main()
{
    if( (segvar = _bheapseg( 1000 )) != _NULLSEG )
    {
        if( (b_string = _bmalloc( segvar, 20 )) != _NULLOFF )
        {
            _fstrcpy( (char _far *)b_string, (char _far *)"This is a test.\n" );
            printf( "%Fs", (char _far *)b_string );
            printf( "Size = %d\n", sizeof b_string );   /* Always 2 */
            _bfree( segvar, b_string );
        }
        else
            puts( "bmalloc failed" );
        _bfreeseg( segvar );
    }
    else
        puts( "_bheapseg failed." );
}
```

First, the program asks for 1,000 bytes in a new based heap segment:

```
if( (segvar = _bheapseg( 1000 )) != _NULLSEG )
```

On failure, the **_bheapseg** function returns **_NULLSEG** (null segment). Otherwise, `segvar` holds the valid address of a segment.

Next, the **_bmalloc** function allocates 20 bytes of memory within the segment base and assigns the offset to `b_string`:

```
if( (b_string = _bmalloc( segvar, 20 )) != _NULLOFF )
```

In this case, **_NULLOFF** means "null offset" and indicates the failure of **_bmalloc**. If all is well, the program continues with this code:

```
_fstrcpy( (char _far *)b_string, (char _far *)"This is a test.\n" );
printf( "%Fs", (char _far *)b_string );
printf( "Size = %d\n", sizeof b_string );   /* always 2 */
```

The standard **strcpy** function won't work because this is a small-model program that expects all pointers to be near. The **_fstrcpy** function allows you to copy to a far string. Then the string and its size are printed.

Finally, the offset memory and the segment memory are freed:

```
_bfree( segvar, b_string );
_bfreeseg( segvar );
```

Pointers Based on a Pointer

A based pointer can use another pointer as its base. In the example below, the variable ip is a pointer to an integer. It serves as the base for both bp (a pointer to an integer) and cp (a pointer to a character).

NOTE *Only pointer variables can be based on a pointer. Nonpointer variables (objects) cannot be based on a pointer.*

To find the actual address to which bp points, you take the address in its base (ip) and add the value in bp. For example, if ip points to location 0x2345 and bp holds a 3, then it points to 0x2348. Changing the value in the base immediately changes the addresses to which the based pointers point.

The following example illustrates pointers based on a pointer:

```
#include <stdio.h>
#include <malloc.h>
#include <stdlib.h>
#include <string.h>

int *ip;              /* int pointer */
int _based(ip) *bp;   /* based on ip */
char _based(ip) *cp;

void main()
{
   int *mem1, *mem2;

   bp = (void *)0;    /* bp equals *(ip+0) */
   cp = (void *)2;    /* cp equals *(ip+2) */

   if( (mem1 = (int *)malloc( 100 )) != NULL )
      if( (mem2 = (int *)malloc( 100 )) != NULL )
      {
         ip = mem1; /* ip points to mem1 */
         *bp = 5;
         strcpy( (char *)cp, "String stored in mem1." );
```

```
        ip = mem2;  /* ip now points to mem2 */
        *bp = 12345;
        strcpy( (char *)cp, "String stored in mem2." );

        ip = mem1;  /* point to mem1 */
        /* which still holds previous values */
        printf( "%s  *bp= %i\n", (char *)cp, *bp );

        ip = mem2;  /* point to mem2 */
        /* display the values there */
        printf( "%s  *bp= %i\n", (char *)cp, *bp );

        free( mem2 );
        free( mem1 );
      }
      else puts( "Second malloc failed." );
    else puts( "First malloc failed." );
}
```

Two calls to **malloc** provide two sections of memory, whose addresses are stored in the variables `mem1` and `mem2`. When `ip` is assigned one of these addresses (`mem1`), the pointers based on `ip` point somewhere within that piece of memory. When `ip` is assigned the address in `mem2`, the effective addresses of `bp` and `cp` also change.

Pointers Based on Void

A third way to declare a based pointer is to give it no base at all—to base it on **void**. This creates a generic pointer that acts as an offset into a segment. Such a based pointer can then be combined with a segment name to specify any address.

NOTE *Only pointer variables can be based on **void**. Nonpointer variables (objects) cannot be based on **void**.*

To combine a segment and an offset, use the "base operator." It consists of a colon and a greater-than symbol (:>). Place it between a segment value and an offset as show in the syntax below:

segment:>*offset*

The address can be dereferenced with the indirection operator (*).

The program below reads the first 40 words of video memory and prints the character values. Within a text mode, the high byte contains the colors and other attributes. The low byte contains the characters.

```c
#include <malloc.h>
#include <stdio.h>
#include <conio.h>

_segment segvar = 0xB800;   /* Substitute 0xB000 for Mono */
int _based(void) *vp = 0;

void main()
{
    int i, screen[40];
    for( i = 0; i < 40; i++, vp++ )
    {
        screen[i] = *(segvar:>vp);
    }
    for( i = 0; i < 40; i++ )
        printf("%c", (char)screen[i] );
}
```

The video segment for color text starts at 0xB800. If you're using a monochrome monitor, substitute 0xB000. The variable vp acts as a generic based pointer. To read through video memory, combine the segment and offset and dereference the pointer:

```c
screen[i] = *(segvar:>vp);
```

In the example above, the value is stored in an array of integers. The character values are then printed out:

```c
for( i = 0; i < 40; i++ )
    printf("%c", (char)screen[i] );
```

Pointers Based on a Self Segment

Another way to declare a based pointer is to use the **_self** keyword cast to a segment value, as in the example below:

```
typedef struct tree TREE;

struct tree
{
    int name;
    TREE _based((_segment)_self) *left;
    TREE _based((_segment)_self) *right;
};

void main()
{
    TREE _based( _segname( "MYSEGMENT" ) ) t1;
}
```

Any based declarations that are based on **_self** must apply to pointers only. Ordinary data objects cannot be self-based.

The example above declares a structure called `tree` and then declares `t1` to be such a structure. The pointers within the structure are self-based, meaning they will point within the segment in which the tree structure is located. This is useful when the entire tree would fit into a single based segment. Note that functions cannot return pointers based on **_self**.

2.5.3 Advantages of Based Pointers

The advantage of near pointers is that they occupy only two bytes in memory. The disadvantage is that they can only address the 65,536 locations in the default data segment.

The advantage of far pointers is that they remove the addressing limit; they can point to any address. The disadvantage is that they need twice as much memory for each pointer: four bytes instead of two.

Based pointers are small and flexible.

Based pointers are as small as near pointers but as flexible as far pointers, they enjoy both of the benefits and neither of the drawbacks of the other pointers. Like a near pointer, a based pointer occupies only two bytes. Like a far pointer, a based pointer can point anywhere in memory. You must, however, provide some extra information about where the base is.

Based pointers don't need the two extra bytes used by far pointers to name the segment. When necessary, the Microsoft C compiler generates the code to switch segments to the new base.

If you write programs that use many far pointers, you may be able to save memory by converting the four-byte far pointers to two-byte based pointers.

Near pointers always give you the fastest code. Far and huge pointers always give you the slowest.

Based pointers can be faster than far pointers.

Based pointers lie somewhere in between. When a function accesses a group of based pointers that have the same base, the extra segment register (ES) may be loaded only once. If you enable full optimization and use the same base for your based pointers, in many cases they will be faster than far pointers and nearly as fast as near pointers.

Based pointers can give you access to the code, data, stack, or constant segments. For example, if you want to use the small memory model, but the data requires more than 64K, you can store some of the constant strings in the code segment (instead of the constant segment).

Another benefit of based pointers is that you can swap data from disk to memory or from one area of memory to another. If a series of variables has the same base, you can easily move the block of memory around without having to reinitialize the variables' address.

Based pointers give you assembler-level access to memory.

If you want to read from or write to areas such as video memory, ROM, or the I/O areas, you can declare based pointers that access these sections of memory.

Using the In-Line Assembler

This chapter explains how to use the Microsoft C in-line assembler. Assembly language serves many purposes, such as improving program speed, reducing memory needs, and controlling hardware. The in-line assembler lets you embed assembly-language instructions directly in your C source programs without extra assembly and link steps. The in-line assembler is built into the compiler—you don't need a separate assembler such as the Microsoft Macro Assembler (MASM).

3.1 Advantages of In-Line Assembly

Because the in-line assembler doesn't require separate assembly and link steps, it is more convenient than a separate assembler. In-line assembly code can use any C variable or function name that is in scope, so it is easy to integrate it with your program's C code. And because the assembly code can be mixed in-line with C statements, it can do tasks that are cumbersome or impossible in C alone.

The uses of in-line assembly include

- Writing functions in assembly language

- Spot-optimizing speed-critical sections of code

- Calling DOS and BIOS routines with the **INT** instruction

- Creating TSR (terminate-and-stay-resident) code or handler routines that require knowledge of processor states

In-line assembly is a special-purpose tool. If you plan to transport an application, you'll probably want to place machine-specific code in a separate module. And because the in-line assembler doesn't support all of MASM's macro and data directives, you may find it more convenient to use MASM for such modules.

3.2 The _asm Keyword

The **_asm** keyword invokes the in-line assembler and can appear wherever a C statement is legal. It cannot appear by itself. It must be followed by an assembly instruction, a group of instructions enclosed in braces, or, at the very least, an empty pair of braces. The term "**_asm** block" here refers to any instruction or group of instructions, whether or not in braces.

Below is a simple **_asm** block enclosed in braces. (The code prints the "beep" character, ASCII 7.).

```
_asm
{
    mov ah, 2
    mov dl, 7
    int 21h
}
```

Alternatively, you can put **_asm** in front of each assembly instruction:

```
_asm mov ah, 2
_asm mov dl, 7
_asm int 21h
```

Since the **_asm** keyword is a statement separator, you can also put assembly instructions on the same line:

```
_asm mov ah, 2   _asm mov dl, 7   _asm int 21h
```

Braces can prevent ambiguity and needless repetition.

All three examples generate the same code, but the first style—enclosing the **_asm** block in braces—has some advantages. The braces clearly separate assembly code from C code and avoid needless repetition of the **_asm** keyword. Braces can also prevent ambiguities. If you want to put a C statement on the same line as an **_asm** block, you must enclose the block in braces. Without the braces, the compiler cannot tell where assembly code stops and C statements begin. Finally, since the text in braces has the same format as ordinary MASM text, you can easily cut and paste text from existing MASM source files.

The braces enclosing an **_asm** block don't affect variable scope, as do braces in C. You can also nest **_asm** blocks, but the nesting doesn't affect variable scope.

3.3 Using Assembly Language in _asm Blocks

The in-line assembler has much in common with other assemblers. For example, it accepts any expression that is legal in MASM, and it supports all 80286 and 80287 instructions. This section describes the use of assembly-language features in **_asm** blocks.

Instruction Set

The in-line assembler supports the full instruction set of the Intel 80286 and 80287 processors. It does not recognize 80386- and 80387-specific instructions. To use 80286 or 80287 instructions, compile with the /G2 option.

Expressions

In-line assembly code can use any MASM expression, that is, any combination of operands and operators that evaluates to a single value or address.

Data Directives and Operators

Although an **_asm** block can reference C data types and objects, it cannot define data objects with MASM directives or operators. Specifically, you cannot use the definition directives **DB**, **DW**, **DD**, **DQ**, **DT**, and **DF**, or the operators **DUP** or **THIS**. Nor are MASM structures and records available. The in-line assembler doesn't accept the directives **STRUC**, **RECORD**, **WIDTH**, or **MASK**.

EVEN and ALIGN Directives

While the in-line assembler doesn't support most MASM directives, it does support **EVEN** and **ALIGN**. These directives put **NOP** (no operation) instructions in the assembly code as needed to align labels to specific boundaries. This makes instruction-fetch operations more efficient for some processors (not including eight-bit processors such as the Intel 8088).

Macros

The in-line assembler is not a macro assembler. You cannot use MASM macro directives (**MACRO, REPT, IRC, IRP**, and **ENDM**) or macro operators (**<>, !, &,** %, and **.TYPE**). An **_asm** block can use C preprocessor directives, however. See Section 3.4, "Using C in **_asm** Blocks" for more information.

Segment References

You must refer to segments by register rather than by name (the segment name **_TEXT** is invalid, for instance). Segment overrides must use the register explicitly, as in ES:[BX].

Type and Variable Sizes

The **LENGTH**, **SIZE**, and **TYPE** operators have a limited meaning in in-line assembly. They cannot be used at all with the **DUP** operator (because you cannot define data with MASM directives or operators). But you can use them to find the size of C variables or types:

- The **LENGTH** operator can return the number of elements in an array. It returns the value 1 for nonarray variables.

- The **SIZE** operator can return the size of a C variable. A variable's size is the product of its **LENGTH** and **TYPE**.

- The **TYPE** operator can return the size of a C type or variable. If the variable is an array, **TYPE** returns the size of a single element of the array.

For instance, if your program has an eight-element **int** array,

```
int arr[8];
```

the following C and assembly expressions yield the size of `arr` and its elements:

_asm	C	Size
LENGTH arr	sizeof(ar)/sizeof(arr[0])	8
SIZE arr	sizeof (arr)	16
TYPE arr	size14(arr[0])	2

Comments

Instructions in an **_asm** block can use assembly-language comments:

```
_asm mov ax, offset buff ; Load address of buff
```

Because C macros expand into a single logical line, avoid using assembly-language comments in macros (see Section 3.8, "Defining **_asm** Blocks as C Macros"). An **_asm** block can also contain C-style comments, as noted below.

The _emit Pseudoinstruction

The **_emit** pseudoinstruction is similar to the **DB** directive of MASM. It allows you to define a single immediate byte at the current location in the current text segment. However, **_emit** can define only one byte at a time, and it can only define bytes in the text segment. It uses the same syntax as the **INT** instruction.

One use for **_emit** is to define 80386-specific instructions, which the in-line assembler does not support. The following fragment, for instance, defines the 80386 **CWDE** instruction:

```
/* Assumes 16-bit mode */
#define cwde _asm _emit 0x66 _asm _emit 0x98
    .
    .
    .
_asm {
    cwde
    }
```

Debugging and Listings

In-line assembly code can be debugged with CodeView.

Programs containing in-line assembly code can be debugged with the CodeView debugger, assuming you compile with the /Zi option.

Within CodeView, you can set breakpoints on both C and assembly-language lines. If you enable mixed assembly and C mode, you can display both the source and disassembled form of the assembly code.

Note that putting multiple assembly instructions or C statements on one line can hamper debugging with CodeView. In source mode, the CodeView debugger lets you set breakpoints on a single line but not on individual statements on the same line. The same principle applies to an **_asm** block defined as a C macro, which expands to a single logical line.

If you create a mixed source and assembly listing with the /Fc compiler option, the listing contains both the source and assembly forms of each assembly-language line. Macros are not expanded in listings, but they are expanded during compilation.

See Chapter 9, "Debugging C Programs with CodeView," for more information.

3.4 *Using C in _asm Blocks*

Because in-line assembly instructions can be mixed with C statements, they can refer to C variables by name and use many other elements of C. An **_asm** block can use the following C language elements:

- Symbols, including labels and variable and function names

- Constants, including symbolic constants and **enum** members

- Macros and preprocessor directives

- Comments (both /* */ and //)

- Type names (wherever a MASM type would be legal)

- **typedef** names, generally used with operators such as **PTR** and **TYPE** or to specify structure or union members

Within an **_asm** block, you can specify integer constants with either C notation or assembler radix notation (0x100 and 100h are equivalent, for instance). This allows you to define (using **#define**) a constant in C, and use it in both C and assembly portions of the program. You can also specify constants in octal by preceding them with a 0. For example, 0777 specifies an octal constant.

3.4.1 *Using Operators*

An **_asm** block cannot use C-specific operators, such as the << operator. However, operators shared by C and MASM, such as the * operator, are interpreted as assembly-language operators. For instance, outside an **_asm** block, square brackets ([]) are interpreted as enclosing array subscripts, which C automatically scales to the size of an element in the array. Inside an **_asm** block, they are seen as the MASM index operator, which yields an unscaled byte offset from any data object or label (not just an array). The following code illustrates the difference:

```
int array[10];

_asm mov array[6], bx ;  Store BX at array+6 (not scaled)

array[6] = 0;           /* Store 0 at array+12 (scaled) */
```

The first reference to `array` is not scaled, but the second is. Note that you can use the **TYPE** operator to achieve scaling based on a constant. For instance, the following statements are equivalent:

```
_asm mov array[6 * TYPE int], 0 ; Store 0 at array + 12

array[6] = 0;                    /* Store 0 at array + 12 */
```

3.4.2 Using C Symbols

An **_asm** block can refer to any C symbol in scope where the block appears. (C symbols are variable names, function names, and labels—in other words, names that aren't symbolic constants or **enum** members.)

A few restrictions apply to the use of C symbols:

- Each assembly-language statement can contain only one C symbol. Multiple symbols can appear in the same assembly instruction only with **LENGTH**, **TYPE**, and **SIZE** expressions.

- Functions referenced in an **_asm** block must be declared (prototyped) earlier in the program. Otherwise, the compiler cannot distinguish between function names and labels in the **_asm** block.

- An **_asm** block cannot use any C symbols with the same spelling as MASM reserved words (regardless of case). MASM reserved words include instruction names such as **PUSH** and register names such as SI.

- Structure and union tags are not recognized in **_asm** blocks.

3.4.3 Accessing C Data

A great convenience of in-line assembly is the ability to refer to C variables by name. An **_asm** block can refer to any symbols—including variable names—that are in scope where the block appears. For instance, if the C variable `var` is in scope, the instruction

```
_asm mov ax, var
```

stores the value of `var` in AX.

If a structure or union member has a unique name, an **_asm** block can refer to it using only the member name, without specifying the C variable or **typedef** name before the period (**.**) operator. If the member name is not unique, however, you must place a variable or **typedef** name immediately before the period (**.**) operator. For instance, the following structure types share same_name as their member name:

```
struct first_type
{
    char *weasel;
    int same_name;
};

struct second_type
{
    int wonton;
    long same_name;
};
```

If you declare variables with the types

```
struct first_type hal;
struct second_type oat;
```

all references to the member same_name must use the variable name, because same_name is not unique. But the member weasel has a unique name, so you can refer to it using only its member name:

```
_asm
{
    mov bx, OFFSET hal
    mov cx, [bx]hal.same_name ; Must use 'hal'
    mov si, [bx].weasel       ; Can omit 'hal'
}
```

Note that omitting the variable name is merely a coding convenience. The same assembly instructions are generated whether or not it is present.

3.4.4 Writing Functions

If you write a function with in-line assembly code, it's a simple matter to pass arguments to the function and return a value from it. The following examples compare a function first written for a separate assembler and then rewritten for the in-line assembler. The function, called power2, receives two parameters, multiplying the first parameter by 2 to the power of the second parameter. Written for a separate assembler, the function might look like this:

```
; POWER.ASM
; Compute the power of an integer
;
        PUBLIC _power2
_TEXT SEGMENT WORD PUBLIC 'CODE'
_power2 PROC

        push bp            ; Save BP
        mov bp, sp         ; Move SP into BP so we can refer
                           ;    to arguments on the stack
        mov ax, [bp+4]     ; Get first argument
        mov cx, [bp+6]     ; Get second argument
        shl ax, cl         ; AX = AX * ( 2 ^ CL )
        pop bp             ; Restore BP
        ret                ; Return with sum in AX

_power2 ENDP
_TEXT   ENDS
        END
```

Function arguments are usually passed on the stack.

Since it's written for a separate assembler, the function requires a separate source file and assembly and link steps. C function arguments usually are passed on the stack, so this version of the power2 function accesses its arguments by their positions on the stack. (Note that the **MODEL** directive, available in MASM and some other assemblers, also allows you to access stack arguments and local stack variables by name.)

The POWER2.C program below writes the power2 function with in-line assembly code:

```
/* POWER2.C */
#include <stdio.h>

int power2( int num, int power );

void main( void )
{
    printf( "3 times 2 to the power of 5 is %d\n", \
            power2( 3, 5) );
}

int power2( int num, int power )
{
    _asm
    {
        mov ax, num     ; Get first argument
        mov cx, power   ; Get second argument
        shl ax, cl      ; AX = AX * ( 2 to the power of CL )
    }
    /* Return with result in AX */
}
```

The in-line version of the `power2` function refers to its arguments by name and appears in the same source file as the rest of the program. This version also requires fewer assembly instructions. Since C automatically preserves BP, the **_asm** block doesn't need to do so. It can also dispense with the **RET** instruction, since the C part of the function performs the return.

Because the in-line version of `power2` doesn't execute a C **return** statement, it causes a harmless warning if you compile at warning levels 2 or higher:

```
warning C4035: 'power2' : no return value
```

The function does return a value, but the compiler cannot tell that in the absence of a **return** statement. Simply ignore the warning in this context.

3.5 Using and Preserving Registers

In general, you should not assume that a register will have a given value when an **_asm** block begins. An **_asm** block inherits whatever register values happen to result from the normal flow of control.

If you use the **_fastcall** calling convention, the compiler passes function arguments in registers instead of the stack. This can create problems in functions with **_asm** blocks, since a function has no way to tell which parameter is in which register. If the function happens to receive a parameter in AX and immediately stores something else in AX, the parameter is lost. In addition, you must preserve the CX and ES registers in any function declared with **_fastcall**.

Don't use the _fastcall calling convention for functions with _asm blocks.

To avoid such register conflicts, don't use the **_fastcall** convention for functions that contain an **_asm** block. If you specify the **_fastcall** convention globally with the /Gr compiler option, declare every function containing an **_asm** block with **_cdecl**. (The **_cdecl** attribute tells the compiler to use the normal C calling convention for that function.) If you are not compiling with /Gr, avoid declaring the function with the **_fastcall** attribute.

As you may have noticed in the POWER2.C example in Section 3.4.4, the `power2` function doesn't preserve the value in the AX register. When you write a function in assembly language, you don't need to preserve the AX, BX, CX, DX, ES, and flags registers. However, you should preserve any other registers you use (DI, SI, DS, SS, SP, and BP).

WARNING   *If your in-line assembly code changes the direction flag using the STD or CLD instructions, you must restore the flag to its original value.*

Functions return values in the AX and DX registers.

The POWER2.C example in Section 3.4.4 also shows that functions return values in registers. This is true whether the function is written in assembly language or in C.

If the return value is short (a **char**, **int**, or **near** pointer), it is stored in AX. The POWER2.C example returned a value by terminating with the desired value in AX.

If the return value is long, store the high word in DX and the low word in AX. To return a longer value (such as a floating-point value), store the value in memory and return a pointer to the value (in AX if **near** or in DX:AX if **far**).

Assembly instructions that appear in-line with C statements are free to alter the AX, BX, CX, and DX registers. C doesn't expect these registers to be maintained between statements, so you don't need to preserve them. The same is true of the SI and DI registers, with some exceptions (see Section 3.9, "Optimizing"). You should preserve the SP and BP registers unless you have some reason to change them—to switch stacks, for instance.

3.6 *Jumping to Labels*

Like an ordinary C label, a label in an **_asm** block has scope throughout the function in which it is defined (not only in the block). Both assembly instructions and C **goto** statements can jump to labels inside or outside the **_asm** block.

Labels in _asm blocks have function scope and are not case sensitive.

Unlike C labels, labels defined in **_asm** blocks are not case sensitive, even when used in C statements. C labels are not case sensitive in an **_asm** block, either. (Outside an **_asm** block, a C label is case sensitive as usual.) The following do-nothing code shows all the permutations:

```
void func( void )
{
    goto C_Dest;  /* legal */
    goto c_dest;  /* error */

    goto A_Dest;  /* legal */
    goto a_dest;  /* legal */

    _asm
    {
        jmp C_Dest ; legal
        jmp c_dest ; legal

        jmp A_Dest ; legal
        jmp a_dest ; legal

        a_dest:    ; _asm label
    }

    C_Dest:        /* C label */
    return;
}
```

Don't use C library function names as labels in **_asm** blocks. For instance, you might be tempted to use `exit` as a label,

```
jne exit
     .
     .
     .
exit:
     ; More _asm code follows
```

forgetting that **exit** is the name of a C library function. The code doesn't cause a compiler error, but it might cause a jump to the **exit** function instead of the desired location.

As in MASM programs, the dollar symbol (**$**) serves as the current location counter—a label for the instruction currently being assembled. In **_asm** blocks, its main use is to make long conditional jumps:

```
jne $+5 ; next instruction is 5 bytes long
jmp farlabel
; $+5
     .
     .
     .
farlabel:
```

3.7 Calling C Functions

An **_asm** block can call C functions, including C library routines. The following example calls the **printf** library routine:

```
#include <stdio.h>

char format[] = "%s %s\n";
char hello[] = "Hello";
char world[] = "world";

void main( void )
{
   _asm
   {
      mov  ax, offset world
      push ax
      mov  ax, offset hello
      push ax
      mov  ax, offset format
      push ax
      call printf
   }
}
```

Since function arguments are passed on the stack, you simply push the needed arguments—string pointers, in the example above—before calling the function. The arguments are pushed in reverse order, so they come off the stack in the desired order. To emulate the C statement

```
printf( format, hello, world );
```

the example pushes pointers to `world`, `hello`, and `format`, in that order, then calls **printf**.

3.8 Defining _asm Blocks as C Macros

C macros offer a convenient way to insert assembly code into C code, but they demand extra care because a macro expands into a single logical line. To create trouble-free macros, follow these rules:

- Enclose the **_asm** block in braces.

- Put the **_asm** keyword in front of each assembly instruction.

- Use old-style C comments (/* comment */) instead of assembly-style comments (; comment) or single-line C comments (// comment).

To illustrate, the following example defines a simple macro:

```
#define BEEP _asm \
/* Beep sound */        \
{                       \
    _asm mov ah, 2      \
    _asm mov dl, 7      \
    _asm int 21h        \
}
```

At first glance, the last three **_asm** keywords seem superfluous. They are needed, however, because the macro expands into a single line:

```
_asm /* Beep sound */ { _asm mov ah, 2  _asm mov dl, 7 _asm int 21h }
```

The third and fourth **_asm** keywords are needed as statement separators. The only statement separators recognized in **_asm** blocks are the newline character and **_asm** keyword. And since a block defined as a macro is one logical line, you must separate each instruction with **_asm**.

The braces are essential as well. If you omit them, the compiler can be confused by C statements on the same line to the right of the macro invocation. Without the closing brace, the compiler cannot tell where assembly code stops, and it sees C statements after the **_asm** block as assembly instructions.

Use C comments in _asm blocks written as macros.

Assembly-style comments that start with a semicolon (;) continue to the end of the line. This causes problems in macros because the compiler ignores everything after the comment, all the way to the end of the logical line. The same is true of single-line C comments (// comment). To prevent errors, use old-style C comments (/* comment */) in **_asm** blocks defined as macros.

An _asm block written as a C macro can take arguments but cannot return a value.

An **_asm** block written as a C macro can take arguments. Unlike an ordinary C macro, however, an **_asm** macro cannot return a value. So you cannot use such macros in C expressions.

Be careful not to invoke macros of this type indiscriminately. For instance, invoking an assembly-language macro in a function declared with the **_fastcall** convention may cause unexpected results. (See Section 3.5, "Using and Preserving Registers.")

You can convert MASM macros to C macros.

Note that some MASM-style macros can be written as C macros. Below is a MASM macro that sets the video page to the value specified in the page argument:

```
setpage    MACRO page
           mov ah, 5
           mov al, page
           int 10h
           ENDM
```

The following code defines setpage as a C macro:

```
#define setpage( page ) _asm   \
    {                                 \
        _asm mov ah, 5                \
        _asm mov al, page             \
        _asm int 10h                  \
    }
```

Both macros do the same job.

3.9 Optimizing

The presence of an **_asm** block in a function affects optimization in a few different ways. First, as you might expect, the compiler doesn't try to optimize the **_asm** block itself. What you write in assembly language is exactly what you get.

Second, the presence of an **_asm** block affects register variable storage. Under normal circumstances (unless you suppress optimization with the /Od option) the compiler automatically stores variables in registers. This is not done, however, in any function that contains an **_asm** block. To get register variable storage in such a function, you must request it with the **register** keyword.

Since the compiler stores register variables in the SI and DI registers, these registers represent variables in functions that request register storage. The first eligible variable is stored in SI and the second in DI. Preserve SI and DI in such functions unless you want to change the register variables.

Keep in mind that the name of a variable declared with **register** translates directly into a register reference (assuming a register is available for such use). For instance, if you declare

```
register int sample;
```

and the variable `sample` happens to be stored in SI, then the **_asm** instruction

```
_asm mov ax, sample
```

is equivalent to

```
_asm mov ax, si
```

If you declare a variable with **register** and the compiler cannot store the variable in a register, the compiler issues a warning to that effect at compile time. The solution is to remove the **register** declaration from that variable.

Register variables form a slight exception to the general rule that an assembly-language statement can contain no more than one C symbol. If one of the symbols is a register variable, for example,

```
register int v1;
int v2;
```

then an instruction can use two C symbols, as in

```
mov v1, v2
```

Finally, the presence of in-line assembly code inhibits the following optimizations for the entire function in which the code appears:

- Loop (/Ol)

- Global register allocation (/Oe)

- Global optimizations and common subexpressions (/Og)

These optimizations are suppressed no matter which compiler options you use.

Controlling Floating-Point Math Operations

This chapter describes how to control the way your Microsoft C programs perform floating-point math operations. It describes the math packages that you can include in C libraries when you run the SETUP program, then discusses the options you can specify in the Programmer's WorkBench (PWB) or on the CL command line to choose the appropriate library for linking and controlling floating-point instructions.

This chapter also explains how to override floating-point options by changing libraries at link time, and how to control use of the Intel math coprocessor (80*x*87) using the NO87 environment variable.

4.1 Declaring Floating-Point Types

Microsoft C supports three floating-point types that conform to the Institute of Electrical and Electronics Engineers (IEEE) standard 754 format:

1. Type **float**, a 32-bit floating-point quantity

2. Type **double**, a 64-bit floating-point quantity

3. Type **long double**, an 80-bit floating-point quantity

You can declare variables as any of these types. You can also declare functions that return any of these types.

4.1.1 Declaring Variables as Floating-Point Types

You can declare variables as **float**, **double**, or **long double**, depending on the needs of your application. The principal differences between the three types are the significance they can represent, the storage they require, and their range. Table 4.1 shows the relationship between significance and storage requirements.

Table 4.1   Floating-Point Types

Type	Significant Digits	Number of Bytes
float	6–7	4
double	15–16	8
long double	19	10

Floating-point variables are represented by a mantissa, which contains the value of the number, and an exponent, which contains the order of magnitude of the number.

Table 4.2 shows the number of bits allocated to the mantissa and the exponent for each floating-point type. The most-significant bit of any **float**, **double**, or **long double** is always the sign bit. If it is 1, the number is considered negative; otherwise, it is considered a positive number.

Table 4.2   Lengths of Exponents and Mantissas

Type	Exponent Length	Mantissa Length
float	8 bits	23 bits
double	11 bits	52 bits
long double	15 bits	64 bits

Because exponents are stored in an unsigned form, the exponent is biased by half its possible value. For type **float**, the bias is 127; for type **double**, it is 1,023; for type **long double**, it is 16,383. You can compute the actual exponent value by subtracting the bias value from the exponent value.

The mantissa is stored as a binary fraction greater than or equal to 1 and less than 2. For types **float** and **double**, there is an implied leading 1 in the mantissa in the most-significant bit position, so the mantissas are actually 24 and 53 bits long, respectively, even though the most-significant bit is never stored in memory.

Instead of the storage method just described, the floating-point package can store binary floating-point numbers as denormalized numbers. Denormalized numbers are nonzero floating-point numbers with reserved exponent values in which the most-significant bit of the mantissa is zero. By using denormalized format, the range of a floating-point number can be extended at the cost of precision. You cannot control whether a floating-point number is represented in normalized or denormalized form; the floating-point package determines the representation. The floating-point packages never use denormalized form unless the exponent becomes less than the minimum that can be represented in a normalized form.

Table 4.3 shows the minimum and maximum value you can store in variables of each floating-point type. The values listed in this table apply only to normalized floating-point numbers; denormalized floating-point numbers have a smaller minimum value. Note that numbers retained in 80x87 registers are always represented in 80-bit normal form; numbers can only be represented in denormal form when stored in 32- or 64-bit floating-point variables (type **float** and type **long**).

Table 4.3   Range of Floating-Point Types

Type	Minimum Value	Maximum Value
float	1.175494351 E − 38	3.402823466 E + 38
double	2.2250738585072014 E − 308	1.7976931348623158 E + 308
long double	3.362103143112093503 E − 4932	1.189731495357231765 E + 4932

If precision is less of a concern than storage, consider using type **float** for floating-point variables. Conversely, if precision is the most important criterion, use type **long double**.

Microsoft C observes type-widening rules.

Floating-point variables can be promoted to a type of greater significance (for example, from type **float** to type **double**). Promotion often occurs when you perform arithmetic on floating-point variables. This arithmetic is always done in as high a degree of precision as the variable with the highest degree of precision. For example, consider the following type declarations:

```
float f_short;
double f_long;
long double f_longer;

f_short = f_short * f_long;
```

In the preceding example, the variable f_short is promoted to type **double** and multiplied by f_long; then the result is rounded to type **float** before being assigned to f_short.

In the example below (which uses the declarations from the preceding example), the arithmetic is done in **float** (32-bit) precision on the variables; the result is then promoted to type **long double**.

```
f_longer = f_short * f_short;
```

4.1.2 *Declaring Functions that Return Floating-Point Types*

You can declare functions that return the floating-point types **float**, **double**, and **long double**. Functions that return types **float** or **double** do not place their return values in registers; they place their return values in a global location called the floating-point accumulator (_ _**fac**).

When declaring a function as a floating-point type in a multithreaded program for OS/2, you should use the **_pascal** keyword to specify the FORTRAN/Pascal calling convention. Declaring the function as **_pascal** causes the return value to be placed on the stack, rather than in the floating-point accumulator, _ _**fac**.

You can write re-entrant functions that return floating-point types.

Using the current thread's private stack to return values allows you to write re-entrant functions by eliminating possible contention between threads for the floating-point accumulator.

NOTE *Functions that return type **long double** always place their return values on the stack. You need not use the **_pascal** keyword with functions declared as **long double**.*

4.2 *C Run-Time Library Support of Type long double*

All of the Microsoft C run-time libraries support type **long double**. Each of the normal floating-point math functions has a special version that supports type **long double**. These functions have the same name as the functions that support type **float** and type **double**, except that they end with **l**. For example, the function that returns the absolute value of a variable of type **float** or type **double** is **fabs**. The **long double** equivalent function is **fabsl**. The two exceptions to this rule are the **_atold** and **_strtodl** functions.

4.3 *Summary of Math Packages*

The Microsoft C compiler offers a choice of the following three math packages for handling floating-point operations:

1. Emulator (default)

2. Math coprocessor (a library that supports the Intel 80*x*87 family of math coprocessors)

3. Alternate math

When you install Microsoft C, the SETUP program allows you to build combined libraries. These libraries include the floating-point math library that you choose. Any programs linked with that library use the math package included in the library; you must use the appropriate PWB or CL option to make sure that the library you want is used at link time.

The following descriptions of these math packages are designed to help you choose the appropriate math option for your needs when you build a library using SETUP. For more information about SETUP and about building combined libraries, see *Installing and Using the Microsoft C Professional Development System*.

Note that this chapter does not describe mode-specific libraries. For simplicity, the base names of libraries are noted in their default form; that is *m*LIBC*f*.LIB, where *m* is the model designator and *f* is the floating-point math package designator. For information about mode-specific libraries, see Chapter 14, "Building OS/2 Applications," or *Installing and Using the Microsoft C Professional Development System*.

4.3.1 Emulator Package

Programs created using the emulator math package automatically detect and use an 80*x*87 numeric coprocessor if one is installed. If no coprocessor is installed, these 80*x*87 instructions are carried out in software. The emulator package is the default math package; SETUP uses it if you do not explicitly choose another package. Also, the emulator math option is the option selected by default by the compiler if no other floating-point math option is specified.

Use the emulator math package to maximize accuracy on systems without math coprocessors or if your program will be run on some systems with coprocessors and some systems without coprocessors.

The emulator package performs basic operations to the same degree of accuracy as a math coprocessor. However, the emulator routines used for transcendental math functions (such as **sin, cos, tan**) differ slightly from the corresponding functions performed on a coprocessor. This difference can cause a slight discrepancy (usually within two bits) between the results of these operations when performed with the software emulation instead of with a math coprocessor.

When you use the emulator package, some floating-point exceptions are masked.

When you use a math coprocessor or the emulator floating-point math package, interrupt-enable, precision, underflow, and denormalized-operand exceptions are masked by default. The remaining floating-point exceptions are unmasked. See the discussion of the **_control87** function in on-line help for more information about 80*x*87 floating-point exceptions.

4.3.2 Math Coprocessor Package

The math coprocessor package utilizes the 80x87 math coprocessor exclusively for floating-point calculations. If you use the math coprocessor package, the machine on which your application is to run must have an 80x87 coprocessor to perform floating-point operations. This package gives you the fastest, smallest programs possible for handling floating-point math.

4.3.3 Alternate Math Package

The alternate math package gives you the smallest and fastest programs possible without a coprocessor. However, the program results are not as accurate as results given by the emulator package.

The alternate math package uses the same format as the IEEE standard-format numbers with less precision and weaker error checking. The alternate math package does not support infinities, NANs ("not a number"), and denormal numbers.

You must always use the alternate math package when developing routines that are to be placed in an OS/2 dynamic-link library (DLL) using LLIBCDLL.LIB. Do not, however, use the alternate math package for building the C run-time DLL using CDLLOBJS.LIB; instead, use the emulator math package. For more information about creating dynamic-link libraries for OS/2, see Chapter 16.

4.4 Selecting Floating-Point Options (/FP)

You can select a floating-point library and the method of accessing floating-point routines by setting options in PWB or by specifying command-line options to CL. You can choose between the emulator, alternate, or math coprocessor library. You can also access the floating-point routines by issuing a function call (or calls) or by generating in-line 80x87 instructions to execute the floating-point operation. The smallest and the fastest floating-point math option is the in-line math coprocessor package because the compiler generates true 80x87 coprocessor instructions. If, however, you cannot depend on the target computer having a coprocessor, you must use either the emulator or alternate math options.

To specify floating-point options on the CL command line, you must specify an option from the list in Table 4.4. You specify these options to CL starting with the floating-point option string /FP.

Based on the floating-point option and the memory-model option you choose, the compiler embeds a library name in the object file that it creates. This library is then considered the default library; that is, the linker searches in the standard places for a library with that name. If it finds a library with that name, the linker uses the library to resolve external references in the object file being linked. Otherwise, it displays a message indicating that it could not find the library.

This mechanism allows the linker to automatically link object files with the appropriate library. However, you can link with a different library in some cases. See Table 4.4 and Section 4.5, "Library Considerations for Floating-Point Options," for more information about linking with different libraries.

Table 4.4 summarizes the floating-point options and their effects. These options are described in detail in the following sections.

Table 4.4   Summary of Floating-Point Options

Option for CL for PWB	Combined Use of Method	Effect	Coprocessor	Libraries Selected
/FPi In-Line Emulation	In-line	Default; larger than /FPi87, but can work without a coprocessor; most efficient way to get maximum precision without a coprocessor	Uses coprocessor if present[1]	*m*LIBCE.LIB[2]
/FPi87 In-Line Math Coprocessor	In-line	Smallest and fastest option available with a coprocessor	Requires coprocessor	*m*LIBC7.LIB
/FPc Calls to Emulator	Calls	Slower than /FPi, but allows use of alternate math library at link time	Uses coprocessor if present[1]	*m*LIBCE.LIB[2,3]
/FPc87 Calls to Math Coprocessor	Calls	Slower than /FPi87, but allows use of alternate math library at link time	Requires co-processor unless library changed at link time[5]	*m*LIBC7.LIB[3,4]
/FPa Alternate Math	Calls	Fastest and smallest option available without a coprocessor, but sacrifices some accuracy for speed	Ignores coprocessor	*m*LIBCA.LIB[2,4]

[1] Use of the coprocessor can be suppressed by setting NO87.

[2] Can be linked explicitly with *m*LIBC7.LIB at link time.

[3] Can be linked explicitly with *m*LIBCA.LIB at link time.

[4] Can be linked explicitly with *m*LIBCE.LIB at link time.

[5] Use of the coprocessor can be suppressed by setting NO87 if you change to the emulator library at link time.

Optimizations such as constant propagation and constant subexpression elimination can cause some expressions to be evaluated at compile time. Such evaluations always use IEEE format and are unaffected by the floating-point option you choose. For more information about optimizing, see Chapter 1, "Optimizing C Programs."

You can specify floating-point options in the Programmer's WorkBench.

To specify floating-point options when using the Programmer's WorkBench, you must modify the C Global Build Options (available on the Options menu). In the C Global Build Options dialog box, select one of the following floating-point math options:

Option	Effect
Emulation Calls	Generates calls; makes emulator math library the default (/FPc)
80x87 Calls	Generates calls; makes math coprocessor library the default (/FPc87)
Fast Alternate Math	Generates calls; makes alternate math library the default (/FPa)
Inline Emulation	Generates in-line instructions; makes emulator math library the default (/FPi); this is the default option
Inline 80x87 Instructions	Generates in-line instructions; selects math coprocessor library (/FPi87)

4.4.1 In-Line Emulator Option (/FPi)

The in-line emulator option (/FPi) generates in-line instructions for an 80x87 coprocessor and places the name of the emulator library (mLIBCE.LIB) in the object file. At link time, you can specify the math coprocessor library (mLIBC7.LIB) instead. If you do not choose a floating-point option, the compiler uses the in-line emulator option by default.

The in-line emulator option is useful if you cannot be sure that an 80x87 coprocessor will be available on the target computer. Programs compiled using the in-line emulator option work as described below:

- If a coprocessor is present at run time, the program uses the coprocessor.

- If no coprocessor is present, the program uses the emulator. In this case, the in-line emulator option offers the most efficient way to get maximum precision in floating-point results.

When you use the in-line emulator option, the compiler does not generate in-line 80*x*87 instructions. For real-mode code, the compiler generates software interrupts to library code, which then fixes up the interrupts to use either the emulator or the coprocessor, depending on whether a coprocessor is present. For protected-mode code, the compiler generates no such interrupts; it generates 80*x*87 instructions. If the target computer does not have a coprocessor, an "unsupported extension" exception occurs, which is vectored to library code. If you want true in-line 80*x*87 instructions, use the in-line math coprocessor option (/FPi87).

NOTE *In an OS/2 dynamic-link library built with LLIBCDLL.LIB, you cannot use code that requires the emulator library. You must use the alternate math library instead.*

4.4.2 In-Line Math Coprocessor Instructions Option (/FPi87)

The in-line math coprocessor instructions option (/FPi87) instructs the compiler to place 80*x*87 coprocessor instructions in your code for many math operations. It also causes the name of a math coprocessor library (*m*LIBC7.LIB) to be embedded in the object file.

If you use the in-line math coprocessor instructions option and link with the library *m*LIBC7.LIB, an 80*x*87 coprocessor must be present at run time, or the program fails and the following error message is displayed:

```
run-time error R6002
- floating point not loaded
```

Compiling with the in-line math coprocessor instructions option results in the smallest, fastest programs possible for handling floating-point results.

4.4.3 Calls to Emulator Option (/FPc)

The calls to emulator option (/FPc) generates floating-point calls to the emulator library and places the names of an emulator library (*m*LIBCE.LIB) in the object file. At link time, you can specify a math coprocessor library (*m*LIBC7.LIB) or an alternate math library (*m*LIBCA.LIB) instead. Thus, the calls to emulator option gives you more flexibility in the libraries you can use for linking than the in-line emulator option.

Using the calls to emulator option is also recommended in the following cases:

■ If you compile modules that perform floating-point operations and plan to include these modules in a library

■ If you compile modules that you want to link with libraries other than the libraries provided with Microsoft C

You cannot link with an alternate math library if your program uses the intrinsic forms of floating-point library routines (that is, if you have compiled the program with the /Oi or /Ox option, selected the Generate Intrinsic Functions option from the Debug Build Options or Release Build Options dialog box in the Programmer's WorkBench, or specified math functions in an **intrinsic** pragma).

4.4.4 Calls to Math Coprocessor Option (/FPc87)

The calls to math coprocessor option (/FPc87) generates function calls to routines in the math coprocessor library (*m*LIBC7.LIB) that issue the corresponding 80*x*87 instructions. As with the in-line math coprocessor instructions option (/FPi87), at link time you can choose to link with an emulator library (*m*LIBCE.LIB). However, /FPc offers more flexibility in choosing libraries, since you can change your mind and link with the appropriate alternate math library as well (*m*LIBCA.LIB).

The disadvantages of using the calls to math coprocessor option as opposed to the in-line coprocessor option are the following:

- Your executable size is larger because a call requires more instructions than a true coprocessor instruction.

- Your program does not execute as fast because you must issue a function call for each floating-point operation.

You cannot link with an alternate math library if your program uses the intrinsic forms of floating-point library routines (that is, if you have compiled the program with the /Oi or /Ox option, selected the Generate Intrinsic Functions option from the Debug Build Options or Release Build Options dialog box in the Programmer's WorkBench, or specified math functions in an **intrinsic** pragma).

You must have a math coprocessor installed to run programs compiled with the /FPc option and linked with a math coprocessor library. Otherwise, the program fails and the following error message is displayed:

```
run-time error R6002
- floating point not loaded
```

NOTE *Certain optimizations are not performed when you use the calls to math coprocessor option. This can reduce the efficiency of your code; also, since arithmetic of different precision can result, there may be slight differences in your results.*

4.4.5 Use Alternate Math Option (/FPa)

The use alternate math option (/FPa) generates floating-point calls and selects the alternate math library for the appropriate memory model (*m*LIBCA.LIB). Calls to this library provide the fastest and smallest option for code intended to run on a machine without an 80*x*87 coprocessor. With this option, you can choose an emulator library (*m*LIBCE.LIB) or a math coprocessor library (*m*LIBC7.LIB) at link time.

You cannot link with an alternate math library if your program uses the intrinsic forms of floating-point library routines (that is, if you have compiled the program with the /Oi or /Ox option, selected the Generate Intrinsic Functions from the Debug Build Options or Release Build Options dialog box in the Programmer's WorkBench, or specified math functions in an **intrinsic** pragma).

4.5 Library Considerations for Floating-Point Options

You may want to use libraries in addition to the default library for the floating-point option you have chosen in your compile options. For example, you may want to create your own libraries (or other collections of subprograms in object-file form), then link these libraries at a later time with object files that you have compiled using different options.

The following sections describe these cases and ways to handle them. Although the discussion assumes that you are putting your object files into libraries, the same considerations apply if you are simply using individual object files.

4.5.1 Using One Standard Library for Linking

You must use only one standard C run-time library when you link. You can control which library is used in one of two ways:

1. In the Programmer's WorkBench, add the name of the C run-time library file you want to the program list using the Edit Program List option from the Make menu. You must also modify the Linker Options (from the Make menu) by specifying No Default Library Search.

2. From the LINK command line, give the /NODEFAULTLIBRARYSEARCH (/NOD) option and then specify the name of the combined library file you want to use in the *link-libinfo* field of the CL command line. This overrides the library names embedded in the object files.

4.5.2 In-Line Instructions or Calls

When deciding on a floating-point option, you should decide whether you want to use in-line instructions. If you do, compile with the in-line math coprocessor instructions (/FPi87) or in-line emulator (/FPi) option. Otherwise, compile for floating-point function calls using the calls to math coprocessor (/FPc87), calls to emulator (/FPc), or alternate math (/FPa) option.

If you choose to use in-line instructions for your precompiled object files, you cannot link with an alternate math library (*m*LIBCA.LIB). However, in-line instructions achieve the best performance from your programs on machines that have an 80*x*87 coprocessor installed.

If you choose to use calls, your programs are slower, but at link time you can switch to any standard C run-time library (that is, any library created by the SETUP program) that supports the memory model you have chosen.

4.6 Compatibility between Floating-Point Options

Each time you compile a source file, you can specify a floating-point option. When you link two or more source files to produce an executable program file, you must ensure that floating-point operations are handled consistently and that the environment is set up properly to allow the linker to find the required library.

If you are building libraries of C routines that contain floating-point operations, the calls to emulator option (/FPc) provides the most flexibility.

The examples that follow illustrate how you can link your program with a library other than the default. The floating-point option and the substitute library are compatible.

The example below compiles the program CALC.C with the medium-model option (/AM). Because no floating-point option is specified, the default in-line emulator option (/FPi) is used. The in-line emulator option generates 80*x*87 instructions and specifies the emulator library MLIBCE.LIB in the object file. The /LINK field specifies the /NODEFAULTLIBRARYSEARCH (/NOD) option and the names of the medium-model math coprocessor library. Specifying the math coprocessor library forces the program to use an 80*x*87 coprocessor; the program fails if a coprocessor is not present.

```
CL /AM CALC.C /link MLIBC7 /NOD
```

The example below compiles CALC.C using the small (default) memory model and the alternate math option (/FPa). The /LINK field specifies the /NOD option and the library SLIBCE.LIB. Specifying the emulator library causes all floating-point calls to refer to the emulator library instead of the alternate math library.

```
CL /FPa CALC.C /link SLIBCE /NOD
```

The example below compiles CALC.C with the calls to math coprocessor option (/FPc87), which places the library name SLIBC7.LIB in the object file. The /LINK field overrides this default-library specification by giving the /NOD option and the name of the small-model alternate math library (SLIBCA.LIB).

```
CL /FPc87 CALC.C /link SLIBCA.LIB/NOD
```

4.7 Using the NO87 Environment Variable

Programs compiled using either the calls to emulator (/FPc) or the in-line emulator (/FPi) option automatically use an $80x87$ coprocessor at run time if one is installed. You can override this and force the use of the software emulator by setting an environment variable named NO87.

Use the NO87 environment variable to suppress use of the 80x87 coprocessor at run time.

If NO87 is set to any value when the program is executed, use of the coprocessor is suppressed. The value of the NO87 setting is printed on the standard output as a message. The message is printed only if a coprocessor is present and suppressed; if no coprocessor is present, no message appears. If you don't want a message to be printed, set NO87 equal to one or more spaces. A blank string for NO87 causes a blank line to be printed.

Note that only the presence or absence of the NO87 definition is important in suppressing use of the coprocessor. The actual value of the NO87 setting is used only for printing the message.

The NO87 variable takes effect with any program linked with an emulator library (*m*LIBCE.LIB). It has no effect on programs linked with math coprocessor libraries (*m*LIBC7.LIB) or programs linked with alternate math libraries (*m*LIBCA.LIB).

When a program that uses an emulator library is executed and an $80x87$ coprocessor is present, the example below causes the message Use of coprocessor suppressed to appear.

```
SET NO87=Use of coprocessor suppressed
```

The syntax below sets the NO87 variable to the space character. Use of the coprocessor is still suppressed, but no message is displayed.

SET NO87=*space*

4.8 Incompatibility Issues

The exception handler in the libraries for 80*x*87 floating-point calculations (*m*LIBCE.LIB and *m*LIBC7.LIB) is designed to work without modification on the IBM PC family of computers and on closely compatible computers, including the WANG® PC, the AT&T® 6300, and the Olivetti® personal computers. Also, the libraries need not be modified for the Texas Instruments® Professional Computer, even though it is not compatible. Any machine that uses nonmaskable interrupts (NMI) for 80*x*87 exceptions will run with the unmodified libraries. If your computer is not one of these, and if you are not sure whether it is completely compatible, you may need to modify the math coprocessor libraries.

All Microsoft languages that support 80*x*87 coprocessors intercept 80*x*87 exceptions in order to produce accurate results and properly detect error conditions. To make the libraries work correctly on incompatible machines, you can modify the libraries. To make this easier, an assembly-language source file, EMOEM.ASM, is included on the C 6.0 distribution disk. Any machine that sends the 80*x*87 exception to an 8259 Priority Interrupt Controller (master or master/slave) can be supported by a simple table change to the EMOEM.ASM module. The source file contains further instructions about how to modify EMOEM.ASM, patch libraries, and executable files.

PART 2

Improving Programmer Productivity

CHAPTERS

Improving Programmer Productivity

The Microsoft C Professional Development System helps you write and debug software rapidly.

Chapter 5 describes the quick compile and incremental compile options, both of which can save you time when compiling programs. Chapter 5 also describes the incremental linker, ILINK, which can save you time when you link your application. Chapter 6 describes NMAKE, a powerful new program maintenance utility that automates your program build process. Chapter 7 describes how to build help files with HELPMAKE, the help-file maintenance utility. When you need to share documentation in a readily accessible form, you can add it to the Microsoft Advisor on-line help system using the information in Chapter 7. Chapter 8 explains how to customize the Programmer's WorkBench to make it a personalized development platform. Chapter 9 offers procedures (and some tips) for using the CodeView debugger to find errors in your programs.

Compiling and Linking Quickly

The fundamental processes of compiling and linking take time to perform. The larger your application grows, the longer it takes to compile and link.

This chapter describes how you can speed up compiling by using the quick compiler and incremental compile option, and how you can speed up linking by using ILINK, the Incremental Linker.

5.1 Compiling Quickly

This section describes two ways to speed up the compiling process: using the quick compiler and using the incremental compile option.

5.1.1 Quick Compiler

The Microsoft C Professional Development System includes two separate C compilers: the full compiler and the quick compiler. If you don't specify otherwise, your program is compiled by the full compiler.

You access the quick compiler by specifying the /qc command-line option for CL or by selecting the Quick Compile option from the C Release Build or C Debug Build Options dialogs in the PWB Options menu.

The quick compiler cannot perform as many optimizations as the full compiler, but it is much faster. You can use it to save time during development, whenever optimizations are not critical. When your application is finished, you can compile with the full compiler, using all the desired optimizations.

On-line help for the /qc option describes which optimizations the quick compiler can perform.

5.1.2 Incremental Compile Option

You can speed up compiling even more by compiling incrementally. Incremental compilation means that the compiler compiles only those functions that have changed since you last compiled.

The incremental compile option is available only with the quick compiler (see the previous section). You can access it from within PWB or from the DOS command line. Within PWB, select the Incremental Compile option in the C Release Build dialog box or in the C Debug Build Options dialog box. From the DOS command line, specify the /Gi option for CL.

The incremental compile option automatically triggers another time-saving feature: the Incremental Linker, which is described in the next section.

5.2 Linking Quickly with ILINK

ILINK links only those modules that have changed since the last link.

The Incremental Linker (ILINK) offers the same advantage in linking that the incremental compile option offers in compiling. Rather than link every module in an application, as LINK does, ILINK links only those modules that have changed since the last link. The more modules your application contains, the more time ILINK can potentially save.

In a normal development scenario, you use LINK at the beginning and end of the process, and use ILINK in the middle. In the early stages of development, when your application contains only a few modules, ILINK offers no speed advantage over LINK. Once your application contains several modules, you can save time by using ILINK.

You must link once with LINK to prepare for incremental linking.

To prepare for incremental linking, you must run LINK using /INCREMENTAL, as described in Section 5.2.1. At the same time, you have the option of adding padding bytes to code or data segments by specifying the /PADCODE and /PADDATA options. Padding allows ILINK to expand a segment without relinking the entire module in which it is contained.

Now you can link with ILINK during the rest of development. If changes in your code require a full link, ILINK invokes LINK automatically. When the application is finished, you link a last time with LINK to produce the final executable file.

You can use ILINK with programs compiled for any memory model except tiny model. (Memory models are described in Chapter 2, "Managing Memory.") Typically, ILINK is not efficient for small- or compact-model programs unless they were compiled with the incremental compile option, which is described in Section 5.1.2.

5.2.1 Preparing for Incremental Linking

There are three LINK options that relate to the use of ILINK. One of them (/INCREMENTAL) is mandatory; the other two (/PADCODE and /PADDATA) are optional. This section explains the LINK options that prepare for ILINK. See on-line help for a complete list of LINK options.

The /INCREMENTAL Option

The /INCREMENTAL (/INC) option prepares an object file for incremental linking. You must always run LINK using this option before using ILINK. When you specify /INC, the linker produces two extra files: a symbol file (.SYM) and an ILINK support file (.ILK). The .SYM and .ILK files tell ILINK which parts of the executable file need to be updated.

You must use /INCREMENTAL whenever you use the /PADCODE and /PADDATA options, which are described below.

The /PADCODE Option

The /PADCODE option causes LINK to add padding bytes at the end of a module's code segment. The padding bytes leave room for the code segment to grow in subsequent links, allowing ILINK to update only that module. You can use the /PADCODE option only when /INC is also specified.

Code padding is usually necessary for programs using the small memory model. It is also recommended for compact- or mixed-model programs. You do not need to specify /PADCODE for other memory models (medium, large, or huge).

If you don't specify /PADCODE, LINK doesn't pad the code segment at all. To add padding, specify the desired number of bytes. The optimum amount of padding depends on how much your code changes from one link to the next. If you expect to add only a little code, choose a relatively small amount of padding, say 32 to 64 bytes. If ILINK issues the message

```
padding exceeded
```

and performs a full link more often than desired, increase the padding by a small amount, say 32 bytes. In any case, remember that the total size of a code segment, including padding bytes, cannot exceed 64K (65,535) bytes.

The /PADDATA Option

Like /PADCODE, the /PADDATA option causes LINK to add padding bytes that leave room for the segment to grow in subsequent links. However, the /PADDATA option pads the end of the data segment rather than the code segment. You can use /PADDATA only when /INC is also specified.

If you don't specify /PADDATA, LINK adds 16 bytes of padding by default. The default padding amount should suffice in many cases, since public variables are added less frequently than code. If you need more padding, specify the desired number of bytes. Remember that the total size of a data segment, including padding bytes, cannot exceed 64K (65,535) bytes.

5.2.2 Incremental Violations

ILINK can generate two kinds of errors: real errors and incremental violations. Real errors are errors such as undefined symbols that cannot be resolved by a full link. If ILINK detects a real error, it displays an error message (real errors are documented in on-line help).

Incremental violations are caused by code changes you have made that go beyond the scope of incremental linking. When an incremental violation occurs, ILINK invokes LINK automatically. The following sections describe the incremental violations.

Changing Libraries

An incremental violation occurs when a library changes. Furthermore, if an altered module shares a code segment with a library, ILINK needs access to the library as well as to the altered module.

If you add a function, procedure, or subroutine call to a library that has never been called before, ILINK invokes LINK automatically.

Exceeding Code/Data Padding

An incremental violation occurs if two or more modules contribute to the same physical segment and either module exceeds its padding. The padding allows the module to increase the specified number of bytes before another full link is required.

Moving or Deleting Data Symbols

An incremental violation occurs if a data symbol is moved or deleted. To add new data symbols without requiring a full link, add the new symbols at the end of all other data symbols in the module.

Deleting Code Symbols

You can move or add code symbols, but an incremental violation occurs if you delete any code symbols from a module. Code symbols can be moved within a module but cannot be moved between modules.

Changing Segment Definitions

An incremental violation results if you add, delete, or change the order of segment definitions.

Adding CodeView₍ᵣ₎ Debugger Information

If you include CodeView debugger information for a module when you fully link (by compiling and linking with CodeView debugger support), ILINK supports CodeView debugger information for the module. ILINK maintains symbolic information for current symbols, and it adds information for any new symbols. However, if you try to add CodeView debugger information for a module that did not previously have CodeView debugger support, an incremental violation occurs. See Chapter 9, "Debugging C Programs with CodeView," for more information about CodeView.

Managing Development Projects with NMAKE

The Microsoft Program-Maintenance Utility (NMAKE) is a sophisticated command processor that can save time and simplify project management. By determining which project files depend on others, NMAKE can automatically execute the commands needed to update your project when any project file has changed.

The advantage of using NMAKE over simple batch files is that NMAKE does only what is needed. You don't waste time rebuilding files that are already up-to-date. NMAKE also has advanced features, such as macros, that help you manage complex projects.

This chapter provides complete documentation for NMAKE. Information about NMAKE is also available in on-line help. If you are familiar with MAKE, the predecessor of NMAKE, be sure to read Section 6.9, "Differences Between NMAKE and MAKE." There are some important differences between the two utilities.

6.1 Overview of NMAKE

NMAKE works by comparing the times and dates of two sets of files, which are called "targets" and "dependents." A target is normally a file that you want to create, such as an executable file. A dependent is a file used to create a target, such as a C source file.

When you run NMAKE, it reads a "description file" that you supply. The description file consists of one or more blocks. Each block typically lists a target, the target's dependents, and the command that builds the target. NMAKE compares the date and time of the target to those of its dependents. If any dependent has changed more recently than the target, NMAKE updates the target by executing the command listed in the block.

NMAKE's main purpose is to help you update applications quickly and simply. However, it can execute any command, so it is not limited to compiling and linking. NMAKE can also make backups, move files, and do many other project management tasks.

6.2 The NMAKE Command

When you run NMAKE, you can supply the description-file name and other arguments using the following syntax:

NMAKE [[*options*]] [[*macros*]] [[*targets*]] [[*descriptfile*]]

All of the command-line fields are optional. If you don't supply any arguments, NMAKE looks for a default description file named MAKEFILE and follows various other defaults that are described in this chapter.

The *options* field lists NMAKE options, which are described in Section 6.4, "Command-Line Options."

The *macros* field lists macro definitions, which allow you to replace text in the description file. Macros are described in Section 6.3.3.

The *targets* field lists targets to build. If you do not list any targets, NMAKE builds only the first target in the description file. (This is a significant departure from the behavior of MAKE, NMAKE's predecessor. See Section 6.9, "Differences between NMAKE and MAKE.")

The *descriptfile* field specifies a description file. If this field is absent, NMAKE automatically looks for a file named MAKEFILE in the current directory. You can also specify the description file with the /F option (for information, see Section 6.4, "Command-Line Options").

Below is a typical NMAKE command:

```
NMAKE /S "program = sample" sort.exe search.exe
```

The command supplies four arguments: an option (/S), a macro definition ("`program = sample`"), and two target specifications (`sort.exe search.exe`).

Because the command does not specify a description file, NMAKE looks for the default description file, MAKEFILE. The /S option tells NMAKE to suppress the display of commands as they are executed. The macro definition performs a text substitution throughout the description file, replacing every instance of `program` with `sample`. The target specifications tell NMAKE to update the targets SORT.EXE and SEARCH.EXE.

6.3 NMAKE Description Files

You must always supply NMAKE with a description file. In addition to description blocks, which tell NMAKE how to build your project's target files, the description file can contain comments, macros, inference rules, and directives. This section describes all the elements of description files.

6.3.1 Description Blocks

Description blocks form the heart of the description file. Figure 6.1 illustrates a typical NMAKE description block, including the three parts: targets, dependents, and commands.

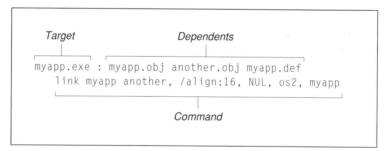

Figure 6.1 Typical Description Block

A target is a file that you want to build. The targets part of the description block lists one or more files to build. The line that lists targets and dependents is called the "dependency line."

The example in Figure 6.1 tells NMAKE to build a single target, MYAPP.EXE. Although single targets are common, you can also list multiple targets; separate each target name with a space. If the rightmost target name is one character long, put a space between the name and the colon.

The target is normally a file, but it can also be a "pseudotarget," a name that allows you to build groups of files or execute a group of commands. See Section 6.3.6, "Pseudotargets."

A dependent is a file used to build a target.
The dependents part of the description block lists one or more files from which the target is built. It is separated from the targets part by a colon. The example in Figure 6.1 lists three dependents:

```
myapp.exe : myapp.obj another.obj myapp.def
```

The example tells NMAKE to build the target MYAPP.EXE whenever MYAPP.OBJ, ANOTHER.OBJ, or MYAPP.DEF has changed more recently than MYAPP.EXE.

If any dependents of a target are listed as targets in other description blocks, then NMAKE builds those files before it builds the original target. Essentially NMAKE evaluates a "dependency tree" for the entire description file. It builds files in the order needed to update the original target, never building a target until all files that depend on it are up-to-date.

The dependent list can also include a list of directories in which NMAKE should search for dependents. The directory list is enclosed in curly braces ({ }) and precedes the dependent list. NMAKE searches the current directory first, then the directories you list:

```
forward.exe : {\src\alpha;d:\proj}pass.obj
```

In the line above, the target, FORWARD.EXE, has one dependent: PASS.OBJ. The directory list specifies two directories:

```
{\src\alpha;d:\proj}
```

NMAKE begins searching for PASS.OBJ in the current directory. If it is not found, NMAKE searches the \ SRC \ ALPHA directory, then the D:\ PROJ directory. If NMAKE cannot find a dependent in the current directory or a listed directory, it looks for an inference rule that describes how to create the dependent (see Section 6.3.4, "Inference Rules").

The commands part of the description block lists the command(s) NMAKE should use to build the target. This can be any command that you can execute from the command line. The example tells NMAKE to build MYAPP.EXE using the following LINK command:

```
LINK myapp another.obj, /align:16, NUL, os2, myapp
```

Notice that the line above is indented. NMAKE uses indentation to distinguish between the dependency line and command line. If the command appears on a separate line, as here, it must be indented at least one space or tab. The dependency line must not be indented (it cannot start with a space or tab).

Many targets are built with a single command, but you can place more than one command after the dependency line. A long command can span several lines if each line ends with a backslash (\ ).

You can also place the command at the end of the dependency line. Separate the command from the rightmost dependent with a semicolon.

In OS/2 description files, NMAKE imposes a slight restriction on the use of the CD, CHDIR, and SET commands. Do not place any of these commands on a command line that uses the ampersand (&) to execute multiple commands. For instance, the following command line is legal in an OS/2 description file,

```
DIR & COPY sample.c backup.c
```

but this line is not legal because it places a CD command after the ampersand:

```
DIR & CD \mydir
```

To use CD, CHDIR, or SET in a description block, place the command on a separate line:

```
DIR
CD \mydir
```

Your OS/2 user's documentation contains more information about using the ampersand in command lines.

Wild Cards

You can use DOS wild-card characters (* and ?) to specify target and dependent file names. NMAKE expands wild cards in target names when it reads the description file. It expands wild cards in the dependent names when it builds the target. For example, the following description block compiles all source files with the .C extension:

```
bondo.exe : *.c
    CL *.c
```

Command Modifiers

Command modifiers provide extra control over the command listed in a description block. They are special characters that appear in front of a command. You can use more than one modifier for a single command. Table 6.1 describes the three NMAKE command modifiers.

Table 6.1   Command Modifiers

Character	Action
At sign (@)	Prevents NMAKE from displaying the command as it executes. In the example below, NMAKE does not display the ECHO command line:

```
sort.exe : sort.obj
  @ECHO sorting
```

The output of the ECHO command appears as usual.

Dash (−)	Turns off error checking for the command. If the dash is followed by a number, NMAKE stops only if the error level returned by the command is greater than the number. In the following example, if the program `sample` returned an error code NMAKE does not stop but continues to execute commands:

```
light.lst : light.txt
  -sample light.txt
```

Exclamation point (!)	Executes the command for each dependent file if the command uses the predefined macros $? or $**. The $? macro refers to all dependent files that are out-of-date with respect to the target. The $** macro refers to all dependent files in the description block (see Section 6.3.3, "Macros"). For example,

```
print:hop.asm skip.bas jump.c
  !print $** lpt1:
```

generates the following commands:

```
print hop.asm lpt1:
print skip.bas lpt1:
print jump.c lpt1:
```

Using Control Characters as Literals

Occasionally, you may need to list a file name that contains a character that NMAKE uses as a control character. These characters are

( ) $ ^ \ { } ! @ −

To use an NMAKE control character as a literal character, place a caret (^) in front of it. For example, say that you define a macro that ends with a backslash:

```
exepath=c:\bin\
```

The line above is intended to define a macro named `exepath` with the value `c:\bin\`. But the second backslash causes unexpected results. Since the backslash is the NMAKE line-continuation character, the line actually defines the macro `exepath` as `c:\bin` followed by whatever appears on the next line of the description file. You can solve the problem by placing a caret in front of the second backslash:

```
exepath=c:\bin^\
```

You can also use a caret to place a literal newline character in a description file. This feature can be useful in macro definitions:

```
XYZ=abc^
def
```

NMAKE interprets the example as if you assigned the C-style string `abc\ndef` to the `XYZ` macro. This effect differs from using the backslash (\\ ) to continue a line. A newline character that follows a backslash is replaced with a space.

Carets that precede noncontrol characters are ignored. The line

```
ign^ore : these ca^rets
```

is interpreted as

```
ignore : these carets
```

A caret that appears in quotation marks is treated as a literal caret character.

Listing a Target in Multiple Description Blocks

You can specify more than one description block for the same target by placing two colons (::) after the target. This feature can be useful for building a complex target, such as a library, that contains components created with different commands. For example,

```
target.lib :: a.asm b.asm c.asm
    CL a.asm b.asm c.asm
    LIB target -+a.obj -+b.obj -+c.obj;
target.lib :: d.c e.c
    CL /c d.c e.c
    LIB target -+d.obj -+e.obj;
```

Both description blocks update the library named TARGET.LIB. If any of the assembly-language files have changed more recently than the library, NMAKE executes the commands in the first block to assemble the source files and update the library. Similarly, if any of the C-language files have changed, NMAKE executes the second group of commands, which compile the C files and update the library.

If you use a single colon in the example above, NMAKE issues an error message. It is legal, however, to use single colons if commands are listed in only one block. In this case, dependency lines are cumulative. For example,

```
target: jump.bas
target: up.c
    echo Building target...
```

is equivalent to

```
target: jump.bas up.c
    echo Building target...
```

6.3.2 Comments

You can place comments in a description file by preceding them with a number sign (#):

```
# This comment appears on its own line
huey.exe : huey.obj dewey.obj # Comment on the same line
    link huey.obj dewey.obj;
```

A comment extends to the end of the line in which it appears. Command lines cannot contain comments.

6.3.3 Macros

Macros allow you to do text replacements throughout the description file.

Macros offer a convenient way to replace a string in the description file with another string. The text is automatically replaced each time you run NMAKE. Macros are useful in a variety of tasks, including the following:

■ To create a standard description file for several projects. The macro represents the file names used in commands. These file names are then defined when you run NMAKE. When you switch to a different project, you can change file names throughout the description file by changing a single macro.

■ To control the options that NMAKE passes to the compiler or linker. When you specify options in a macro, you can change options throughout the description file in one easy step.

You can define your own macros or use predefined macros. This section begins by describing user-defined macros.

User-Defined Macros

You can define a macro with

macroname = string

The *macroname* can be any combination of letters, digits, and the underscore (_) character. Macro names are case sensitive. NMAKE interprets `MyMacro` and `MYMACRO` as different macro names.

The *string* can be any string, including a null string. For example,

```
command = LINK
```

defines a macro named `command` and assigns it the string `LINK`.

You can define macros in the description file or on the command line. In the description file, you must define each macro on a separate line; the line cannot start with a space or tab. The *string* can contain embedded spaces, and NMAKE ignores spaces on either side of the equal sign. You do not need to enclose *string* in quotation marks (if you do, they become part of the string).

Slightly different rules apply when you define a macro on the command line, because of the way that the command line handles spaces. You must enclose *string* in quotation marks if it contains embedded spaces. No spaces can surround the equal sign. You can also enclose the entire macro definition, *macroname* and *string*, in quotation marks. For example,

```
NMAKE "program=sample"
```

defines the macro `program`, assigning it the value `sample`.

Once you have defined a macro, you can "undefine" it with the !UNDEF directive (see Section 6.3.5, "Directives").

Invoking Macros

You invoke a macro by enclosing its name in parentheses preceded by a dollar sign ($). (The parentheses are optional if *macroname* is one character long.) For example, you can invoke the `command` macro defined above as

```
$(command)
```

When NMAKE runs, it replaces every occurrence of `$(command)` with `LINK`. The following description file defines and uses three macros:

```
program = sample
c = LINK
options =

$(program).exe : $(program).obj
   $c  $(options)  $(program).obj;
```

NMAKE interprets the description block as

```
sample.exe : sample.obj
   LINK    sample.obj;
```

NMAKE replaces every occurrence of `$(program)` with `sample`, every instance of `$c` with `LINK`, and every instance of `$(options)` with a null string. Because `c` is only one character long, you do not need to enclose it in parentheses.

If you invoke a macro that is not defined, NMAKE treats the macro as a null string.

Occasionally, you may need to use the dollar sign ($) as a literal character. Use two signs ($$), or precede it with a caret (^$).

Predefined Macros

NMAKE provides several predefined macros, which represent various file names and commands. Predefined macros are useful in their own right, and they are also employed in predefined inference rules, which are described later in this chapter. Table 6.2 lists NMAKE predefined macros.

Table 6.2   Predefined Macros

Macro	Meaning
$@	The current target's full name.
$*	The current target's base name (full name minus the file extension).
$**	The dependents of the current target.
$?	The dependents that are out-of-date with respect to the current target.
$$@	The target that NMAKE is currently evaluating. You can only use this macro to specify a dependent.
$<	The dependent file that is out-of-date with respect to the current target (evaluated only for inference rules).
$(CC)	The command to invoke the C compiler. By default, **$(CC)** is predefined as `CC = cl`, which invokes the optimizing compiler.
$(AS)	The command that invokes the Microsoft Macro Assembler. NMAKE predefines this macro as `AS = masm`.

Table 6.2   (*continued*)

Macro	Meaning
$(MAKE)	The name with which the NMAKE utility is invoked. This macro is used to invoke NMAKE recursively. It causes the line on which it appears to be executed even if the /N option is on. You can redefine this macro if you want to execute another program.

The **$(MAKE)** macro is useful for building different versions of a program. The following description file invokes NMAKE recursively to build targets in the VERS1 and VERS2 directories.

```
all :vers1 vers2

vers1 :
  cd vers1
  $(MAKE)
  cd ..

vers2 :

  cd vers2
  $(MAKE)
  cd ..
```

The example changes to the VERS1 directory, then invokes NMAKE recursively, causing NMAKE to process the file MAKEFILE in that directory. Then it changes to the VERS2 directory and invokes NMAKE again, processing the file MAKEFILE in that directory.

Deeply recursive build procedures can exhaust NMAKE's run-time stack, causing a run-time error. To eliminate the error, use the EXEHDR utility to increase NMAKE's run-time stack. The following command, for example, gives NMAKE.EXE a stack size of 16,384 (0x4000) bytes:

```
exehdr /stack:0x4000 nmake.exe
```

Macro	Meaning
$(MAKEFLAGS)	The NMAKE options currently in effect. If you invoke NMAKE recursively, you should use the command: `$(MAKE)  $(MAKEFLAGS)`. You cannot redefine this macro.
$(MAKEDIR)	The directory from which NMAKE is invoked.

Like user-defined macro names, predefined macro names are case sensitive. NMAKE interprets `CC` and `cc` as different macro names.

*Macro modifiers allow
you to specify parts
of predefined macros
representing file names.*

You can append characters to any of the first six macros in Table 6.2 to modify its meaning. Appending a **D** specifies the directory part of the file name only, an **F** specifies the file name, a **B** specifies just the base name, and an **R** specifies the complete file name without the extension. If you add one of these characters, you must enclose the macro name in parentheses. (The predefined macros **$$@** and **$**** are the only exceptions to the rule that macro names more than one character long must be enclosed in parentheses.)

For example, assume that **$@** has the value C:\SOURCE\PROG\SORT.OBJ. The list below shows the effect of combining the special characters with **$@**:

Macro	Value
$(@D)	C:\SOURCE\PROG
$(@F)	SORT.OBJ
$(@B)	SORT
$(@R)	C:\SOURCE\PROG\SORT

For example, in the code below, the macro **$?** represents the names of all dependents that are more recent than the target. The exclamation point causes NMAKE to execute the LIB command once for each dependent in the list. As a result, the LIB command is executed up to three times, each time replacing a module with a newer version.

```
trig.lib : sin.obj cos.obj arctan.obj
        !LIB trig.lib -+$?;
```

In the following example, NMAKE updates a group of include files:

```
# Include files depend on versions in current directory
DIR=c:\include
$(DIR)\globals.h : globals.h
        COPY globals.h $@
$(DIR)\types.h : types.h
        COPY types.h $@
$(DIR)\macros.h : macros.h
        COPY macros.h $@
```

Each of the files GLOBALS.H, TYPES.H, and MACROS.H in the directory C:\INCLUDE depends on its counterpart in the current directory. If one of the include files is out-of-date, NMAKE replaces it with the file of the same name from the current directory.

Substitution within Macros

Just as macros allow you to substitute text in a description file, you can also substitute text within a macro itself. Use the following form:

$(*macroname*:*string1* = *string2*)

You can replace text in a macro, as well as in the description file.

Every occurrence of *string1* is replaced by *string2* in the macro *macroname*. Do not put any spaces or tabs between *macroname* and the colon. Spaces between the colon and *string1* are made part of *string1*. If *string2* is a null string, all occurrences of *string1* are deleted from the *macroname* macro.

The following description file illustrates macro substitution:

```
SRCS = prog.c sub1.c sub2.c
prog.exe : $(SRCS:.c=.obj)
        LINK  $**;

DUP : $(SRCS)
        !COPY $** c:\backup
```

The predefined macro **$**** stands for the names of all the dependent files (see the previous section). If you invoke the example file with a command line that specifies both targets, NMAKE executes the following commands:

```
LINK prog.obj sub1.obj sub2.obj;

COPY prog.c c:\backup
COPY sub1.c c:\backup
COPY sub2.c c:\backup
```

The macro substitution does not alter the definition of the SRCS macro, rather, it simply replaces the listed characters. When NMAKE builds the target PROG.EXE, it gets the definition for the predefined macro **$**** (the dependent list) from the dependency line, which specifies the macro substitution in SRCS. The same is true for the second target, DUP. In this case, however, no macro substitution is requested, so SRCS retains its original value, and **$**** represents the names of the C source files. (In the example above, the target DUP is a pseudotarget; Section 6.3.6 describes pseudotargets.)

You can also perform substitution in the following predefined macros: **$@**, **$***, **$****, **$?**, and **$<**. The principle is the same as for other macros. The command in the following description block substitutes within a predefined macro:

```
target.abc : depend.xyz
    echo $(@:targ=blank)
```

If dependent `depend.xyz` is out-of-date relative to target `target.abc`, then NMAKE executes the command

```
echo blanket.abc
```

The example uses the predefined macro **$@**, which equals the full name of the current target (`target.abc`). It substitutes `blank` for `targ` in the target, resulting in `blanket.abc`. Note that you do not put the usual dollar sign in front of the predefined macro. The example uses

```
$(@:targ=blank)
```

instead of

```
$($@:targ=blank)
```

to substitute within the predefined macro **$@**.

Inherited Macros

When NMAKE executes, it creates macros equivalent to every current environment variable. These are called "inherited" macros because they have the same names and values as the corresponding environment variables. (The inherited macro is all uppercase, however, even if the corresponding environment variable is not.)

Inherited macros can be used like other macros. You can also redefine them. The following example redefines the inherited macro `PATH`:

```
PATH = c:\tools\bin

sample.obj : sample.c
    CL /c sample.c
```

Inherited macros take their definitions from environment variables.

No matter what value PATH had in the DOS environment, it has the value `c:\tools\bin` when NMAKE executes the CL command in this description block. Redefining the inherited macro does not affect the original environment variable; when NMAKE terminates, PATH has its original value.

The /E option defeats macro inheritance. If you supply this option, NMAKE ignores any attempt to redefine a macro that derives from an environment variable.

Precedence among Macro Definitions

If you define the same macro in more than one place, NMAKE uses the macro with the highest precedence. The precedence from highest to lowest is as follows:

1. Macros defined on the command line

2. Macros defined in a description file or include file

3. Inherited macros

4. Macros defined in the TOOLS.INI file

5. Predefined macros such as **CC** and **AS**

The /E option defeats any attempt to redefine inherited macros. If you run NMAKE with this option, macros inherited from environment variables override any same-named macros in the description file.

6.3.4 Inference Rules

Inference rules are templates that NMAKE uses to create files with a given extension. For instance, when NMAKE encounters a description block with no commands, it tries to apply an inference rule that tells how to create the target from the dependent files, given the two extensions. Similarly, if a dependent file does not exist, NMAKE tries to apply an inference rule that tells how to create the missing dependent from another file with the same base name.

Inference rules tell NMAKE how to create files with a certain extension.

Inference rules provide a convenient shorthand for common operations. For instance, you can use an inference rule to avoid repeating the same command in several description blocks.

You can define your own inference rules or use predefined inference rules. This section begins by describing user-defined inference rules.

User-Defined Inference Rules

You can define inference rules in the description file or in the TOOLS.INI file. An inference-rule definition lists two file extensions and one or more commands. For instance, the following inference rule tells NMAKE how to build a .OBJ file using a .C file:

```
.C.OBJ:
    CL /c $<;
```

The first line lists two extensions. The second extension (.OBJ) specifies the type of the desired file and the first (.C) specifies the type of the desired file's dependent. The second line lists the command used to build the desired file. Here, the predefined macro $< represents the name of a dependent that is out-of-date relative to the target.

NMAKE could apply the above inference rule to the following description block:

```
sample.obj :
```

The description block lists only a target, SAMPLE.OBJ. Both the dependent and the command are missing. However, given the target's base name and extension, plus the above inference rule, NMAKE has enough information to build the target. NMAKE first looks for a .C file with the same base name as the target. If SAMPLE.C exists, NMAKE compares its date to that of SAMPLE.OBJ (the comparison is triggered by the predefined macro $<). If SAMPLE.C has changed more recently, NMAKE compiles it using the CL command listed in the inference rule:

```
CL/c sample.c
```

NOTE *NMAKE applies an inference rule only if the base name of the file it is trying to create matches the base name of a file that already exists. Thus, inference rules are useful only when there is a one-to-one correspondence between the desired file and its dependent. You cannot define an inference rule that replaces several modules in a library, for example.*

Extension Search Paths

If an inference rule does not specify a search path, as in the example above, NMAKE looks for files in the current directory. You can specify a single path for each of the extensions, using the following form:

{ *frompath* }. *fromext* { *topath* }. *toext* :
    commands

NMAKE searches in the *frompath* directory for files with the *fromext* extension. It uses *commands* to create files with the *toext* extension in the *topath* directory.

Predefined Inference Rules

NMAKE provides predefined inference rules to perform these common development tasks:

- Creating an .OBJ file by compiling a .C file

- Creating an .OBJ file by assembling an .ASM file

- Creating an .EXE file by compiling a .C file and linking the resulting .OBJ file

Table 6.3 describes the predefined inference rules.

Table 6.3   Predefined Inference Rules

Inference Rule	Command	Default Action
.c.obj	$(CC) $(CFLAGS) /c $*.c	cl /c $*.c
.asm.obj	$(AS) $(AFLAGS) $*;	masm $*;
.c.exe	$(CC) $(CFLAGS) $*.c	cl $*.c

For example, say that you have the following description file:

```
sample.exe :
```

Like the previous example, this description block lists a target without any dependents or commands. NMAKE looks at the target's extension (.EXE) and checks for an inference rule that describes how to create a .EXE file. The last rule in Table 6.3 provides this information:

```
.c.exe:
    $(CC) $(CFLAGS) $*.c
```

To apply this rule, NMAKE first looks for a file with the same base name as the target (SAMPLE) and the .C extension. If SAMPLE.C exists in the current directory, NMAKE executes the CL command given in the rule. The command compiles SAMPLE.C and links the resulting file SAMPLE.OBJ to create SAMPLE.EXE.

Precedence among Inference Rules

If the same inference rule is defined in more than one place, NMAKE uses the rule with the highest precedence. The precedence from highest to lowest is

1. Inference rules defined in the description file

2. Inference rules defined in the TOOLS.INI file

3. Predefined inference rules

NMAKE uses a predefined inference rule only if no user-defined inference rule exists for the desired operation.

6.3.5 Directives

Directives allow you to write description files that are similar to batch files. Directives can execute commands conditionally, display error messages, include other files, and turn on or off certain options.

NMAKE directives are similar to C preprocessor directives.

A directive begins with an exclamation point (!), which must appear at the beginning of the line. You can place spaces between the exclamation point and the directive keyword. (See Table 6.4.)

Table 6.4   Directives

Directive	Description
!CMDSWITCHES {+|−}*opt...*	Turns on or off one of four NMAKE options: /D, /I, /N, and /S. If no options are specified, the options are reset to the way they were when NMAKE started. Turn an option on by preceding it with a plus sign (+), or turn it off by preceding it with a minus sign (−). Using this keyword updates the **MAKEFLAGS** macro.
!ELSE	Executes the statements between the **!ELSE** and **!ENDIF** keywords if the statements preceding the **!ELSE** keyword were not executed.
!ENDIF	Marks the end of the **!IF**, **!IFDEF**, or **!IFNDEF** block of statements.
!ERROR *text*	Causes *text* to be printed and then stops execution.
!IF *constantexpression*	Executes the statements between the **!IF** keyword and the next **!ELSE** or **!ENDIF** keyword if *constant expression* evaluates to a nonzero value.
!IFDEF *macroname*	Executes the statements between the **!IFDEF** keyword and the next **!ELSE** or **!ENDIF** keyword if *macroname* is defined. NMAKE considers a macro with a null value to be defined.
!IFNDEF *macroname*	Executes the statements between the **!IFNDEF** keyword and the next **!ELSE** or **!ENDIF** keyword if *macroname* is not defined.
!INCLUDE *filename*	Reads and evaluates the file *filename* before continuing with the current description file. If *filename* is enclosed by angle brackets (< >), NMAKE searches for the file in the directories specified by the **INCLUDE** macro. Otherwise, it looks only in the current directory. The **INCLUDE** macro is initially set to the value of the INCLUDE environment variable.
!UNDEF *macroname*	Marks *macroname* as being undefined in NMAKE's symbol table.

The *constantexpression* used with the !IF directive can consist of integer constants, string constants, or program invocations. Integer constants can use the C unary operators for numerical negation (–), one's complement (∼), and logical negation (!). They can also use any of the C binary operators listed in Table 6.5.

Table 6.5   Directive Operators

Operator	Description
+	Addition
–	Subtraction
*	Multiplication
/	Division
%	Modulus
&	Bitwise AND
|	Bitwise OR
∧∧	Bitwise XOR
&&	Logical AND
||	Logical OR
<<	Left shift
>>	Right shift
==	Equality
!=	Inequality
<	Less than
>	Greater than
<=	Less than or equal to
>=	Greater than or equal to

You can group expressions using parentheses. NMAKE treats numbers as decimal unless they start with 0 (octal) or 0x (hexadecimal). Use the equality (==) operator to compare two strings for equality or the inequality (!=) operator to compare for inequality. Enclose strings with quotes. Program invocations must be in square brackets ([ ]).

The following example illustrates directives:

```
!INCLUDE <infrules.txt>
!CMDSWITCHES +D
winner.exe:winner.obj
!IFDEF debug
!   IF "$(debug)"=="y"
        LINK /CO winner.obj;
!   ELSE
        LINK winner.obj;
!   ENDIF
!ELSE
!   ERROR Macro named debug is not defined.
!ENDIF
```

The !INCLUDE directive causes NMAKE to insert the file INFRULES.TXT into the description file. The !CMDSWITCHES directive turns on the /D option, which displays the dates of the files as they are checked. If WINNER.EXE is out-of-date with respect to WINNER.OBJ, the !IFDEF directive checks to see if the macro debug is defined. If it is defined, the !IF directive checks to see if it is set to y. If it is, the linker is invoked with the /CO option; otherwise it is invoked without. If the debug macro is not defined, the !ERROR directive prints the message and NMAKE stops.

6.3.6 Pseudotargets

Pseudotargets are useful for building a group of files or executing a group of commands.

A "pseudotarget" is similar to a target, but it is not a file. It is a name that serves as a "handle" for building a group of files or executing a group of commands. In the following example, UPDATE is a pseudotarget.

```
UPDATE: *.*
        !COPY $** a:\product
```

When NMAKE evaluates a pseudotarget, it always considers the dependents to be out-of-date. In the example, NMAKE copies each of the dependent files to the specified drive and directory.

Like macro names, pseudotarget names are case sensitive. Predefined pseudo-target names are all uppercase.

The pseudotargets in Table 6.6 are predefined to provide special rules in a description file. You can use their names on the command line, in a description file, or in the TOOLS.INI file. You need not specify them as targets; NMAKE uses the rules they define no matter where they appear.

Table 6.6 Pseudotargets

Pseudotarget	Action
.IGNORE:	Ignores exit codes returned by programs called from the description file. Same effect as invoking NMAKE with the /I option.
.PRECIOUS: *target(s)*	Tells NMAKE not to delete *target(s)* if the commands that build it are quit or interrupted. Using this pseudo-target overrides the NMAKE default. By default, NMAKE deletes the target if it cannot be sure the target is built successfully.
	The .PRECIOUS pseudotarget is rarely needed. Like most professional tools, Microsoft language tools clean up by themselves when errors occur.
.SILENT:	Does not display lines as they are executed. Same effect as invoking NMAKE with the /S option.
.SUFFIXES:*list*	Lists file suffixes for NMAKE to try when building a target file for which no dependents are specified. This list is used together with inference rules. See Section 6.3.4, "Inference Rules."
	When NMAKE finds a target without any dependents, it searches the current directory for a file with the same base name as the target and a suffix from the list. If NMAKE finds such a file, and if an inference rule applies to the file, then NMAKE treats the file as a dependent of the target. The order of the suffixes in the list defines the order in which NMAKE searches for the file. The list is predefined as follows:
	`.SUFFIXES: .obj .exe .c .asm`
	To add suffixes to the list, specify `.SUFFIXES :` followed by the new suffixes. To clear the list, specify `.SUFFIXES:`

6.3.7 PWB's extmake Syntax

NMAKE description files can use the same syntax as the **extmake** switch of PWB (see Chapter 8, "Customizing the Microsoft Programmer's WorkBench"). This syntax allows you to determine the drive, path, base name, and extension of the first dependent, information that is not otherwise available. The file name, and parts of its name, are represented using the syntax

*%|parts*F

where *parts* is one or more of the following:

Letter	Description
d	Drive
e	File extension
f	File base name
p	Path
s	Complete name

The following example uses **extmake** syntax:

```
sample.obj : sample.c
    CL /Fod:%|pfF %|dfeF
```

In this example, the sequence `%|pfF` represents the path and base name of the first dependent file, while the sequence `%|dfeF` represents the drive, base name, and extension of the same file. The example, then, compiles the file and writes the output to a file on the same path but with the default .OBJ extension.

The percent symbol (%) is a replacement character in DOS and OS/2 command lines in the description file. To use **extmake** syntax in command-line arguments, specify each percent symbol as a double percent symbol (%%).

6.4 Command-Line Options

NMAKE accepts a number of options, which are listed in Table 6.7. You can specify options in uppercase or lowercase and use either a slash or dash. For example, –A, /A, –a, and /a all represent the same option.

Table 6.7   NMAKE Options

Option	Action
/A	Builds all of the requested targets even if they are not out-of-date.
/C	Suppresses nonfatal error or warning messages and the NMAKE logo display.
/D	Displays the modification date of each file.
/E	Causes environment variables to override macro definitions in description files. See Section 6.3.3, "Macros."
/F *filename*	Specifies *filename* as the name of the description file. If you supply a dash (–) instead of a file name, NMAKE gets input from the standard input device instead of the description file.
/HELP	Calls the QuickHelp utility. If the QuickHelp program is not available, NMAKE displays the most commonly used NMAKE options.
/I	Ignores return codes from commands listed in the description file. NMAKE processes the whole description file even if errors occur.
/N	Displays but does not execute the description file's commands. This option is useful for debugging description files and checking which targets are out-of-date.
/NOLOGO	Suppresses the NMAKE logo display.
/P	Displays all macro definitions and target descriptions on the standard output device.
/Q	Returns zero if the target is up-to-date and nonzero if it is not. This option is useful when running NMAKE from a batch file.
/R	Ignores inference rules and macros that are predefined or defined in the TOOLS.INI file.
/S	Suppresses the display of commands listed in the description file.
/T	Changes the modification dates for out-of-date target files to the current date.
/X *filename*	Sends all error output to *filename*, which can be a file or a device. If you supply a dash (–) instead of a file name, the error output is sent to the standard output device.
/Z	Used for internal communication between NMAKE and PWB.
/?	Displays a brief summary of NMAKE syntax and exits to the operating system.

The following command specifies two NMAKE options:

```
NMAKE /f sample.mak /c targ1 targ2
```

The /f option tells NMAKE to read the description file SAMPLE.MAK. The /c option tells NMAKE not to display nonfatal error messages and warnings. The command lists two targets (`targ1` and `targ2`) to update.

```
NMAKE  /D /N targ1 targ1.mak
```

In the example above, NMAKE updates the target `targ1`. If the current directory does not contain a file named MAKEFILE, NMAKE reads the file TARG1.MAK as the description file. The /D option displays the modification date of each file; the /N option displays the commands without executing them.

6.5 NMAKE Command Files

Occasionally, you may need to give NMAKE a long list of command-line arguments that exceeds the maximum length of a command line (128 characters in DOS, 256 in OS/2). To do this, place the command arguments in a file, then give the name of the file when you run NMAKE.

For instance, say that you create a file named UPDATE, which consists of this line:

```
/S "program = sample" sort.exe search.exe
```

If you start NMAKE with the command

```
NMAKE @update
```

NMAKE reads its command-line arguments from UPDATE. The at sign (@) tells NMAKE to read arguments from the file. The effect is the same as if you typed the arguments directly on the command line:

```
NMAKE /S "program = sample" sort.exe search.exe
```

Within the file, line breaks between arguments are treated as spaces. Macro definitions that contain spaces must be enclosed in quotation marks, just as if you typed them on the command line. You can continue a macro definition across multiple lines by ending each line except the last with a backslash (\ ):

```
/S "program \
= sample" sort.exe search.exe
```

This file is equivalent to the first example. The backslash in the example allows the macro definition (`"program = sample"`) to span two lines.

6.6 The TOOLS.INI File

You can customize NMAKE by placing commonly used macros and inference rules in the TOOLS.INI initialization file. Settings for NMAKE must follow a line that begins with [NMAKE]. This part of the initialization file can contain macro definitions, .SUFFIXES lists, and inference rules. For example,

```
[NMAKE]
CC=cl
CFLAGS=-Gc -Gs -W3 -Oat
.c.obj:
    $(CC) -c $(CFLAGS) $*.c
```

If TOOLS.INI contains the code above, NMAKE reads and applies the lines following [NMAKE]. The example defines the macros **CC** and **CFLAGS** and redefines the inference rule for making .OBJ files from .C sources.

NMAKE looks for TOOLS.INI in the current directory. If it is not found there, NMAKE searches the directory specified by the INIT environment variable.

6.7 In-Line Files

NMAKE can write "in-line files," which can contain any text you specify. One use for in-line files is to write a response file for another utility such as LIB. (Response files are useful when you need to supply a program with a long list of arguments that exceeds the maximum length of the command line.)

Use this syntax to create an in-line file:

target **:** *dependents*
  command << [[*filename*]]
inlinetext
<<[[KEEP | NOKEEP]]

All of the text between the two sets of double angle brackets (<<) is placed in the in-line file. The *filename* is optional. If you don't supply *filename*, NMAKE gives the in-line file a unique name. NMAKE places the in-line file in the current directory or, if the TMP environment variable is defined, in the directory specified by TMP.

The in-line file can be temporary or permanent. If you don't specify otherwise, or if you specify **NOKEEP**, it is temporary. Specify **KEEP** to retain the file.

The following example creates a LIB response file named LIB.LRF:

```
math.lib : add.obj sub.obj mul.obj div.obj
  LIB @<<lib.lrf
math.lib
-+add.obj-+sub.obj-+mul.obj-+div.obj
listing
<<KEEP
```

The resulting response file tells LIB which library to use, the commands to execute, and the listing file to produce:

```
math.lib
-+add.obj-+sub.obj-+mul.obj-+div.obj
listing
```

The in-line file specification can create more than one in-line file. For instance,

```
target.abc : depend.xyz
  cat <<file1 <<file2
I am the contents of file1.
<<KEEP
I am the contents of file2.
<<KEEP
```

The example creates two in-line files named FILE1 and FILE2; then NMAKE executes the command:

```
CAT file1 file2
```

The **KEEP** keywords tell NMAKE not to delete FILE1 and FILE2 when done.

6.8 NMAKE Operations Sequence

If you are writing a complex description file, you may need to know the exact order of steps that NMAKE follows. This section describes those steps in order.

When you run NMAKE from the command line, its first task is to find the description file, following these steps:

1. If NMAKE is invoked with the /F option, it uses the file name specified in the option.

2. If /F is not specified, NMAKE looks for a file named MAKEFILE in the current directory. If such a file exists, it is used as a description file.

3. If MAKEFILE is not in the current directory, NMAKE parses the command line for the first string that is not an option or a macro definition and treats this string as a file name. If the file-name extension does not appear in the .SUFFIXES list, NMAKE uses the file as the description file. If the extension appears in the .SUFFIXES list, NMAKE tries additional strings until it finds a suitable file. (See Section 6.3.6, "Pseudotargets," for a description of the .SUFFIXES list.)

4. If NMAKE still has not found a description file, it returns an error.

NMAKE stops searching for a description file as soon as it finds one, even if other potential description files exist. If you specify /F, NMAKE uses the file specified by that option even if MAKEFILE exists in the current directory. Similarly, if NMAKE uses MAKEFILE, any description file listed in the command line is treated as a target.

If you do not specify targets, NMAKE updates only the first target in the description file.

Next, NMAKE updates every target listed on the command line. If none is listed, NMAKE updates only the first target in the description file. (This behavior differs from the older MAKE program's default; see Section 6.9, "Differences between NMAKE and MAKE.")

NMAKE then applies macro definitions and inference rules in the following order, from highest to lowest priority:

1. Macros defined on the command line

2. Macros defined in a description file or include file

3. Inherited macros

4. Macros defined in the TOOLS.INI file

5. Predefined macros such as **CC** and **AS**

Definitions in later steps take precedence over definitions in earlier steps. The /E option, however, causes inherited macros to override macros defined on the command line. The /R option causes NMAKE to ignore macros and inference rules that are predefined or defined in TOOLS.INI.

Now NMAKE updates each target in the order in which it appears in the description file. It compares the date and time of each dependent with that of the target and performs the commands needed to update the target. If you specify the /A option or if the target is a pseudotarget, NMAKE updates the target even if its dependents are not out-of-date.

If the target has no explicit dependents, NMAKE looks in the current directory for one or more files whose extensions are in the .SUFFIXES list. If it finds such files, NMAKE treats them as dependents and updates the target according to the commands.

If no commands are given to update the target or if the dependents cannot be found, NMAKE applies inference rules to build the target. By default, it tries to build .EXE files from .OBJ files; and it tries to build .OBJ files from .C and .ASM sources. In practice, this means you should specify .OBJ files as dependents, because NMAKE compiles your source files when it can't find the .OBJ files.

NMAKE normally quits processing the description file when a command returns an error. In addition, if it cannot tell that the target was built successfully, NMAKE deletes the partially created target. If you use the /I command-line option, NMAKE ignores exit codes and attempts to continue processing. The .IGNORE pseudotarget has the same effect. To prevent NMAKE from deleting the partially created target, specify the target name in the .PRECIOUS pseudotarget.

Alternatively, you can use the dash (–) command modifier to ignore the error code for an individual command. An optional number after the dash tells NMAKE to continue if the command returns an error code that is less than or equal to the number, and to stop if the error code is greater than the number.

You can help document errors by using the !ERROR directive to print descriptive text. The directive causes NMAKE to print some text, then stop, even if you use /I, .IGNORE, or the dash (–) modifier.

6.9 Differences between NMAKE and MAKE

As its name implies, NMAKE is a new utility that replaces the older Microsoft MAKE program. NMAKE differs from MAKE in the following ways:

- NMAKE does not evaluate targets sequentially. Instead, NMAKE updates the targets you specify when you invoke it, regardless of their positions in the description file. If no targets are specified, NMAKE updates only the first target in the file.

- NMAKE accepts command-line arguments from a file.

- NMAKE provides more command-line options.

- NMAKE provides more predefined macros.

- NMAKE permits substitutions within macros.

- NMAKE supports directives placed in the description file.

- NMAKE allows you to specify include files in the description file.

The first item in the list deserves special emphasis. While MAKE normally builds every target, working from beginning to end of the description file, NMAKE expects you to specify targets on the command line. If you do not, NMAKE builds only the first target in the description file.

The difference is clear if you run NMAKE using a typical MAKE description file, which lists a series of subordinate targets followed by a higher-level target that depends on the subordinates:

```
pmapp.obj : pmapp.c
    CL /c /G2sw /W3 pmapp.c

pmapp.exe : pmapp.obj pmapp.def
    LINK pmapp, /align:16, NUL, os2, pmapp
```

MAKE builds both targets (PMAPP.OBJ and PMAPP.EXE), but NMAKE builds only the first target (PMAPP.OBJ).

Because of these performance differences, you may want to convert MAKE files to NMAKE files. MAKE description files are easy to convert. A simple method is to create a new description block at the beginning of the file. Give this block a pseudotarget named ALL and list the top-level target as a dependent of ALL. To build ALL, NMAKE must update every target upon which the target of ALL depends:

```
ALL : pmapp.exe

pmapp.obj : pmapp.c
    CL /c /G2sw /W3 pmapp.c

pmapp.exe : pmapp.obj pmapp.def
    LINK pmapp, /align:16, NUL, os2, pmapp
```

If the above file is named MAKEFILE, you can update the target PMAPP.EXE with the command

```
NMAKE
```

or the command

```
NMAKE ALL
```

Note that it is not necessary to list PMAPP.OBJ as a dependent of ALL. NMAKE builds a dependency tree for the entire description file, and builds whatever files are needed to update PMAPP.EXE. So if PMAPP.C is out-of-date with respect to PMAPP.OBJ, NMAKE compiles PMAPP.C to create PMAPP.OBJ, then links PMAPP.OBJ to create PMAPP.EXE.

The same technique is suitable for description files with more than one top-level target. List all of the top-level targets as dependents of ALL:

```
ALL : pmapp.exe second.exe another.exe
```

The example updates the targets PMAPP.EXE, SECOND.EXE, and ANOTHER.EXE.

If the description file lists a single, top-level target, you can use an even simpler technique. Move the top-level block to the beginning of the file:

```
pmapp.exe : pmapp.obj pmapp.def
    LINK pmapp, /align:16, NUL, os2, pmapp

pmapp.obj : pmapp.c
    CL /c /G2sw /W3 pmapp.c
```

NMAKE updates the second target (PMAPP.OBJ) whenever needed to keep the first target (PMAPP.EXE) current.

Creating Help Files with HELPMAKE

If you have used PWB or other Microsoft language products such as QuickC, you are familiar with the many advantages of on-line help. The Microsoft Help-File-Creation Utility (HELPMAKE) allows you to create your own help files for use with Microsoft products. It also allows you to customize the help files supplied with Microsoft language products.

HELPMAKE translates help text files into a help database accessible from within the following:

- Microsoft C 6.0 Programmer's WorkBench (PWB)

- QuickHelp Utility

- Microsoft Editor 1.02

- Microsoft QuickC 2.0

- Microsoft QuickPascal 1.0

- Microsoft QuickBASIC 4.5

This chapter describes how to create and modify help files using the HELPMAKE utility.

7.1 Structure and Contents of a Help Database

HELPMAKE creates a help database from one or more input files that contain information formatted for the help system. This section defines some of the terms involved in formatting and outlines the formats that HELPMAKE can process.

7.1.1 Contents of a Help File

As you might expect, each help text file starts with a topic and some information about the topic, then lists another topic and some information about it, and so on. In HELPMAKE terminology, topics are called "contexts"; the information is called "topic text."

The **.context** command introduces a context. In the source file for C 6.0 help, for example, this line introduces help for the **open** function:

```
.context open
```

The **.context** command and other formatting elements are described in Section 7.5, "Help Text Conventions."

Whether a context is one or several words depends on the application. Quick-BASIC, for example, considers spaces to be delimiters, so in QuickBASIC help files contexts are limited to a single word. Other applications, such as the Microsoft Editor, can handle contexts that span several words. Either way, the application simply hands the context to an internal "help engine," which searches the database for information.

Often, especially with library routines, the same information applies to more than one subject. For example, the string-to-number functions **strtod**, **strtol**, and **stroul** share the same help text. The help file lists all three function names as contexts for one block of topic text. The converse, however, is not true. You cannot specify different blocks of topic text, in different places in the help file, to describe a single subject.

Cross-references help you navigate through a help database.

Cross-references make it possible to view information about related topics, including header files and code examples. The help for the **open** function, for example, references the **access** function and the ASCII header file FCNTL.H. Cross-references can point to other contexts in the same help database, to contexts in other help databases, or to ASCII files outside the database.

Help files can have two kinds of cross-references:

- Implicit
- Explicit, or hyperlinks

Implicit cross-references are coded with an ordinary .context command.

The word "open" is an implicit cross-reference throughout C 6.0 help. If you select the word "open" anywhere in C 6.0 help, the help system displays information on the **open** function. As illustrated above, the context for **open** begins with an ordinary **.context** command. As a result, anywhere that you select "open," the help system references this context.

Hyperlinks are explicit cross-references marked by invisible text.

A "hyperlink" is an explicit cross-reference tied to a word or phrase at a specific location in the help file. You create hyperlinks when you write the help text. The hyperlink consists of a word or phrase followed by invisible text that gives the context to which the hyperlink refers.

For example, to cause an instance of the word "formatting" to display help on the **printf** function, you would create an explicit cross-reference from the word "formatting" to the context "printf." Elsewhere in the file, "formatting" has no special significance but, at that one position, it references the help for **printf**. Section 7.5.4 describes how to create hyperlinks.

Formatting flags let you change the appearance of text.

Help text can also include formatting flags to control the appearance of the text on the screen. Using these flags, you can make certain words appear in various colors, inverse video, and so forth, depending on the application displaying help and the graphics capabilities of the host computer.

7.1.2 Help File Formats

You can create help files using any of three formats:

- QuickHelp format
- Rich Text Format (RTF)
- Minimally formatted ASCII

In addition, you can reference unformatted ASCII files, such as include files, from within a help database.

An entire help system (such as the one supplied with Microsoft C or Quick-BASIC) can use any combination of files formatted with different format types. With C, for example, the README.DOC information file is encoded as minimally formatted ASCII; the help files for the PWB, C language, and run-time library are encoded in the QuickHelp format. The database also cross-references the header (include) files, which are unformatted ASCII files stored outside the database.

QuickHelp

QuickHelp format is the default and is the format into which HELPMAKE decodes help databases. Use any text editor to create a QuickHelp-format help text file. QuickHelp format also lends itself to a relatively easy automated translation from other document formats.

QuickHelp files can contain any kind of cross-reference or formatting attribute. Typically, you use QuickHelp format for any changes to a database supplied by Microsoft.

RTF

Rich Text Format (RTF) is a Microsoft word-processing format that many other word processors also support. You can create RTF help text with any word processor that generates RTF output. You can also use any utility program that takes word-processor output and produces an RTF file.

Use RTF when you want to transfer help files from one application to another while retaining formatting information. You can format RTF files directly with the word-processing program; you need not edit them to insert any special commands or tags. Like QuickHelp files, RTF files can contain formatting attributes and cross-references.

Minimally Formatted ASCII

Minimally formatted ASCII files simply define contexts and their topic text. These files cannot contain screen-formatting commands or explicit cross-references (implicit cross-references are allowed). They are often used to display text such as README.DOC and small help files that do not require compression.

Unformatted ASCII

Unformatted ASCII files are exactly what their name implies: regular ASCII files with no special formatting commands, context definitions, or special information. An unformatted ASCII file does not become part of the help database. Only its name is used as the object of a cross-reference. The standard C header (include) files are unformatted ASCII files used for cross-references by the help system for the C run-time library. Unformatted ASCII files are also useful for storing program examples.

7.2 Invoking HELPMAKE

The HELPMAKE program can encode or decode help files, allowing you to create new help files or modify existing ones. Encoding converts a text file to a compressed help database. HELPMAKE can encode text files written in QuickHelp, RTF, and minimally formatted ASCII format. Decoding converts a help database to a text file for editing. HELPMAKE always decodes a help database into a QuickHelp format text file.

Invoke HELPMAKE with the following syntax:

HELPMAKE [[*options*]] { /E*n* | /D } { *sourcefiles* }

The *options* modify the action of HELPMAKE; they are described in Section 7.3.

Use the /E option to encode with HELPMAKE and use the /D option to decode.

You must supply either the /E (encode) or the /D (decode) option. When encoding (/E) to create a help database, you must use the /O option to specify the file name of the database.

The *sourcefile* field is required. It specifies the input file for HELPMAKE. If you use the /D (decode) option, *sourcefile* can be one or more help database files (such as QC.HLP). HELPMAKE decodes the database files into a single text file. If you use the /E (encode) option, *sourcefile* can be one or more help text files (such as QC.SRC). Separate file names with a space. Standard wild-card characters can also be used.

The example below invokes HELPMAKE with the /V, /E, and /O options (see Section 7.3.1, "Options for Encoding"). HELPMAKE reads input from the text file `my.txt` and writes the compressed help database in the file `my.hlp`. The /E option causes maximum compression. Note that the DOS redirection symbol (>) sends a log of HELPMAKE activity to the file `my.log`. You may find it helpful to redirect the log file because, in its more verbose modes (given by /V), HELPMAKE may generate a lengthy log.

```
HELPMAKE /V /E /Omy.hlp my.txt > my.log
```

The example below invokes HELPMAKE to decode the help database `my.hlp` into the text file `my.src`, given with the /O option. Once again, the /V option results in verbose output, and the output is directed to the log file `my.log`. Section 7.3.2 describes additional options for decoding.

```
HELPMAKE /V /D /Omy.src my.hlp > my.log
```

7.3 HELPMAKE Options

HELPMAKE accepts a number of command-line options, which are described below. You can specify options in uppercase or lowercase letters, and precede them with either a forward slash (/) or a dash (–). For example, –L, /L, –l, and /l all represent the same option. Most options apply only to encoding; others apply only to decoding; and a few apply to both.

7.3.1 *Options for Encoding*

When you encode a file—that is, when you build a help database—you must specify the /E option. In addition, you can supply various other options that control the way HELPMAKE works. All the options that apply when encoding are listed below:

Option	Action
/A*c*	Specifies *c* as an application-specific control character for the help database file. The character marks a line that contains special information for internal use by the application. For example, QuickC uses the colon (:).
/C	Indicates that the context strings for this help file are case sensitive. At run time, all searches for help topics are case sensitive if the help database was built with the /C option in effect.
/E[[*n*]]	Creates (encodes) a help database from a specified text file. The optional *n* indicates the amount of compression to take place. If *n* is omitted, HELPMAKE compresses the file as much as possible, thereby reducing the size of the file by about 50%. The more compression requested, the longer HELPMAKE takes to create a database file. The value of *n* is a number in the range 0 – 15. It is the sum of successive powers of 2 representing various compression techniques, as listed below:

Value	Technique
0	No compression
1	Run-length compression
2	Key word compression
4	Extended key word compression
8	Huffman compression

Add values to combine compression techniques. For example, use /E3 to get run-length and key word compression. This is useful in the testing stages of creating a help database when you need to create the database quickly and are not too concerned with size.

| /H | Displays a summary of HELPMAKE syntax and exits. |

/HELP

Invokes QH.EXE, the QuickHelp utility, for help about HELPMAKE. If QuickHelp is not available, displays the same information as the /H option.

/K *filename*

Optimizes key word compression by supplying a list of characters that act as word separators. The *filename* is a file containing your list of separator characters.

When you select key word compression, HELP-MAKE scans the help file to identify "key words." A key word is any word that occurs often enough to justify replacing it with a shorter character sequence. HELPMAKE normally uses the following characters as word separators:

- All characters from 0–32 (including the space)

- !"#&'()*+'–,/:;<=>?@[\]^_'{|}~

- 127

When performing key word compression, HELP-MAKE treats as a word any series of characters not appearing in the separator list.

Depending on the content of your help file, you may be able to improve key word compression by using the /K option to specify a different list of separator characters. For instance, the default separator list contains the number sign (#). If your help file contains **#include** directives, HELPMAKE normally treats **#include** as the word **include** without a number sign. To cause HELPMAKE to treat **#include** as a word, you could specify the following separator list:

```
!"&'()*+'-,/:;<=>?@[\]^_'{|}~
```

The list above does not include the number sign. HELPMAKE always treats characters in the range 0–32 as separators, so you do not need to include them. Your list must include all the other characters you want HELPMAKE to use as separators, including the space.

/L

Locks the generated file so that it cannot be decoded by HELPMAKE at a later time.

/O*destfile*

Specifies *destfile* as the name of the help database.

/S*n*	Specifies the type of input file, according to the following *n* values:

Option	File Type
/S1	Rich Text Format (RTF)
/S2	QuickHelp (default)
/S3	Minimally formatted ASCII

/T	Translates dot commands into internal format. If your help file contains dot commands other than **.context**, you should supply this option when encoding it. Dot commands are described in Section 7.6.1, "QuickHelp Format," and in later sections.

/V[[*n*]]	Indicates the verbosity of diagnostic and informational output, depending on the value of *n*. Increasing the value adds more information to the output. If you omit this option or specify only /V, HELPMAKE gives you its most verbose output. The possible values of *n* are listed below:

Option	Effect
/V	Maximum diagnostic output
/V0	No diagnostic output and no banner
/V1	Prints only HELPMAKE banner (default)
/V2	Prints pass names
/V3	Prints contexts on first pass
/V4	Prints contexts on each pass
/V5	Prints any intermediate steps within each pass
/V6	Prints statistics on help file and compression

/W*width*	Indicates the fixed width of the resulting help text in number of characters. The values of *width* can range from 11 to 255. If the /W option is omitted, the default is 76. When encoding RTF source (/S1), HELPMAKE automatically formats the text to *width*. When encoding QuickHelp (/S2) or minimally formatted ASCII (/S3) files, HELPMAKE truncates lines to this width.

7.3.2 Options for Decoding

To decode a help database into QuickHelp files, you must use the /D option. In addition, HELPMAKE accepts other options to control the decoding process. The list below shows all the options that are valid when decoding:

Option	Action
/D[[*letter*]]	Decodes the input file into its original text or component parts. If a destination file is not specified with the /O option, the help file is decoded to **stdout**. HELPMAKE decodes the file differently depending on the letter specified:

Letter	Effect
/D	"Decode." Fully decodes the help database, leaving all cross-references and formatting information intact.
/DS	"Decode split." Splits the concatenated, compressed help database into its components using their original names. If the database was created without concatenation (the default), HELPMAKE simply copies it to a file with its original name. No decompression occurs.
/DU	"Decode unformatted." Decompresses the database and removes all screen formatting and cross-references. The output can still be used later for input and recompression, but all screen formatting and cross-references are lost.

Option	Action
/H	Displays a summary of HELPMAKE syntax and exits without encoding or decoding any files.
/HELP	Invokes QH.EXE, the QuickHelp utility, for information about HELPMAKE. If QuickHelp is not available, displays the same information as the /H option.

| /O*destfile* | Specifies *destfile* for the decoded output from HELPMAKE. If *destfile* is omitted, the help database is decoded to **stdout**. HELPMAKE always decodes help database files into QuickHelp format. |

| /T | Translates dot commands from internal format into dot-command format. You should always supply this option when decoding a help database that contains dot commands other than **.context**. |

| /V[[*n*]] | Indicates the verbosity of diagnostic and informational output depending on the value of *n*. The possible values are listed below. If you omit this option or specify only /V, HELPMAKE gives you its most verbose output. |

Option	Effect
/V	Maximum diagnostic output
/V0	No diagnostic output and no banner
/V1	Prints only the HELPMAKE banner
/V2	Prints pass names
/V3	Prints contexts on first pass

7.4 Creating a Help Database

You can create a Microsoft-compatible help database by either of two methods.

The first method is to decompress an existing help database, modify the resulting help text file, and recompress the help text file to form a new database.

The second and simpler method is to append a new help database to an existing help database. This method involves the following steps:

1. Create a help text file in QuickHelp format, RTF, or minimally formatted ASCII.

2. Use HELPMAKE to create a help database file. The example below invokes HELPMAKE, using SAMPLE.TXT as the input file and producing a help database file named `sample.hlp`:

   ```
   HELPMAKE /V /E /Osample.hlp sample.txt > sample.log
   ```

3. Make a backup copy of the existing database file (for safety's sake).

4. Append the new help database file to the existing help database. The example below concatenates the new database `sample.hlp` onto the end of the CLANG.HLP database:

```
COPY clang.hlp /b + sample.hlp /b
```

5. Test the database. The `sample.hlp` database contains the context `sample`. If you type the word "sample" in the PWB and request help on it, the help window displays the text associated with the context `sample`.

7.5 Help Text Conventions

Microsoft help databases have a common structure and follow certain organizational conventions. You should follow the same conventions to create Microsoft-compatible help files.

7.5.1 Structure of the Help Text File

The help-retrieval capability that is built into Microsoft products is simply a data-retrieval tool. It imposes no restrictions on the content and format of the help text. The HELPMAKE utility and the display routines built into Microsoft language environments, however, make certain assumptions about the format of help text. This section provides some guidelines for creating help text files compatible with those assumptions.

In all three help text formats, the help text source file is a sequence of topics, each preceded by one or more unique context definitions. The following list specifies the various formats and the corresponding context definition statements:

Format	Context Definition
QuickHelp	**.context** *context*
RTF	\ par >>*context* \ par
Minimally formatted	>>*context*
ASCII	(none)

In QuickHelp format, each topic begins with one or more **.context** statements that define the context strings that map to the topic text. Subsequent lines up to the next **.context** statement constitute the topic text.

In RTF format, each context definition must be in a paragraph of its own (denoted by \ par), beginning with the help delimiter (>>). Subsequent paragraphs up to the next context definition constitute the topic text.

In minimally formatted ASCII, each context definition must be on a separate line, and each must begin with the help delimiter (>>). As in RTF and QuickHelp files, subsequent lines up to the next context definition constitute the topic text.

See Section 7.6, "Using Help Database Formats," for detailed information about these three formats.

7.5.2 *Local Contexts*

Context strings that begin with an "at" sign (@) are defined as "local" and have no implicit cross-references. They are used in cross-references instead of the context string that otherwise is generated.

When you use a local context, HELPMAKE does not generate a global context string (a context string that is known throughout the help file). Instead, it embeds an encoded cross-reference that has meaning only within the current context. For example,

```
.context normal
This is a normal topic, accessible by the context string "normal."
[button\v@local\v] is a cross-reference to the following topic.

.context @local

This topic can be reached only if the user browses
sequentially through the file or uses the cross-reference
in the previous topic.
```

In the example above, the text `[button\v@local\v]` defines `local` as a local context. If the user selects the text `[button]` or scrolls through the file, the help system displays the topic text that follows the context definition for `local`. Because `local` is defined with the "at" sign (@), it can be accessed only by a hyperlink within the help file or by sequentially browsing through the file. Making a context local saves file space and speeds access.

7.5.3 Context Prefixes

Microsoft help databases use several context prefixes. A "context prefix" is a single letter followed by a period. It appears before a context string that has a predefined meaning. If you decode a Microsoft help database, many of these contexts may appear in the resulting text file.

Most context prefixes are internal. Except for the h. prefix, which is described below, context prefixes are internal. You do not need to add them in help files that you write.

You can use the h. prefix to identify standard help-file contexts. For instance, h.default identifies the default help screen: the screen that normally appears when you select "top-level" help. Table 7.1 lists the standard h. contexts.

Table 7.1   Standard h. Contexts

Context	Description
h.contents	The table of contents for the help file. You should also define the string "contents" for direct reference to this context.
h.default	The default help screen, typically displayed when the user presses SHIFT+F1 at the "top level" in most applications. The contents are generally devoted to information about using help.
h.index	The index for the help file. You can also define the string "index" for direct reference to this context.
h.notfound	The help text that is displayed when the help system cannot find information about the requested context. The text could be an index of contexts, a topical list, or general information about using help.
h.pg#	A specific page within the help file. This is used in response to a "go to page #" request.
h.pg$	The help text that is logically last in the file. This is used by some applications in response to a "go to the end" request made within the help window.
h.pg1	The help text that is logically first in the file. This is used by some applications in response to a "go to the beginning" request made within the help window.
h.title	The title of the help database.

The context prefixes in Table 7.2 are internal to Microsoft products. They appear in decompressed databases, but you do not need to use them.

Table 7.2   Microsoft Product Context Prefixes

Prefix	Purpose
d.	Dialog box. Each dialog box is assigned a number. Its help context string is d. followed by the number (for example, `d.12`).
e.	Error number. If a product supports the error-numbering scheme used by Microsoft languages, it displays help for each error using this prefix. For example, the context `e.c1234` refers to the C compiler error message number C1234.
m.	Menu item. Contexts that relate to product menu items are defined by their accelerator keys. For example, the Exit selection on the FILE menu item is accessed by ALT+F X and is referenced in help by `m.f.x`.
n.	Message number. Each message box is assigned a number. Its help context string is n. plus the number (for example, `n.5`).

7.5.4 Hyperlinks

Explicit cross-references, or hyperlinks, in the help text file are marked with invisible text. A hyperlink comprises a word or phrase followed by invisible text that gives the context to which the hyperlink refers.

The keystroke that activates the hyperlink depends on the application. Consult the documentation for each product to find the specific keystroke needed.

When the user activates the hyperlink, the help system displays the topic named by the invisible text. The invisible cross-reference text is formatted as one of the following:

Hyperlink Text	Action
contextstring	Causes the help topic associated with *contextstring* to be displayed. For example, `exeformat` results in the display of the help topic associated with the context `exeformat`.
filename!	Treats *filename* as a single topic to be displayed. For example, `$INCLUDE:stdio.h!` searches the INCLUDE environment variable for file STDIO.H and displays it as a single help topic.

filename!*contextstring*   Works the same way as *contextstring* above, except that only the help file *filename* is searched for the context. If the file is not already open, the help system finds it (by searching either the current path or an explicit environment variable) and opens it. For example, `$BIN:readme.doc!patches` searches for `readme.doc` in the BIN environment variable and displays the topic associated with `patches`.

In the following example, the word `Example` is a hyperlink:

```
\bSee also:\p    \uExample\p\vopen.ex\v
```

The hyperlink refers to `open.ex`. If you select any of the letters of `Example`, the help system displays the topic whose context is `open.ex`. On the screen, this line appears as follows:

```
See also:    Example
```

An application might display `See also:` and `Example` in different colors or character types, depending on such factors as your default color selection and type of monitor.

When a hyperlink needs to cross-reference more than one word, you must use an anchor, as in the following example:

```
\bSee also:\p    \uExample\p\vprintf.ex\v, fprintf, scanf, sprintf,
vfprintf, vprintf, vsprintf
            \aformatting table\vprintf.table\v
```

This part of the example is an anchored hyperlink:

```
\aformatting table\vprintf.table\v
```

Anchored hyperlinks must fit on a single line.

The \a flag creates an anchor for the cross-reference. In the example, the phrase following the \a flag (`formatting table`) is the hyperlink. It refers to the context `printf.table`. The first \v flag marks both the end of the hyperlink and the beginning of the invisible text. The name `printf.table` is invisible; it does not appear on the screen when the help is displayed. The second \v flag ends the invisible text.

7.6 Using Help Database Formats

The text format of the database can be any of three types. The list below briefly describes these types. Sections 7.6.1–7.6.3 describe the formatting types in detail.

An entire help system (such as the one supplied with the Professional Development System or QuickC) can use any combination of files formatted with different format types. With C, for example, the README.DOC information file is encoded as minimally formatted ASCII; and the help files for the C language and run-time library are encoded in the QuickHelp format. The database also cross-references the header (include) files, which are unformatted ASCII files stored outside the database.

Type	Characteristics
QuickHelp	Uses dot commands and embedded formatting characters (the default formatting type expected by HELPMAKE); supports highlighting, color, and cross-references. This format must be compressed before using.
Minimally formatted ASCII	Uses a help delimiter (>>) to define help contexts; does not support highlighting, color, or cross-references. This format can be compressed, but compression is not required.
RTF	Uses a subset of standard RTF; supports highlighting, color, and cross-references; supports dot commands. This format must be compressed before using.

7.6.1 QuickHelp Format

The QuickHelp format uses a dot command and embedded formatting flags to convey information to HELPMAKE.

QuickHelp Dot Commands

QuickHelp supports a number of dot commands, which identify topics and convey other topic-related information to the help system. If your help file contains dot commands other than **.context**, you must supply the /T option when encoding and decoding with HELPMAKE.

You can define more than one context for a single topic.

The most important dot command is the **.context** command. Every topic in a QuickHelp file begins with one or more **.context** commands. Each **.context** command defines a context string for the topic text. You can define more than one context for a single topic, as long as you do not place any topic text between them.

Typical dot commands are shown below. The first defines a context for the **#include** C preprocessor directive. The second set illustrates multiple contexts for one block of topic text. In this case, the same topic text explains all of the string-to-number conversion routines in C.

```
.context #include
     .
     . description of #include goes here
     .
.context strtod
.context strtol
.context strtoul
     .
     . description of string-to-number functions goes here
     .
```

The QuickHelp format supports several other dot commands. Table 7.3 lists all of the dot commands available in QuickHelp format.

Table 7.3   QuickHelp Dot Commands

Command	Action
.category *string*	Lists the category in which the current topic appears and its position in the list of topics. The category name is used by the QuickHelp Topic command, which brings up the list of topics to which the current topic belongs. Some applications, such as the PWB, use this name as a pointer to the applicable table of contents.
.command	Indicates that the topic text is not a displayable help topic. Use this command to hide hyperlink topics and other internal information. Hyperlink topics are described in Section 7.5.5, "Hyperlink Commands."
.comment *string*	The *string* is a comment that appears only in the help source file. Comments are especially useful for documenting the purpose of cross-references.
	Because comments are not inserted in the help database, they are not restored when you decompress a help file.
.context *string*	The *string* introduces a topic.

Table 7.3   (*continued*)

Command	Action
.end	Ends a paste section. See the **.paste** command below.
.freeze *numlines*	Indicates that the first *numlines* lines should be frozen as the top line of the help screen. This is normally used to freeze a row of cross-reference buttons at the top of a help topic that might be scrolled.
.length *topiclength*	Indicates the default window size, in *topiclength* lines, of the topic about to be displayed. This command is always the first line in the topic if present.
.list	Indicates that the current topic contains a list of topics. QuickHelp displays a highlighted line; you can choose a topic by moving the highlighted line over the desired topic and pressing **ENTER**. Help searches for the first word of the line.
.mark *name* [[*column*]]	Defines a mark immediately preceding the following line of text. This command can be used in help script commands to indicate that the display of a particular topic begins at the marked line. The *name* identifies the mark. The optional *column* value is an integer that indicates a column location within the specified line.
.next *context*	Tells the help system to look up the next topic using *context* instead of the next topic's name. You can use this command to skip large blocks of **.command** or **.popup** topics.
.previous *context*	Tells the help system to look up the previous topic using *context* instead of the previous topic's name. You can use this command to skip large blocks of **.command** or **.popup** topics.
.paste *pastename*	Begins a paste section. The *pastename* appears in the QuickHelp Paste menu.
.popup	Tells the help system to display the current topic as a popup instead of a normal, scrollable topic.
.ref *string(s)*	Tells the help system to display the list of *string* topics in the Reference menu. You can list as many topics as needed; separate each additional *string* with a comma.
.topic *text*	Defines *text* as the name or title to be displayed in place of the context string if the application help displays a title. This command is always the first line in the context unless you also use the **.length** command.

QuickHelp Formatting Flags

The QuickHelp format supports a number of formatting flags that are used to highlight parts of the help database and to mark hyperlinks in the help text.

Each formatting flag consists of a backslash (\ ) followed by a character. Table 7.4 lists the formatting flags.

Table 7.4   Formatting Flags

Formatting Flag	Action
\a	Anchors text for cross-references
\b, \B	Turns boldface on or off
\i, \I	Turns italics on or off
\p, \P	Turns off all attributes
\u, \U	Turns underlining on or off
\v, \V	Turns invisibility on or off (hides cross-references in text)
\\	Inserts a single backslash in text

On monochrome monitors, text labeled with the bold, italic, and underlining attributes appears in various ways, depending on the application (for example, high intensity and reverse video are commonly displayed). On color monitors, these attributes are translated by the application into suitable colors, depending on the user's default color selections.

The \b, \i, \u, and \v options are toggles, turning on and off their respective attributes. You can use several of these on the same text. Use the \p attribute to turn off all attributes. Use the \v attribute to hide cross-references and hyperlinks in the text.

HELPMAKE truncates the lines in QuickHelp files to the width specified with the /W option. (See Section 7.3.1, "Options for Encoding," for more information.) Only visible characters count toward the character-width limit. Lines that begin with an application-specific control character are truncated to 255 characters regardless of the width specification. See Section 7.3.1 for more information about application-specific control characters.

In the example below, the \b flag initiates boldface text for Returns:, and the \p flag that follows the word reverts to plain text for the remainder of the line.

```
\bReturns:\p    a handle if successful, or -1 if not.
            errno:  EACCES, EEXIST, EMFILE, ENOENT
```

In the example below, \a anchors text for the hyperlink Example. The \v flags define the cross-reference to be sample_prog and cause the text between the flags to be invisible. Cross-references are described in the following section.

```
\aExample \vsample_prog\v
```

QuickHelp Cross-References

Help databases contain two types of cross-references: implicit cross-references and explicit cross-references. They are described in Section 7.1.1, "Contents of a Help File."

An implicit cross-reference is any word that appears both in the topic text and as a context in the help file. For example, any time you request help on the word "close," the help window displays help on the **close** function. You don't need to code implicit cross-references in your help text files.

Insert formatting flags to mark explicit cross-references.

Explicit cross-references (hyperlinks) are words or phrases on the screen that are associated with a context. For example, the word "Example" in the initial help-screen area for any C function is an explicit cross-reference to the C program example for that function. You must insert formatting flags in your help text files to mark explicit cross-references.

If the hyperlink consists of a single word, you can use invisible text to flag it in the source file. The \v formatting flag creates invisible text, as follows:

hyperlink\vcontext\v

Specify the first \v flag immediately following the word you want to use as the hyperlink. Following the flag, insert the context that the hyperlink cross-references. The second \v flag marks the end of the context; that is, the end of the invisible text. HELPMAKE generates a cross-reference whose context is the invisible text, and whose hyperlink is the entire word.

If the hyperlink consists of a phrase, rather than a single word, you must use anchored text to create explicit cross-references. Use the \a and \v flags to create anchored text as follows:

\ahyperlink-words\vcontext\v

The \a flag marks an anchor for the cross-reference. The text that follows the \a flag is the hyperlink. The hyperlink must fit entirely on one line. The first \v flag marks both the end of the hyperlink and the beginning of the invisible text that contains the cross-reference context. The second \v flag marks the end of the invisible text.

The following example contains three implicit cross-references to the C routines **abs**, **cabs**, and **fabs**.

```
See also: abs, cabs, fabs
```

The following example shows the encoding for an explicit cross-reference to an example program and a function template from the help database for the C runtime library:

```
See also: Example\vopen.ex\v, Template\vopen.tm\v, close
```

Here, the hyperlinks are `Example` and `Template`, which reference the contexts `open.ex` and `open.tm`. The example also contains an implicit cross-reference to the **close** function.

The following example shows the encoding for an explicit cross-reference to an entire family of functions:

```
See also: \ais... functions\vis_functions\v, atoi
```

The cross-reference uses anchored text to associate a phrase, rather than just a word, with a context. In this example, the hyperlink is the anchored phrase `is... functions`, and it cross-references the context `is_functions`. In addition, the example contains an implicit cross-reference to the **atoi** routine.

The code below is an example in QuickHelp format that contains a single entry:

```
.context open
.length 13
\bInclude:\p   <fcntl.h>, <io.h>, <sys\\types.h>, <sys\\stat.h>

\bPrototype:\p  int open(char *path, int flag[, int mode]);
          flag:  O_APPEND O_BINARY O_CREAT O_EXCL O_RDONLY
                 O_RDWR   O_TEXT    O_TRUNC O_WRONLY
                 (can be joined by |)
          mode:  S_IWRITE S_IREAD   S_IREAD | S_IWRITE

\bReturns:\p    a handle if successful, or -1 if not.
          errno:  EACCES, EEXIST, EMFILE, ENOENT

\bSee also:\p  \uExample\p\vopen.ex\v, \uTemplate\p\vopen.tp\v,
          access, chmod, close, creat, dup, dup2, fopen, sopen, umask
```

The **.length** command near the beginning of the example specifies the size of the initial window for the help text. Here, the initial window displays 13 lines.

The manifest constants (such as **O_WRONLY** and **EEXIST**), the C keywords (such as **int** and **char**), and the other functions (such as **sopen** and **access**) are implicit cross-references. The words `Example` and `Template` are explicit cross-references to the example `open.ex` and to the **open** template `open.tp`, respectively. Note the use of double backslashes in the include file names.

7.6.2 Minimally Formatted ASCII Format

A minimally formatted ASCII text file comprises a sequence of topics, each preceded by one or more unique context definitions. Each context definition must be on a separate line beginning with a help delimiter (>>). Subsequent lines up to the next context definition constitute the topic text.

Minimally formatted ASCII files cannot contain highlighting.

Minimally formatted ASCII files can be used in two ways. You can compress the file with HELPMAKE, creating a help database, or an application can access the uncompressed file directly. Uncompressed files are somewhat larger and slower to search, however. Minimally formatted ASCII files are of fixed width, and they cannot contain highlighting (or other nondefault attributes) or cross-references.

The following example, coded in minimally formatted ASCII, shows the same text as the QuickHelp example in the previous section. The first line of the example defines `open` as a context string. The minimally formatted ASCII help file must begin with the help delimiter (>>), so that HELPMAKE or the application can verify that the file is indeed an ASCII help file.

```
>>open

Include:    <fcntl.h>, <io.h>, <sys\types.h>, <sys\stat.h>

Prototype:  int open(char *path, int flag[, int mode]);
      flag: O_APPEND  O_BINARY  O_CREAT  O_EXCL  O_RDONLY
            O_RDWR    O_TEXT    O_TRUNC  O_WRONLY
            (can be joined by |)
      mode: S_IWRITE  S_IREAD    S_IREAD | S_IWRITE

Returns:    a handle if successful, or -1 if not.
            errno:  EACCES, EEXIST, EMFILE, ENOENT

See also:  access, chmod, close, creat, dup, dup2, fopen, sopen, umask
```

When displayed, the help information appears exactly as it is typed into the file. Any formatting codes are treated as ASCII text. Note that you do not need to escape backslashes in minimally formatted ASCII files.

If you compress minimally formatted ASCII files, they are smaller and faster to search.

7.6.3 *Rich Text Format (RTF)*

RTF is a Microsoft word-processing format supported by many other word processors. It allows documents to be transferred from one application to another without losing any formatting information. The HELPMAKE utility recognizes a subset of the full RTF syntax. If your file contains any RTF code that is not part of the subset, HELPMAKE ignores the code and strips it out of the file.

Certain word-processing and file-conversion programs generate the RTF code automatically as output. You need not worry about inserting RTF codes yourself; you can simply format your help files directly with a word-processor that generates RTF, using the attributes supported by the subset. The only items you need to insert are the help delimiter (>>) and context string that start each entry.

HELPMAKE recognizes the subset of RTF listed below:

RTF Code	Action
\b	Boldface. The application decides how to display this; often it is intensified text.
\fi *<nnn>*	Paragraph first-line indent.
\i	Italic. The application decides how to display this; often it is reverse video.
\li *<nnn>*	Paragraph indent from left margin.
\line	New line (not new paragraph).
\par	End of paragraph.
\pard	Default paragraph formatting.
\plain	Default attributes. On most screens this is nonblinking normal intensity.
\tab	Tab character.
\ul	Underline. The application decides how to display this; some adapters that do not support underlining display it as blue text.
\v	Hidden text. Hidden text is used for cross-reference information and for some application-specific communications; it is not displayed.

Using the word-processing program, you can break the topic text into paragraphs. When HELPMAKE compresses the file, it formats the text to the width given with the /W option, ignoring the paragraph formats.

As with the other text formats, each entry in the database source consists of one or more context strings, followed by topic text. An RTF file can contain Quick-Help dot commands.

The help delimiter (>>) at the beginning of any paragraph denotes the beginning of a new help entry. The text that follows on the same line is defined as a context for the topic. If the next paragraph also begins with the help delimiter, it also defines a context string for the same topic text. You can define any number of contexts for a block of topic text. The topic text comprises all subsequent paragraphs up to the next paragraph that begins with the help delimiter.

The code below is an example of a help database that contains a single entry using subset RTF text. Note that RTF uses curly braces ({ }) for nesting. Thus, the entire file is enclosed in curly braces, as is each specially formatted text item.

```
{\rtf1
\pard >>open\par
  {\b Include:}      <fcntl.h>, <io.h>, <sys\\types.h>, <sys\\stat.h>\par
\par
  {\b Syntax:}      int open( char * filename, int oflag[, int pmode ] );\par
             oflag:  O_APPEND  O_BINARY  O_CREAT  O_EXCL  O_RDONLY\par
                     O_RDWR     O_TEXT      O_TRUNC  O_WRONLY\par
                     (may be joined by |)\par
             pmode:  S_IWRITE  S_IREAD    S_IREAD | S_IWRITE\par
\par
  {\b Returns:}    a handle if successful, or -1 if not.\par
             errno:  EACCES, EEXIST, EMFILE, ENOENT\par
\par
  {\b See also:}  Examples{\v open.ex}, access, chmod, close, creat, dup,\par
             dup2, fopen, sopen, umask\par
>>open.ex\par
To build this help file, use the following command:\par
\par
HELPMAKE /S1 /E15 /OOPEN.HLP OPEN.RTF\par
\par

        < Back >{\v !B}
}
```

Actual RTF output normally contains additional information that is not visible to the user; HELPMAKE ignores this extra information.

Customizing the Microsoft Programmer's WorkBench

Designed with flexibility in mind, the Microsoft Programmer's WorkBench (PWB) provides a highly extensible development platform for the Microsoft C Professional Development System. Using PWB it is easy to change basic environment features such as screen colors and key assignments, and you can add powerful new functions of your own using macros and C-language extensions.

This chapter explains four methods for customizing the Programmer's WorkBench: setting switches, assigning keystrokes, writing macros, and writing C extensions. While it explains customization methods, the chapter does not document every customizable feature of the Programmer's WorkBench. Use on-line help as your primary source of information about these and other PWB features.

This chapter assumes you are familiar with basic PWB operations and terminology. If you are not, read "Using the Programmer's WorkBench" in *Installing and Using the Microsoft C Professional Development System*.

8.1 Setting Switches

The Programmer's WorkBench has a number of "switches," or user-configurable options, that control features such as screen colors. Each switch has a name and can be assigned a value.

There are two ways to set PWB switches. The easiest way is by choosing Editor Settings in the Options menu. You can also edit the TOOLS.INI initialization file. These methods can also be used for more elaborate customizations, such as writing macros.

8.1.1 Editing the <assign> Pseudofile

If you choose Editor Settings in the Options menu, PWB changes to the **<assign>** pseudofile and displays it in the current window. (A pseudofile is constructed dynamically by PWB; it exists only in memory.) The **<assign>** file lists all the current PWB settings.

To change a switch, edit the line where it appears. For instance, the **vscroll** switch controls how many lines PWB scrolls vertically; its default setting is 1. To change it, move to the corresponding line:

```
vscroll:1
```

Change the 1 to 3 and move the cursor to another line. PWB highlights the line to indicate the change is legal. (If you make an illegal change, PWB signals an error.) The change takes effect immediately: now PWB scrolls text three vertical lines at a time.

If you don't explicitly save a change, it disappears at the end of the current session. You can save a change by saving **<assign>** as you would any other file (by pressing ALT+A ALT+A F2). When you exit PWB, you are asked if you want to save TOOLS.INI, the PWB initialization file, which records customizations. Answer yes (type Y) to save the change.

You can also use this method for more elaborate customizations, such as writing macros (see Section 8.3, "Writing Macros"). Simply insert a few blank lines in **<assign>** and enter the new information in them. Note that PWB only pays attention to lines you change or add to **<assign>**. Deleting a line has no effect.

8.1.2 Editing the TOOLS.INI Initialization File

Another way to customize PWB is by editing TOOLS.INI, the initialization file used by PWB and other Microsoft language tools. This method is useful if you customize PWB extensively.

While the **<assign>** file lists every customizable PWB item, the TOOLS.INI file contains lines only for items you have customized. Those items not mentioned in TOOLS.INI are set to a default value.

Dividing TOOLS.INI into Sections

Since several tools can use TOOLS.INI, the file may contain information that doesn't relate to PWB. If you customize more than one tool, TOOLS.INI is divided into sections, one for each tool. Each section begins with a tag consisting of the tool's base name enclosed in square brackets: [PWB] for PWB.EXE, [NMAKE] for NMAKE.EXE, and so on.

For example, say you set the **vscroll** switch to 3 and save the change, but you have not customized PWB in any other way. Your TOOLS.INI file will contain this section:

```
[PWB]
vscroll:3
```

Settings following this tag are put in effect by PWB every time it starts.

You can also create sections of TOOLS.INI that PWB reads only in certain circumstances. You can create sections for different video adapters, file-name extensions, and operating system versions.

If you use more than one video display, TOOLS.INI can have a different section for each display:

- [PWB-mono]

- [PWB-cga]

- [PWB-ega]

- [PWB-vga]

After each tag, you can set different screen colors, dimensions, and other display-specific switches.

You can also create a section for files with specific extensions. For instance, your TOOLS.INI file could contain a section beginning with the tag

```
[PWB-.C]
```

for C source files, and

```
[PWB-.ASM]
```

for assembly-language (.ASM) source files. Each time you load a file with the designated extension, PWB reads the appropriate section of TOOLS.INI. For each file type, you could use a different set of macros and other customizations.

TOOLS.INI can also contain sections specific to operating system versions. The following tag introduces a section specific to DOS version 3.20, for instance:

```
[PWB-3.20]
```

You can combine tags as needed. For example, the tag

```
[PWB-3.20 PWB-10.10R]
```

applies to DOS version 3.20 and OS/2 version 1.1 real mode.

You can also create a section in TOOLS.INI containing switches for a user-written extension. See Section 8.4.3, "Describing Functions and Switches." On-line help contains additional information about TOOLS.INI tags.

8.2 Assigning Keystrokes

PWB allows you to assign any editing function to almost any keystroke. Reassigning keystrokes doesn't change PWB graphic interface, however.

Keystrokes, like switches, are listed in the **<assign>** pseudofile (choose Key Assignments in the Options menu) and can be changed there. For example, say you want to assign the **home** cursor function to the SHIFT+HOME keystroke. The default keystroke assignment for **home** is:

```
home:ctrl+home
```

If you change the assignment to

```
home:shift+home
```

SHIFT+HOME moves the cursor to the home (upper left) window position.

It is legal to assign more than one keystroke to the same function. For example, many keystrokes invoke the **select** function, which selects a text region. Thus, the previous example adds a new keystroke (SHIFT+HOME) for the **home** function; it does not remove the previous assignment (CTRL+HOME).

There are two limitations on keystroke assignments:

- You can't reassign a keystroke that PWB is using for a menu. For instance, if ALT+F pulls down the File menu, PWB ignores any attempt to reassign ALT+F.

- You can't reassign ALT plus the number keys 1 – 9 (ALT+1, ALT+2, and so on). These keystrokes are reserved for the file history menu items.

Each keystroke can only invoke one function. If you mistakenly assign a keystroke to more than one function, PWB uses the most recent assignment. For example,

```
home:ctrl+a
setfile:ctrl+a
```

assigns the CTRL+A keystroke to two different functions, **home** and **setfile**. The second assignment overrides the first, assigning CTRL+A to **setfile**.

Occasionally, you may want to "unassign," or disable, a keystroke. This is done by assigning the **unassigned** function to the keystroke. For example,

```
unassigned:ctrl+a
```

disables CTRL+A. PWB signals an error when you press any unassigned key.

8.3 Writing Macros

The fastest way to create a new editing function for PWB is to write a macro. The function can be as simple as inserting a long word or phrase, or it can perform complex tasks by invoking PWB functions and other macros.

8.3.1 Macro Syntax

A macro can contain any combination of PWB functions, literal text, and macro operators. You can define as many as 1,024 macros at one time.

Literal text is case sensitive.   Literal text is anything inside double quotes. Inside literal text, you can represent a double quote as \" and a backslash as \\. Text is case sensitive inside quotes and case insensitive outside them.

The following macro comments out a line of C source code:

```
comment:=begline "/* " endline " */"
comment:alt+c
```

The first line names the macro and tells what it does. The **begline** and **endline** editor functions move the cursor, while the text inside quotes is printed at the current cursor position. The second line assigns a keystroke (ALT+C) to the macro.

A macro definition must fit on one logical line. If necessary, you can use the backslash (\ ) to continue the definition on the next line. For instance, the definition

```
comment:=begline "/* " endline " */"
```

could be written as

```
comment:=begline  \
"/* " endline  \
" */"
```

Notice the extra space before each backslash. If you want a space between the end of one line and the beginning of the other, you must precede the backslash with two spaces.

You can use the **arg** function to pass arguments to functions. For example, the following macro passes the argument 15 to the **plines** function (which scrolls text down):

```
movedown:=arg "15" plines
```

Because **arg** precedes the literal text, the text doesn't appear on the screen. Instead, it is passed as an argument to the next function, **plines**. The macro scrolls the current text down 15 lines.

Arguments can use regular expression syntax, as well (regular expressions are documented in on-line help):

```
endword:=arg arg "( !.!$!\\:!;!\\)!\\(!,)" psearch
```

The **arg arg** sequence directs the **psearch** function to treat the text argument as a regular expression search pattern. This search pattern tells PWB to search for the next period, end of line ($), colon, semicolon, close parenthesis, open parenthesis, or comma.

A macro can invoke other macros:

```
lcomment:= "/* "
rcomment:= " */"
commentout:=begline lcomment endline rcomment
commentout:alt+z
```

The `commentout` macro invokes the previously defined macros `lcomment` and `rcomment`.

In addition to standard PWB functions, macros can invoke user-defined (extension) functions. See Section 8.4, "Writing and Building C Extensions."

8.3.2 Macro Responses

Some PWB functions ask you for confirmation. For example, the **meta exit** (quit without saving) function normally asks if you really want to exit. Such questions always take the answer "yes" (y) or "no" (n).

When you invoke such a function in a macro, the function assumes an answer of yes and does not ask for confirmation. For example, the macro definition

```
quit:=meta exit
quit:alt+x
```

invokes **meta exit** when you press ALT+X. Because the **meta exit** function is invoked from a macro, PWB exits without asking for confirmation.

The following operators allow you to restore normal prompting or change the default responses:

Operator	Description
<	Asks for confirmation; if not followed by another < operator, prompts for all further questions
<y	Assumes a response of yes
<n	Assumes a response of no

A response operator applies to the function immediately preceding it. For instance, you can add the < operator to the `quit` macro definition to restore the usual prompt:

```
quit:=meta exit <
quit:alt+x
```

Now the macro prompts for a response before it exits.

8.3.3 Macro Arguments

If you enter an argument in PWB and then invoke a macro, the argument is passed to the first function in the macro that takes an argument:

```
tripleit:=copy paste paste
```

The `tripleit` macro invokes the **copy** and **paste** editing functions. If you highlight a text area and then invoke the macro, your highlighted argument is passed to the **copy** function, which copies the argument to the clipboard. The macro then invokes **paste** twice. The effect is to insert two copies of the highlighted text.

You cannot pass more than one argument from PWB to a macro.

You cannot pass more than one argument from PWB to a macro, even if the macro invokes more than one function that can accept an argument. The argument always goes to the first function in the macro that takes an argument.

You can also prompt for input inside a macro and pass the input as an argument using the **prompt** function as shown below:

```
newfile:=arg "Next file: " prompt setfile <
newfile:alt+n
```

The `newfile` macro prompts for a file name and then switches to the specified file. The sequence `arg "Next file: "` passes a text argument to **prompt**, which prints the text on the dialog line and waits for input. The input is passed as a text argument to the **setfile** function, which switches to that file. For more information on the **prompt** function, see on-line help.

8.3.4 Macro Conditionals

Macros can take different actions depending on certain conditions. Such macros take advantage of the fact that PWB editing functions generally return values—a TRUE (nonzero) value if successful or FALSE (zero) if unsuccessful.

Macros can use four conditional operators:

Operator	Description
:>*label*	Defines a *label* that can be targeted by other operators
=>*label*	Jumps to *label*
+>*label*	Jumps to *label* if the previous function returns TRUE
–>*label*	Jumps to *label* if the previous function returns FALSE

For example, the `leftmarg` macro moves the cursor to the left margin of the editing window:

```
leftmarg:=:>leftmore left +>leftmore
```

The macro above invokes the **left** function repeatedly (jumping to the label `leftmore`) until it returns FALSE, indicating the cursor has reached the left margin.

The label must appear immediately after the conditional operator, with no intervening spaces. A conditional operator without a label exits the macro immediately if the condition is true. If the condition is false, the macro continues execution. The following example demonstrates this:

```
turnon:=insertmode +> insertmode
```

This macro turns on insert mode regardless of whether insert mode is currently on or off. If insert mode is off, the first invocation of **insertmode** toggles the mode on and returns TRUE, causing the **+>** operator to terminate the macro. If insert mode is currently on, the first invocation of **insertmode** turns insert mode off and returns FALSE. The macro then invokes **insertmode** a second time, turning insert mode back on.

8.3.5 Temporary Macros

Occasionally, you may want to create a macro that lasts only through the current session. This can be done with the **assign** function. For example, the following steps create the `comment` macro described above.

To create the macro:

- Press ALT+A
- Type `comment:=begline "/* " endline " */"`
- Press ALT+=

To assign the ALT+C keystroke to the macro:

- Press ALT+A
- Type `comment:alt+c`
- Press ALT+=

The macro is available immediately and then disappears at the end of the current session.

8.3.6 Macro Recordings

Another way to create a macro is by recording your own actions. The entire sequence of actions is saved and can be replayed later by pressing a key.

You start the recording by invoking the **record** function. PWB names the resulting macro **recordvalue** by default, but you can use other names as well. To record a macro:

- Choose Record On from the Edit menu to start the recording.

- Perform the actions you want to record.

- Choose Record On again to end the recording.

- If **recordvalue** is not already assigned, assign it to a keystroke as described above.

After you complete these steps, a macro named **recordvalue** is available through the keystroke you assigned in the last step above. When you press this key, PWB replays the actions you recorded.

If you don't do anything more, the recorded macro is temporary—it disappears when you exit PWB. To save the macro permanently:

- Open the **<record>** pseudofile (press ALT+A, type `<record>`, press F2).

- Copy the macro definition in **<record>**.

- Paste the definition into the `[PWB]` section of your TOOLS.INI file.

Studying recorded macros can teach you a lot about macros and editor functions. If you open the **<record>** pseudofile in a second window before you record, you can watch PWB write the macro definition function by function.

If you save a recorded macro, you'll want to name it something other than **recordvalue,** the default name. To do this, pass the new name as an argument when you start the recording:

- Press ALT+A ALT+A.

- Type the new name.

- Choose Record On from the Edit menu to start recording.

- Complete the recording as usual.

You can expand an existing macro using the same process. If you supply the name of an existing macro, PWB appends the recorded commands to the macro instead of replacing it.

You can record a series of actions without executing them.

You can also make a "silent" recording, which records a series of actions without executing them. Start the recording with a **meta record** command (press F9 SHIFT+CTRL+R). Then complete the recording process as described above.

8.4 Writing and Building C Extensions

An "extension" is a file containing one or more user-written functions. PWB loads extensions at run time. Once the extension has been loaded, its functions can be assigned their own keystrokes, given arguments, and invoked in macros, exactly like other PWB functions.

User-written functions execute more quickly than macros.

The ability to load and call user-written functions makes PWB highly extensible. Because they consist of compiled C code, your functions can perform more complex jobs than macros can, and they execute many times faster.

An extension contains executable code, but it differs from a normal executable file in some important ways:

- It does not contain the usual C start-up code.

- It contains special data structures that describe its functions to PWB.

- Its functions are declared in a form that allows PWB to call them and pass arguments to them.

- Its functions can call native PWB functions, and some, but not all, C library functions.

This section explains how to build, load, and invoke a PWB extension. The example, CENTER.C, serves as a basis for discussion throughout the rest of this chapter.

The CENTER.C extension contains one extension function, `CenterLine`, which centers a line or range of lines in the current file.

```c
/* CENTER.C: Sample PWB extension */

#define LINE_LENGTH 80 /* Assumes 80-column screen */

#include <string.h>
/* PWB extension header file */
#include "ext.h"

PWBFUNC CenterLine( unsigned argData,
                    ARG _far *pArg,
                    flagType fMeta );

/* Switch Table */
struct swiDesc   swiTable[] =
{
    { NULL, NULL, 0 }
};

/* Command Table */
struct cmdDesc   cmdTable[] =
{
    { "CenterLine", CenterLine, 0, NOARG | LINEARG },
    { NULL, NULL, 0, 0 }
};

/* Initialization Function */
void EXTERNAL WhenLoaded( void )
{
    DoMessage( "Loading Center extension" );
}

/* Extension (user-written) function */
PWBFUNC CenterLine( unsigned argData,
                    ARG _far *pArg,
                    flagType fMeta )
{
    PFILE pFile;
    LINE  yStart, yEnd;
    int   len;
    char *pBuf, buf[BUFLEN];
```

```
/* Get a handle to the current file */
pFile = FileNameToHandle( "", "" );

/* Handle various argument types */
switch( pArg->argType )
{
   case NOARG:   /* No argument. Center current line */
      yStart = yEnd = pArg->arg.noarg.y;
      break;

   case LINEARG:  /* Center range of lines */
      yStart = pArg->arg.linearg.yStart;
      yEnd = pArg->arg.linearg.yEnd;
      break;
}

/* Center current line or range of lines */
for( ; yStart <= yEnd; yStart++ )
{
   /* Get a line from the current file */
   len = GetLine( yStart, buf, pFile );

   if( len > 0 )
   {
      /* Center the text in this line */
      pBuf = buf + strspn( buf, " \t" );
      len = strlen( pBuf );
      memmove( buf+(LINE_LENGTH-len) / 2, pBuf, len+1 );
      memset( buf, ' ', (LINE_LENGTH - len) / 2 );

      /* Write modified line back to the current file */
      PutLine( yStart, buf, pFile );
   }
}
return TRUE;
}
```

Building and using a PWB extension involves four basic steps:

1. Compiling

2. Linking

3. Loading the extension into PWB

4. Assigning a keystroke to each function in the extension

You can build extensions for both real mode (DOS) and OS/2 protected mode.

8.4.1 Building Real-Mode Extensions

This section describes how to build extensions for real mode.

Compiling

The source (.C) file for an extension must include EXT.H, the extension header file. Since an extension is not a stand-alone executable file, it doesn't have a **main** function; so its source file is compiled with the /c (compile, but don't link) option:

```
CL /c /Gs /ACw CENTER.C
```

The /Gs option turns off stack checking; the /ACw option selects the required custom memory model.

PWB extension interface is designed for C programmers. However, you can write extensions in assembly language or other languages if you simulate the required C memory model (in which SS is not assumed to equal DS).

Linking

The first object file in the link command must be the stub EXTHDR.OBJ:

```
link exthdr center, center.mxt;
```

PWB can load a file with any name, but most programmers use the .MXT extension to distinguish a PWB extension from a normal .EXE file.

Loading the Extension

Once the extension is built, you can cause PWB to load it by adding a **load** command to your TOOLS.INI file:

```
load:center
```

You don't need to supply a file extension; PWB assumes the correct file extension. To specify a path, supply the path name preceded by a dollar sign ($):

```
load:$INIT:center
```

The example tells PWB to search the directories specified in the INIT environment variable. If listed, the environment variable must be in uppercase.

TOOLS.INI can contain multiple **load** commands for different extensions. However, loading each extension involves a certain amount of memory overhead, and there is no way to unload an extension from memory. To conserve memory, place all frequently used functions in a single extension and load only that extension.

Assigning Keystrokes to Functions

After an extension has been loaded, you must provide some way to invoke its functions from inside PWB. A keystroke is the most common means, although extension functions, like native PWB functions, can be invoked in various ways.

You can assign the ALT+C keystroke to the `CenterLine` function with:

```
CenterLine:alt+c
```

Once the `CenterLine` function has been assigned to this keystroke, you can invoke it by pressing ALT+C.

8.4.2 Building Protected-Mode Extensions

The build process for OS/2 protected mode differs only slightly from the real-mode build process.

Compiling

The source (.C) file for an extension must include EXT.H, the extension header file. Since an extension is not a stand-alone executable file, it doesn't have a **main** function; so its source file is compiled with the /c (compile, but don't link) option:

```
CL /c /Gs /ACw CENTER.C
```

The /Gs option turns off stack checking; the /ACw option selects the required custom memory model.

PWB extension interface is designed for C programmers. However, you can write extensions in assembly language or other languages if you simulate the required C memory model (in which SS is not assumed to equal DS).

Linking

Link with EXTHRDP.OBJ instead of EXTHDR.OBJ. Specify the .PXT extension for the output file. List the EXT.DEF definitions file:

```
link exthdrp center, center.pxt,, os2, ext.def
```

Loading the Extension

In protected mode, PWB assumes the .PXT file extension. If your extension is not found, PWB assumes the .DLL file extension.

You cannot create a bound extension. There is no way to create a bound extension (one that runs in both real and protected mode). However, you can build separate versions of an extension and use a single TOOLS.INI **load** command to load the correct extension in each mode. PWB loads the real-mode file (.MXT) in real mode and the protected-mode file (.PXT or .DLL) in protected mode.

Assigning Keystrokes to Functions

After an extension has been loaded, you must provide some way to invoke its functions from inside PWB. A keystroke is the most common means, although extension functions, like native PWB functions, can be invoked in various ways.

You can assign the ALT+C keystroke to the `CenterLine` function with:

```
CenterLine:alt+c
```

Once the `CenterLine` function has been assigned to this keystroke, you can invoke it by pressing ALT+C.

8.4.3 *Describing Functions and Switches*

To call functions in your extension, PWB must know certain information about each function, such as the name and address of the function, what types of arguments it accepts, and what switches (if any) it employs. You provide this information in a pair of arrays—**cmdTable** and **swiTable**—that must be present in every PWB extension.

The cmdTable Array

Every extension must contain an array of structures named **cmdTable**. This array provides the information PWB needs to call the extension's functions.

The **cmdTable** array is an array of structures of type **cmdDesc** (which is declared in EXT.H). Each structure in the array describes one function in the extension. The array is terminated with a structure whose members are all null.

For instance, the CENTER.C extension has one function, named `CenterLine`, so its **cmdTable** array contains two structures (one for `CenterLine` and the other to terminate the table):

```
struct cmdDesc cmdTable[] =
{
    { "CenterLine", CenterLine, 0, NOARG | LINEARG },
    { NULL, NULL, 0, 0 }
};
```

Each **cmdDesc** structure in **cmdTable** contains these members:

- The function's name

- The function's address

- Reserved item (must be 0)

- The argument types the function accepts

The last member in the list is an integer containing bitflags representing types of arguments that your function accepts. You can combine more than one bitflag using the **OR (|)** operator.

For instance, the `CenterLine` function can handle an argument of the type **LINEARG**, or no arguments (**NOARG**). So it lists the types:

```
NOARG | LINEARG
```

There are many argument types in addition to these. For information about specific argument types, see the Extensions topic in on-line help.

The swiTable Array

Extension functions, such as native PWB functions, can respond to user-configurable switches. From the viewpoint of an extension function, a switch is usually a variable that the user can change at run time. Your function must be ready to respond to these changes, and PWB must have some way to convey them. The vehicle for this interchange is an array of structures named **swiTable**.

The **swiTable** array is similar to the **cmdTable** array described above. It is an array of structures, terminated by a structure whose members are all null. Each structure in **swiTable** describes one switch used by a function in your extension.

The CENTER.C extension doesn't take any switches, so its **swiTable** array only contains a terminating null structure:

```
struct swiDesc swiTable[] =
{
    { NULL, NULL, 0 }
};
```

Each structure in **swiTable** is of type **swiDesc**, whose members are

- A pointer to the switch name

- A pointer to the switch or a function

- A flag that indicates the type of the switch

A switch can be one of three types: **SWI_BOOLEAN** for TRUE/FALSE conditions, **SWI_NUMERIC** for numerics, or **SWI_SPECIAL** for strings.

The second member of **swiDesc** is a pointer. It points to the switch itself if the switch is type **SWI_BOOLEAN** or **SWI_NUMERIC**, or to a string-handling function if the switch is type **SWI_SPECIAL**.

For instance, the following code creates a numeric switch with the default value 27:

```
static int n = 27;

struct swiDesc swiTable[] =
{
    { "newswitch", &n, SWI_NUMERIC | RADIX10 },
    { NULL,  NULL, 0 }
};
```

The first structure in the example above contains the name of the switch (`"newswitch"`), a pointer to the variable that contains the switch's value (`&n`), and the switch's type (**SWI_NUMERIC**).

In this example, the third structure member contains another constant, **RADIX10**. If a switch is type **SWI_NUMERIC**, you must supply a second constant to tell PWB whether to interpret user-assigned values as decimal (**RADIX10**) or hexadecimal (**RADIX16**) numbers.

If the switch is type **SWI_SPECIAL**, the second member of **swiDesc** is a pointer to an additional string-handling function that you write. This function must be of type **int far _pascal**. Each time the text switch changes, PWB calls your function, passing it the address of the updated string as a **char far** pointer. The following code stores the updated string in a buffer named `mystring`:

```
char mystring[BUFLEN];

int far _pascal setstr( char far *ptr )
{
    strcpy( mystring, ptr );
}
```

If desired, you can list switches for extension functions separately from other switches. Whenever PWB loads an extension, it looks in TOOLS.INI for a section with this form:

[PWB-*ext*]

where *ext* is the base name of the extension. If the extension exists, PWB recognizes the settings immediately following the tag. For instance, if your extension SAMPLE.MXT uses a numeric switch named `numbills`, you can set `numbills` to the value 66 with:

```
[PWB-SAMPLE]
numbills:66
```

8.4.4 *Initializing Functions*

Every PWB extension must contain a function named **WhenLoaded**, which PWB calls immediately after loading the extension. The **WhenLoaded** function provides a chance to do any initialization that your functions require. (If your functions don't need any initialization, they can simply return.)

The CENTER.C extension uses **WhenLoaded** to display a loading message:

```
void EXTERNAL WhenLoaded( void )
{
    DoMessage( "Loading Center extension" );
}
```

DoMessage is a PWB function that displays a message on the dialog line. Section 8.4.7, "Calling PWB Functions," lists PWB functions and explains how to call them.

8.4.5 Prototyping Functions

To be called by PWB, each extension function must be declared as type **PWBFUNC** and accept the parameters **argData**, **pArg**, and **fMeta**. The CenterLine function in the section of CENTER.C code below follows this model:

```
PWBFUNC CenterLine( unsigned argData,
                    ARG _far *pArg,
                    flagType fMeta )
```

The **PWBFUNC** type is actually a macro that evaluates to **flagType _pascal _loadds _far**. The **flagType** return type declares that the function returns either TRUE (nonzero) or FALSE (zero). Your function should return a value so that it can be used in a macro with conditionals. The modifiers **_pascal**, **_loadds**, and **_far** specify the calling conventions PWB expects editor functions to have.

8.4.6 Receiving Parameters

Like native PWB functions, extension functions can receive parameters from the user. The CENTER.C example allows you to select a range of lines to center, for example. The selected range is passed as a parameter to the CenterLine function.

Extension functions receive parameters in much the same way ordinary C programs receive command-line parameters. In both cases, the parameters are passed in a predefined data construct—**argc** and **argv** for a normal C program, and the following parameters for an extension function:

Parameter	Description
argData	The keystroke used to invoke your function
pArg	A pointer to a structure containing arguments passed to your function
fMeta	TRUE (nonzero) if **meta** precedes the argument, otherwise FALSE (zero)

The first parameter is rarely used. Most extension functions receive all their parameter data in the second parameter, **pArg**. This parameter is a pointer to a structure of type **ARG**, which contains:

Parameter	Description
argType	An integer that indicates the argument type
arg	A union of structures, one structure for each argument type

Typically, your function tests **pArg–>argType** to find out what type of parameter PWB has passed. Once the type is known, the function responds accordingly. The following code from CENTER.C handles two argument types:

```
switch( pArg->argType )
{
   case NOARG:   /* No argument. Center current line */
      yStart = yEnd = pArg->arg.noarg.y;
      break;

   case LINEARG:   /*  Center range of lines */
      yStart = pArg->arg.linearg.yStart;
      yEnd = pArg->arg.linearg.yEnd;
      break;
}
```

PWB rejects invalid arguments. If your function takes only one argument, it doesn't need to test **pArg–>argType** at all. PWB knows beforehand what argument types your function accepts (via **cmdDesc**) and rejects any invalid arguments.

Once the argument type is known, your function can access the parameters through **pArg–>arg**, a structure whose members differ for each argument type. In the **NOARG** (no arguments) case, it contains *x* and *y* values identifying the cursor position in the current file:

```
struct noargType
{              /* no argument   */
   LINE y;  /* cursor line    */
   COL  x;  /* cursor column  */
};
```

The CENTER.C example uses the *y* value in this structure (**noarg.y**, the cursor line) to center the current line:

```
case NOARG:   /* No argument. Center current line */
   yStart = yEnd = pArg->arg.noarg.y;
   break;
```

Similarly, in the **LINEARG** case, the **pArg–>arg** structure contains three values:

```
struct lineargType
{                    /* line argument specified */
    int  cArg;       /* count of args pressed   */
    LINE yStart;     /* starting line of range  */
    LINE yEnd;       /* ending line of range    */
};
```

The CENTER.C example uses the starting and ending values in this structure (**yStart** and **yEnd**) to center a range of selected lines:

```
case LINEARG:  /*  Center range of lines */
    yStart = pArg->arg.linearg.yStart;
    yEnd = pArg->arg.linearg.yEnd;
    break;
```

The method is the same for other argument types. The **pArg–>arg** structures for all argument types are described in on-line help.

8.4.7 Calling PWB Functions

Many of PWB's internal functions are public. Your extension function can call them for the same purposes that PWB itself does. This section demonstrates the most commonly used PWB functions—those that manipulate the current file.

A list of callable PWB functions appears near the end of this section. For complete information on specific PWB functions, consult on-line help.

Getting a File Handle

Extension functions can do many different tasks, but they typically manipulate a file in some way. The extension function in the CENTER.C example rewrites a line or lines in the current file, for example. The current file is the one that appears in the editing window. Since it is already open for editing, you can access the current file without opening it. Simply assign its file handle to a variable in your function.

Table 8.1   (*continued*)

Category	Function	Description
	pFileToTop	Make specified file the current file
	RemoveFile	Remove file from memory
Keyboard	**KbHook**	Restore keyboard control to PWB
	KbUnHook	Remove keyboard control from PWB
	ReadChar	Get information on next keystroke
Format	**ReadCmd**	Get keystroke information in **CmdDesc**
Line	**FileLength**	Get length of file
	GetLine	Get line from file
	PutLine	Write line to file
List	**GetListEntry**	Get item from list
	ScanList	Process list
Memory	**Falloc**	Allocate far memory
	Fdalloc	Deallocate far memory
Miscellaneous	**fExecute**	Execute macro
	FindSwitch	Get information about switch
	GetEditorObject	Get internal PWB data item
	GetString	Get input from dialog line
	mgetenv	Get environment string
	NameToFunc	Get information about function or macro
	NameToKeys	Get key(s) assigned to specified function
	Replace	Replace character
	SetEditorObject	Set internal PWB data item
	SetKey	Assign function to keystroke
Search	**REsearch**	Search for regular expression
	search	Search for string

Table 8.1   (*continued*)

Category	Function	Description
Virtual Memory	**fpbtoVM**	Copy data to virtual memory
	VMalloc	Allocate virtual memory
	VMFree	Free virtual memory
	VMtofpb	Copy data from virtual memory
Window	**CloseWnd**	Close window
	Resize	Resize window
	SplitWnd	Split window

8.4.8 *Calling C Library Functions*

You can write many useful extension functions using only PWB functions listed in the previous section. It is also possible to call C library routines, with some limitations. An extension written for OS/2 protected mode can call any C library routine if it is linked with EXTHDRP.OBJ and the .DLL C run-time library. The list of usable routines is shorter for real-mode (DOS) extensions linked with the non-.DLL run-time library.

Before you call a C library routine, ask whether the task can be done with a PWB function. If the answer is yes, you should always call a PWB function in preference to the C library routine. This practice ensures compatibility between your functions and PWB.

The following categories of C library routines are always safe to use in real mode:

■ Buffer manipulation

■ Character classification and conversion

■ Data conversion

■ String manipulation

This list includes the library routines you are most likely to need in an extension function. If your extension function calls C library functions, you must link with the compact-model C library.

The following routines should not be used in real mode:

- Routines that need C start-up support (most input/output functions)
- Memory management routines, such as **malloc**, and routines that call them
- Process control routines such as **spawn** and **exec**

If you are in doubt about a particular C library routine, you can always use it and see what happens. If the linker displays the following message,

```
error L2044: __acrtused : symbol multiply defined, use /NOE
```

the routine requires C start-up support and should not be used.

Debugging C Programs with CodeView

Even experienced programmers occasionally find bugs in their programs. This chapter explores techniques that will help you locate these errors quickly, using the Microsoft CodeView debugger.

This chapter describes:

- How to display and modify variables and memory

- How to control the flow of execution while debugging

- Advanced CodeView debugging techniques

- How to control CodeView's behavior with command-line switches and the TOOLS.INI file

CodeView supports the Microsoft mouse (or any fully compatible pointing device). All operations are described first using the mouse; the keyboard command follows.

For information about debugging OS/2 programs that use threads or processes, see Chapter 15, "Creating OS/2 Multithread Applications."

9.1 Understanding CodeView Windows

CodeView divides the screen into logically separate sections called windows, so that a large amount of information can be displayed in an organized and easy-to-read fashion. Each window is a discrete section of the display that operates independently of the other windows.

Each window displays a different type of data.

Each CodeView window has a distinct function. The name of each window described below appears in the top of the window's frame:

- The Source window displays the source code. You can open a second Source window to view an include file, another source file, or the same source file at a different location.

- The Command window accepts debugging commands.

- The Watch window displays the current values of selected variables.

- The Local window lists the values of all variables local to the current function or block.

- The Memory window shows the contents of memory. You can open a second Memory window to view a different section of memory.

- The Register window displays the contents of the microprocessor's registers, as well as the processor flags.

- The 8087 window displays the registers of the coprocessor or its software emulator.

CodeView starts running with three windows displayed. The Local window is at the top, the Source window fills the middle of the screen, and the Command window is at the bottom.

There are two ways to open windows. You can choose the desired window from the View menu. (Note that you can open more than one of certain windows, such as Source or Memory.) In addition, some operations (such as selecting a Watch variable) open the appropriate window automatically, if it is not already open.

All displays are updated automatically.

CodeView continually and automatically updates the contents of all windows. However, if you want to interact with a particular window (for instance, to enter a command, set a breakpoint, or modify a variable), you must select that window as the focus of user interaction.

The selected window is called the "current" window. The current window is marked in three ways:

- The window's name is highlighted in white.

- The text cursor appears in the window.

- The vertical and horizontal scroll bars are moved into the window.

To select a new current window, click left in the window (position the mouse cursor in the window and press the left mouse button) that you want to be current. You can also press F6 or SHIFT+F6 to move the focus from one window to the next.

Windows often contain more information than can be displayed in the area allotted to the window. There are two ways to view these additional contents. You can drag on the window's horizontal or vertical scroll bars. (Position the mouse pointer on the bar and, while holding down the left mouse button, drag the mouse in the appropriate direction.) You can also use the direction keys (LEFT, RIGHT, UP, DOWN) to move the text cursor.

Typing commands into the Source window causes CodeView to temporarily shift its focus to the Command window. Whatever you type is appended to the last line in the Command window. If the Command window is closed, CodeView beeps in response to your entry and ignores the input.

Adjusting the Windows

Although you cannot change the relative positions of the windows, you can change their size or remove them. The Maximize, Size, and Close commands from the View menu perform these functions, or you can press CTRL+F10, CTRL+F8, and CTRL+F4, respectively. Window manipulations are especially easy with a mouse:

- To maximize a window (enlarge it so it fills the screen), click left on the up arrow at the right end of the window's top border. To restore the window to its previous size and position, click left on the double arrow at the right end of the top border.

- To change the size of a window, position the mouse pointer anywhere along the white line at the top of the window. Press and hold down the left mouse button. When two double arrows appear on the line, you can drag the mouse to enlarge or reduce the window. The same action on a vertical border widens or narrows the window.

- To close a window, click left on the dot at the left end of the top border. You can also close any window in the View menu whose name has a dot next to it by selecting that window from the menu or by pressing that window's acclerator key. The adjacent windows automatically expand to recover the empty space.

CodeView stores session information in a file called CURRENT.STS, which is created in the directory pointed to by the INIT environment variable. The session information includes such items as the name of the program being debugged, which CodeView windows were open, and the breakpoint locations. This information becomes the default status the next time you run CodeView.

9.2 Overview of Debugging Techniques

There is no single best approach to debugging for all programs or users. CodeView offers a variety of debugging tools that let you pick a method appropriate to the program or your work habits. The following section may help you decide how to approach a particular program.

Broadly speaking, two things can go wrong in a program:

- The program doesn't manipulate the data the way you expected it to.

- The flow of execution is incorrect.

These problems occasionally overlap. Incorrect execution can corrupt the data, and bad data can cause execution to take an unexpected turn. Because CodeView allows you to trace program execution *and* display whatever combination of variables you want simultaneously, you don't have to know ahead of time whether the problem is bad data manipulation, a bad execution path, or some combination of these.

CodeView has features that deal specifically with the problems of bad data and incorrect execution:

- You can view and modify any program variable, any section of memory, or any processor register.

- You can monitor the path of execution and precisely control where execution pauses.

The following sections explain how to view and modify data and describe how execution is controlled.

9.3 Viewing and Modifying Program Data

The CodeView debugger offers a variety of ways to display program variables, processor registers, and memory. You can also modify the values of all these items as the program executes. This section shows how to display and modify variables, registers, and memory.

9.3.1 Displaying Variables in the Watch Window

To add a variable to the Watch window, position the cursor on the name of the variable using either the mouse or the direction keys (LEFT, RIGHT, UP, DOWN). Then select the Add Watch command from the Watch menu, or press CTRL+W.

A dialog box appears with the selected variable's name displayed in the Expression field. If you don't want to watch the variable shown, type in the name of the variable you want to watch. Pressing ENTER or clicking left on the OK button adds this variable to the Watch window.

The Watch window appears at the top of the screen. Adding a Watch variable automatically opens the Watch window if the window doesn't already exist.

A newly added variable may be followed by the message:

```
<Watch Expression Not in Context>
```

This message appears when program execution has not yet reached the block where the variable is defined. (A block is a section of code enclosed in curly braces.) Global variables (those declared outside C functions) never cause CodeView to display this message; they can be watched from anywhere in the program.

To remove a variable from the Watch window, use the Delete Watch command from the Watch menu, and select the variable to be removed using the list in the dialog box. You can also position the cursor on any line in the Watch window and press CTRL+Y to delete the line.

There is no limit to how many variables you can watch.

You can place as many variables as you like in the Watch window; the quantity is limited only by available memory. You can scroll through the Watch window to position it at those variables you want to view. CodeView automatically updates all watched variables as the program runs, including those not currently visible.

Loops (**do**, **for**, or **while**) cause problems when they don't terminate correctly. Displaying loop variables in the Watch window is an easy way to determine whether a loop variable achieves its proper value.

9.3.2 Displaying Expressions in the Watch Window

You may have noticed that the Add Watch dialog box prompts for an expression, not simply a variable name. As this suggests, you can enter an expression (that is, any valid combination of variables, constants, and operators) for CodeView to evaluate and display.

Expressions can use the syntax of other languages.

You are not limited to evaluating C expressions. The Language command of the Options menu offers a choice of BASIC or FORTRAN expression evaluation, if one of these languages better suits your needs. The ability to select the language evaluator is especially useful when debugging mixed-language programs. Remember that C-specific features, such as type casting or pointer conversions, are not available in other languages.

You can display more information with expressions than with individual variables.

By reducing several variables to a single, easily read value, an expression can be easier to interpret than the components that make it up. Imagine a **for** loop with two variables whose ratio is supposed to remain constant. You suspect that one of these variables (you aren't sure which) sometimes takes the wrong value. With (var1 / var2) displayed as an expression in the Watch window, you can easily see when this single value changes; you don't have to mentally divide two numbers.

You can also display Boolean expressions. For example, if a variable is never supposed to be larger than 100 or less than 25, (var < 25 || var > 100) evaluates to 1 (true) when var goes out-of-bounds.

9.3.3 Displaying Arrays and Structures

Most program variables are scalar quantities—a single character or a single integer or floating-point value. These appear in the Watch window with the variable name to the left, followed by an equal sign (=) and the current value.

You can view arrays and structures in expanded form.

Arrays and structures contain multiple values, arranged in one or more layers. They are often referred to as "aggregate" data items. CodeView lets you control how much of these variables is shown; that is, whether all, part, or none of their internal structure is displayed.

An array initially appears in the Watch window in this form:

```
+wordholder[]  = [...]
```

The brackets indicate that this variable contains more than one element. The plus sign (+) indicates that the variable has not yet been expanded to display its components.

To expand the array, double-click anywhere on the line. You can also position the cursor on the line and press ENTER. For example, if wordholder is a six-character array containing the word "Basic," the Watch window display changes to the following :

```
-wordholder[]
   [0]  =   66 'B'
   [1]  =   97 'a'
   [2]  =  115 's'
   [3]  =  105 'i'
   [4]  =   99 'c'
   [5]  =    0 ' '
```

Note that both the individual character values and their ASCII decimal equivalents are listed. The minus sign (–) indicates no further expansion is possible. To contract the array, double-click on its line (or position the cursor on the line and press ENTER) again.

If it is inconvenient to view a character array in this form, cast the variable's name to a character pointer by placing (char *) in front of the name. The character array is then displayed as a string delimited by apostrophes.

You can display arrays with more than one dimension. Imagine a 5 x 5 integer array named matrix, whose diagonal elements are the numbers 1 through 5 and whose other elements are zero. Unexpanded, the array is displayed like this:

```
+matrix[]  = [...]
```

Double-clicking on matrix (or pressing ENTER) changes the display:

```
-matrix[]
  +[0][]  =  [...]
  +[1][]  =  [...]
  +[2][]  =  [...]
  +[3][]  =  [...]
  +[4][]  =  [...]
```

The actual values of the elements are not shown yet. You have to descend one more level to see them. To view the elements of the third row of the array, position the cursor anywhere on the fourth line and press ENTER:

```
-matrix[]
  +[0][]  =  [...]
  +[1][]  =  [...]
  -[2][]
     [0]  = 0
     [1]  = 0
     [2]  = 3
     [3]  = 0
     [4]  = 0
  +[3][]  =  [...]
  +[4][]  =  [...]
```

Expanding the fifth row of the array produces this display:

```
-matrix[]
  +[0][]  =  [...]
  +[1][]  =  [...]
  -[2][]
     [0]  = 0
     [1]  = 0
     [2]  = 3
     [3]  = 0
     [4]  = 0
  +[3][]  =  [...]
  -[4][]
     [0]  = 0
     [1]  = 0
     [2]  = 0
     [3]  = 0
     [4]  = 5
```

You can view individual elements instead of the entire array.

Any element of an array (or structure) can be independently expanded or contracted. If you only want to view one or two elements of a large array, specify the particular array or structure elements in the Expression field of the Add Watch dialog box; you need not display every element of the variable.

You can dereference pointers.

You can dereference a pointer in the same way as you expand an array or structure. The pointer address is displayed, followed by all the elements of the variable to which the pointer currently refers. Multiple levels of indirection (that is, pointers referencing other pointers) can be displayed simultaneously.

9.3.4 Displaying Array Elements Dynamically

You do not have to display every element of an array. If specific subscripts are given, the corresponding element is displayed.

You can also specify a dynamic array element, which changes as some other variable changes. For example, suppose that the loop variable p is a subscript for the array variable catalogprice. The Watch window expression catalogprice[p] displays only the array element currently specified by p, not the entire array.

You can mix constant and variable subscripts. For example, the expression bigarray[3][i] displays only the element in the third row of the array to which the index variable i points.

9.3.5 Using Quick Watch

Selecting the Quick Watch command from the Watch menu (or pressing SHIFT+F9) displays the Quick Watch dialog box. If the text cursor is in the Source, Local, or Watch window, the variable at the current cursor position appears in the dialog box. If this is not the item you wish to display, type in the desired expression or variable, then press ENTER. The selected item is displayed immediately.

The Quick Watch display automatically expands arrays and structures to their first level. For example, an array with three dimensions is expanded to the first dimension. You can expand or contract an element just as you would in the Watch window: position the cursor on the appropriate line and press ENTER. If the array needs more lines than the Quick Watch window can display, drag the mouse along the scroll bar, or press DOWN or PGDN to view the rest of the array.

You can add Quick Watch variables to the Watch window.

If you decide to add a Quick Watch item to the Watch window, select the Add Watch button. Arrays and structures appear in the Watch window expanded as they were displayed in the Quick Watch box.

Quick Watch is a convenient way to take a quick look at a variable or expression. Since only one Quick Watch variable can be viewed at a time, you would not use Quick Watch for most of the variables you want to view.

9.3.6 Displaying Memory

Selecting the Memory command from the View menu opens a Memory window. Up to two Memory windows can be open at one time.

By default, memory is displayed as hexadecimal byte values, with 16 bytes per line. At the end of each line is a second display of the same memory in ASCII form. Values that correspond to printable ASCII characters (decimal 32 through 127) are displayed in that form. Values outside this range are shown as periods.

You can display memory values in any form.

Byte values are not always the most convenient way to view memory. If the area of memory you're examining contains character strings or floating-point values, you might prefer to view them in a directly readable form. The Memory Window command of the Options menu displays a dialog box with a variety of display options:

- ASCII characters

- Byte, word, or double-word binary values

- Signed or unsigned integer decimal values

- Short (32 bit), long (64 bit), or ten-byte (80 bit) floating-point values

You can also directly cycle through these display formats by pressing F3.

If a section of memory cannot be displayed as a valid floating-point number, the number shown includes the characters NAN (not a number).

Displaying Variables with a Live Expression

Section 9.3.4, "Displaying Array Elements Dynamically," explains how to display a specific array element by adding the appropriate expression to the Watch window. It is also possible to watch a particular memory area that your program uses to store data in the Memory window. This CodeView display feature is called a "live expression."

"Live" means that the area of memory displayed changes to reflect the value of a pointer or subscript. For example, if buffer is an array and pbuf is a pointer to that array, then *pbuf points to the array element currently referenced. A live expression displays the section of memory beginning with this element. If your program changes the value of pbuf, CodeView dynamically adjusts the Memory window display.

Live expressions are displayed in a Memory window, not in the Watch window. To create a live expression, select the Memory Window command of the Options menu, then select the Live Expression check box. Enter the name of the element you want to view. For example, if strgptr is a pointer to an array of characters, and you want to see what it currently points at, enter *strgptr. Then select the OK button or press ENTER to view that memory area.

A new Memory window opens. The first memory location in the window is the first memory location of the live expression. The section of memory displayed changes to the section the pointer currently references.

You can use the Memory Window command of the Options menu to display the value of the live expression in a directly readable form. This is especially convenient when the live expression represents strings or floating-point values, which are difficult to interpret in hexadecimal form.

It is usually more convenient to view an item in the Watch window than as a live expression. However, some items are more easily viewed as live expressions. For example, you can examine what is currently on top of the stack. Enter SS:SP as the live expression.

9.3.7 Displaying the Processor Registers

Selecting the Register command from the View menu (or pressing F2) opens a window on the right side of the screen. The current values of the microprocessor's registers appear in this window.

At the bottom of the window is a group of mnemonics representing the processor flags. When you first open the Register window, all values are shown in normal-intensity video. Any subsequent changes are marked in high-intensity video. For example, suppose the overflow flag is not set when the Register window is first opened. The corresponding mnemonic is NV and it appears in light gray. If the overflow flag is subsequently set, the mnemonic changes to OV and appears in bright white.

Selecting the 386 Instructions command from the Options menu displays the registers as 32-bit values, but only if your computer uses an 80386 processor, and only when running the real-mode version of CodeView. Selecting this command a second time toggles back to a 16-bit display.

You can also display the registers of an 8087/287/387 coprocessor in a separate window by selecting the 8087 command from the View menu. If your program uses the coprocessor emulator, the emulated registers are displayed instead.

9.3.8 Modifying the Values of Variables, Registers, and Memory

You can easily change the values of variables, memory locations, or registers displayed in the Watch, Local, Memory, Register, or 8087 windows. Simply position the cursor at the value you want to change and edit it to the appropriate value. If you change your mind, press ALT+BKSP to undo the last change you made.

The starting address of each line of memory displayed is shown at the left of the Memory window, in CS:IP form. Altering the address automatically shifts the display to the corresponding section of memory. If that section is not used by your program, memory locations are displayed as double question marks (??).

Byte display form is different from other forms. When you select Byte display from the Memory Window Options dialog box, CodeView presents both a hexadecimal and an ASCII representation of the data in memory. (Byte display is the default.) You can change data in memory either by entering new hex values over the hexadecimal representation of your data or by entering character values over the character representation.

To toggle a processor flag, click left on its mnemonic. You can also position the cursor on a mnemonic, then press any key (except TAB or SPACE). Repeat to restore the flag to its previous setting.

Be cautious when modifying memory or a register. The effect of changing a register, flag, or memory location may vary from no effect at all, to crashing the operating system. You should be cautious when altering "machine-level" values; most of the items you would want to change can be altered from the Watch window.

One instance where direct manipulation of register values can be valuable is when you are debugging in-line assembly code. You can change register values to test assumptions before making changes in your source code and recompiling.

9.4 Controlling Execution

There are two forms of program execution under CodeView:

- Continuous; the program executes until either a previously specified "breakpoint" has been reached or the program terminates normally.

- Single-step; the program pauses after each line of code has been executed.

Sections 9.4.1 and 9.4.2 explain how each form of execution works and the most effective way to use each.

9.4.1 Continuous Execution

Continuous execution lets you quickly execute the bug-free sections of code, which would otherwise take a long time to execute a single step at a time.

The simplest form of continuous execution is to click right (position the mouse pointer and press the right mouse button) anywhere on the line of code you want to debug or examine in more detail. The program executes at full speed up to the beginning of this line, then pauses. You can do the same thing by positioning the text cursor on this line, then pressing F7.

You can also pause execution at a specific line of code with a "breakpoint." There are several types of breakpoints. Breakpoints are explained in the following section.

Selecting Breakpoint Lines

Breakpoints can be tied to lines of code.

You can skip over the parts of the program that you don't want to examine by specifying one or more lines as "breakpoints." The program executes at full speed up to the first breakpoint, then pauses. Pressing F5 continues program execution up to the next breakpoint, and so on. (You can halt execution at any time by pressing CTRL+BREAK or ALT+SYSRQ.)

There is no limit to the number of breakpoints.

You can set as many breakpoints as you like (limited only by available memory). There are several ways to set breakpoints:

- Double-click anywhere on the desired breakpoint line. The selected line is highlighted to show that it is a breakpoint. To remove the breakpoint, double-click on the line a second time.

- Position the cursor anywhere on the line at which you want execution to pause. Press F9 to select the line as a breakpoint. (CodeView highlights lines that have been selected as breakpoints.) Press F9 a second time to remove the breakpoint.

■ Display the Set Breakpoint dialog box by selecting Set Breakpoint from the Watch menu. Choose one of the breakpoint options that permits a line ("location") to be specified. The line on which the text cursor currently rests is the default breakpoint line in the Location field. If this line is not the desired breakpoint, enter the line number desired. (The line number must begin with a period.) Use F9 or the Edit Breakpoints screen of the Watch menu to remove the breakpoint.

Not every line can be a breakpoint. A breakpoint line must be a program line that represents executable code. You cannot select a blank line, a comment line, or a declaration line (such as a variable declaration or a preprocessor statement) as a breakpoint.

A breakpoint can also be set at a function or an explicit address. To set a breakpoint at a function, simply enter its name in the Set Breakpoint dialog box. To set a breakpoint at an address, enter the address in CS:IP form.

> **NOTE** By default, Microsoft compilers optimize your code. In the process of optimization, some lines of code may be repositioned or reorganized for more efficient execution. These changes can prevent CodeView from recognizing the corresponding lines of source code as breakpoints. Therefore, it is a good idea to disable optimization during development (use the /Od switch). You can restore optimization once debugging is completed.

Once execution has paused, you can continue execution by pressing F5 or clicking left on the <F5> button in the display.

Setting Breakpoint Values

Breakpoints can be tied to variables. Breakpoints are not limited to specific lines of code. CodeView can also break execution when a variable reaches a particular value, or just changes value. You can also combine these value breakpoints with line breakpoints, so that execution stops at a specific line only if a variable has simultaneously reached a particular value, or changed value. You must use the check boxes in the Set Breakpoint dialog box to select these other types of breakpoints.

To pause execution when an expression reaches a particular value, enter that expression in the Expression field of the Set Breakpoint dialog box. For example, assume you have declared a tree structure as follows:

```
struct Tagtree
{
    char * s;                  /* Pointer to a string */
    struct TAGtree * left;     /* Pointer to left branch */
    struct TAGtree * right;    /* Pointer to right branch */
};

struct TAGtree t;
```

You can then pause execution when your tree traversal reaches a terminal node by entering the expression (t.left == NULL) || (t.right == NULL).

To pause execution when a variable changes value, you need to enter only the name of the variable in the Expression field. For large variables (such as arrays or character strings), you can specify the number of bytes you want checked (up to 32K) in the Length field.

NOTE *When a breakpoint is tied to a variable, CodeView must check the variable's value after each machine instruction is executed. This slows execution greatly. For maximum speed when debugging, either tie conditional breakpoints to specific lines, or set conditional breakpoints only after you have reached the section of code that needs to be debugged.*

Using Breakpoints

Here are several examples that show how breakpoints can help you find the cause of a problem.

One of the most common bugs is a **for** loop that executes too many or too few times. If you set a breakpoint that encloses the loop statements, the program pauses after each iteration. With the loop variable or critical program variables in the Watch or Local windows, it should be easy to see what the loop is doing wrong.

You can specify how many times a breakpoint line is executed.

You do not have to pause at a breakpoint the first time execution reaches it. CodeView lets you specify the number of times you want to ignore the breakpoint condition before pausing. Enter the decimal number in the Pass Count field of the Set Breakpoint dialog box of the Watch menu.

For example, suppose your program repeatedly calls a function to create a binary tree. You suspect that something goes wrong with the process about halfway through. You could mark the line that calls the function as the breakpoint, then specify how many times this line is to execute before execution pauses. Running the program creates a representative (but unfinished) tree structure that can be examined from the Watch window. You can then continue your analysis using single-stepping.

Another programming error is erroneously assigning a value to a variable. Enter the variable in the Expression field of the Set Breakpoint dialog box. Execution breaks whenever this variable changes value.

You can assign new values to variables while execution is paused.

Breakpoints are a convenient way to pause the program so you can assign new values to variables. For example, if a limit value is set by a variable, you can change the value to see whether program execution is affected. Similarly, you can pass a variety of values to a **switch** statement to see if they are correctly processed.

This ability to alter variables is an especially convenient way to test new functions without having to write a stand-alone test program.

9.4.2 Single-Stepping

In single-stepping, CodeView pauses after each line of code is executed. (If a line contains more than one executable statement, CodeView executes all the statements on the line before pausing.) The next line to be executed is highlighted in reverse video.

There are two ways to single-step.

You can single-step through a program with the Step and Trace functions. Step (executed by pressing F10) steps over function calls. All the code in the function is executed but, to you, the function appears to execute as a single step. Trace (executed by pressing F8) traces through every step of all functions for which CodeView has symbolic information. Each line of the function is executed as a separate step. (CodeView has no symbolic information about run-time functions; therefore, they are executed as a single step.)

You can alternate between Trace and Step as you like. The method you use depends only on whether you want to see what happens within a particular function.

You can Trace through the program continuously (without having to press F8), using the Animate command of the Run menu. The speed of execution is controlled by the Trace Speed command from the Options menu. You can halt animated execution at any time by pressing any key.

9.5 Replaying a Debug Session

CodeView can automatically create a "tape" (a disk file) with all the debugging instructions and input data you entered when testing a program. The tape is then "replayed" to repeat the debugging process. This dynamic replay feature is unique to the CodeView debugger and is activated by selecting the History On command from the Run menu. Selecting History On a second time terminates recording.

You can use the recording as a bookmark. You can quit after a long debugging session, then pick up the session later in the same place.

Dynamic replay makes it easy to correct a mistake.

The principal use of dynamic replay is to allow you to back up when you make an error or overshoot the section of code with the bug. This feature is important because not all bugs are located when executing the program in a linear fashion.

For example, you may have to manually execute a function many times before its bug appears. If you then enter a command that alters the machine's or program's status and thereby lose the information you need to find the cause of the bug, you would have had to restart the program and manually repeat every debugging step to return to that point. Even worse, if you don't remember the exact sequence of events that exposed the bug, it could take hours to find your way back.

Dynamic replay eliminates this problem. Selecting the Undo command from the Run menu automatically restarts the program and rapidly executes every debug command up to (but not including) the last one you entered. You can repeat this process as many times as you like until you return to the desired point in execution.

To add additional steps to an existing tape, select History On, then select Replay. When replay has completed, perform whatever new debugging steps you want, then select History On a second time to terminate recording. The new tape contains both the original and the added commands.

NOTE *CodeView records only those mouse commands that apply to CodeView. Mouse commands recognized by the application being debugged are not recorded.*

Replay Limitations under OS/2

There are some limitations to dynamic replay when debugging under OS/2:

- The program must not respond to asynchronous events.

- Breakpoints must be specified at specific source lines or for specific symbols (rather than by absolute addresses), or replay may fail.

- Single-thread programs behave normally during replay. However, one of the threads in a multithread program may cause an asynchronous event, violating the first restriction. Multithread programs are, therefore, more likely to fail during replay.

- Multiprocess replay will fail. Each new process invokes a new CodeView session. The existence of multiple sessions makes it impractical to record the sequence of events if you execute commands in a session other than the original.

- Replay under Presentation Manager is not currently supported because it violates the first restriction.

9.6 Advanced CodeView Techniques

Once you are comfortable displaying and changing variables, stepping through the program, and using dynamic replay, you might want to experiment with the advanced techniques explained below.

Setting Command-Line Arguments

If your program retrieves command-line arguments, you can specify them with the Set Runtime Arguments command from the Run menu. Enter the arguments in the Command Line field before you begin execution. (Arguments entered after execution begins cause an automatic restart.)

Multiple Source Windows

You can open two Source windows at the same time. The windows can display two different sections of the same program, or one can show the high-level listing and the other the assembly-language listing. In the latter case, the contents of the windows track, with the next assembly-language instruction to be executed matching the next line of source code.

You can move freely between these windows, executing a single line of source code or a single assembly instruction at a time. The assembly-language window must be opened in CS:IP mode.

Calling Functions

Any C function in your program (whether user-written or from the library) can be called from the Command window or the Watch window, using the following format:

?funcname (varlist)

The function is evaluated and the returned value is displayed in the Command window.

The function does not have to be called by your program to be available for evaluation. For example, all the .OBJ code specified in the linker input response file is linked. The functions in this code can then be evaluated from the Command window.

This feature allows you to run functions from within CodeView that you would not normally include in the final version of your program. For example, you could include the OS/2 API functions that control semaphores, then execute them from the Command window to manipulate the run-time environment at any point in the debugging process.

Checking for Undefined Pointers

Until a pointer has been explicitly assigned a value, its value is undefined. That is, its value may be completely random, or it may be some consistent value that does not point to a useful data address (such as −1).

Accessing data through an uninitialized pointer will cause unpredictable program behavior and, under OS/2, will usually result in a protection violation. Because many C programs use pointers heavily, tracking down exactly which pointer variable was left uninitialized is tedious.

CodeView can help locate the problem quickly. If you use an uninitialized pointer (or "null pointer" under OS/2) the operating system will generate a protection violation. By examining the Calls menu, you can determine the last line of your code that was executed before the protection violation occurred.

Under DOS, you can take advantage of the fact that global or static variables are initialized to 0 to track down uninitialized pointers. Set a conditional breakpoint that stops when location 0 changes, then start execution. Execution will pause when your program makes an assignment to that location.

NOTE   *For near pointers, location 0 is DS:0000; for far pointers, location 0 is 0000:0000.*

Using Breakpoints Efficiently

Breakpoints slow execution when debugging. You can increase CodeView's speed by using the /R command-line switch if you have an 80386-based computer. This switch enables the 386's four debug registers, which support breakpoint checking in hardware rather than in software.

Printing Selected Items

You can print all or part of the contents of any window with the Print command from the File menu. The check box lets you print the complete contents of the window, only the material that is currently viewable in the window, or selected text from the window. Text is selected by dragging the mouse across it, or by holding down the SHIFT key and pressing the direction keys (LEFT, RIGHT, UP, DOWN).

By default, print output is to the file CODEVIEW.LST in the current directory. You can choose whether the new material will be appended to an existing file or overwrite it, using the Append/Overwrite check box. If you would like print output to go to a different file, type its name in the To File Name field. If you want the output to go to a printer, enter the appropriate device name, such as LPT1 or COM2.

Handling Register Variables

A register variable is stored in one of the microprocessor's registers, rather than in RAM. This speeds access to the variable.

There are two ways for a conventional variable to become a register variable. One way is declaring the variable as a register variable; if a register is free, the compiler will store the variable there. The other way occurs during optimization, when the compiler stores an often-used variable (such as a loop variable) in a register to speed up execution.

Register variables can cause problems during debugging. As with local variables, they are only visible within the function where they are defined. In addition, a register variable may not always be displayed with its current value.

In general, it is a good idea to turn off all optimization and to avoid declaring register variables until the program has been fully debugged. Any side effects produced by optimization or register variables can then be easily isolated.

Redirecting CodeView Input and Output

The Command window accepts DOS-like commands that redirect input and output. These commands can also be included on the command line that invokes CodeView. Whatever follows the /C option in the command line is treated as CodeView commands that are immediately executed at start-up.

```
CV/c "infile; t >outfile" myprog
```

Input is redirected to `infile`, which can contain start-up commands for CodeView. When CodeView exhausts all commands in the input file, focus automatically shifts to the command window. Output is sent to `outfile` and echoed to the Command window. The `t` must precede the `>` command for output to be sent to the Command window.

Redirection is a useful way to automate CodeView start-up. It also lets you keep a viewable record of command-line input and output, a feature not available with dynamic replay. (No record is kept of mouse operations.) Some applications (particularly interactive ones) may need modification to allow for redirection of input to the application itself.

Using CodeView with Additional Memory

If your computer uses expanded or extended memory, you can increase CodeView's functionality by selecting the /X or /E option. CodeView moves as much as it can of itself, the debugging table, and the program to higher memory (above the first megabyte).

The /X option uses extended memory and gives the greatest speed increase. This option requires the HIMEM.SYS driver, which is included on your distribution disks. Add `DEVICE = HIMEM.SYS` to your CONFIG.SYS file to load HIMEM.SYS at boot time.

The /E option uses expanded memory. The speed increase is not as great as that supplied by the /X option. The expanded memory manager (EMM) must be LIM 4.0, and no single module's debug information can exceed 48K. If the symbol table exceeds this limit, try reducing file-name information by not specifying paths at compile time and using /Zi only with those sections of the program that need debugging (use /Zd otherwise).

If you do not specify either /X or /E (or the /D disk-overlay option), CodeView automatically searches for the HIMEM.SYS driver and extended memory so it can implement the /X option. If it fails, CodeView searches for expanded memory to implement the /E option. If that search fails, CodeView uses a default disk overlay of 64K. (See the description of the /D option below.)

9.7 Controlling CodeView with Command-Line Options

The following options can be added to the command line that invokes CodeView:

Option	Effect
/2	Two-monitor debugging. The display adapters must be configured for different addresses. One display shows the output of the application; the other shows CodeView.
/25	Display in 25-line mode.
/43	Display in 43-line mode (EGA or VGA only).
/50	Display in 50-line mode (VGA only).
/B	Display in black and white. This assures that the display is readable when a color display is not used.
/C*commands*	All items following this switch are treated as CodeView commands to be executed immediately on start-up. Commands must be separated with a semicolon (;).
/D[[*ddd*]]	Use disk overlays, where *ddd* is the decimal size of the overlay buffer, in kilobytes. The acceptable range is 16K to 128K. The default size is 64K. DOS only.
/E	Use expanded memory for symbolic information. DOS only.
/F	Flip screen video pages. When your application does not use graphics, eight video screen pages are available. Switching from CodeView to the output screen is accomplished more quickly than swapping (/S) by directly selecting the appropriate video page. Cannot be used with /S. DOS only.
/I*number*	Turns nonmaskable interrupts and 8259-interrupt trapping on (/I1) or off (/I2).

/K	Disables installation of keyboard monitors for the program being debugged.
/L*dlls*	Load DLLs specified. DLLs must be separated by a semicolon (;). OS/2 only.
/M	Disable the mouse.
/N*number*	/N0 tells CodeView to trap; /N1 tells it not to.
/O	Debug child processes ("offspring"). OS/2 only.
/R	Use 386 hardware debug registers. DOS only.
/S	Swap screen in buffers. When your program uses graphics, all eight screen buffers must be used. Switching from CodeView to the output screen is accomplished by saving the previous screen in a buffer. Cannot be used with /F. DOS only.
/X	Use extended memory for symbolic information. DOS only.

9.8 Customizing CodeView with the TOOLS.INI FILE

The TOOLS.INI file customizes the behavior and user interface of several Microsoft products. The TOOLS.INI file is a plain ASCII text file. You should place it in a directory pointed to the INIT environment variable. (If you do not use the INIT environment variable, CodeView looks for TOOLS.INI only in its source directory.)

The CodeView section of TOOLS.INI is preceded by the following line:

```
[cv]
```

If you are running the protected-mode version of CodeView, use `[cvp]` instead. If you run both versions, include both: `[cv cvp]`.

Most of the TOOLS.INI customizations control screen colors, but you can also specify such things as start-up commands or the name of the file that receives CodeView output. On-line help contains full information about all TOOLS.INI switches for CodeView.

PART 3

Special Environments

CHAPTERS

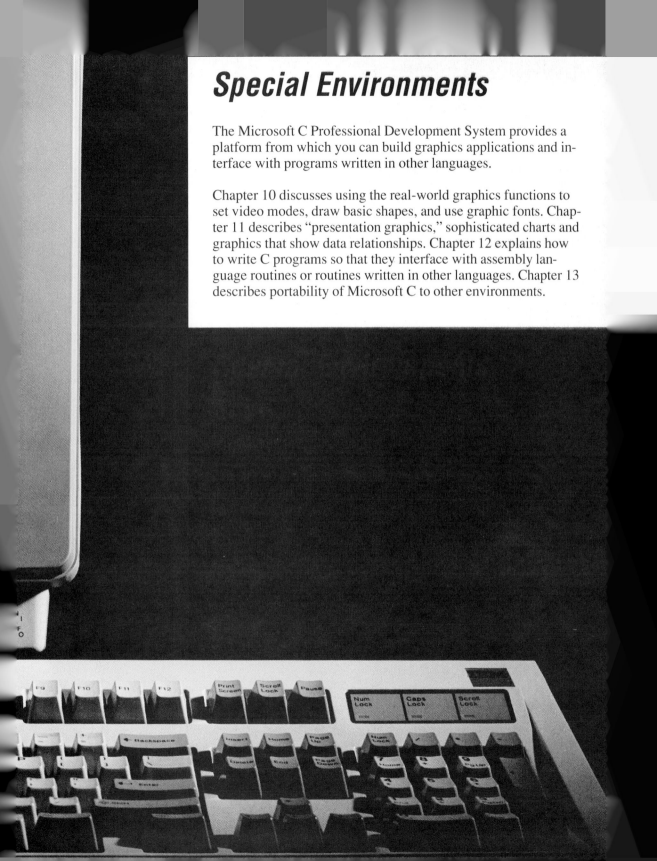

Special Environments

The Microsoft C Professional Development System provides a platform from which you can build graphics applications and interface with programs written in other languages.

Chapter 10 discusses using the real-world graphics functions to set video modes, draw basic shapes, and use graphic fonts. Chapter 11 describes "presentation graphics," sophisticated charts and graphics that show data relationships. Chapter 12 explains how to write C programs so that they interface with assembly language routines or routines written in other languages. Chapter 13 describes portability of Microsoft C to other environments.

CHAPTER 10

Communicating with Graphics

A map, a chart, an illustration, a graph, or some other visual aid often can communicate more information more quickly and more vividly than would several screens of text.

The extensive Microsoft C graphics library allows you to communicate your ideas graphically. The functions range from the simple to the complex; from functions that turn on a pixel to functions that draw graphs and charts complete with labels and legends.

This chapter describes low-level graphics functions that draw basic shapes such as lines, circles, and rectangles. It introduces video modes, color palettes, coordinate systems, and synopses of the graphics and font functions. For complete function prototypes and example programs, use on-line help.

NOTE   *The ANSI C standard does not define any standard graphics functions. The functions described in this section are unique to Microsoft C and are not portable to other implementations of C.*

10.1 *Video Modes*

Graphics adapters are boards or cards inside the computer that are responsible for displaying text and graphics on the screen. Commonly used adapters include:

- CGA (Color Graphics Adapter)

- EGA (Enhanced Graphics Adapter)

- HGC (Hercules Graphics Card)

■ MCGA (Multicolor Graphics Array)

■ MDPA (Monochrome Display Printer Adapter)

■ VGA (Video Graphics Array)

In addition, there are Olivetti versions of the CGA, EGA, and VGA (called OCGA, OEGA, and OVGA in this chapter).

The video modes available at run time depend on your graphics adapter and monitor.

Adapters can enter one or more "video modes." The video mode controls the resolution and number of colors on the video display. Microsoft C supports 17 video modes, which fall into two broad categories:

■ "Text modes," where characters are displayed

■ "Graphics modes," where individual pixels can be turned on and off

The graphics adapter and the type of monitor in use determine which of the 17 video modes are available at run time. See Section 10.1.2 for a list of video modes.

10.1.1 Sample Low-Level Graphics Program

The program ERESBOX.C below shows, in a few lines, the steps you follow to enter and exit a graphics mode. It sets the video mode **_ERESCOLOR**, draws a box, waits for a keypress, and returns to default mode, which is the video mode in effect when the program began running.

```
/* ERESBOX.C -- Enters _ERESCOLOR mode and draws a box */

#include <graph.h> /* graphics functions */
#include <stdio.h> /* puts */
#include <conio.h> /* getch */

main()
{
    if( _setvideomode( _ERESCOLOR ) ) /* EGA 640x350 mode */
    {
        _rectangle( _GBORDER, 10, 10, 110, 110 ); /* draw */
        getch(); /* wait for a keypress */
        _setvideomode( _DEFAULTMODE ); /* return to default */
    } else puts( "Can't enter _ERESCOLOR graphics mode." )
}
```

The program above illustrates the steps you follow to display graphics:

- Include the header file GRAPH.H. It contains function prototypes, macros, useful structures, and symbolic constants such as **_ERESCOLOR**, **_GBORDER**, and **_DEFAULTMODE**.

  ```
  #include <graph.h>
  ```

- Call the **_setvideomode** function, which sets the desired video mode. The function returns 0 if the hardware does not support the requested mode. (See Section 10.1.2, "Setting a Video Mode.")

  ```
  if( _setvideomode( _ERESCOLOR ) )
  ```

- Draw the graphics on the screen. The example program calls the **_rectangle** function. (See Section 10.4.3, "Drawing Points, Lines, and Shapes.")

  ```
  _rectangle( _GBORDER, 10, 10, 110, 110 )
  ```

- Exit the graphics mode and return to whatever video mode was in effect before the program began. Call **_setvideomode**, passing the constant **_DEFAULTMODE**. In some cases, you might want to skip this step, exiting the program with the graphics screen still in place.

  ```
  _setvideomode( _DEFAULTMODE );
  ```

In addition, you must link with the GRAPHICS.LIB library, which contains the function code. If you use window-coordinate functions (which require floating-point calculations) and if you have not created a standard combined library containing a floating-point component, you must explicitly link with a floating-point math library.

10.1.2 Setting a Video Mode

The **_setvideomode** function turns on one of the 17 available video modes. Pass it a single integer that tells it which mode to display. The constants in Table 10.1 are defined in the GRAPH.H file. The dimensions are listed in pixels for video graphics mode and in columns for video text mode.

Table 10.1   Constants that Represent Video Modes

Constant (Name)	Description	Mode/Hardware
_DEFAULTMODE	Restores the original mode	All/All
_ERESCOLOR	640 × 350, 4 or 16 color	Graphics/EGA
_ERESNOCOLOR	640 × 350, BW	Graphics/EGA
_HRES16COLOR	640 × 200, 16 color	Graphics/EGA

Table 10.1   (*continued*)

Constant (Name)	Description	Mode/Hardware
_HERCMONO*	720 × 348, BW	Graphics/HGC
_HRESBW	640 × 200, BW	Graphics/CGA
_MAXCOLORMODE	Graphics mode with the most colors	Graphics/All[†]
_MAXRESMODE	Graphics mode with the highest resolution	Graphics/All[†]
_MRES4COLOR	320 × 200, 4 color	Graphics/All
_MRES16COLOR	320 × 200, 16 color	Graphics/EGA
_MRES256COLOR	320 × 200, 256 color	Graphics/VGA
_MRESNOCOLOR	320 × 200, 4 gray	Graphics/CGA
_ORESCOLOR	640 × 400, 1 of 16 colors	Graphics/Olivetti
_TEXTBW40	40 column text, 16 gray	Text/CGA
_TEXTBW80	80 column text, 16 gray	Text/CGA
_TEXTC40	40 column text, 16/8 color	Text/CGA
_TEXTC80	80 column text, 16/8 color	Text/CGA
_TEXTMONO	80 column text, BW	Text/MDPA
_VRES2COLOR	640 × 480, BW	Graphics/VGA
_VRES16COLOR	640 × 480, 16 color	Graphics/VGA

[*] Before attempting to enter **_HERCMONO** mode, you must install the terminate-and-stay-resident program MSHERC.COM, which comes in the Microsoft C package. If you have both a Hercules adapter and an additional graphics adapter in the same computer, use the /H option to put the Hercules into **HALF** mode to avoid unpredictable and undesirable results.

[†] **_MAXRESMODE** and **_MAXCOLORMODE** support all adapters except the MDPA. See Section 10.1.4, "Maximizing Resolution or Color," for definitions of these two modes.

If the hardware does not support the selected mode, **_setvideomode** returns 0.

Some graphics adapters are able to enter additional video modes:

- EGA adapters can display all CGA modes.

- HGC adapters can enter **_TEXTMONO** mode.

- MCGA adapters can display all CGA modes, plus **_VRES2COLOR** and **_MRES256COLOR**.

- VGA adapters can display all EGA and CGA modes.

10.1.3 Reading the videoconfig Structure

At any time, you can inquire about the current video configuration by passing the **_getvideoconfig** function a structure of type **videoconfig**. The structure contains 11 members, all of which are short integers. They are listed in Table 10.2.

Table 10.2   Members of a videoconfig Structure

Member	Description
adapter*	Active display adapter
bitsperpixel	Number of bits per pixel
memory	Adapter video memory in kilobytes
mode*	Current video mode
monitor*	Active display monitor
numcolors	Number of color indexes
numtextcols	Number of text columns available
numtextrows	Number of text rows available
numvideopages	Number of video pages available
numxpixels	Number of pixels on the x axis
numypixels	Number of pixels on the y axis

* Possible values for the mode, adapter, and monitor items are listed in the GRAPH.H file.

The **_getvideoconfig** function initializes these values. Most of the values are self-explanatory. For example, if **numxpixels** holds 640, the current video mode contains 640 horizontal pixels, numbered 0 – 639.

The READVC.C example program below illustrates how to initialize and examine a **videoconfig** structure:

```
/* READVC.C -- Reads the videoconfig structure */

#include <graph.h>
#include <stdio.h>

main()
{
    struct videoconfig vc;

    _getvideoconfig( &vc );
    printf( "Text Rows = %i.\n", vc.numtextrows );
}
```

First, the program declares a structure `vc` of type **videoconfig**. Next, it calls **_getvideoconfig** to initialize the structure. Finally, it prints a member of the structure.

10.1.4 *Maximizing Resolution or Color*

Two symbolic constants are new to Microsoft C 6.0: **_MAXRESMODE** and **_MAXCOLORMODE**. The first selects the highest possible resolution for the graphics adapter and monitor currently in use. The second selects the graphics mode with the greatest number of colors. The constants work with all graphics adapters except the MDPA. (See Table 10.3.)

Table 10.3   Constants for Maximum Resolution and Color

Adapter/Monitor	_MAXRESMODE	_MAXCOLORMODE
CGA	_HRESBW	_MRES4COLOR
EGA color	_HRES16COLOR	_HRES16COLOR
EGA ecd 64K	_ERESCOLOR	_HRES16COLOR
EGA ecd 256K	_ERESCOLOR	_ERESCOLOR
EGA mono	_ERESNOCOLOR	_ERESNOCOLOR
HGC	_HERCMONO	_HERCMONO
MCGA	_VRES2COLOR	_MRES256COLOR
MDPA	Fails	Fails
OCGA	_ORESCOLOR	_MRES4COLOR
OEGA color	_ORESCOLOR	_ERESCOLOR
VGA/OVGA	_VRES16COLOR	_MRES256COLOR

10.1.5 *Selecting Your Own Video Modes*

A program that will run only on a single machine with a known graphics adapter can enter the appropriate video mode immediately. However, if you attempt to run the program on another machine with a different adapter, it may not run correctly, if at all.

If your program might run on a variety of computers and you prefer to select your own video modes, initialize a **videoconfig** structure by calling the **_getvideoconfig** function. Then check the **adapter** member and use a **switch** statement to enter the selected video mode.

For example, suppose you know that a program will run on monochrome systems equipped with either an EGA adapter or a Hercules adapter. To enter the appropriate mode, use code such as this:

```
struct videoconfig vc;

_getvideoconfig( &vc );

switch( vc.adapter )
{
    case _EGA:
        _setvideomode( _ERESNOCOLOR );
        break;
    case _HGC:
        _setvideomode( _HERCMONO );
        break;
}
```

10.2 Mixing Colors and Changing Palettes

Depending on the graphics card installed and the video mode in effect, you can display 2, 4, 8, 16, or 256 colors on the screen at the same time. You specify a color by selecting a color index (sometimes called a "pixel value" or "color attribute"). The color indexes are numbered from 0 to $n-1$, where n is the number of colors in the palette.

CGA adapters offer four different palettes containing predefined fixed color sets.

All video modes that support color offer a color palette.

EGA, MCGA, and VGA adapters have palettes that can be redefined to suit your needs. You can change the visible color associated with any color index by re-mapping to a color index a color value that describes the true color (the amount of red, green, and blue) you want to display.

Olivetti adapters (OCGA, OEGA, and OVGA) support the standard CGA, EGA, and VGA modes (and palettes), plus an additional Olivetti mode described in Section 10.2.2, "Olivetti Palettes."

NOTE *The distinction between a color index and a color value is important. A color index is always a short integer. A color value is always a long integer. The only exception to this rule involves **_setbkcolor**, which uses a color index cast to a long integer in CGA and text modes.*

10.2.1 CGA Palettes

The CGA (Color Graphics Adapter) supports two color video modes: _MRES4COLOR and _MRESNOCOLOR, which display four colors selected from one of several predefined palettes of colors. They display these foreground colors against a background color that can be any one of the 16 available colors. With the CGA hardware, the palette of foreground colors is predefined and cannot be changed. Each palette number is an integer. (See Table 10.4.)

Table 10.4   CGA Palettes in _MRES4COLOR Mode

Palette Number	Color Index		
	1	2	3
0	Green	Red	Brown
1	Cyan	Magenta	Light Gray
2	Light Green	Light Red	Yellow
3	Light Cyan	Light Magenta	White

_MRESNOCOLOR produces palettes with shades of gray on monochrome monitors.

The **_MRESNOCOLOR** video mode produces palettes containing various shades of gray on monochrome monitors. However, the **_MRESNOCOLOR** mode displays colors when used with a color display. Only two palettes are available in this mode. Table 10.5 shows the colors available in the two palettes.

Table 10.5   CGA Palettes in _MRESNOCOLOR Mode

Palette Number	Color Index		
	1	2	3
0	Blue	Red	Light Gray
1	Light Blue	Light Red	White

You can use the **_selectpalette** function only in the **_MRES4COLOR**, **_MRESNOCOLOR**, and **_ORESCOLOR** graphics modes. To change palettes in other video modes, use the **_remappalette** or **_remapallpalette** functions.

10.2.2 Olivetti® Palettes

Olivetti graphics adapters are found in most Olivetti computers (including the M24, M28, M240, M280, and M380) and in the AT&T 6300 series computers. These adapters function the same as their non-Olivetti equivalents; that is, the OCGA, OEGA, and OVGA adapters support CGA, EGA, and VGA modes, respectively. In addition, Olivetti adapters can enter the high resolution **_ORESCOLOR** mode.

In **_ORESCOLOR** mode, you can choose one of 16 foreground colors by passing a value in the range 0–15 to the **_selectpalette** function. The background color is always black.

10.2.3 VGA Palettes

Depending on the video mode currently in effect, a VGA (Video Graphics Array) screen has 2, 16, or 256 color indexes chosen from a pool of 262,144 (256K) color values.

To name a color value, specify a level of intensity ranging from 0–63 for each of the red, green, and blue components. The long integer that defines a color value contains four bytes (32 bits):

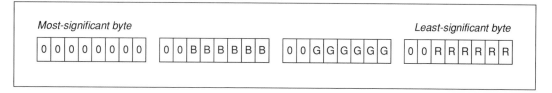

The most-significant byte should contain zeros. The two high bits in the remaining three bytes should also be zero (these bits are ignored).

To mix a light red (pink), turn red all the way up, and mix in some green and blue:

The number 0x0020203FL represents this value in hexadecimal notation. You can also use the following macro:

```
#define RGB ( r, g, b ) (0x3F3F3FL & ((long)(b) << 16 | (g) << 8 | (r)))
```

To create pure yellow (100% red plus 100% green) and assign it to a variable `yel`, use this line:

```
yel = RGB( 63, 63, 0 );
```

For white, turn all the colors on: `RGB( 63, 63, 63)`. For black, set all colors to 0: `RGB( 0, 0, 0 )`.

Once you have the color value,

- Call **_remappalette**, passing a color index and a color value.
- Call **_setcolor** to make that color index the current color.
- Draw something.

The program YELLOW.C below shows how to remap a color. It draws a rectangle in color index 3 and then changes index 3 to the color value 0x00003F3FL (yellow).

```
/* YELLOW.C -- Draws a yellow box on the screen */
/* Requires VGA or EGA */

#include <graph.h> /* graphics functions */
#include <conio.h> /* getch */

main()
{
    short int index3 = 3;
    long int yellow = 0x00003F3FL;
    long int old3;
```

```
if( _setvideomode( _HRES16COLOR ) )
{
        /* set current color to index 3*/
    _setcolor( index3 );
        /* draw a rectangle in that color */
    _rectangle( _GBORDER, 10, 10, 110, 110 );
        /* wait for a keypress */
    getch();
        /* change index 3 to yellow */
    old3 = _remappalette( index3, yellow );
        /* wait for a keypress */
    getch();
        /* restore the old color */
    _remappalette( index3, old3 );
    getch();
         /* back to default mode */
    _setvideomode( _DEFAULTMODE );
} else _outtext( "This program requires EGA or VGA." );
}
```

10.2.4 MCGA Palettes

In terms of color mixing, the MCGA (Multicolor Graphics Array) adapter is the same as the VGA. It can display any of 256K colors. It cannot enter all of the VGA video modes, however. It is limited to CGA modes and **_VRES2COLOR** and **_MRES256COLOR**.

10.2.5 EGA Palettes

Mixing colors in EGA (Enhanced Graphics Adapter) is similar to the VGA mixing described in Section 10.2.3, but there are fewer levels of intensity for the red, green, and blue (RGB) components. In the modes that offer 64 colors, the RGB values include two bits and can range in value from 0 – 3. The long integer that defines a color value looks like this:

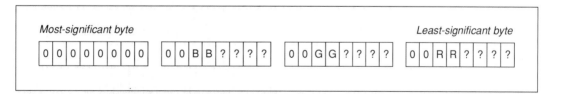

The bits marked 0 should be zeros; the bits marked ? are ignored. EGA color values are defined this way to maintain compatibility with VGA color values.

To form a pure red color value, use the constant 0x00000030L. For cyan (blue plus green), use 0x00303000L. The RGB macro defined above for VGA color mixing can be used as is, or you can modify it for EGA monitors:

```
#define EGARGB( r, g, b ) (0x303030L & ((long)(b) << 20 | (g) << 12 | (r << 4)))
```

In this macro, you would pass values in the range 0 –3 instead of 0 – 63.

For an example program that remaps a color index to a color value, see YELLOW.C in Section 10.2.3, "VGA Palettes."

10.2.6 Symbolic Constants

The GRAPH.H file defines the following constants, which can be used as ready-made color values for EGA and VGA adapters:

_BLACK	_GREEN	_LIGHTYELLOW
_BLUE	_LIGHTBLUE	_MAGENTA
_BRIGHTWHITE	_LIGHTCYAN	_RED
_BROWN	_LIGHTGREEN	_WHITE
_CYAN	_LIGHTMAGENTA	
_GRAY	_LIGHTRED	

For example, to change color index 1 to red, use the line

```
_remappalette( 1, _RED );
```

which causes any object currently drawn with color index 1 to change to red. The default color value associated with index 1 is blue.

10.3 Specifying Points within Coordinate Systems

A coordinate system describes points on the screen in terms of their horizontal (x) and vertical (y) positions. You specify a certain location by providing two values that map to a unique position.

Graphics functions usually use viewport and window coordinates.

Coordinates on the physical screen never change. Only five functions, listed in Section 10.3.1, use physical coordinates. All other graphics functions use one of these two coordinate systems:

- Viewport coordinates (short integers)

- Window coordinates (double-precision floating-point numbers)

Viewports and windows can occupy all of the physical screen or just part of it. The three coordinate systems and conventions for naming points and regions of the screen are described below.

10.3.1 Physical Coordinates

Within the physical screen, the upper left corner is called the "origin." The x and y coordinates for the origin are always (0, 0). The x axis extends in the positive direction left to right, while the y axis extends in the positive direction top to bottom.

For example, the video mode **_VRES16COLOR** has a resolution of 640×480, which means the x axis contains the values $0 - 639$ (left to right), and the y axis contains $0 - 479$ (top to bottom). (See Figure 10.1.)

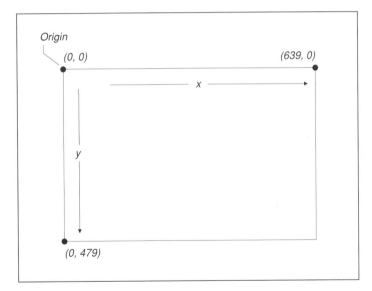

Figure 10.1 Physical Screen Coordinates

Only five functions use physical coordinates: **_setcliprgn**, **_setvieworg**, **_setviewport**, **_getviewcoord**, and **_getphyscoord**.

The **_setcliprgn** function establishes a "clipping region." Attempts to draw inside the region succeed, while attempts to draw outside the region are clipped (ignored). When you first enter a graphics mode, the clipping region defaults to the entire screen.

The **_setvieworg** function changes the current location of the origin. When a program first enters a graphics mode, the physical origin and the viewport origin are in the upper left corner. The following code moves the viewport origin to the physical screen location (50, 100):

```
_setvieworg( 50, 100 );
```

The effect on the screen is illustrated in Figure 10.2. Note that the number of pixels remains constant, but the range of legal *x* values changes from a range of 0 to 639 (physical screen) to –50 to 589. The legal *y* values change as well.

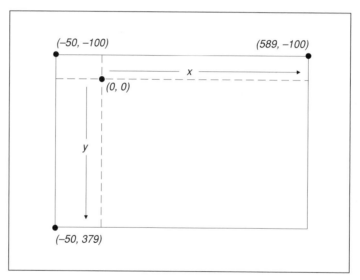

Figure 10.2 Coordinates Changed by _setvieworg

All graphics functions are affected by the new origin, including **_arc**, **_ellipse**, **_lineto**, **_moveto**, **_outgtext**, **_pie**, and **_rectangle**.

The third function that uses physical coordinates is **_setviewport**, described below, which establishes the boundaries of the current viewport.

10.3.2 Viewport Coordinates

The default viewport coordinate system is identical to the physical screen coordinate system. The **_setviewport** function creates a new viewport within the boundaries of the physical screen. A standard viewport has two distinguishing features:

- The origin of a viewport initially lies in the upper left corner of the viewport, not the upper left corner of the physical screen.

- The clipping region matches the outer boundaries of the viewport.

Graphics output functions require viewport or window coordinate values.

In other words, the **_setviewport** function does the same thing as would two separate calls to **_setvieworg** and **_setcliprgn**. All graphics output functions require values that are either viewport coordinates or window coordinates.

For example,

```
_setviewport( 50, 50, 200, 100 );
```

creates the viewport illustrated in Figure 10.3. The values passed to the **_setviewport** function are physical screen locations of opposite corners. After the viewport is created, the viewport origin lies in the upper left corner.

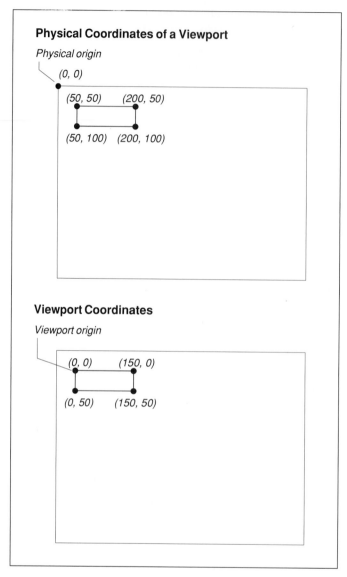

Figure 10.3 A Viewport

10.3.3 Window Coordinates

The **_setwindow** function allows you to use floating-point coordinates instead of integers. More importantly, it scales the screen coordinates to almost any size within the current viewport. Window functions take double-precision arguments and have names that end with the suffixes **_w** or **_wxy**. The function **_lineto_w** is the window-coordinate equivalent of the viewport function **_lineto**.

To create a window for charting 12 months of average temperatures ranging from −40 to 100, use this line:

```
_setwindow( TRUE, 1.0, -40.0, 12.0, 100.0 );
```

The first argument is the invert flag, which puts the lowest *y* value at the bottom of the screen instead of the top. The minimum and maximum coordinates follow. The new organization of the screen is shown in Figure 10.4.

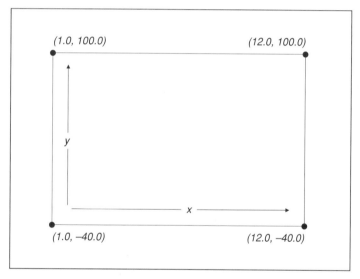

Figure 10.4 Window Coordinates

If you plot a point with **_setpixel_w** or draw a line with **_lineto_w**, the values are automatically scaled to the established window.

Window-coordinate graphics provide a lot of flexibility. You can fit an axis into a small range (such as 151.25 to 151.45) or into a large range (–50,000 to 80,000), depending on the type of data to be graphed. In addition, by changing the window coordinates and redrawing a figure, you can create the effects of zooming in or panning across a figure.

10.3.4 Screen Locations

A coordinate system needs two values (a horizontal and a vertical position) to describe the location of a point on the screen. There are times, however, when it is more convenient to use one variable instead of two.

Some graphics functions require you to pass the location of a point on the screen. Others return a value that represents a location. The GRAPH.H file defines two structures that allow you to refer to a point with a single variable.

- An **xycoord** structure contains two short integers called **xcoord** and **ycoord** for use in viewport graphics.

- A **_wxycoord** structure contains two **doubles** called **wx** and **wy** for use in window-coordinate graphics.

For example, you pass four **doubles** to the **_rectangle_w** function: an *x* and *y* position for the upper left corner of the window and an *x* and *y* position for the lower right corner. The **_rectangle_wxy** function takes two **_wxycoord** structures.

10.3.5 Bounding Rectangles

Certain figures such as arcs and ellipses are centered within a "bounding rectangle," specified by two points that define the opposite corners of the rectangle. The center of the rectangle becomes the center of the figure, and the rectangle's borders determine the size of the figure. Figure 10.5 shows start and end vectors and a bounding rectangle in which a pie shape has been drawn with the **_pie** function. The first two sets of coordinates are *x1*, *y1*, *x2*, and *y2*. They define the boundaries of the rectangle. The pie shape needs two other points, *x3*, *y3*, *x4*, and *y4*, which indicate the starting and ending lines.

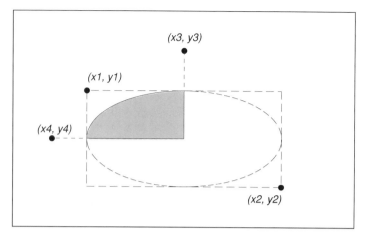

Figure 10.5 Bounding Rectangle

10.3.6 The Pixel Cursor

A "pixel cursor" is a location on the screen. The **_moveto** function positions this cursor at a given spot. Nothing visible appears. If you call **_lineto**, a line is drawn from the current pixel cursor to another point. The **_lineto** function also changes the location of the pixel cursor. When you call **_outgtext** to display fonted text, the characters are drawn at the current pixel cursor location.

To draw a series of connected lines, call **_lineto** several times.

The **_getcurrentposition** function returns the cursor location in an **xycoord** structure.

10.4 Graphics Functions

This section lists the functions that work in one or more bit-mapped graphics modes. Most of these functions are present in several forms. The function names that end with **_w** use **double** values as arguments and the window coordinate system. Functions that end with **_wxy** use the window coordinate system and a **_wxycoord** structure to define the coordinates. Functions with no suffix use the viewport coordinate system.

10.4.1 Controlling Video Modes

The functions described below affect the current video mode, coordinate systems, clipping regions, viewports, and windows. For more information, use on-line help.

_clearscreen   Erases the text or graphics screen and fills it with the current background color (note that setting the video mode automatically clears the screen). Pass one of the constants **_GCLEARSCREEN**, **_GVIEWPORT**, or **_GWINDOW**. No return value.

_getphyscoord   Converts viewport coordinates to physical coordinates. Pass an *x* and *y* coordinate from the viewport. The function returns an **xycoord** structure, which includes an *x* and a *y* position from the physical screen.

_getvideoconfig   Obtains the status of the current graphics environment. Pass it the address of a structure of type **_videoconfig**. See Section 10.1.3. "Reading the videoconfig Structure."

_getviewcoord   Converts physical coordinates to viewport coordinates. Pass two integers: an *x* and *y* coordinate. The function returns an **xycoord** structure containing the equivalent position within the viewport.

_getviewcoord_w   Converts window coordinates to viewport coordinates. Pass two **doubles** that name points within the window. Returns the equivalent viewport coordinates as an **xycoord** structure.

_getviewcoord_wxy   Converts window coordinates to viewport coordinates in an **xycoord** structure. Pass a **_wxycoord** structure.

_getwindowcoord   Converts viewport coordinates to window coordinates. Pass two integers representing viewport coordinates. Returns a **_wxycoord** structure.

_setcliprgn   Limits graphic output to part of the screen, called the "clipping region." Pass four values: the *x* and *y* coordinate of the upper left corner (on the physical screen) and the coordinates of the lower right corner. The default clipping region is the entire screen. See Section 10.3.1, "Physical Coordinates."

_setvideomode   Selects an operating mode for the display screen. Pass a constant, such as **_HRES16COLOR**. Returns 0 if the video mode selected is not supported by the hardware. See Section 10.1.2, "Setting a Video Mode."

_setvideomoderows   Sets the video mode and the number of rows for text operations. Pass two values: a video mode and the desired number of text rows (25, 30, 43, 50, or 60). Pass the symbolic constant **_MAXTEXTROWS** to get the largest available number of rows. Returns the number of rows or 0 if unsuccessful.

_setvieworg   Repositions the viewport origin. Pass an *x* and *y* position: the physical screen location that will become the new origin. Returns the previous origin in an **xycoord** structure.

_setviewport   Creates a viewport, including a clipping region and a new origin in the upper left corner of the viewport. Subsequent calls to graphics routines will be limited to the viewport area. Pass four short integers that indicate the physical screen locations of the *x* and *y* coordinates in the upper left and lower right corners of the viewport. No return value.

_setwindow   Defines a window coordinate system. Pass five values: a short invert flag (TRUE or FALSE) and four **doubles** that represent the extreme values in the upper left and lower right portions of the current viewport. See Section 10.3.3, "Window Coordinates."

10.4.2 Changing Colors

The functions below control colors and color palettes. For an introduction to this topic, see Section 10.2, "Mixing Colors and Changing Palettes." For function prototypes and more information, consult on-line help.

_getbkcolor   Reports the current background color as a long integer. In EGA, MCGA, and VGA video modes, this is a color value. In CGA and text modes, it is a color index.

_getcolor   Returns the current color index.

_remapallpalette   Assigns new color values to all color indexes. Pass a pointer to an array of color values. Returns 0 if unsuccessful.

_remappalette   Assigns a color value to a specific color index. Pass a short color index and a long color value (which specifies the amount of red, green, and blue). Returns the previous color value for that index or –1 if unsuccessful. See Section 10.2.1, "CGA Palettes."

_selectpalette   Selects a predefined palette. This function applies only to the CGA video modes **_MRES4COLOR** and **_MRESNOCOLOR** and the Olivetti graphics mode **_ORESCOLOR**. To change palettes in other color video modes, use **_remappalette** instead. Pass a short integer in the range 0 – 4 for CGA, or 0 –15 for Olivetti mode. Returns the value of the previous palette.

_setbkcolor   Sets the current background color. Always pass a long integer. In EGA, MCGA, and VGA modes, this value is a color value. In CGA and text modes, this is a color index cast to a long integer. Returns the old background color or –1 if unsuccessful.

_setcolor   Sets the color index to be used for graphic output. It affects later calls to functions such as **_arc**, **_ellipse**, **_floodfill**, **_lineto**, **_outgtext**, **_outtext**, **_pie**, **_rectangle**, and **_setpixel**. Returns the previous color or –1 if unsuccessful.

10.4.3 Drawing Points, Lines, and Shapes

The functions described below draw points, lines, and shapes. For a definition of bounding rectangle and pixel cursor, see Sections 10.3.5 and 10.3.6.

_arc   Draws an elliptical arc. Pass eight short integers: four pairs of x and y coordinates. The first two pairs are the corners of the bounding rectangle. The third and fourth are the starting and ending points of the arc. Returns 0 if unsuccessful.

_arc_wxy   Draws an arc within the window. Pass four **wxycoord** structures. The first two are the corners of the bounding rectangle. The third and fourth are the starting and ending points of the arc. Returns 0 if unsuccessful.

_ellipse   Draws an ellipse or a circle. Pass a short fill flag (**_GBORDER** or **_GFILLINTERIOR**) and four short integers representing the corners of the bounding rectangle. Returns 0 if unsuccessful.

_ellipse_w   Draws an ellipse or a circle within a window. Pass a short fill flag (**_GBORDER** or **_GFILLINTERIOR**) and four **doubles** representing the corners of the bounding rectangle. Returns 0 if unsuccessful.

_ellipse_wxy   Draws an ellipse or a circle. Pass a short fill flag (**_GBORDER** or **_GFILLINTERIOR**) and two **_wxycoord** structures representing the two corners of the bounding rectangle. Returns 0 if unsuccessful.

_getcurrentposition   Returns the current pixel cursor position in viewport coordinates as an **xycoord** structure. The current position can be changed by **_arc**, **_lineto**, and **_moveto**. The default position is the center of the viewport.

_getcurrentposition_w   Returns the current position of the pixel cursor as a **_wxycoord** structure containing the *x* and *y* coordinates. Pass nothing.

_getpixel   Returns a pixel's color index. Pass a short *x* and *y* coordinate (in viewport coordinates). If the point is outside the clipping region, the function returns -1.

_getpixel_w   Returns a pixel's color index. Pass two doubles: an *x* and *y* coordinate.

_lineto   Draws a line from the current pixel cursor position to a specified point. Pass a short *x* and a short *y* position. Returns 0 if unsuccessful.

_lineto_w   Draws a line from the current pixel position to a specified window coordinate point. Pass a **double** *x* and *y* position. Returns 0 if unsuccessful.

_moveto   Moves the pixel cursor to a specified point (with no graphic output). Pass an *x* and *y* position. Returns the coordinates of the previous position in an **xycoord** structure.

_moveto_w   Moves the pixel cursor to a specified point in a window. Pass two doubles: an *x* and a *y* coordinate. Returns the previous position as a **_wxycoord** structure.

_ pie   Draws a figure shaped like a pie slice. Pass a short fill flag and eight short integers. The first four describe the bounding rectangle. The final four represent the starting vector and ending vector. Returns 0 if unsuccessful.

_ pie_wxy   Draws a pie-slice figure within a window. Pass a short fill flag and four **_wxycoord** structures. The first two describe the bounding rectangle. The second two represent the starting vector and ending vector. Returns 0 if unsuccessful.

_rectangle   Draws a rectangle in the current line style. Pass a short fill flag (**_GFILLINTERIOR** or **_GBORDER**) and four short integers: the *x* and *y* coordinates of opposite corners. Returns 0 if unsuccessful.

_rectangle_w   Draws a rectangle in the current line style. Pass a short fill flag (**_GFILLINTERIOR** or **_GBORDER**) and four doubles: the *x* and *y* window coordinates of opposite corners. Returns 0 if unsuccessful.

_rectangle_wxy   Draws a rectangle in the current line style. Pass a short fill flag (**_GFILLINTERIOR** or **_GBORDER**) and two **_wxycoord** structures describing the *x* and *y* coordinates of opposite corners. Returns 0 if unsuccessful.

_setpixel   Sets a pixel to the current color (which is selected by **_setcolor**). Pass it integer *x* and *y* coordinates. Returns the previous value of the pixel or −1 if unsuccessful.

_setpixel_w   Sets a pixel to the current color (which is selected by **_setcolor**). Pass it **double** *x* and *y* coordinates describing a position within the window. Returns the previous value of the pixel or −1 if unsuccessful.

10.4.4 Defining Patterns

The following functions control the style in which straight lines are drawn and the fill pattern used for solid shapes. For more information, use on-line help.

_floodfill   Fills a bounded shape with the fill pattern set by **_setfillmask** in the current color established by **_setcolor**. Pass an *x* and *y* coordinate and a boundary color (the color index that marks the edge of the shape to be filled). Returns 0 if unsuccessful.

_floodfill_w   Fills a bounded shape with the fill pattern set by **_setfillmask**. Pass **doubles** that describe an *x* and *y* position within the window and a boundary color (the color index that marks the edge of the shape to be filled). Returns 0 if unsuccessful.

_getfillmask   Returns the address of the current fill mask, an eight-character array, or 0 if the fill mask is not currently defined.

_getlinestyle   Returns the line style, a short integer whose bits correspond to the screen pixels turned on or off within a line.

_setfillmask   Sets the current fill mask used by **_floodfill** and functions that draw solid shapes (**_ellipse**, **_pie**, and **_rectangle**). Pass the address of an array of eight unsigned characters, where each bit represents a pixel. The pixels are drawn in the current color. No return value.

_setlinestyle   Sets the current style, which is used to draw the straight lines within **_lineto**, **_rectangle**, and **_pie**. Pass an unsigned short integer within which the bits correspond to the pixels on screen. For example, 0xFFFF represents a solid line, 0xAAAA is a dotted line, and 0xF0F0 is dashed.

10.4.5 *Manipulating Images*

The functions described below can be used to create animated graphics. The **_getimage** and **_putimage** functions act like a rubber stamp; after capturing a shape, you can make copies anywhere on the screen.

_getimage   Stores a screen image in memory. Pass four integers (the coordinates of the bounding rectangle) and a pointer to a storage buffer. Call **_imagesize** to find out how much memory is required. No return value.

_getimage_w   Stores a screen image in memory. Pass four **doubles** (the coordinates of the bounding rectangle) and a pointer to a storage buffer. Call **_imagesize_w** to find out how much memory is required. No return value.

_getimage_wxy   Same as **_getimage_w**, but you pass two **_wxycoord** structures and a pointer to memory.

_imagesize   Returns a long integer representing the size of an image in bytes. Call this function in preparation for a call to **_getimage**. Pass four integers: the x and y coordinates of opposite corners of the portion of the screen to be saved.

_imagesize_w   Returns the size of an image in bytes in preparation for a call to **_getimage_w** and **_putimage_w**. Pass four doubles: the x and y window coordinates of opposite corners of the portion of the screen to be saved.

_imagesize_wxy   Same as **_imagesize_w**, but you pass two **_wxycoord** structures.

_putimage   Retrieves an image from memory and displays it on the active screen page. The image should previously have been saved to memory with **_getimage**. Pass two short integers (coordinates where the image is to be placed), a pointer to the image, and a short integer indicating what kind of action to take: **_GAND, _GOR, _GPRESET, _GPSET,** or **_GXOR**. No return value.

_putimage_w   Displays an image from memory within a window. The image should previously have been saved to memory with **_getimage_w**. Pass two **doubles** (coordinates where the image is to be placed), a pointer to the image, and a short integer indicating what kind of action to take: **_GAND, _GOR, _GPRESET, _GPSET,** or **_GXOR**. No return value.

10.5 *Using Graphic Fonts*

A "font" is a collection of stylized text characters. Each font consists of a type-face with several type sizes.

A "typeface" is the name of the displayed text—Courier, for example, or Roman. The list on the next page shows six of the typefaces available with the Microsoft C font library.

"Type size" measures the screen area occupied by individual characters in units of screen pixels. For example, "Courier 12 × 9" denotes text of Courier typeface, with each character occupying a screen area of 12 vertical pixels by 9 horizontal pixels.

A font's spacing can be fixed or proportional. "Fixed" means that all characters have the same width in pixels. "Proportional" means the width varies. An *i*, for example, is thinner than an *M*.

The Microsoft C font functions use two methods to create fonts. The first technique generates Courier, Helv, and Tms Rmn fonts through a "bit-mapping" (or "raster-mapping") technique. Bit-mapping defines character images with binary data. Each bit in the map corresponds to a screen pixel. If a bit is 1, its associated pixel is set to the current screen color.

The second method creates the remaining three type styles—Modern, Script, and Roman—as "vector-mapped" fonts. Vector-mapping represents each character in terms of lines and arcs.

Each method has advantages and disadvantages. Bit-mapped characters are more completely formed since the pixel mapping is predetermined. However, they cannot be scaled. Vector-mapped text can be scaled to any size, but the characters tend to lack the solid appearance of the bit-mapped characters.

The following list shows six sample typefaces:

Typeface	**Sample Text**
Courier	ABCDEFGHIJKLMNOPQRSTUVWXYZ abcdefghijklmnopqrstuvwxyz
Helv	ABCDEFGHIJKLMNOPQRSTUVWXYZ abcdefghijklmnopqrstuvwxyz
Tms Rmn	ABCDEFGHIJKLMNOPQRSTUVWXYZ abcdefghijklmnopqrstuvwxyz
Modern	ABCDEFGHIJKLMNOPQRSTUVWXYZ abcdefghijklmnopqrstuvwxyz
Script	ABCDEFGHIJKLMNOPQRSTUVWXYZ abcdefghijklmnopqrstuvwxyz
Roman	ABCDEFGHIJKLMNOPQRSTUVWXYZ abcdefghijklmnopqrstuvwxyz

Table 10.6 lists available sizes for each font. Note that the bit-mapped fonts come in preset sizes as measured in pixels. The vector-mapped fonts can be scaled to any size.

Table 10.6   Typefaces and Type Sizes in the C Library

Typeface	Mapping	Size (in pixels)	Spacing
Courier	Bit	10×8, 12×9, 15×12	Fixed
Helv	Bit	10×5, 12×7, 15×8, 18×9, 22×12, 28×16	Proportional
Tms Rmn	Bit	10×5, 12×6, 15×8, 16×9, 20×12, 26×16	Proportional
Modern	Vector	Scaled	Proportional
Script	Vector	Scaled	Proportional
Roman	Vector	Scaled	Proportional

10.5.1 *Using the C Font Library*

Data for both bit-mapped and vector-mapped fonts reside in .FON files. For example, the files MODERN.FON, ROMAN.FON, and SCRIPT.FON hold data for the three vector-mapped fonts.

You can use Microsoft Windows .FON files. The Microsoft C .FON files are identical to the .FON files used in the Microsoft Windows operating environment. If you have access to Windows, you can use any of its .FON files with Microsoft C font functions. In addition, several vendors offer software that creates or modifies .FON files, allowing you to design your own fonts.

Your programs should follow these three steps to display fonted text:

1. Register the fonts.

2. Set the current font from the register.

3. Display text using the current font.

The following sections describe each of the three steps in detail. An example program in Section 10.5.5 demonstrates these steps.

10.5.2 Registering the Fonts

The fonts must first be organized into a list in memory, a process called "registering." Register fonts by calling the function **_registerfonts**. This function reads header information from specified .FON files, building a list of file information but not reading any mapping data from the files.

The GRAPH.H file prototypes the **_registerfonts** function as

```
short far _registerfonts( unsigned char far * );
```

The argument points to a string containing a file name. The file name is the name of the .FON file for the desired font. The file name can include wild cards, allowing you to register several fonts with one call to **_registerfonts**.

If it successfully reads one or more .FON files, **_registerfonts** returns the number of fonts. If the function fails, it returns a negative error code.

10.5.3 Setting the Current Font

Call the function **_setfont** to select a current font. This function checks to see if the requested font is registered, then reads the mapping data from the appropriate .FON file. A font must be registered and marked current before your program can display text in that font.

The GRAPH.H file prototypes the **_setfonts** function as

```
short far _setfont( unsigned char far * );
```

The function's argument is a pointer to a character string. The string consists of letter codes that describe the desired font, as outlined here:

Option Code	Meaning
b	The best fit from the registered fonts. This option instructs **_setfont** to accept the closest-fitting font if a font of the specified size is not registered.
	If at least one font is registered, the **b** option always sets a current font. If you do not specify the **b** option and an exact matching font is not registered, the **_setfont** function will fail. In this case, any existing current font remains current. Refer to on-line help for a description of error codes returned by **_setfont**.
	The **_setfont** function uses four criteria for selecting the best fit. In descending order of precedence, the four criteria are pixel height, typeface, pixel width, and spacing (fixed or proportional). If you request a vector-mapped font, **_setfont** sizes the font to correspond with the specified pixel height and width. If you request a raster-mapped (bit-mapped) font, **_setfont** chooses the closest available size. If the requested type size for a raster-mapped font fits exactly between two registered fonts, the smaller size takes precedence.
f	Fixed-spaced font.
hy	Character height, where y is the height in pixels.
nx	Font number x, where x is less than or equal to the value returned by **_registerfonts**. For example, the option **n3** makes the third registered font current, if three or more fonts are registered.
p	Proportional-spaced font.

r	Raster-mapped (bit-mapped) font.
t'*fontname*'	Typeface of the font in single quotes. The *fontname* string is one of the following:

courier	modern
helv	script
tms rmn	roman

Note the space in tms rmn. Additional font files use other names for *fontname*. Refer to the vendor's documentation for these names.

v	Vector-mapped font.
w*x*	Character width, where *x* is the width in pixels.

Option codes are not case sensitive and can be listed in any order. You can separate codes with spaces or any other character that is not a valid option code. The **_setfont** function ignores all invalid codes.

The **_setfont** function updates a data area with parameters of the current font. The data area is in the form of a structure, defined in GRAPH.H as follows:

```
struct _fontinfo
{
    int     type;           /* set = vector,clear = bit map */
    int     ascent;         /* pix dist from top to base */
    int     pixwidth;       /* character width in pixels */
    int     pixheight;      /* character height in pixels */
    int     avgwidth;       /* average character width */
    char    filename[81];   /* file name including path */
    char    faceName[32];   /* font name */
};
```

If you want to retrieve the parameters of the current font, call the function **_getfontinfo**.

10.5.4 *Displaying Text*

The last step, displaying text, consists of two parts. First you must select a screen position for the text with the graphics function **_moveto**. Then display fonted text at that position with the function **_outgtext**. The **_moveto** function takes pixel coordinates as arguments. The coordinates locate the top left of the first character in the text string.

10.5.5 A Sample Program

The program SAMPLER.C displays sample text in all the available fonts, then exits when a key is pressed. Make sure the .FON files are in the current directory before running the program.

```
/* SAMPLER.C: Displays sample text in various fonts. */

#include <stdio.h>
#include <conio.h>
#include <stdlib.h>
#include <graph.h>
#include <string.h>
#define NFONTS 6

main()

{
    static unsigned char *text[2*NFONTS] =
    {
        "COURIER",        "courier",
        "HELV",           "helv",
        "TMS RMN",        "tms rmn",
        "MODERN",         "modern",
        "SCRIPT",         "script",
        "ROMAN",          "roman"
    };
    static unsigned char *face[NFONTS] =
    {
        "t'courier'",
        "t'helv'",
        "t'tms rmn'",
        "t'modern'",
        "t'script'",
        "t'roman'"
    };

static unsigned char list[20];
    struct videoconfig vc;
    int mode = _VRES16COLOR;
    register i;
```

```
    /*   Read header info from all .FON files in
     *   current directory
     */

    if( _registerfonts( "*.FON" ) < 0 )
    {
       _outtext( "Error: can't register fonts" );
       exit( 0 );
    }

    /*   Set highest available video mode */

    if( _setvideomode( _MAXRESMODE ) == 0 )
       exit ( 0 );

    /*   Copy video configuration into structure vc */

    _getvideoconfig( &vc );              .

    /*   Display six lines of sample text */

    for( i = 0; i < NFONTS; i++ )
    {
       strcpy( list, face[i] );
       strcat( list, "h30w24b" );

       if( _setfont( list ) >= 0 )
       {
           _setcolor( i + 1 );
           _moveto( 0, (i * vc.numypixels) / NFONTS );
           _outgtext( text[i * 2] );
           _moveto( vc.numxpixels / 2,
                       (i * vc.numypixels) / NFONTS );
           _outgtext( text[(i * 2) + 1] );
       }
       else
       {
           _setvideomode( _DEFAULTMODE );
           _outtext( "Error: can't set font" );
           exit( 0 );
       }
    }

getch();
    _setvideomode( _DEFAULTMODE );

    /* Return memory when finished with fonts */

    _unregisterfonts();
    exit( 0 );
}
```

10.5.6 Using Fonts Effectively

Displaying fonts is simply another form of graphics; using fonts effectively requires little programming effort. Still, there are a few things to watch:

- Remember that the video mode should be set only once. If you generate an image with presentation graphics and want to add text to it, do not reset the video mode prior to calling the font routines. Doing so will blank the screen, destroying the original image.

- The _setfont function reads specified .FON files to obtain mapping data for the current font. Each call to _setfont causes a disk access and overwrites the old font data in memory. If you want to show text of different styles on the same screen, display all text of one font before moving on to the others. Minimizing the number of calls to _setfont saves time spent in disk I/O and memory reloads.

- When your program finishes using the fonts library, you may want to free the memory occupied by the register list by calling **_unregisterfonts**. This function frees the memory allocated by **_registerfonts**. The register information for each type size of each font takes up approximately 140 bytes of memory.

- Aesthetic suggestions for the printed page also apply to screen text. Typefaces are more effective when they do not compete with each other for attention. Restricting the number of styles per screen to one or two generally results in a more pleasing, less cluttered image.

Creating Charts and Graphs

The low-level graphics functions described in Chapter 10, "Communicating with Graphics," draw points, lines, and shapes. Although it is possible to use them to generate charts and graphs, an additional set of high-level graphics functions is better suited to this task.

"Presentation graphics" is a set of high-level functions that displays presentation-quality graphics. These functions transform numeric data into pie charts, bar and column charts, line graphs, and scatter diagrams.

This chapter describes how to use presentation graphics.

11.1 Overview of Presentation Graphics

The presentation graphics library PGCHART.LIB contains 22 functions. They are listed in Table 11.1 for convenient reference.

Table 11.1   Presentation Graphics Function

Primary Functions	Secondary Functions	
_pg_chart	_pg_analyzechart	_pg_hlabelchart
_pg_chartms	_pg_analyzechartms	_pg_resetpalette
_pg_chartpie	_pg_analyzepie	_pg_resetstyleset
_pg_chartscatter	_pg_analyzescatter	_pg_setchardef
_pg_chartscatterms	_pg_analyzescatterms	_pg_setpalette
_pg_defaultchart	_pg_getchardef	_pg_setstyleset
_pg_initchart	_pg_getpalette	_pg_vlabelchart
	_pg_getstyleset	

The seven primary functions initialize variables and display selected chart types.

In most cases, you will be using only seven "primary functions." These functions initialize variables and display selected chart types. The 15 "secondary functions" of presentation graphics do not directly display charts. Most of them retrieve or set data in the presentation graphics chart environment.

Among the secondary functions are the "analysis functions," identified by the prefix **_pg_analyze**. These five functions calculate default values that pertain to a given chart type and data set. Calling an analysis function has the same effect as calling a corresponding primary function, except that the chart is not displayed. This allows you to pass on to the library the burden of calculating values. You can then make modifications to the resulting values and call a primary routine to display the chart.

Use the **_pg_hlabelchart** and **_pg_vlabelchart** functions to display text that is not part of a title or axis label on your chart. These functions enable you to attach notes or other messages to your chart.

11.2 Parts of a Graph

This section describes the terms used to refer to the different kinds of information that can be plotted. The various types of charts and graphs are also defined.

Data Series

Data that are related by a common idea or purpose constitute a "series." For example, the prices of a futures commodity over the course of a year form a single series of data. The volume forms a second data series.

When you include several series in one chart, characteristics such as color and pattern can help distinguish one from another. You can more readily differentiate series on a color monitor than you can on a monochrome monitor. The number of series that can appear on the same chart depends on the chart type and the number of available colors.

Categories

"Categories" are nonnumeric data. A set of categories forms a frame of reference for the comparison of numeric data. For example, the months of the year are categories against which numeric data such as inches of rainfall can be plotted.

Regional sales provide another example. A chart can compare a company's sales in different parts of the country. Each region forms a category.

Values

"Values" are numeric data. Sales, stock prices, air temperatures, and populations are all series of values that can be plotted against categories or against other values.

Presentation graphics allows you to overlay different series of value data on a single graph. For example, average monthly temperatures or monthly sales of heating oil during different years—or a combination of temperatures and sales—can be plotted together on the same graph.

Pie Charts

"Pie charts" are used to represent data by showing the relationship of each part to the whole. A good example is a company's annual budget. A pie chart allows you to view each area of revenue or spending by its relative size within the context of the entire company budget.

Presentation graphics can display either a standard or an "exploded" pie chart. The exploded view shows the pie with one or more pieces separated for emphasis. You can label each slice of a pie chart with a percentage figure if you wish.

Bar and Column Charts

As the name implies, a "bar chart" shows data as horizontal bars. Bar charts show comparisons among items rather than absolute value.

"Column charts" are vertical bar charts. Column charts are frequently used to show variations over a period of time, since they suggest time flow better than a bar chart.

Line Graphs

"Line graphs" illustrate trends or changes in data. They show how a series of values varies against a particular category—for example, average temperatures throughout one year.

Traditionally, line graphs show a collection of data points connected by lines. Presentation graphics can also plot points that are not connected by lines.

Scatter Diagrams

A "scatter diagram" is the only type of graph available in presentation graphics that directly compares values with values. A scatter diagram simply plots points.

Scatter diagrams illustrate the relationship between numeric values in different groups of data. They graphically show trends and correlations not easily detected from rows and columns of raw numbers.

Scatter diagrams are most useful with large amounts of data. Consider, for example, the relationship between personal income and family size. If you poll one thousand wage earners for their income and family size, you have a scatter diagram with one thousand points. If you combine your results so that you are left with one average income for each family size, you have a line graph.

Axes

All presentation graphics charts except pie charts are displayed with two perpendicular reference axes. The vertical, or *y*, axis runs from top to bottom of the chart and is placed against the left side of the screen. The horizontal, or *x*, axis runs from left to right across the bottom of the screen.

The chart type determines the axis used for category data and the axis for value data.

The *x* axis is the category axis for column and line charts and the value axis for bar charts. The *y* axis is the value axis for column and line charts and the category axis for bar charts.

Chart Windows

The "chart window" defines that part of the screen on which the chart is drawn. By default, the window fills the entire screen, but presentation graphics allows you to resize the window for smaller graphs. By redefining the chart window to different screen locations, you can view separate graphs together on the same screen.

Data Windows

While the chart window defines the entire graph including axes and labels, the "data window" defines only the actual plotting area. This is the portion of the graph to the right of the *y* axis and above the *x* axis. You cannot specify or adjust the size of the data window. Presentation graphics automatically determines its size based on the dimensions of the chart window.

Chart Styles

Each of the five types of presentation graphics charts can appear in two different "chart styles," as described in Table 11.2.

Table 11.2 Presentation Graphics Chart Styles

Chart Type	Chart Style #1	Chart Style #2
Pie	With percentages	Without percentages
Bar	Side-by-side	Stacked
Column	Side-by-side	Stacked
Line	Points with lines	Points only
Scatter	Points with lines	Points only

Bar and column charts have only one style when displaying a single series of data. The styles "side-by-side" and "stacked" are applicable when more than one series appears on the same chart. The first style arranges the bars or columns for the different series side by side, showing relative heights or lengths. The stacked style, illustrated for a column chart in Figure 11.3, emphasizes relative sizes between bars or columns.

Legends

Legends help identify individual data series.

When displaying more than one data series on a chart, presentation graphics uses different colors, line styles, or patterns to differentiate them. Presentation graphics also can display a "legend" that labels the different series of a chart. For a pie chart, the legend labels individual slices of the pie.

A sample of the color and pattern used to graph the series appears next to the series label. This identifies the set of data to which the labels belong.

You may change the font displayed by calling the **_registerfonts** and **_setfont** functions (see Section 10.5 for more information about using fonts). If you don't select a font, presentation graphics defaults to an internal font.

11.3 *Writing a Presentation Graphics Program*

To write a C program that uses presentation graphics, follow these steps:

1. Include the required header files, GRAPH.H and PGCHART.H, as well as any other header files your program may need.

2. Set the video mode to a graphics mode. See Chapter 10, "Communicating with Graphics," for a description of video modes.

3. Initialize the presentation graphics chart environment. Presentation graphics places charting parameters in data structures. The amount of initialization that must be done by your program depends on how extensively it relies on the defaults.

4. Assemble the plot data. Data can be collected in a variety of ways: by calculating it elsewhere in the program, reading it from files, or entering it from the keyboard. All plot data must be assembled in arrays because the presentation graphics functions locate them through pointers.

5. Call presentation graphics functions to display the chart. Pause while the chart is on the screen.

6. Reset the video mode. When your program detects the signal to continue, it should reset the video to its original (default) mode.

After compiling the program, link it to the library modules PGCHART.LIB and GRAPHICS.LIB.

The sample programs in Sections 11.3.1–11.3.3 use 5 of the 22 presentation graphics functions: **_pg_initchart**, **_pg_defaultchart**, **_pg_chartpie**, **_pg_chart**, and **_pg_chartscatter**. Each program is commented so that you can recognize the steps given in this section.

11.3.1 Pie Chart

The following program uses presentation graphics to display a pie chart for monthly sales of orange juice over a year. The chart, which is shown in Figure 11.1, remains on the screen until a key is pressed.

```c
/* PIE.C:  Create sample pie chart.  */

#include <conio.h>
#include <string.h>
#include <graph.h>
#include <pgchart.h>

#define MONTHS 12

typedef enum {FALSE, TRUE} boolean;

float far value[MONTHS] =
{
    33.0, 27.0, 42.0, 64.0,106.0,157.0,
   182.0,217.0,128.0, 62.0, 43.0, 36.0
};
char far *category[MONTHS] =
{
    "Jan", "Feb", "Mar", "Apr",
    "May", "Jun", "Jly", "Aug",
    "Sep", "Oct", "Nov", "Dec"
};
short far explode[MONTHS] = {0};

main()
{
    chartenv env;
    int mode = _VRES16COLOR;
```

```
/* Set highest video mode available */

if( _setvideomode( _MAXRESMODE ) == 0 )
   exit( 0 );

/* Initialize chart library and a default pie chart */

_pg_initchart();
_pg_defaultchart( &env, _PG_PIECHART, _PG_PERCENT );

/* Add titles and some chart options */

strcpy( env.maintitle.title, "Good Neighbor Grocery" );
env.maintitle.titlecolor = 6;
env.maintitle.justify = _PG_RIGHT;
strcpy( env.subtitle.title, "Orange Juice Sales" );
env.subtitle.titlecolor = 6;
env.subtitle.justify = _PG_RIGHT;
env.chartwindow.border = FALSE;

/* Parameters for call to _pg_chartpie are:
 *
 *    env        - Environment variable
 *    category   - Category labels
 *    value      - Data to chart
 *    explode    - Separated pieces
 *    MONTHS     - Number of data values
 */
if( _pg_chartpie( &env, category, value,
                  explode, MONTHS ) )
{
   _setvideomode( _DEFAULTMODE );
   _outtext( "Error:  can't draw chart" );
}
else
{
   getch();
   _setvideomode( _DEFAULTMODE );
}
return( 0 );
}
```

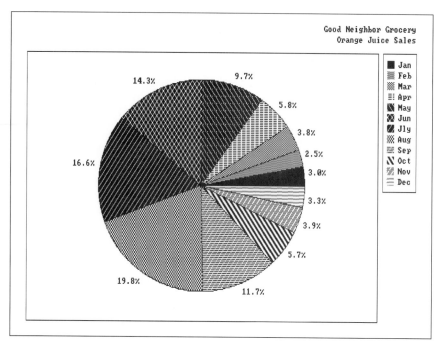

Figure 11.1 Example Pie Chart

11.3.2 Bar, Column, and Line Charts

The code for the PIE.C program needs only minor alterations to produce bar, column, and line charts for the same data:

- Replace the call to **_pg_chartpie** with **_pg_chart**. This function produces bar, column, and line charts depending on the value of the second argument for **_pg_defaultchart**.

- Give new arguments to **_pg_defaultchart** that specify chart type and style.

- Assign titles for the *x* axis and *y* axis in the structure env.

- Remove references to array explode, which is applicable only to pie charts.

The following example produces a bar chart for the store owner's data. The result is shown in Figure 11.2.

```c
/* BAR.C:  Create sample bar chart. */

#include <conio.h>
#include <string.h>
#include <graph.h>
#include <pgchart.h>

#define MONTHS 12

typedef enum {FALSE, TRUE} boolean;

float far value[MONTHS] =
{
    33.0, 27.0, 42.0, 64.0,106.0,157.0,
    182.0,217.0,128.0, 62.0, 43.0, 36.0
};
char far *category[MONTHS] =
{
    "Jan", "Feb", "Mar", "Apr",
    "May", "Jun", "Jly", "Aug",
    "Sep", "Oct", "Nov", "Dec"
};

main()
{
    chartenv env;
    int mode = _VRES16COLOR;

    /* Set highest video mode available */

    if( _setvideomode( _MAXRESMODE ) == 0 )
      exit( 0 );

    /* Initialize chart library and a default bar chart */
    _pg_initchart();
    _pg_defaultchart( &env, _PG_BARCHART, _PG_PLAINBARS );

    /* Add titles and some chart options */

    strcpy( env.maintitle.title, "Good Neighbor Grocery" );
    env.maintitle.titlecolor = 6;
    env.maintitle.justify = _PG_RIGHT;
    strcpy( env.subtitle.title, "Orange Juice Sales" );
    env.subtitle.titlecolor = 6;
    env.subtitle.justify = _PG_RIGHT;
    strcpy( env.yaxis.axistitle.title, "Months" );
    strcpy( env.xaxis.axistitle.title, "Quantity (cases)" );
    env.chartwindow.border = FALSE;
```

```
/* Parameters for call to _pg_chart are:
 *    env       - Environment variable
 *    category  - Category labels
 *    value     - Data to chart
 *    MONTHS    - Number of data values
 */
if( _pg_chart( &env, category, value, MONTHS ) )
{
   _setvideomode( _DEFAULTMODE );
   _outtext( "Error:  can't draw chart" );
}
else
{
   getch();
   _setvideomode( _DEFAULTMODE );
}
return( 0 );
}
```

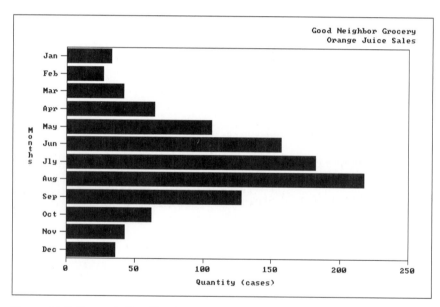

Figure 11.2 Example Bar Chart

The grocer's bar chart becomes a column chart in two easy steps. Simply specify the new chart type when calling **_pg_defaultchart** and change the axis titles. To produce a column chart for the grocer's data, replace the call to **_pg_defaultchart** with

```
_pg_defaultchart( &env, _PG_COLUMNCHART, _PG_PLAINBARS );
```

Replace the last two calls to **strcpy** with

```
strcpy( env.xaxis.axistitle.title, "Months" );
strcpy( env.yaxis.axistitle.title, "Quantity (cases)" );
```

Note that now the *x* axis is labeled "Months" and the *y* axis is labeled "Quantity (cases)." Figure 11.3 shows the resulting column chart.

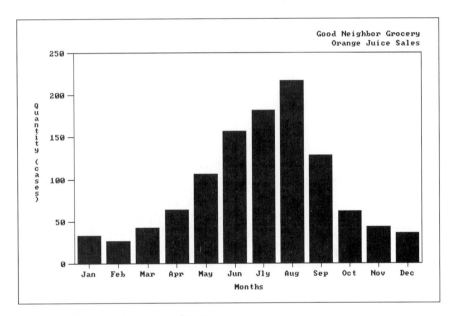

Figure 11.3 Example Column Chart

Creating an equivalent line chart requires only one change. Use the same code as for the column chart and replace the call to **_pg_defaultchart** with

```
_pg_defaultchart( &env, _PG_LINECHART, _PG_POINTANDLINE );
```

Figure 11.4 shows the line chart for the grocer's data.

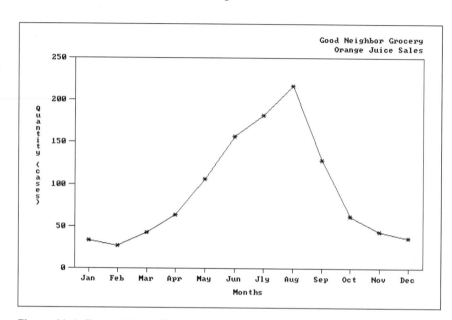

Figure 11.4 Example Line Chart

11.3.3 Scatter Diagram

The program SCATTER.C displays a scatter diagram that illustrates the relationship between the sales of orange juice and hot chocolate throughout a 12-month period. Figure 11.5 shows the results of SCATTER.C. Notice that the scatter points form a slightly curved line, indicating that a correlation exists between the sales of the two products. The demand for orange juice is roughly inverse to the demand for hot chocolate.

```
/* SCATTER.C:  Create sample scatter diagram. */

#include <conio.h>
#include <string.h>
#include <graph.h>
#include <pgchart.h>

#define MONTHS 12

typedef enum {FALSE, TRUE} boolean;
```

```
/* Orange juice sales */

float far xvalue[MONTHS] =
{
    33.0, 27.0, 42.0, 64.0,106.0,157.0,
  182.0,217.0,128.0, 62.0, 43.0, 36.0
};

/* Hot chocolate sales */

float far yvalue[MONTHS] =
{
  37.0, 37.0, 30.0, 19.0, 10.0,  5.0,
   2.0,  1.0,  7.0, 15.0, 28.0, 39.0
};

main()
{
    chartenv env;
    int mode = _VRES16COLOR;

    /* Set highest video mode available */

    if( _setvideomode( _MAXRESMODE ) == 0 )
       exit( 0 );
    /* Initialize chart library and default
     * scatter diagram
     */
    _pg_initchart();
    _pg_defaultchart( &env, _PG_SCATTERCHART,
                      _PG_POINTONLY );

    /* Add titles and some chart options */

    strcpy( env.maintitle.title, "Good Neighbor Grocery" );
    env.maintitle.titlecolor = 6;
    env.maintitle.justify = _PG_RIGHT;
    strcpy( env.subtitle.title,
            "Orange Juice vs Hot Chocolate" );
    env.subtitle.titlecolor = 6;
    env.subtitle.justify = _PG_RIGHT;
    env.yaxis.grid = TRUE;
    strcpy( env.xaxis.axistitle.title,
            "Orange Juice Sales" );
    strcpy( env.yaxis.axistitle.title,
            "Hot Chocolate Sales" );
    env.chartwindow.border = FALSE;
```

```
/* Parameters for call to _pg_chartscatter are:
 *      env        - Environment variable
 *      xvalue     - X-axis data
 *      yvalue     - Y-axis data
 *      MONTHS     - Number of data values
 */
if( _pg_chartscatter( &env, xvalue,
                         yvalue, MONTHS ) )
{
   _setvideomode( _DEFAULTMODE );
   _outtext( "Error:  can't draw chart" );
}
else
{
   getch();
   _setvideomode( _DEFAULTMODE );
}
return( 0 );
}
```

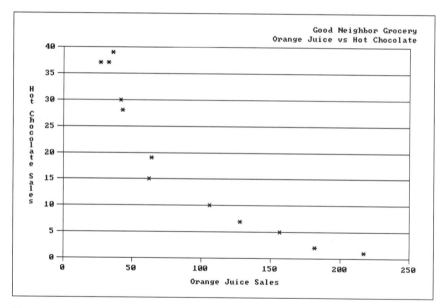

Figure 11.5 Example Scatter Diagram

11.4 *Manipulating Colors and Patterns*

Presentation graphics displays each data series in a way that makes it discernible from other series. It does this by defining a separate "palette" for every data series in a chart. Palettes consist of entries that determine color, line style, fill pattern, and point character used to graph the series.

Presentation graphics maintains its palettes as an array of structures. The header file PGCHART.H defines the palette structures as shown below:

```
/* Typedef for pattern bitmap */
typedef unsigned char fillmap[8];

/* Typedef for palette entry definition */
typedef struct
{
    unsigned short color;
    unsigned short style;
    fillmap        fill;
    char           plotchar;
} paletteentry;

/* Typedef for palette definition */
typedef paletteentry palettetype[_PG_PALETTELEN];
```

Do not confuse the presentation graphics palettes with the adapter display palettes, which are register values kept by the video controller. The function **_selectpalette** described in Chapter 10, "Communicating with Graphics," sets the display palette. It does not define the data series palettes used by presentation graphics.

11.4.1 *Color Pool*

The color pool determines the colors of graphic elements (axes, labels, legends, titles).

Presentation graphics organizes all chart colors into a "color pool." The color pool holds the color index values valid for the current graphics mode. (Refer to Chapter 10, "Communicating with Graphics," for more information about the color index.) Palette structures contain color codes that refer to the color pool. A palette's color index determines the colors used to graph the data series associated with the palette. The colors of labels, titles, legends, and axes are determined by the contents of the color pool.

The first element of the color pool is always 0, which is the color index for the screen background color. The second element is always the highest color index available for the graphics mode. The remaining elements repeat the sequences of available pixel values, beginning with 1.

As shown in the example in Section 11.4, the first member of a palette data structure is

```
unsigned short color;
```

This member defines the color index for the data series associated with the palette.

An example should make this clearer. A graphics mode of **_MRES4COLOR** (320 by 200 pixels) provides four colors for display. Color index values from 0 to 3 determine the possible colors—say, black, green, red, and brown, respectively. The first eight elements of this color pool are shown below.

Color Pool Index	Color Index	Color
0	0	Black
1	3	Brown
2	1	Green
3	2	Red
4	3	Brown
5	1	Green
6	2	Red
7	3	Brown

Notice that the sequence of available foreground colors repeats from the third element. The first data series in this case would be plotted in brown, the second series in green, the third series in red, the fourth series again in brown, and so forth.

Video adapters such as the EGA or the Hercules® InColor™ Card allow 16 on-screen colors. This allows presentation graphics to graph more series without duplicating colors.

11.4.2 Style Pool

Presentation graphics matches the color pool with a collection of different line styles called the "style pool." Entries in the style pool define the appearance of lines such as axes and grids. Lines can be solid, dotted, dashed, or some combination of styles.

The second member of a palette structure defines a style code as

```
unsigned short style;
```

Each palette contains a style code that refers to an entry in the style pool in the same way that it contains a color code that refers to an entry in the color pool. The style code value in a palette is applicable only to line graphs and lined scatter diagrams. The style code determines the appearance of the lines drawn between points.

Use the different line styles in the style pool to differentiate series.

The palette's style code adds further variety to the lines of a multiseries graph. It is most useful when the number of lines in a chart exceeds the number of available colors. For example, a graph of nine different data series must repeat colors if only three foreground colors are available for the display. However, the style code for each color repetition will be different, ensuring that none of the lines looks the same.

11.4.3 *Pattern Pool*

Presentation graphics also maintains a pool of "fill patterns" that determine the fill design for column, bar, and pie charts. The third member of the palette structure holds the fill pattern. The pattern member is an array:

```
fillmap fill;
```

where `fillmap` is type-defined as

```
typedef unsigned char fillmap[8];
```

Each fill pattern array holds an 8-by-8 bit map that defines the fill pattern for the data series associated with the palette. Table 11.3 shows how a fill pattern of diagonal stripes is created with the `fill` pattern array.

The bit map in Table 11.3 corresponds to screen pixels. Each of the eight layers of the map is a binary number, where a solid circle signifies 1 and an open circle signifies 0. Thus the first layer of the map—that is, the first byte—represents the binary number 10011001, which is the decimal number 153.

Table 11.3   Fill Patterns

Bit Map	Value in Fill
● ○ ○ ● ● ○ ○ ●	`fill[0]` = 153
● ● ○ ○ ● ● ○ ○	`fill[1]` = 204
○ ● ● ○ ○ ● ● ○	`fill[2]` = 102
○ ○ ● ● ○ ○ ● ●	`fill[3]` = 51
● ○ ○ ● ● ○ ○ ●	`fill[4]` = 153
● ● ○ ○ ● ● ○ ○	`fill[5]` = 204
○ ● ● ○ ○ ● ● ○	`fill[6]` = 102
○ ○ ● ● ○ ○ ● ●	`fill[7]` = 51

For example, if you want to create the pattern in Table 11.3 for your chart's first data series, you must reset the fill array for the first palette structure. You can do this in five steps:

1. Declare a structure of type **palettetype** to hold the palette parameters.

2. Call **_pg_initchart** to initialize the palettes with default values.

3. Call the presentation graphics function **_pg_getpalette** to retrieve a copy of the current palette data.

4. Assign the values given in Table 11.3 to the array fill for the first palette.

5. Call the presentation graphics function **_pg_setpalette** to load the modified palette values.

The following lines of code demonstrate these five steps:

```
/* Declare a structure array for palette data. */

palettetype palette_struct;
.
.
.
/* Initialize chart library */

_pg_initchart();
.
.
.
/* Copy current palette data into palette_struct */

_pg_getpalette( palette_struct );

/* Reinitialize fill pattern for first palette using
   values in Table 11.3 */

palette_struct[1].fill[0] = 153;
palette_struct[1].fill[1] = 204;
palette_struct[1].fill[2] = 102;
palette_struct[1].fill[3] =  51;
palette_struct[1].fill[4] = 153;
palette_struct[1].fill[5] = 204;
palette_struct[1].fill[6] = 102;
palette_struct[1].fill[7] =  51;

/* Load new palette data */

_pg_setpalette( palette_struct );
```

Now when you display your bar or column chart, the first series appears filled with the striped pattern shown in Table 11.3.

Palette structures are used differently with pie charts. Instead of clarifying multiple series, fill patterns, line styles, and colors, palette structures are used to distinguish individual slices in a pie chart. Palettes are recycled if the number of slices exceeds **_PG_PALETTELEN**. Thus, the first palette dictates not only the appearance of the first slice, but of slice number **_PG_PALETTELEN** as well. The second palette determines the appearance of both the second slice and of slice number **_PG_PALETTELEN** + 1, and so forth.

11.4.4 Character Pool

The last member of a palette structure is an index number in a pool of ASCII characters:

```
char plotchar;
```

The member **plotchar** represents plot points on line graphs and scatter diagrams. Each palette uses a different character to distinguish plot points between data series.

11.5 Customizing the Chart Environment

The presentation graphics functions are designed to be flexible. You can use the system of default values to produce professional-looking charts with a minimum of programming effort. Or you can fine-tune the appearance of your charts by overriding default values and initializing variables explicitly in your program.

The header file PGCHART.H defines a structure type **chartenv**, which organizes the chart environment variables. The chart environment describes everything about a chart except the plots themselves. It is the blank page, in other words, ready for plotting data. The environment determines the appearance of text, axes, grid lines, and legends.

Colors and line styles in the chart environment are taken from palettes. In this way, the appearance of titles and axis lines matches the colors and line styles of plotted data series.

You can reset any variable in the environment.

Calling the **_pg_defaultchart** function fills the chart environment with default values. Presentation graphics allows you to reset any variable in the environment before displaying a chart. Except for adjusting the palette values, all initialization of data is done through a **chartenv** type structure.

The sample chart programs provided in Section 11.3, "Writing a Presentation Graphics Program," illustrate how to adjust variables in the chart environment. These programs create a structure `env` of type **chartenv**. The structure `env` contains the chart environment variables, initialized by the call to the **_pg_defaultchart** function. Environment variables such as the chart title are then given specific values, as in

```
strcpy( env.maintitle.title, "Good Neighbor Grocery" );
```

Environment variables that determine colors and line styles deserve special mention. The chart environment holds several such variables, which can be recognized by their names. For example, the variable **titlecolor** specifies the color of title text. Similarly, the variable **gridstyle** specifies the line style used to draw the chart grid.

These variables are index numbers, but do not refer directly to the color pool or line pool. They correspond instead to palette numbers. If you set **titlecolor** to 2, presentation graphics uses the color code in the second palette to determine the title's color. Thus, the title in this case would be the same color as the chart's second data series. If you change the color code in the palette, you'll also change the title's color.

A structure of type **chartenv** consists of four types of secondary structures. The file PGCHART.H type-defines these secondary structures: **titletype**, **axistype**, **windowtype**, and **legendtype**.

The remainder of this section describes the chart environment of presentation graphics. It first examines structures of the four secondary structures that make up the chart environment structure. The section concludes with a description of the **chartenv** structure type. Each section begins with a brief explanation of the structure's purpose, followed by a listing of the structure type definition as it appears in the PGCHART.H file. All symbolic constants are defined in the file PGCHART.H.

11.5.1 *titletype Structures*

Structures of type **titletype** determine text, color, and placement of titles appearing in the graph. The PGCHART.H file defines the structure type as

```
typedef struct
{
   char     title[_PG_TITLELEN];   /* Title text */
   short    titlecolor;            /* Palette color
                                      for title text */
   short    justify;               /* _PG_LEFT, _PG_CENTER,
                                      _PG_RIGHT */
} titletype;
```

The following list describes **titletype** members:

Member Variable	Description
justify	An integer specifying how the title is justified within the chart window. The symbolic constants defined in PGCHART.H for this variable are **_PG_LEFT**, **_PG_CENTER**, and **_PG_RIGHT**.
titlecolor	An integer between 1 and **_PG_PALETTELEN** that specifies a title's color. The default value for *titlecolor* is 1.
title[**_PG_TITLELEN**]	A character array containing title text. For example, if env is a structure of type **chartenv**, then env.maintitle.title holds the character string used for the main title of the chart. Similarly, env.xaxis.axistitle.title contains the *x* axis title. The number of characters in a title must be one less than **_PG_TITLELEN** to allow room for a null terminator.

11.5.2 axistype Structures

Structures of type **axistype** contain variables for the axes such as color, scale, grid style, and tick marks. The PGCHART.H file defines the structure type as the following:

```
typedef struct
{
    short       grid;           /* TRUE=grid lines drawn;
                                   FALSE=no lines */
    short       gridstyle;      /* Style bytes for grid */
    titletype   axistitle;      /* Title definition
                                   for axis */
    short       axiscolor;      /* Color for axis */
    short       labeled;        /* TRUE=ticks marks and titles
                                   drawn */
    short       rangetype;      /* _PG_LINEARAXIS,
                                   _PG_LOGAXIS */
    float       logbase;        /* Base used if log axis */
    short       autoscale;      /* TRUE=next 7 values
                                   calculated by system */
    float       scalemin;       /* Minimum value of scale */
    float       scalemax;       /* Maximum value of scale */
    float       scalefactor;    /* Scale factor for data on
                                   this axis */
    titletype   scaletitle;     /* Title definition for
                                   scaling factor */
    float       ticinterval;    /* Distance between tick marks
                                   (world coord.) */
    short       ticformat;      /* _PG_EXPFORMAT or
                                   _PG_DECFORMAT */
    short       ticdecimals;    /* Number of decimals for tick
                                   labels (max=9) */
} axistype;
```

The following list describes **axistype** member variables:

Member Variable	Description
autoscale	A Boolean variable. If *autoscale* is set to **TRUE**, presentation graphics automatically determines values for *scalefactor*, *scalemax*, *scalemin*, *scaletitle*, *ticdecimals*, *ticformat*, and *ticinterval* (see below). If *autoscale* equals **FALSE**, these seven variables must be specified in your program.
axiscolor	An integer between 1 and **_PG_PALETTELEN** that specifies the color used for the axis and parallel grid lines. (See description for *gridstyle* below.) Note that this member does not determine the color of the axis title. That selection is made through the **axistitle** structure.
axistitle	A **titletype** structure that defines the title of the associated axis. The title of the *y* axis displays vertically to the left of the *y* axis, and the title of the *x* axis displays horizontally below the *x* axis.
grid	A Boolean true/false value that determines whether grid lines are drawn for the associated axis. Grid lines span the data window perpendicular to the axis.
gridstyle	An integer between 1 and **_PG_PALETTELEN** that specifies the grid's line style. Lines can be solid, dashed, dotted, or some combination. The default value for *gridstyle* is 1. Note that the color of the parallel axis determines the color of the grid lines. Thus, the *x* axis grid is the same color as the *y* axis, and the *y* axis grid is the same color as the *x* axis.
labeled	A Boolean value that determines whether tick marks and labels are drawn on the axis. Axis labels should not be confused with axis titles. Axis labels are numbers or descriptions such as "23.2" or "January" attached to each tick mark.
logbase	If *rangetype* is logarithmic, the *logbase* variable determines the log base used to scale the axis. The default value is 10.
rangetype	An integer that determines whether the scale of the axis is linear or logarithmic. The variable *rangetype* applies only to value data.

Specify a linear scale with **_PG_LINEARAXIS**. A linear scale is best when the difference between axis minimum and maximum is relatively small. For example, a linear axis range 0 – 10 results in 10 tick marks evenly spaced along the axis.

Use **_PG_LOGAXIS** to specify a logarithmic *rangetype*. Logarithmic scales are useful when the range is very large or when the data varies exponentially. Line graphs of exponentially varying data can be made straight with a logarithmic *rangetype*.

scalefactor

All numeric data are scaled by dividing each value by *scalefactor*. For relatively small values, *scalefactor* should be 1, which is the default. But data with large values should be scaled by an appropriate factor. For example, data in the range 2 million – 20 million should be plotted with *scalemin* set to 2, *scalemax* set to 20, and *scalefactor* set to 1 million.

If *autoscale* is set to **TRUE**, presentation graphics automatically determines a suitable value for *scalefactor* based on the range of data to be plotted. Presentation graphics selects only values that are a factor of 1 thousand—that is, values such as 1 thousand, 1 million, or 1 billion. It then labels the *scaletitle* appropriately (see below). If you desire some other value for scaling, you must set *autoscale* to **FALSE** and set *scalefactor* to the desired scaling value.

scalemax

Highest value represented by the axis.

scalemin

Lowest value represented by the axis.

scaletitle

A **titletype** structure defining a string of text that describes the value of *scalefactor*. If *autoscale* is **TRUE**, presentation graphics automatically writes a scale description to *scaletitle*. If *autoscale* equals **FALSE** and *scalefactor* is 1, *scaletitle.title* should be blank. Otherwise your program should copy an appropriate scale description to *scaletitle.title*, such as "(× 1000)," "(in millions of units)," or "times 10 thousand dollars."

For the *y* axis, the *scaletitle* text displays vertically between the axis title and the *y* axis. For the *x* axis, the scale title appears below the *x* axis title.

ticdecimals	Number of digits to display after the decimal point in tick labels. Maximum value is 9. (This variable applies only to axes with value data and is ignored for the category axis.)
ticformat	An integer that determines format of the labels assigned to each tick mark. Set *ticformat* to **_PG_EXPFORMAT** for exponential format or to **_PG_DECFORMAT** for decimal. The default is **_PG_DECFORMAT**. (This variable applies only to axes with value data and is ignored for the category axis.)
ticinterval	Sets interval between tick marks on the axis. The tick interval is measured in the same units as the numeric data associated with the axis. For example, if 2 sequential tick marks correspond to the values 20 and 25, the tick interval between them is 5. (This variable applies only to axes with value data and is ignored for the category axis.)

11.5.3 *windowtype Structures*

Structures of type **windowtype** contain sizes, locations, and color codes for the three windows produced by presentation graphics: the chart window, the data window, and the legend. Windows are located on the screen relative to the screen's logical origin. By changing the logical origin, you can display charts that are partly or completely off the screen.

The PGCHART.H file defines **windowtype** as the following:

```
typedef struct
{
    short   x1;              /* Left edge of window in
                               pixels */
    short   y1;              /* Top edge of window in
                               pixels */
    short   x2;              /* Right edge of window in
                               pixels */
    short   y2;              /* Bottom edge of window in
                               pixels */
    short   border;         /* TRUE for border, FALSE
                               otherwise */
    short   background;     /* Internal palette color for
                               window background */
    short   borderstyle;    /* Style bytes for window
                               border */
    short   bordercolor;    /* Internal palette color for
                               window border */
} windowtype;
```

The following list describes **windowtype** member variables:

Member Variable	Description
background	An integer between 1 and **_PG_PALETTELEN** that specifies the window's background color. The default value for *background* is 1.
border	A Boolean variable that determines whether a border frame is drawn around a window.
bordercolor	An integer between 1 and **_PG_PALETTELEN** that specifies the color of the window's border frame. The default value is 1.
borderstyle	An integer between 1 and **_PG_PALETTELEN** that specifies the line style of the window's border frame. The default value is 1.
x1, y1, x2, y2	Window coordinates in pixels. The ordered pair (*x1*, *y1*) specifies the coordinate of the upper left corner of the window. The ordered pair (*x2*, *y2*) specifies the coordinate of the lower right corner.
	The reference point for the coordinates depends on the type of window. The chart window is located relative to the logical origin, usually the upper left corner of the screen. The data and legend windows are located relative to the upper left corner of the chart window. This allows you to change the position of the chart window without having to redefine coordinates for the other two windows.

11.5.4 *legendtype Structures*

Structures of type **legendtype** contain size, location, and colors of the chart legend. The PGCHART.H file defines the structure type as the following:

```
typedef struct
{
    short        legend;           /* TRUE=draw legend;
                                      FALSE=no legend */
    short        place;            /* _PG_RIGHT, _PG_BOTTOM,
                                      _PG_OVERLAY */
    short        textcolor;        /* Palette color for text*/
    short        autosize;         /* TRUE=system calculates
                                      legend size */
    windowtype legendwindow;       /* Window definition for
                                      legend */
} legendtype;
```

The following list describes **legendtype** member variables:

Member Variable	Description
autosize	A Boolean true/false variable that determines whether presentation graphics is to automatically calculate the size of the legend. If *autosize* equals **FALSE**, the legend window must be specified in the *legendwindow* structure (see below).
legend	A Boolean true/false variable that determines whether a legend is to appear on the chart. The *legend* variable is ignored by functions that graph single-series charts.
legendwindow	A **windowtype** structure that defines coordinates, background color, and border frame for the legend. Coordinates given in *legendwindow* are ignored if *autosize* is set to **TRUE**.
place	An integer that specifies the location of the legend relative to the data window. Setting *place* equal to the constant **_PG_RIGHT** positions the legend to the right of the data window. Setting *place* to **_PG_BOTTOM** positions the legend below the data window. Setting *place* to **_PG_OVERLAY** positions the legend within the data window.
	These settings influence the size of the data window. If *place* equals **_PG_RIGHT** or **_PG_BOTTOM**, presentation graphics automatically sizes the data window to accommodate the legend. If *place* equals **_PG_OVERLAY**, the data window is sized without regard to the legend.
textcolor	An integer between 1 and **_PG_PALETTELEN** that specifies the color of text within the legend window.

11.5.5 chartenv Structures

A structure of type **chartenv** defines the chart environment. The following listing shows that a **chartenv** type structure consists almost entirely of structures of the four types described above.

The PGCHART.H file defines the **chartenv** structure type as the following:

```
typedef struct
{
    short        charttype;        /* Chart type */
    short        chartstyle;       /* Chart style */
    windowtype   chartwindow;      /* Window definition for
                                      overall chart */
    windowtype   datawindow;       /* Window definition for data
                                      part of chart */
    titletype    maintitle;        /* Main chart title */
    titletype    subtitle;         /* Chart subtitle */
    axistype     xaxis;            /* Definition for x axis */
    axistype     yaxis;            /* Definition for y axis */
    legendtype   legend;           /* Definition for legend */
} chartenv;
```

Initialize the chart environment with the _pg_defaultchart function. The data in a **chartenv** type structure is initialized by calling the function **_pg_defaultchart**. If your program does not call **_pg_defaultchart**, it must explicitly define every variable in the chart environment—a tedious procedure. The recommended method for adjusting the appearance of your chart is to initialize variables for the proper chart type by calling the **_pg_defaultchart** function, and then to reassign selected environment variables such as titles.

The following list describes **chartenv** member variables:

Member Variable	Description
chartstyle	An integer that determines the style of the chart (see Table 11.2). Legal values for *chartstyle* are **_PG_PERCENT** and **_PG_NOPERCENT** for pie charts; **_PG_PLAINBARS** and **_PG_STACKEDBARS** for bar and column charts; and **_PG_POINTONLY** and **_PG_POINTANDLINE** for line graphs and scatter diagrams. This variable corresponds to the third argument for the **_pg_defaultchart** function.
charttype	An integer that determines the type of chart displayed. The value of *charttype* is **_PG_BARCHART**, **_PG_COLUMNCHART**, **_PG_LINECHART**, **_PG_SCATTERCHART**, or **_PG_PIECHART**. This variable corresponds to the second argument for the **_pg_defaultchart** function.
chartwindow	A **windowtype** structure that defines the appearance of the chart window.
datawindow	A **windowtype** structure that defines the appearance of the data window.

legend	A **legendtype** structure that defines the appearance of the legend window.
maintitle	A **titletype** structure that defines the appearance of the main title of the chart.
subtitle	A **titletype** structure that defines the appearance of the chart's subtitle.
xaxis	An **axistype** structure that defines the appearance of the x axis. (This variable is not applicable for pie charts.)
yaxis	An **axistype** structure that defines the appearance of the y axis. (This variable is not applicable for pie charts.)

Programming with Mixed Languages

There are times when your Microsoft C programs need to call programs written in other languages or when programs written in other languages need to call your C functions. This is called mixed-language programming. For example, when a particular subprogram is available commercially in a language other than C or when algorithms are described more naturally in a different language, you need to use more than one language.

This chapter describes the elements of mixed-language programming—how to make calls from programs written in one language to routines written in another.

12.1 Making Mixed-Language Calls

Mixed-language programming always involves a call to a function, procedure, or subroutine. For example, a BASIC main module may need to execute a specific task that you would like to program separately. Instead of calling a BASIC subprogram, however, you decide to call a C function.

Mixed-language calls involve calling functions in separate modules. Instead of compiling all of your source modules with the same compiler, you use different compilers. In the instance mentioned above, you would compile the main-module source file with the BASIC compiler, another source file (written in C) with the C compiler, and then link the two object files.

Figure 12.1 illustrates how the syntax of a mixed-language call works, using the instance mentioned above.

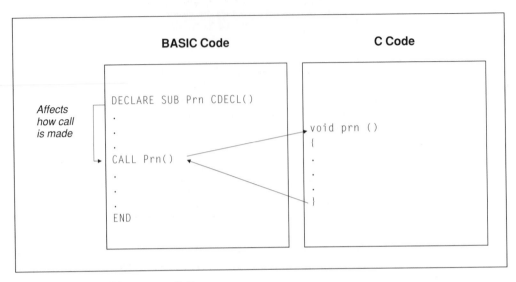

Figure 12.1 Mixed-Language Call

In Figure 12.1, the BASIC call to C is `CALL Prn`, similar to a call to a BASIC subprogram. There are two differences between this mixed-language call and a call between two BASIC modules:

1. The subprogram `Prn` is implemented in C, using standard C syntax.

2. The implementation of the call in BASIC is affected by the **DECLARE** statement, which uses the **CDECL** keyword to create compatibility with C. The **DECLARE** statement (which is described in detail in the *Microsoft BASIC Language Reference* and the *Microsoft BASIC Programmer's Guide*) is an example of a mixed-language "interface" statement. These interface statements override default naming and calling conventions. Each language provides its own form of interface.

You can make mixed-language calls to routines regardless of whether they have return values. (In this chapter, "routine" refers to any function, procedure, or subroutine that can be called from another module.)

Table 12.1 shows the correspondence between calls to routines in different languages.

Table 12.1   Language Equivalents for Routine Calls

Language	Return Value	No Return Value
Assembly Language	Procedure	Procedure
BASIC	FUNCTION procedure	Subprogram
C	function	(**void**) function
FORTRAN	FUNCTION	SUBROUTINE
Pascal	Function	Procedure

For example, a C module can make a subprogram call to a FORTRAN subroutine. You can prototype a FORTRAN subroutine as a function with a **void** type.

NOTE   *BASIC **DEF FN** functions and **GOSUB** subroutines cannot be called from another language.*

12.2 *Language Convention Requirements*

To mix languages, the calling program must observe the same conventions as the called program. The conventions described in this section govern the following:

- How compilers treat identifiers, including function and variable names (naming convention)

- How the subprogram call is implemented (calling convention)

- How parameters are passed (parameter-passing convention)

12.2.1 *Naming Convention Requirement*

Both the calling program and the called subprogram must agree on the names of identifiers. Identifiers can refer to subprograms (functions, procedures, and subroutines) or to variables that have a public or global scope. Each language alters the names of identifiers.

The term "naming convention" refers to the way a compiler alters the name of the routine before placing it in an object file. Languages may alter the identifier names differently. You can choose between several naming conventions to ensure that the names in the calling program agree with those in the called program. If the names of called routines are stored differently in each object file, the linker will not be able to find a match. It will instead report unresolved external references.

Microsoft compilers place machine code into object files; they also place the names of all publicly accessed routines and variables in object files. The linker can then compare the name of a routine called in one module with the name of a routine defined in another module, and recognize a match. Names are stored in the ASCII (American Standard Code for Information Interchange) character set.

Some languages translate names to uppercase. BASIC, FORTRAN, and Pascal use similar naming conventions. They translate each letter to uppercase. BASIC type declaration characters (%, &, !, #, $) are dropped.

Each language recognizes a different number of characters. FORTRAN recognizes the first 31 characters of any name (unless identifier names are truncated), Pascal the first 8, and BASIC the first 40. If a name is longer than the language will recognize, additional characters are simply not placed in the object file.

NOTE *Versions of Microsoft FORTRAN previous to version 5.0 truncated identifiers to six characters. As of version 5.0, FORTRAN retains up to 31 characters of significance unless you use the /4Yt option.*

C is a case-sensitive language. The C compiler does not translate any letters to uppercase. It inserts a leading underscore (_) in front of the name of each routine. C recognizes the first 31 characters of a name.

Differences in naming conventions are dealt with automatically by mixed-language keywords, as long as you follow two rules:

1. If you use any FORTRAN routines that were compiled with the /4Yt command-line option or with the **$TRUNCATE** metacommand enabled, make all names 6 characters or less. Make all names 6 characters or less when using FORTRAN routines compiled with versions of the FORTRAN compiler prior to 5.0.

2. Do not use the /NOIGNORECASE linker option (which causes the linker to treat identifiers in a case-sensitive manner). With C modules, this means that you must be careful not to rely upon differences between uppercase and lowercase letters when programming.

   CL automatically uses the /NOIGNORECASE option when linking. To solve the problems created by this behavior, either link separately with the LINK utility, or use all lowercase letters in your C function names and public variables (global variables that are not declared as static).

NOTE   *If you use the command-line option /Gc (generate Pascal-style function calls) when you compile, or if you declare a function or variable with the **_pascal** keyword, the compiler will translate your identifiers to uppercase.*

Figure 12.2 illustrates a complete mixed-language development example, showing how naming conventions enter into the process.

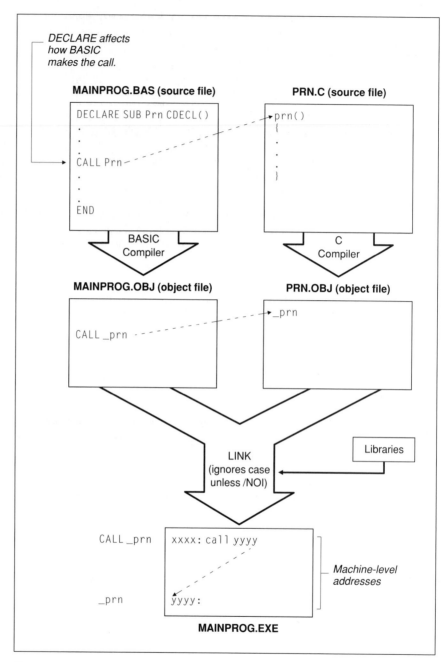

Figure 12.2 Naming Convention

In Figure 12.2, note that the BASIC compiler inserts a leading underscore in front of `Prn` as it places the name into the object file, because the **CDECL** keyword directs the BASIC compiler to use the C naming convention. BASIC will also convert all letters to lowercase when this keyword is used. (Converting letters to lowercase is not part of the C naming convention; however, it is consistent with the programming style of many C programs.)

12.2.2 *Calling Convention Requirement*

The term "calling convention" refers to the way a language implements a call. The choice of calling convention affects the machine instructions that a compiler generates to execute (and return from) a function, procedure, or subroutine call.

It is crucial that the two routines concerned (the routine issuing a call and the routine being called) use the same protocol. Otherwise, the processor may receive inconsistent instructions, causing the program to behave incorrectly.

The use of a calling convention affects programming in three ways:

1. The calling routine uses a calling convention to determine the order in which to pass arguments (parameters) to another routine. This convention can be specified in a mixed-language interface statement or declaration.

2. The called routine uses a calling convention to determine the order in which to receive the parameters passed to it. In most languages, this convention can be specified in the routine's heading. BASIC, however, always uses its own convention to receive parameters.

3. Both the calling routine and the called routine must agree on which of them is responsible for adjusting the stack after all parameters are removed.

In other words, each call to a routine uses a certain calling convention; each routine heading specifies or assumes some calling convention. The two conventions must be compatible. With all languages except BASIC, it is possible to change the calling convention at the point of the call or at the declaration of the called routine. Usually, however, it is easier to adopt the convention of the called routine. For example, a C function would use its own convention to call another C function, and would use the Pascal convention to call Pascal.

BASIC, FORTRAN, and Pascal use the same standard calling convention. C uses a different convention.

Effects of Calling Conventions

Calling conventions dictate three things:

1. The way parameters are communicated from one routine to another (in Microsoft mixed-language programming, parameters or pointers to the parameters are passed on the stack)

2. The order in which parameters are passed from one routine to another

3. The part of the program responsible for adjusting the stack

Some languages pass parameters in a different order than C. The BASIC, FORTRAN and Pascal calling conventions push parameters onto the stack in the order in which they appear in the source code. For example, the BASIC statement

```
CALL Calc( A, B )
```

pushes argument A onto the stack before it pushes B. These conventions also specify that the stack is adjusted by the called routine just before returning control to the caller.

The C calling convention pushes parameters onto the stack in the reverse order from their appearance in the source code. For example, the C function call

```
calc( a, b );
```

pushes b onto the stack before it pushes a. In contrast with the other high-level languages, the C calling convention specifies that a calling routine always adjusts the stack immediately after the called routine returns control.

The BASIC, FORTRAN, and Pascal conventions produce slightly less object code. However, the C convention makes calling with a variable number of parameters possible. (Because the first parameter is always the last one pushed, it is always on the top of the stack; therefore it has the same address relative to the frame pointer, regardless of how many parameters were actually passed.)

NOTE *The __fastcall__ keyword, which specifies that parameters are to be passed in registers, is incompatible with programs written in other languages. Avoid using __fastcall__ or the /Gr command-line option for C functions that you intend to make public to BASIC, FORTRAN, or Pascal programs.*

12.2.3 *Parameter-Passing Requirement*

Your programs must agree on the calling convention and the naming convention; they must also agree on the order in which they pass parameters. It is important that your routines send parameters in the same way to ensure proper data transmission and correct program results.

Microsoft compilers support three methods for passing a parameter:

Method	Description
Near reference	Passes a variable's near (offset) address. This address is expressed as an offset from the default data segment.
	This method gives the called routine direct access to the variable itself. Any change the routine makes to the parameter changes the variable in the calling routine.
Far reference	Passes a variable's far (segmented) address.
	This method is similar to passing by near reference, except that a longer address is passed. This method is slower than passing by near reference, but is necessary when you pass data that is outside the default data segment. (This is an issue in BASIC or Pascal only if you have specifically requested far memory.)
Value	Passes only the variable's value, not its address.
	With this method, the called routine knows the value of the parameter but has no access to the original variable. Changes to a value passed by a parameter have no affect on the value of the parameter in the calling routine.

These different parameter-passing methods mean that you must consider the following when programming with mixed languages:

- You need to make sure that the called routine and the calling routine use the same method for passing each parameter (argument). In most cases, you will need to check the parameter-passing defaults used by each language and possibly make adjustments. Each language has keywords or language features that allow you to change parameter-passing methods.

- You may want to choose a specific parameter-passing method rather than using the defaults of any language.

Table 12.2 summarizes the parameter-passing defaults for each language.

Table 12.2   Parameter-Passing Defaults

Language	Near Reference	Far Reference	By Value
BASIC	All	---	---
C	Near arrays	Far arrays	All data except arrays
FORTRAN	All (medium model)	All (large model)	With attributes[1]
Pascal	**VAR, CONST**	**VARS, CONSTS**	Other parameters

[1] When a PASCAL or C attribute is applied to a FORTRAN routine, passing by value becomes the default.

12.3 Compiling and Linking

After you have written your source files and decided on a naming convention, a calling convention, and a parameter-passing convention, you are ready to compile and link individual modules.

12.3.1 Compiling with Correct Memory Models

With BASIC, FORTRAN, and Pascal, no special options are required to compile source files that are part of a mixed-language program.

With C, not all memory models are compatible with other languages.

BASIC, FORTRAN, and Pascal use only far (segmented) code addresses. Therefore, you must use one of two techniques with C programs that call one of these languages: compile C modules in medium, large, or huge model (using the /A*X* command-line options), because these models also use far code addresses; or apply the **_far** keyword to the definitions of C functions you make public. If you use the /A*X* command-line option to specify medium, large, or huge model, all your function calls become far by default. This means you don't have to declare your functions explicitly with the **_far** keyword.

Choice of memory model affects the default data pointer size in C and FORTRAN, although this default can be overridden with the **_near** and **_far** keywords. With C and FORTRAN, choice of memory model also affects whether data objects are located in the default data segment; if a data object is not located in the default data segment, it cannot be passed by near reference.

For more information about code and data address sizes in C, refer to Chapter 2, "Managing Memory."

12.3.2 Linking with Language Libraries

In most cases, you can easily link modules compiled with different languages. Do any of the following to ensure that all required libraries link in the correct order:

- Put all language libraries in the same directory as the source files.

- List directories containing all needed libraries in the LIB environment variable.

- Let the linker prompt you for libraries.

In each of the cases above, the linker finds libraries in the order that it requires them. If you enter the library names on the command line, make sure you enter them in an order that allows the linker to resolve your program's external references. Here are some points to observe when specifying libraries on the command line:

- If you are using FORTRAN to write one of your modules, you need to link with the /NOD (no default libraries) option and explicitly specify all the libraries you need on the link command line. You can also specify these libraries with an automatic-response file (or batch file), but you cannot use a default-library search.

- If your program uses both FORTRAN and C, specify the library for the most recent of the two language products first. In addition, make sure that you choose a C-compatible library when you install FORTRAN.

- If you are listing BASIC libraries on the LINK command line, specify those libraries first.

The following example shows how to link two modules, `mod1` and `mod2`, with a user library, GRAFX, the C run-time library, LLIBCE, and the FORTRAN run-time library, LLIBFORE:

```
LINK /NOD mod1 mod2,,,GRAFX+LLIBCE+LLIBFORE
```

12.4 C Calls to High-Level Languages

Just as you can call Microsoft C routines from other Microsoft languages, you can call routines written in Microsoft FORTRAN and Pascal from C. With FORTRAN, Pascal, and C, freestanding routines can be written with no restriction. When calling BASIC routines, however, you must write the main program in BASIC; any subprograms are free to call one another, whether they are written in C or BASIC.

For information about how to pass particular kinds of data, see Section 12.9, "Handling Data in Mixed-Language Programming."

Executing a Mixed-Language Call

The C interface to other languages uses standard C prototypes, with the **_fortran** or **_pascal** keyword. Using either of these keywords causes the routine to be called with the FORTRAN/Pascal naming and calling convention. (The FORTRAN/Pascal convention also works for BASIC.) Here are the recommended steps for executing a mixed-language call from C:

1. Write a prototype for each mixed-language routine called. The prototype should declare the routine **extern** for the purpose of program documentation.

   Instead of using the **_fortran** or **_pascal** keyword, you can simply compile with the Pascal calling convention option (/Gc). The /Gc option causes all functions in the module to use the FORTRAN/Pascal naming and calling conventions, except where you apply the **_cdecl** keyword.

2. Pass the values of variables or pointers to variables. You can obtain a pointer to a variable with the address-of (**&**) operator.

   In C, array names are always passed as pointers to the first element of the array; they are always passed by reference.

   The prototype you declare for your function ensures that you are passing the correct length address (that is, near or far).

3. Issue a function call in your program as though you were calling a C function.

4. Always compile the C module in either medium, large, or huge model, or use the **_far** keyword in your function prototype. This ensures that a far (intersegment) call is made to the routine.

Using the _fortran or _pascal Keyword

There are two rules of syntax that apply when you use the **_fortran** or **_pascal** keyword:

1. The **_fortran** and **_pascal** keywords modify only the item immediately to their right.

2. The **_near** and **_far** keywords can be used with the **_fortran** and **_pascal** keywords in prototypes. The sequences **_fortran _far** and **_far _fortran** are equivalent.

The keywords **_pascal** and **_fortran** have the same effect on the program; using one or the other makes no difference except for internal program documentation. Use **_fortran** to declare a FORTRAN routine, **_pascal** to declare a Pascal routine, and either keyword to declare a BASIC routine.

The following examples demonstrate the syntax rules presented above.

The example below declares **func** to be a BASIC, Pascal, or FORTRAN function taking two **short** parameters and returning a **short** value.

```
short _pascal func( short sarg1, short sarg2 );
```

The example below declares **func** to be pointer to a BASIC, Pascal, or FORTRAN routine that takes a **long** parameter and returns no value. The keyword **void** is appropriate when the called routine is a BASIC subprogram, Pascal procedure, or FORTRAN subroutine, since it indicates that the function returns no value.

```
void ( _fortran * func )( long larg );
```

The example below declares **func** to be a **_near** BASIC, Pascal, or FORTRAN routine. The routine receives a **double** parameter by reference (because it expects a pointer to a **double**) and returns a **short** value.

```
short _near _pascal func( _near double * darg );
```

The example below is equivalent to the preceding example (**_pascal _near** is equivalent to **_near _pascal**).

```
short _pascal _near func( _near double * darg );
```

You can make C adopt the conventions of other languages.

When you call a BASIC subprogram, you must use the FORTRAN/Pascal conventions to make the call. When you call FORTRAN or Pascal, however, you have a choice. You can make C adopt the conventions described in the previous section, or you can make the FORTRAN or Pascal routine adopt the C conventions.

To make a FORTRAN or Pascal routine adopt the C conventions, put the **C** attribute in the heading of the routine's definition. The following example shows the syntax for the **C** attribute in a FORTRAN subroutine-definition heading:

```
SUBROUTINE FFROMC [C] (N)
INTEGER*2 N
```

The following example shows the syntax for the **C** attribute in a Pascal procedure-definition heading:

```
PROCEDURE Pfromc( n : INTEGER ) [C];
```

To make a C function adopt the FORTRAN/Pascal conventions, declare the function as **_fortran** or **_pascal**. For example,

```
void _pascal CfromP( int n );
```

12.5 C Calls to BASIC

No BASIC routine can be executed unless the main program is in BASIC, because a BASIC routine requires the environment to be initialized in a way that is unique to BASIC. No other language will perform this special initialization.

However, your program can start up in BASIC, call a C function that does most of the work of the program, and then call BASIC subprograms and function procedures as needed. Figure 12.3 illustrates how to do this.

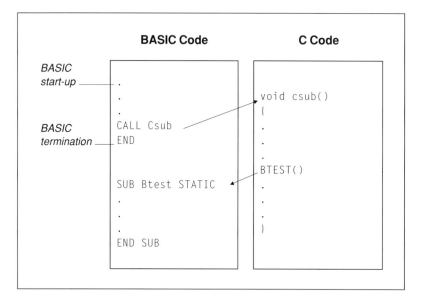

Figure 12.3 C Call to BASIC

Follow these rules when you call BASIC from C:

1. Start up in a BASIC main module. You will need to use the **DECLARE** statement to provide an interface to the C module.

2. In the C module, write a prototype for the BASIC routine and include type information for parameters. Use either the **_fortran** or **_pascal** keyword to modify the routine itself.

3. Make sure that all data are passed as near pointers. BASIC can pass data in a variety of ways but is unable to receive data in any form other than near reference. With near pointers, the program assumes that the data are in the default data segment. If you want to pass data that are not in the default data segment, copy the data to a variable in the default data segment.

4. Compile the C module in medium or large model to ensure far (intersegment) calls.

The example below demonstrates a BASIC program that calls a C function. The C function then calls a BASIC function that returns twice the number passed to it and a BASIC subprogram that prints two numbers.

```
' BASIC source
'
' The main program is in BASIC because of BASIC's start-up
' requirements.  The BASIC main program calls the C function
' Cprog.
'
' Cprog calls the BASIC subroutine Dbl.
'
DEFINT A-Z
DECLARE SUB Cprog CDECL()
CALL Cprog
END
'
FUNCTION Dbl(N) STATIC
    Dbl = N*2
END FUNCTION
'
SUB Printnum(A,B) STATIC
    PRINT "The first number is ";A
    PRINT "The second number is ";B
END SUB


/* C source; compile in medium or large model */

int _fortran dbl( int _near * N );
void _fortran printnum( int _near * A, int _near * B );

void cprog()
{
int a = 5;
int b = 6;

    printf( "%d times 2 is %d\n", a, dbl( &a ) );
    printnum( &a, &b );
}
```

In the previous example, note that the addresses of a and b are passed, since BASIC expects to receive addresses for parameters. This is important because C passes parameters by value unless you use the address-of (**&**) operator to obtain the address, or are passing an array. Also note that the function prototype for printnum declares the parameters as near pointers. The prototype causes the variables to be passed by near reference. If `a` or `b` is declared as **_far**, the C compiler issues a warning that you are converting a far pointer to a near pointer and that a segment was lost in the conversion.

Calling and naming conventions are resolved by the **CDECL** keyword in the BASIC declaration of **Cprog**, and by the **_fortran** keyword in the C declaration of `dbl` and `printnum`.

BASIC can invoke one of your functions as part of the termination procedure.

Versions of QuickBASIC later than 4.0 provide a "user entry point," **B_OnExit**, which can be called directly from C. The **B_OnExit** function enables you to make sure you have performed an orderly termination. The following code shows how to use **B_OnExit**.

```
#include <malloc.h>    /* For declaration of _fmalloc */
#include <stdlib.h>    /* For declaration of onexit_t */

/* The prototype for B_OnExit declares it as a function
 * returning type onexit_t that takes one parameter. The
 * parameter is a far pointer to a function that returns
 * no value.
 */
extern onexit_t _pascal _far B_OnExit( onexit_t );
void TermProc( void );

int * p_IntArray;

void InitProc( void )
{
    /* Allocate far space for 20-integer array */

    p_IntArray = (int *)_fmalloc( 20 * sizeof( int ) );

    /* Log termination routine (TermProc) with BASIC. */

    B_OnExit( TermProc );
}

void TermProc( void )
{
    free( p_IntArray );    /* Release far space allocated */
                           /* previously by InitProc.    */
}
```

12.6 C Calls to FORTRAN

This section shows two examples of C-FORTRAN programs. There are two types of subprogram calls to FORTRAN routines: calls to subroutines and calls to functions. Functions return a value, while subroutines do not. The examples in the next sections illustrate how to handle the difference between function and subroutine calls.

12.6.1 Calling a FORTRAN Subroutine from C

The example below demonstrates a C main module calling a FORTRAN sub-routine, **MAXPARAM**. This subroutine adjusts the lower of two arguments to be equal to the higher argument.

```c
/* C source file - calls FORTRAN subroutine
 * Compile in medium or large model
 */

extern void _fortran maxparam( int _near * I, int _near * J );

/* Declare as void, because there is no return value.
 * FORTRAN keyword causes C to use FORTRAN/Pascal
 * calling and naming conventions.
 * Two integer parameters, passed by near reference.
 */

main()
{
    int a = 5;
    int b = 7;

    printf( "a = %d, b = %d", a, b );
    maxparam( &a, &b );
    printf( "a = %d, b = %d", a, b );
}
```

```fortran
C    FORTRAN source file, subroutine MAXPARAM
C
$NOTRUNCATE

     SUBROUTINE MAXPARAM (I, J)
     INTEGER*2 I [NEAR]
     INTEGER*2 J [NEAR]
C
C    I and J received by near reference,
C    because of NEAR attribute
C
     IF (I .GT. J) THEN
         J = I
     ELSE
         I = J
     ENDIF
     END
```

In the previous example, the C program adopts the naming convention and calling convention of the FORTRAN subroutine. The two programs must agree on whether parameters are to be passed by reference or by value. The following keywords affect how the two programs interface:

- The **_fortran** keyword directs C to call `maxparam` with the FORTRAN/Pascal naming convention (as `MAXPARAM`); **_fortran** also directs C to call `maxparam` with the FORTRAN/Pascal calling convention.

- Since the FORTRAN subroutine `MAXPARAM` may alter the value of either parameter, both parameters must be passed by reference. In this case, near reference was chosen; this method is specified in C by the use of near pointers, and in FORTRAN by applying the **NEAR** keyword to the parameter declarations.

  Far reference could have been specified by using far pointers in C. In that case, you would not declare the FORTRAN subroutine `MAXPARAM` with the **NEAR** keyword. If you compile the FORTRAN program in medium model, declare `MAXPARAM` using the **FAR** keyword.

12.6.2 Calling a FORTRAN Function from C

The example below demonstrates a C main module calling the FORTRAN function `fact`. This function returns the factorial of an integer value.

```
/* C source file - calls FORTRAN function.
 * Compile in medium or large model.
 */

int _fortran fact( int N );

/* FORTRAN keyword causes C to use FORTRAN/Pascal
 * calling and naming conventions.
 * Integer parameter passed by value.
 */

main()
{
        int x = 3;
        int y = 4;

    printf( "The factorial of x   is %4d", fact( x ) );
    printf( "The factorial of y   is %4d", fact( y ) );
    printf( "The factorial of x+y is %4d", fact( x + y ) );
}
```

```
C   FORTRAN source file - factorial function
C
$NOTRUNCATE
    INTEGER*2 FUNCTION FACT (N)
    INTEGER*2 N [VALUE]
C
C   N is received by value, because of VALUE attribute
C
        INTEGER*2 I
        FACT = 1
        DO 100 I = 1, N
            FACT = FACT * I
100     CONTINUE
        RETURN
        END
```

In the example above, the C program adopts the naming convention and calling convention of the FORTRAN subroutine. Both programs must agree on whether parameters are passed by reference or by value. Note that the C program passes the parameters by value rather than by reference. Passing parameters by value is the default for C. To accept parameters passed by value, the keyword **VALUE** is used in the declaration of N in the FORTRAN function. The **_fortran** keyword directs C to call fact with the FORTRAN/Pascal naming convention (as FACT); **_fortran** also directs C to call fact with the FORTRAN/Pascal calling convention.

When passing a parameter that should not be changed, pass the parameter by value. Passing by value is the default method in C and is specified in FORTRAN by applying the **VALUE** attribute to the parameter declaration.

12.7 C Calls to Pascal

This section shows two examples of C-Pascal programs. There are two types of subprogram calls to Pascal routines: calls to procedures and calls to functions. Functions return a value, while procedures do not. The examples in the next sections illustrate how to handle the difference between function and procedure calls.

12.7.1 Calling a Pascal Procedure from C

The following example demonstrates a C main module calling a Pascal procedure, maxparam. This procedure adjusts the lower of two arguments to be equal to the higher argument.

```
/* C source file - calls Pascal procedure.
 * Compile in medium or large model.
 */

void _pascal maxparam( int _near * a, int _near * b );

/* Declare as void, because there is no return value.
 * The _pascal keyword causes C to use FORTRAN/Pascal
 * calling and naming conventions.
 * Two integer params, passed by near reference.
 */

main()
{
    int a = 5;
    int b = 7;

    printf( "a = %d, b = %d", a, b );
    maxparam( &a, &b );
    printf( "a = %d, b = %d", a, b );
}

{ Pascal source code - Maxparam procedure. }

MODULE Psub;
PROCEDURE Maxparam( VAR a:INTEGER; VAR b:INTEGER );

{ Two integer parameters are received by near reference. }
{ Near reference is specified with the VAR keyword. }

    BEGIN
        if a > b THEN
            b := a
        ELSE
            a := b
    END;
END.
```

In the example above, the C program adopts the Pascal naming convention and calling convention. Both programs must agree on whether parameters are passed by reference or by value; the following keywords affect the conventions:

- The **_pascal** keyword directs C to call Maxparam with the FORTRAN/Pascal naming convention (as MAXPARAM); **_pascal** also directs C to call Maxparam with the FORTRAN/Pascal calling convention.

■   Since the procedure `Maxparam` can alter the value of either parameter, both
    parameters must be passed by reference. In this case, near reference is used;
    this method is specified in C by the use of near pointers, and in Pascal with
    the **VAR** keyword.

    Far reference could have been specified by using far pointers in C. To specify
    far reference in Pascal, use the **VARS** keyword instead of **VAR**.

12.7.2 Calling a Pascal Function from C

The example below demonstrates a C main module calling Pascal function
`fact`. This function returns the factorial of an integer value.

```
/* C source file - calls Pascal function.
 * Compile in medium or large model.
 */

int _pascal fact(int n);

/* PASCAL keyword causes C to use FORTRAN/Pascal
 * calling and naming conventions.
 * Integer parameter passed by value.
 */

main()
{
    int x = 3;
    int y = 4;

    printf( "The factorial of x   is %4d", fact( x ) );
    printf( "The factorial of y   is %4d", fact( y ) );
    printf( "The factorial of x+y is %4d", fact( x + y ) );
}

{ Pascal source code - factorial function. }

MODULE Pfun;
FUNCTION Fact (n : INTEGER) : INTEGER;

{Integer parameters received by value, the Pascal default. }

    BEGIN
        Fact := 1;
        WHILE n > 0 DO
            BEGIN
                Fact := Fact * n;
                n := n - 1;              {Parameter n modified.}
            END;
    END;
END.
```

In the example above, the C program adopts the Pascal naming convention and calling convention. Both programs must agree on whether parameters are passed by reference or by value. The **_pascal** keyword directs C to call `fact` with the FORTRAN/Pascal naming convention (as `FACT`); **_pascal** also directs C to call `fact` with the FORTRAN/Pascal calling convention.

The Pascal function `fact` should receive a parameter by value. Otherwise, the Pascal function will corrupt the parameter's value in the calling module. Passing by value is the default method for both C and Pascal.

12.8 C Calls to Assembly Language

In Microsoft C, Version 6.0, you can write assembly-language programs either by using the in-line assembler or by creating a stand-alone module using the Microsoft Macro Assembler (MASM). If you use the in-line assembler, you do not need to take any special precautions other than those outlined in Chapter 3, "Using the In-Line Assembler." This section explains the techniques for interfacing your assembly-language routines with your C program.

When deciding whether to use the in-line assembler or MASM, there are several considerations. Here is a list of advantages MASM provides over the in-line assembler:

- MASM supports declaration of data in MASM format; in-line assembly does not.

- MASM has a more powerful macro capability than in-line assembly.

- Modules written for MASM can be interfaced more easily with modules written in more than one Microsoft high-level language.

- MASM assembles large assembly-language programs more quickly than the in-line assembler.

- MASM supports assembly-language code written prior to the existence of the in-line assembler.

- MASM error messages and warnings are more complete than those of the in-line assembler.

The in-line assembler is far more efficient for some assembly-language programming tasks. Here are some of the benefits of the in-line assembler:

- You can do spot optimizations by including short sections of assembly-language code in your C programs with the in-line assembler.

- Code written in in-line assembler does not necessarily incur the overhead of a function call; code assembled using MASM always does.

- You can include in-line assembly code in your C source files; code written for MASM must be in a separate file.

12.8.1 Writing the Assembly-Language Procedure

You must write your assembly-language procedure so that it uses the same calling conventions and naming conventions as your C program. If you follow these conventions, you will be able to write recursive procedures (procedures that call themselves), and you will be able to use the CodeView debugger to locate errors in the code.

NOTE *This section discusses only the simplified segment directives provided with the Microsoft Macro Assembler, version 5.0. If you are using a version prior to 5.0, you have to specify complete **SEGMENT** directives.*

The standard assembly-language interface method consists of these steps:

1. Setting up the procedure

2. Entering the procedure

3. Allocating local data (optional)

4. Preserving register values

5. Accessing parameters

6. Returning a value (optional)

7. Exiting the procedure

The next sections describe each of these steps in detail.

12.8.2 Setting Up the Procedure

The linker cannot combine the assembly-language procedure with the C program unless you define compatible segments and declare the procedure properly. Perform the following steps to set up the procedure:

1. Use the **.MODEL** directive at the beginning of the source file; this directive automatically causes the appropriate kind of returns to be generated (**NEAR** for tiny, small or compact models, **FAR** for medium, large, or huge models).

   If you are using a version of MASM prior to 5.0, declare the procedure **NEAR** for small or compact model, **FAR** for medium, large, or huge models.

2. Use the simplified segment directives **.CODE** and **.DATA** to declare the code and data segments.

   If you are using a version of MASM prior to 5.0, declare the segments using the **SEGMENT**, **GROUP**, and **ASSUME** directives. These directives are described in the *Microsoft Macro Assembler Reference* .

3. Use the **PUBLIC** directive to declare the procedure label public. This declaration makes the procedure visible to other modules. Also declare any data you want to make public as **PUBLIC**.

4. Use the **EXTRN** directive to declare any global data or procedures accessed by the routine as external. The safest way to use **EXTRN** is to place the directive outside any segment definition; however, place near data inside the data segment.

5. Observe the C naming convention; precede all procedure names and global data names with an underscore.

12.8.3 *Entering the Procedure*

When you enter the procedure, in most cases you will want to set up a "stack frame." This allows you to access parameters passed on the stack and to allocate local data on the stack. You do not need to set up the stack frame if your procedure accepts no arguments and does not use the stack.

To set up the stack frame, issue the instructions:

```
push    bp
mov     bp,sp
```

This sequence establishes BP as the frame pointer. You cannot use SP for this purpose because it is not an index or base register. Also, the value of SP may change as more data are pushed onto the stack. However, the value of the base register BP remains constant for the life of the procedure unless your program changes it, so each parameter can be addressed as an offset from BP.

The instruction sequence above preserves the value of BP, since it will be needed in the calling procedure as soon as your assembly-language procedure returns. It then transfers the value in SP to BP to establish a stack frame on entry to the procedure.

12.8.4 *Allocating Local Data*

Your assembly-language procedure can use the same technique for allocating temporary storage for local data that is used by high-level languages. To set up local data space, decrease the contents of SP just after setting up the stack frame. (To ensure correct execution, always increase or decrease SP by an even number.) Decreasing SP reserves space on the stack for local data. You must restore the space at the end of the procedure as follows:

```
push    bp
mov     bp,sp
sub     sp,space
```

In the example above, `space` is the total size in bytes of the local data you want to allocate. Local variables are then accessed as fixed negative displacements from BP.

In the following example, the entry sequence establishes a stack frame and allocates temporary local storage for two words (4 bytes) of data. Later in the example, the program accesses the local storage, initializing both to 0.

```
push    bp          ; Save old stack frame.
mov     bp,sp       ; Set up new stack frame.
sub     sp,4        ; Allocate 4 bytes of local storage.
.
.
.
mov     WORD PTR [bp-2],0
mov     WORD PTR [bp-4],0
```

Note that local variables are also called dynamic, stack, or automatic variables.

12.8.5 *Preserving Register Values*

A procedure called from C should preserve the values of SI, DI, SS, and DS (in addition to BP, which is already saved). You should push any register value that your procedure modifies onto the stack after setting up the stack frame and allocating local storage, but prior to entering the main body of the procedure. Registers that your procedure does not alter need not be preserved.

WARNING   *Routines that your assembly-language procedure calls must not alter the SI, DI, SS, DS, or BP registers. If they do, and you have not preserved the registers, they can corrupt the calling program's register variables, segment registers, and stack frame, causing program failure. If your procedure modifies the direction flag using the* **STD** *or* **CLD** *instructions, you must preserve the flags register.*

The example below shows an entry sequence that sets up a stack frame, allocates 4 bytes of local data space on the stack, then preserves the SI, DI, and flags registers.

```
push    bp          ; Save caller's stack frame.
mov     bp,sp       ; Establish new stack frame.
sub     sp,4        ; Allocate local data space.
push    si          ; Save SI and DI registers.
push    di
pushf               ; Save the flags register.
    .
    .
    .
```

In the example above, you must exit the procedure with the following code:

```
popf                ; Restore the flags register.
pop     di          ; Restore the old value in the DI
                    ;   register.
pop     si          ; Restore the old value in the SI
                    ;   register.
mov     sp,bp       ; Restore the stack pointer.
pop     bp          ; Restore the frame pointer.
ret                 ; Return to the calling routine.
```

If you do not issue the instructions above in the order shown, you will place incorrect data in registers. Follow the rules below when restoring the calling program's registers, stack pointer, and frame pointer:

- Pop all registers that you preserve in the reverse order from which they were pushed onto the stack. So, in the example above, SI and DI are pushed, and DI and SI are popped.

- Restore the stack pointer by transferring the value of BP into SP before restoring the value of the frame pointer.

- Always restore the frame pointer last.

12.8.6 Accessing Parameters

Once you have established the frame pointer, allocated local storage (if required), and pushed any registers that need to be preserved, you can write the main body of the procedure. Figure 12.4 shows how functions that observe the C calling convention use the stack frame.

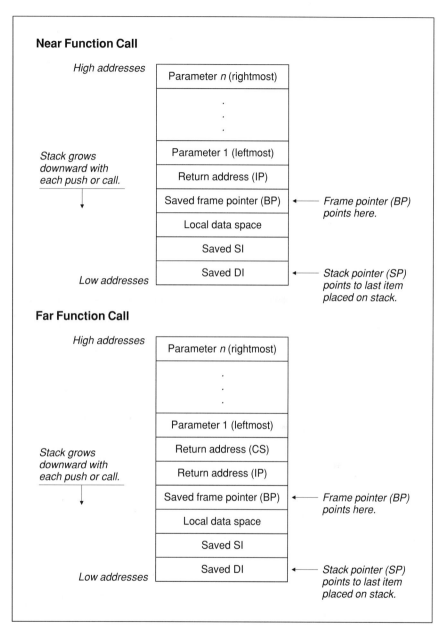

Figure 12.4 C Stack Frame

The stack frame for the assembly-language procedure shown in Figure 12.4 is established by the following:

1. The calling program pushes each of the parameters onto the stack, after which SP points to the last parameter pushed.

2. The calling program issues a **CALL** instruction, which causes the return address (the place in the calling program to which control will ultimately return) to be placed on the stack. This address can be either two bytes long (for near calls) or four bytes long (for far calls). SP now points to this address.

3. The first instruction of the called procedure saves the old value of BP, with the instruction `push bp`. SP now points to the saved copy of BP.

4. BP is used to hold the current value of SP, with the instruction `mov bp,sp`. BP therefore now points to the old value of BP (saved on the stack).

5. While BP remains constant throughout the procedure, SP is often decreased to provide room on the stack for local data or saved registers.

In general, the displacement (from BP) for a parameter x is equal to the size of return address plus 2 plus the total size of parameters between x and BP.

To calculate the size of parameters between x and BP, you must start with the rightmost parameter because C pushes parameters from right to left. For example, consider a **FAR** procedure that has one argument of type **int** (two bytes). The displacement of the parameter is

```
Argument's displacement = size of far return address + 2
                        = 4 + 2
                        = 6
```

The argument can thus be loaded into BP with the following instruction:

```
mov    bx,[bp+6]
```

Once you determine the displacement of each parameter, you can use **EQU** directives or structures to refer to the parameter with a single identifier name in your assembly source code. For example, you can use a more readable name to reference the parameter at `BP+6` if you put the following statement at the beginning of the assembly source file:

```
Arg1    EQU    [bp+6]
```

You can then refer to the first parameter in your source as `Arg1` in any instruction. Use of this feature is optional.

For far (segmented) addresses, Microsoft C pushes the segment address before pushing the offset address. When pushing arguments larger than two bytes, high-order words are always pushed before low-order words, and parameters larger than two bytes are stored on the stack in most-significant, least-significant order.

This standard for pushing segment addresses before pushing offset addresses facilitates the use of the assembly-language instructions **LDS** (load data segment) and **LES** (load extra segment).

12.8.7 Returning a Value

Your assembly-language procedure can return a value to a C calling program. All return values of four bytes or less are passed in registers. Far pointers to return values larger than four bytes are returned in the DX and AX registers. The DX register contains the segment address; the AX register contains the offset relative to the segment contained in DX.

Table 12.3 shows the register conventions for returning simple data types to a C program.

Table 12.3   Register Conventions for Simple Return Values

Data Type	Registers
char	AL
int, short, _near *	AX
long, _far *	High-order portion (or segment address) in DX; low-order portion (or offset address) in AX

Your procedures can return structures. To return a structure from a procedure that uses the C calling convention, you must copy the structure to a global variable, then return a pointer to that variable in the AX register (DX:AX, if you compiled in compact, large, or huge model).

Procedures that use the FORTRAN/Pascal calling convention return structures similarly, with the following exceptions:

- The calling program allocates space for the return value on the stack.

- The calling program passes a pointer to the location where the return value is to be placed in a hidden parameter.

- Instead of copying your structure into a global data item, you copy it into the location pointed to by the hidden parameter.

- You must still return the pointer to that location in the AX register (or DX:AX for far data models).

You can return floating-point values from your procedures.

Procedures that use the C calling convention and return type **float** or type **double** must always copy their return values into the global variable _ _**fac**. To return floating-point values from procedures declared with the FORTRAN/Pascal calling convention, you must return the result on the stack, just as you would a structure.

To return a value of type **long double**, you must place the value on the NDP(80x87) stack using the **FLD** instruction. The C run-time math routines guarantee that the only value on the NDP stack is a return value; your routines must observe the same rule.

12.8.8 Exiting the Procedure

Before you exit your assembly-language procedure, you must perform several steps to restore the calling program's environment. Some of these steps are dependent on actions you took in allocating space for local variables and preserving registers.

You must follow these steps (if appropriate to your procedure) in the order shown:

1. If you saved any of the registers SS, DS, SI, or DI, they must be popped off the stack in the reverse order from which they were saved. If you pop these registers in any other order, your program will behave incorrectly.

2. If you allocated local data space at the beginning of the procedure, you must restore SP with the instruction mov s p ,bp.

3. Restore BP with the instruction pop bp. This step is always necessary.

4. Return to the calling program by issuing the **ret** instruction.

The following example shows the simplest possible entry and exit sequence. In the entry sequence, no registers are saved and no local data space is allocated.

```
push    bp
mov     bp,sp    ; Set up the new stack frame.
.
.
.
pop     bp       ; Restore the caller's stack frame.
ret
```

The following example shows an entry and exit sequence for a procedure that saves SI and DI and allocates local data space on the stack.

```
push    bp
mov     bp,sp      ; Establish local stack frame.
sub     sp,4       ; Allocate space for local data.
push    si         ; Preserve the SI and DI registers.
push    di
.
.
.
pop     di         ; Pop saved registers.
pop     si
mov     sp,bp      ; Free local data space.
pop     bp         ; Restore old stack frame.
ret
```

12.9 Handling Data in Mixed-Language Programming

This section contains detailed information about naming and calling conventions in a mixed-language program. It also describes how various languages represent strings, numerical data, arrays, and logical data.

12.9.1 Default Naming and Calling Conventions

Each language has its own default naming and calling conventions (Table 12.4).

Table 12.4   Default Naming and Calling Conventions

Language	Calling Convention	Naming Convention	Parameter Passing
BASIC	FORTRAN/Pascal	Case insensitive	Near reference
C	C	Case sensitive	Value (scalar variables), reference (arrays and pointers)
FORTRAN	FORTRAN/Pascal	Case insensitive	Reference
Pascal	FORTRAN/Pascal	Case insensitive	Value

BASIC Conventions

When you call BASIC routines from C, you must pass all arguments by near reference (near pointer). You can modify the conventions observed by BASIC routines that interface with C functions by using the **DECLARE**, **BYVAL**, **SEG**, and **CALLS** keywords. For more information on these keywords, see the *Microsoft BASIC Language Reference* or the *Microsoft BASIC Programmer's Guide*.

FORTRAN Conventions

You can modify the conventions observed by FORTRAN routines that call C functions by using the **INTERFACE, VALUE, PASCAL,** and **C** keywords. For more information about the use of these keywords, see the *Microsoft FORTRAN Reference*.

Pascal Conventions

You can modify the conventions observed by Pascal routines that interface with C functions by using the **VAR, CONST, ADR, VARS, CONSTS, ADRS,** and **C** keywords. For more information about the use of these keywords, see the *Microsoft Pascal Compiler User's Guide*.

12.9.2 Numeric Data Representation

Table 12.5 shows how to declare numeric variables of similar type in different languages.

Table 12.5   Equivalent Numeric Data Types

BASIC	C	FORTRAN	Pascal
$x\%$	short	INTEGER*2	INTEGER2
INTEGER	int	---	INTEGER (default)
---	unsigned short[1]	---	WORD
---	unsigned	---	---
$x\&$	long	INTEGER*4	INTEGER4
LONG	---	INTEGER (default)	---
---	unsigned long[1]	---	---
$x!$	float	REAL*4	REAL4
x (default)	---	REAL	REAL (default)
SINGLE	---	---	---
$x\#$	double	REAL*8	REAL8
DOUBLE	---	DOUBLE PRECISION	---
---	long double	REAL*16	REAL16
---	unsigned char	CHARACTER*1[2]	CHAR

[1] Types **unsigned short** and **unsigned long** are not supported by BASIC or FORTRAN. Type **unsigned long** is not supported by Pascal. A signed integral type can be substituted, but the maximum range will be less.

[2] The FORTRAN type **CHARACTER*1** is not the same as **LOGICAL**.

The FORTRAN types **COMPLEX∗8** and **COMPLEX∗16** are not implemented in C but can be represented with structures.

The FORTRAN types **LOGICAL∗2** and **LOGICAL∗4** are not implemented in C. **LOGICAL∗2** is stored as a one-byte Boolean indicator followed by an unused byte; **LOGICAL∗4** is stored as a one-byte Boolean indicator followed by three unused bytes.

12.9.3 Strings

Each language implements strings differently. This section describes the ways that strings are implemented in Microsoft languages.

C String Format

C stores strings as arrays of bytes and uses a null character (`'\0'`) as an end-of-string delimiter. For example, consider the following string:

```
char c_string[] = "C text string";
```

This string is represented in memory as follows:

Because `c_string` is an array like any other, C passes it by reference in function calls.

BASIC String Format

BASIC stores strings as four-byte descriptors pointing to the actual string data. The format of the descriptor is as follows:

The first field of the string descriptor contains an integer indicating the length (in bytes) of the string. The second field contains the address of the string in the default data segment.

Do not attempt to alter the length of BASIC strings, because they are managed by BASIC string-space management routines. You cannot count on a particular string remaining at a given offset during the execution of a BASIC program because the BASIC string-space management routines allocate strings to different areas of memory depending on program requirements.

The format of the string at DS:*Address* is a simple array of characters. The string is exactly the length indicated in the descriptor.

To pass a BASIC string to C, append a null character.

Because C needs the null character to delimit the end of the string, you should append `chr$( 0 )` to your BASIC string before passing it to your C function. For example,

```
A$ = "I am a BASIC string"
A$ = A$ + chr$( 0 )

CALL CFunc( SADD(A$) )
```

Note that the BASIC call is made by near reference using the **SADD** keyword.

Use a string descriptor to pass a C string to BASIC.

To pass a C string to BASIC, create a structure for the string descriptor. For example,

```
char c_string[] = "C String Data";

struct tagBASICStringDes
{
    char *   sd_addr;
    int      sd_len;
} str_des;

str_des.sd_addr = c_string;
str_des.sd_len = strlen( c_string );

BASICFunction( &str_des );
```

FORTRAN String Format

FORTRAN stores strings as a series of bytes at a fixed location in memory. There is no delimiter at the end of the string. Consider the string declared as follows:

```
STR = 'FORTRAN STRING'
```

The string is stored in memory as follows:

FORTRAN passes strings by reference, as it does all other data.

NOTE *FORTRAN's variable length strings cannot be used in mixed-language programming because the temporary variable used to communicate string length is not accessible to other languages.*

To pass a C string to FORTRAN (or Pascal), pass the variable by reference as you normally would. In your FORTRAN or Pascal routine, you must specify the length of the string; strings that are passed as arguments from one language to another must be of fixed length.

Pascal String Format

Pascal represents strings as fixed-length arrays of **CHAR** or as strings with a length byte followed by the string data.

To pass a fixed-length string to C, append a null character.

To pass a fixed-length string to a C function, use the concatenation operator (∗) to append a null character. Then pass the string to the C function by reference (by declaring the string as **CONST**, **CONSTS**, **VAR**, or **VARS**). For example,

```
PROGRAM PasStr( input, output );
type
     stype15 = string(15);  { fixed-length }
var
     str : stype15;

PROCEDURE PasStrToC( VAR s1 : stype15 ) [C]; EXTERN;

BEGIN
     str := 'Pass this to C' * chr( 0 );
     PasStrToC( str );
END.
```

A more flexible way to pass Pascal strings to C functions is to declare them as type **ADRMEM** or **ADSMEM**, then pass the address of the string. For example,

```
PROCEDURE PasStrToC( s1adr : ADRMEM ) [C]; EXTERN;
```

Then you can call the C function with this code:

```
PasStrToC( ADR str );
```

Using this method, you can pass strings of different lengths to C functions.

> **NOTE** *The Pascal type **LSTRING** is not compatible with C; you can pass a string declared as **LSTRING** by first assigning it to another variable of type **STRING**, then passing that variable.*

Whenever you pass a variable of type **STRING** or type **LSTRING** by value, Pascal pushes the whole string onto the stack and passes the length of the string as another parameter. C cannot access strings passed in this manner.

Before passing a string from C to Pascal, make sure enough space is allocated.

Passing a string from a C function to a Pascal function or procedure is identical to passing a string from a C function to a FORTRAN routine. The only provision you must make is to specify the length of the string to your Pascal function.

12.9.4 Arrays

When you use an array in a program written in a single language, the method for array handling is consistent. When you mix languages, you need to be aware of the differences between array-handling techniques in various languages.

Unlike most Microsoft languages, BASIC keeps an array descriptor, which is similar to the BASIC string descriptor discussed in Section 12.9.3, "Strings." This array descriptor is necessary because BASIC handles memory allocation for arrays dynamically (at run time). Dynamic allocation requires BASIC to shift arrays in memory.

To pass a BASIC array to a C function, use the VARPTR and VARSEG keywords.

The **VARPTR** and **VARSEG** keywords obtain the address of the first element of the array and its segment, respectively. The example below shows how to call a C function with a near reference and a far reference to an array:

```
DIM ARRAY%( 20 )
DECLARE CNearArray CDECL( BYVAL Addr AS INTEGER )
DECLARE CFarArray CDECL( BYVAL Addr AS INTEGER, BYVAL Seg AS
INTEGER )
.
.
.
CALL CNearArray( VARPTR( ARRAY%(0) ) )
CALL CFarArray( VARPTR( ARRAY%(0) ), VARSEG( ARRAY%(0) ) )
```

The C functions receiving `ARRAY` can be declared as follows:

```
_cdecl CNearArray( int * array );
_cdecl CFarArray( int far * array );
```

The routine that receives the array must not make a call back to BASIC. If it does, the location of the array data could change, and the address that was passed to the routine would become meaningless.

If you only need to pass one member of the array from BASIC to your C function, you can pass it by value as follows:

```
CALL CFunc( ARRAY%(8) )
```

12.9.5 Array Declaration and Indexing

Each language varies in the way that arrays are declared and indexed. Array indexing is a source-level consideration and involves no transformation of data. There are two differences in the way elements are indexed by each language:

1. The value of the lower array bound is different among Microsoft languages.

   By default, FORTRAN indexes the first element of an array as 1. BASIC and C index it as 0. Pascal lets you begin indexing at any integer value. Recent versions of BASIC and FORTRAN also give you the option of specifying lower bounds at any integer value.

2. Some languages vary subscripts in row-major order; others vary subscripts in column-major order.

   This issue only affects arrays with more than one dimension. With row-major order (used by C and Pascal), the rightmost dimension changes first. With column-major order (used by FORTRAN, and BASIC by default), the left-most dimension changes first. Thus, in C, the first four elements of an array declared as `X[3][3]` are

   ```
   X[0][0]    X[0][1]    X[0][2]    X[1][0]
   ```

   In FORTRAN, the four elements are

   ```
   X(1,1)    X(2,1)    X(3,1)    X(1,2)
   ```

   The C and FORTRAN arrays shown above illustrate the difference between row-major and column-major order as well as the difference in the assumed lower bound between C and FORTRAN. Table 12.6 shows equivalences for array declarations in each language. In this table, r is the number of elements of the row dimension (which changes most slowly), and c is the number of elements of the column dimension (which changes most quickly).

Table 12.6   Equivalent Array Declarations

Language	Array Declaration	Notes
BASIC	**DIM** $x(r-1, c-1)$	With default lower bounds of 0
C	type $x[r][c]$ **struct** { *type* $x[r][c]$; } x	When passed by reference When passed by value
FORTRAN	*type* $x(c, r)$	With default lower bounds of 1
Pascal	x : **ARRAY** [$a..a+r-1$, $b..b+c-1$] **OF** *type*	

The order of indexing extends to any number of dimensions you declare. For example, the C declaration

```
int arr1[2][10][15][20];
```

is equivalent to the FORTRAN declaration

```
INTEGER*2 ARR1( 20, 15, 10, 2 )
```

The constants used in a C array declaration represent dimensions, not upper bounds as they do in other languages. Therefore, the last element in the C array declared as `int arr[5][5]` is `arr[4][4]`, not `arr[5][5]`.

12.9.6 *Structures, Records, and User-Defined Types*

The C **struct** type, the BASIC user-defined type, the FORTRAN record (defined with the **STRUCTURE** keyword), and the Pascal **record** type are equivalent. Therefore, these data types can be passed between C, FORTRAN, Pascal, and BASIC.

These types can be affected by the storage method. By default, C, FORTRAN, and Pascal use word alignment for types shorter than one word (type **char** and **unsigned char**). This storage method specifies that occasional bytes can be inserted as padding so that word and double-word objects start on an even boundary. (In addition, all nested structures and records start on a word boundary.)

If you are passing a structure or record across a mixed-language interface, your calling routine and called routine must agree on the storage method and parameter-passing convention. Otherwise, data will not be interpreted correctly.

Because Pascal, FORTRAN, and C use the same storage method for structures and records, you can interchange data between routines without taking any special precautions unless you modify the storage method. Make sure the storage methods agree before interchanging data between C, FORTRAN, and Pascal.

BASIC packs user-defined types, so your C function must also pack structures (using the /Zp command-line option or the **pack** pragma) to agree.

You can pass structures as parameters by value or by reference. Both the calling program and the called program must agree on the parameter-passing convention. See Section 12.2.3, "Parameter-Passing Requirement," for more information about the language you are using.

12.9.7 External Data

External data refers to data that is both static and public; that is, the data is stored in a set place in memory as opposed to being allocated on the stack, and the data is visible to other modules.

External data can be defined in C, Pascal, and assembly language. Note that a data definition is distinct from an external declaration. A data definition causes a compiler to create a data object; an external declaration informs a compiler that the object is to be found in another module. FORTRAN can only define external data in COMMON blocks. (See Section 12.9.9, "Common Blocks," for more information about sharing external data with FORTRAN programs.)

There are three requirements for programs that share external data between languages:

1. One of the modules must define the data.

   You can define a static data object in a C module by defining a data object outside all functions. (If you use the **static** keyword in C, however, the data object will not be made public.)

2. The other modules that will access the data must declare the data as external.

   In C, you can declare data as external by using an **extern** declaration, similar to the **extern** declaration for functions. In FORTRAN and Pascal, you can declare data as external by adding the **EXTERN** attribute to the data declaration.

3. Resolve naming-convention differences.

   In C, you can adopt the FORTRAN/Pascal naming convention by applying **_fortran** or **_pascal** to the data declaration. In FORTRAN and Pascal, you can adopt the C naming convention by applying the **C** attribute to the data declaration.

12.9.8 Pointers and Address Variables

Rather than passing data directly, you may want to pass the address of a piece of data. Passing the address amounts to passing the data by reference. In some cases, such as in BASIC arrays, there is no other way to pass a data item as a parameter.

C programs always pass array variables by address. All other types are passed by value unless you use the address-of (**&**) operator to obtain the address.

The Pascal **ADR** and **ADS** types are equivalent to near and far pointers, respectively, in C. You can pass **ADR** and **ADS** variables as **ADRMEM** or **ADSMEM**. BASIC and FORTRAN do not have formal address types. However, they do provide ways for storing and passing addresses.

BASIC programs can access a variable's segment address with the **VARSEG** function and its offset address with the **VARPTR** function. The values returned by these intrinsic functions should then be passed or stored as ordinary integer variables. If you pass them to another language, pass by value. Otherwise you will be attempting to pass the address of the address, rather than the address itself.

To pass a near address, pass only the offset; if you need to pass a far address, you may have to pass the segment and the offset separately. Pass the segment address first, unless **CDECL** is in effect.

FORTRAN programs can determine near and far addresses with the **LOC** and **LOCFAR** functions. Store the result of the **LOC** function as **INTEGER∗2** and the result of the **LOCFAR** function as **INTEGER∗4**.

As with BASIC, if you pass the result of **LOC** or **LOCFAR** to another language, be sure to pass by value.

12.9.9 Common Blocks

You can pass individual members of a FORTRAN or BASIC common block in an argument list, just as you can any data item. However, you can also give a different language module access to the entire common block at once.

C modules can reference the items of a common block by first declaring a structure with fields that correspond to the common-block variables. Having defined a structure with the appropriate fields, the C module must then connect with the common block itself. The next two sections present methods for gaining access to common blocks.

Passing the Address of a Common Block

To pass the address of a common block, simply pass the address of the first variable in the block. (In other words, pass the first variable by reference.) The receiving C module should expect to receive a structure by reference.

In the example below, the C function `initcb` receives the address of the variable `N`, which it considers to be a pointer to a structure with three fields:

```
C       FORTRAN SOURCE CODE
C
        COMMON /CBLOCK/N, X, Y
        INTEGER*2 N
        REAL*8    X, Y
.
.
.
        CALL INITCB( N )


/* C source code */


/* Explicitly set structure packing to word-alignment */
#pragma pack( 2 );

struct block_type
{
    int     n;
    double  x;
    double  y;
};

initcb( struct block_type * block_hed )
{
    block_hed-n = 1;
    block_hed-x = 10.0;
    block_hed-y = 20.0;
}
```

Accessing Common Blocks Directly

You can access FORTRAN common blocks directly by defining a structure with the appropriate fields and then using the methods described in Section 12.9.7, "External Data." Here is an example of accessing common blocks directly:

```
struct block_type
{
    int    n;
    double x;
    double y;
};

extern struct block_type fortran cblock;
```

You cannot access common blocks directly using BASIC common blocks.

Note that the technique of accessing common blocks directly works with FORTRAN common blocks, but not with BASIC common blocks. If your C module must work with both FORTRAN and BASIC common blocks, pass the address of the common block as a parameter to the function.

12.9.10 Using a Varying Number of Parameters

Some C functions (for example **printf**) accept a variable number of parameters. To call such a function from another language, you need to suppress the type-checking that normally forces a call to be made with a fixed number of parameters. In BASIC, you can remove this type-checking by omitting a parameter list from the **DECLARE** statement. In FORTRAN or Pascal, you can call routines with a variable number of parameters by including the **VARYING** attribute in your interface to the routine, along with the **C** attribute. You must use the **C** attribute because a variable number of parameters is feasible only with the C calling convention.

Writing Portable Programs

Because C compilers exist on a variety of computers, some C applications developed for one computer system can be ported to other systems. However, some aspects of language behavior depend on how a particular C compiler is implemented and how a specific computer operates. Therefore, when designing a program to be ported to another system, it is important that you examine programming assumptions.

This chapter describes programming assumptions that can affect writing portable programs.

The American National Standards Institute Standard for the C Language (the ANSI Standard) details every instance where language behavior is defined by the implementation. Appendix C summarizes implementation-defined behavior for Microsoft C.

13.1 Assumptions about Hardware

To make C programs portable, you must examine two aspects of your code: hardware assumptions and compiler dependency. This section deals with hardware assumptions. Section 13.2, "Assumptions about the Compiler," deals with compiler dependency.

13.1.1 Size of Basic Types

In C, the size of basic types (**char**, **signed int**, **unsigned int**, **float**, **double**, and **long double**) is implementation-defined, so relying on a particular data type to be a given size reduces the portability of a program.

Don't make assumptions about the size of data types. Because the size of basic types is left to the implementation, do not make assumptions about the size or alignment of data types within aggregate types. Use only the **sizeof** operator to determine the size or amount of storage required for a variable or a type.

Following are some rules governing the size of data types.

Type char

Type **char** is the smallest of the basic types, but it must be large enough to hold any of the characters in the implementation's basic character set. Normally, variables of type **char** are one byte.

Type int and Type short int

Type **int** and type **short int** often correspond to the register size of the target machine. Both **int** and **short** are greater than or equal to the size of type **char** but less than or equal to the size of type **long**.

If you assume that type **int** is a certain size, your code may not be portable because

- An **int** can be defined as a 16-bit (two-byte) or a 32-bit quantity.

- An **int** is not always large enough to hold array indexes. For large arrays, you must use **unsigned int**; for extremely large arrays, use **long**. To be certain your code is portable, define your array indexes as type **size_t**. You may not know, before porting your code, the maximum value to expect an array index of type **int** to hold. The file LIMITS.H contains manifest constants, listed below, for the maximum and minimum values of each basic integral type.

Constant	Value
CHAR_BIT	Number of bits in a variable of type **char**
CHAR_MIN	Minimum value a variable of type **char** can hold
CHAR_MAX	Maximum value a variable of type **char** can hold
SCHAR_MIN	Minimum value a variable of type **signed char** can hold
SCHAR_MAX	Maximum value a variable of type **signed char** can hold
UCHAR_MAX	Maximum value a variable of type **unsigned char** can hold

SHRT_MIN	Minimum value a variable of type **short** can hold
SHRT_MAX	Maximum value a variable of type **short** can hold
USHRT_MAX	Maximum value a variable of type **unsigned short** can hold
INT_MIN	Minimum value a variable of type **int** can hold
INT_MAX	Maximum value a variable of type **int** can hold
UINT_MAX	Maximum value a variable of type **unsigned int** can hold
LONG_MIN	Minimum value a variable of type **long** can hold
LONG_MAX	Maximum value a variable of type **long** can hold
ULONG_MAX	Maximum value a variable of type **unsigned long** can hold

Type float, Type double, and Type long double

Type **float** is the smallest of the basic floating-point types. Type **double** is usually larger than type **float**, and type **long double** is usually the largest of the floating-point types. You can make only these portability assumptions about floating-point types:

- Any value that can be represented as type **float** can be represented as type **double** (type **float** is a subset of type **double**).

- Any value that can be represented as type **double** can be represented as type **long double** (type **double** is a subset of type **long double**).

The file FLOAT.H contains manifest constants, listed below, for the maximum and minimum values of each basic floating-point type.

Constant	Value
DBL_DIG	Number of decimal digits of precision a variable of type **double** can hold
DBL_MAX	Maximum value a variable of type **double** can hold
DBL_MAX_10_EXP	Maximum value (base 10) the exponent of a variable of type **double** can hold

DBL_MAX_EXP	Maximum value (base 2) the exponent of a variable of type **double** can hold
DBL_MIN	Minimum positive value a variable of type **double** can hold
DBL_MIN_10_EXP	Minimum value (base 10) the exponent of a variable of type **double** can hold
DBL_MIN_EXP	Minimum value (base 2) the exponent of a variable of type **double** can hold
FLT_DIG	Number of decimal digits of precision a variable of type **float** can hold
FLT_MAX	Maximum value a variable of type **float** can hold
FLT_MAX_10_EXP	Maximum value (base 10) the exponent of a variable of type **float** can hold
FLT_MAX_EXP	Maximum value (base 2) the exponent of a variable of type **float** can hold
FLT_MIN	Minimum positive value a variable of type **float** can hold
FLT_MIN_10_EXP	Minimum value (base 10) the exponent of a variable of type **float** can hold
FLT_MIN_EXP	Minimum value (base 2) the exponent of a variable of type **float** can hold
LDBL_DIG	Number of decimal digits of precision a variable of type **long double** can hold
LDBL_MAX	Maximum value a variable of type **long double** can hold
LDBL_MAX_10_EXP	Maximum value (base 10) the exponent of a variable of type **long double** can hold
LDBL_MAX_EXP	Maximum value (base 2) the exponent of a variable of type **long double** can hold

LDBL_MIN	Minimum positive value a variable of type **long double** can hold
LDBL_MIN_10_EXP	Minimum value (base 10) the exponent of a variable of type **long double** can hold
LDBL_MIN_EXP	Minimum value (base 2) the exponent of a variable of type **long double** can hold

Microsoft C Type Sizes

Table 13.1 summarizes the size of the basic types in Microsoft C.

Table 13.1   Size of Basic Types in Microsoft C

Type	Number of Bytes
char, unsigned char	1
int, short, unsigned int, unsigned short	2
near pointer	2
long, unsigned long	4
far pointer	4
float	4
double	8
long double	10

13.1.2 Storage Order and Alignment

The C language does not define any specific layout for the storage of data items relative to one another. The layout for storage of structure elements, or unions within a structure or union, is defined by the implementation.

Some processors require that data longer than one byte be word-aligned (aligned to an even-byte address). Other processors, such as the 80x86 family, do not have such a restriction.

Structure Order and Alignment

The example below illustrates how alignment can affect your program. In the example, a structure is cast to type **long** because the programmer knew the order in which a particular implementation stored data.

```
/* Nonportable code */
struct time
{
    char hour;      /* 0 < hour < 24   -- fits in a char */
    char minute;    /* 0 < minute < 60 -- fits in a char */
    char second;    /* 0 < second < 60 -- fits in a char */
};

    .
    .
    .
    struct time now, alarm_time;
    .
    .
    .
    if ( (long)now >= (long)alarm_time )
    {
        /* sound an alarm */
    }
```

The preceding code makes these nonportable assumptions:

- The data for `hour` will be stored in a higher order position than `minute` or `second`. Because C does not guarantee storage order or alignment of structures or unions, the code may not be portable to other machines.

- Three variables of type **char** will be shorter than or the same length as a variable of type **long**. Thus, the code is not portable according to the rules governing the size of basic types, as described in Section 13.1.1.

If either of these assumptions proves false, the comparison (**if** statement) is invalid.

You can write code that makes no assumptions about storage order.

To make the program in the preceding example portable, you can break the comparison between the two long integers into a component-by-component comparison. This technique is illustrated in the following example:

```
/* Portable code */
struct time
{
    char hour;      /* 0 < hour < 24    -- fits in a char */
    char minute;    /* 0 < minute < 60 -- fits in a char */
    char second;    /* 0 < second < 60 -- fits in a char */
};

        .
        .
        .
    struct time now, alarm_time;
        .
        .
        .
    if ( time_cmp( now, alarm_time ) >= 0 )
    {
        /* sound an alarm */
    }
        .
        .
        .

int time_cmp( struct time t1, struct time t2 )
{
    if( t1.hour != t2.hour )
        return( t2.hour - t1.hour );
    if( t1.minute != t2.minute )
        return( t2.minute - t1.minute );
    return( t2.second - t1.second );
}
```

Union Order and Alignment

Programmers use unions most often for two purposes: to store data whose exact type is not known until run time or to access the same data in different ways.

Unions falling into the second category are usually not portable. For example, the union below is not portable:

```
union tag_u
{
        char bytes_in_long[4];
        long a_long;
};
```

The intent of the union above is to access the individual bytes of a variable of type **long**. However, the union may not work as intended when ported to other computers because

- It relies on a constant size for type **long**.

- It may assume byte ordering within a variable of type **long**. (Byte ordering is described in detail in Section 13.1.3, "Byte Order in a Word.")

The first problem can be addressed by coding the union as follows:

```
union tag_u
{
        char bytes_in_long[sizeof( long ) / sizeof( char )];
        long a_long;
};
```

Note the use of the **sizeof** operator to determine the size of a data type.

13.1.3 Byte Order in a Word

The order of bytes within a word (**int** or **short**) or a double word (**long**) can vary among machines. Code that assumes an internal order is not portable, as shown by this example:

```
/*
 * Nonportable structure to access an
 * int in bytes.
 */
struct tag_int_bytes
{
    char lobyte;
    char hibyte;
};
```

A more portable way to access the individual bytes in a word is to define two macros that rely on the constant **CHAR_BIT**, defined in LIMITS.H:

```
#define LOBYTE(a) (char)((a) & 0xff)
#define HIBYTE(a) (char)((unsigned)(a) >> CHAR_BIT)
```

The **LOBYTE** macro is still not completely portable. It assumes that a **char** is eight bits long, and it uses the constant $0xff$ to mask the high-order eight bits. Because portable programs cannot rely on a given number of bits in a byte, consider the revision below:

```
#define LOBYTE(a) (char)((a) & ((unsigned)~0>>CHAR_BIT))
#define HIBYTE(a) (char)((unsigned)(a) >> CHAR_BIT)
```

The new **LOBYTE** macro performs a bitwise complement on 0; that is, all zero bits are turned into ones. It then takes that unsigned quantity and shifts it right far enough to create a mask of the correct length for the implementation.

The following code assumes that the order of bytes in a word will be least-significant first:

```
    int c;
    .
    .
    .
    fread( &c, sizeof( char ), 1, fp );
```

The code attempts to read one byte as an **int**, without converting it from a **char**. However, the code will fail in any implementation where the low-order byte is not the first byte of an **int**. The following solution is more portable. In the example below, the data is read into an intermediate variable of type **char** before being assigned to the integer variable.

```
    int c;
    char ch;
    .
    .
    .
    fread( &ch, sizeof( char ), 1, fp );
    c = ch;
```

The example below shows how to use the C run-time function **fgetc** to return the value. The **fgetc** function returns type **char**, but the value is promoted to type **int** when it is assigned to a variable of type **int**.

```
int c;
 .
 .
 .
c = fgetc( fp );
```

Microsoft C Specific

Microsoft C normally aligns data types longer than one byte to an even-byte address for improved performance. See the /Zp compiler option and the **pack** pragma in the *Microsoft C Reference* and in on-line help for information about controlling structure packing in Microsoft C.

13.1.4 Reading and Writing Structures

Many C programs read data from disk into structures and write data to disk from structures. The functions that perform disk I/O in C require you to specify the number of bytes to be transferred. You should always use the **sizeof** operator to obtain the size of the data to be read or written because differing data type sizes or alignment schemes may alter the size of a given structure. For example,

```
fread( &my_struct, sizeof(my_struct), 1, fp );
```

Microsoft C Specific

When performing disk input and output in Microsoft C, structures may be different sizes depending on the structure-packing option you have selected (see the /Zp compiler option and the **pack** pragma in the *Microsoft C Reference*).

13.1.5 Bit Fields in Structures

The Microsoft C compiler implements bit fields. However, many C compilers do not.

Bit fields allow you to access the individual bits within a data item. While the practice of accessing the bits in a data item is inherently nonportable, you can improve your chances of porting a program that uses bit fields if you make no assumptions about order of assignment, or size and alignment of bit fields.

Order of Assignment

The order of assignment of bit fields in memory is left to the implementation, so you cannot rely on a particular entry in a bit field structure to be in a higher order position than another. (This problem is similar to the portability constraint imposed by alignment of basic data types in structures. The C language does not define any specific layout for the storage of data items relative to one another.) See Section 13.1.2, "Storage Order and Alignment" for more information.

Size and Alignment of Bit Fields

The Microsoft C compiler supports bit fields up to the size of the type **long**. Each individual member of the bit field structure can be up to the size of the declared type. Some compilers do not support bit field-structure elements that are longer than type **int**.

The example below defines a bit field, short_bitfield, that is shorter than type **int**:

```
struct short_bitfield
{
    unsigned usr_bkup : 1; /* 0  <= usr_bkup <  1 */
    unsigned usr_sec  : 4; /* 9 <= usr_sec < 16 */
};
```

The example below defines a bit field, long_bitfield, that has elements longer than type **int**:

```
struct long_bitfield
{
    unsigned long disk_pos : 22;  /* 0 <= disk_pos   < 4,194,304 */
    unsigned long rec_no   : 10;  /* 0 <= rec_no < 1,024 */
};
```

The bit field short_bitfield is likely to be supported by more implementations than long_bitfield.

Microsoft C Specific

The example below introduces another portability issue: alignment of data defined in bit fields. The Microsoft C compiler does not allow an element in a structure to extend across two words. The first two elements, day and month, take up nine bits. The third, year, would extend across a word boundary, so it must begin on the next word boundary.

```
struct long_bitfield
{
    unsigned int day    : 5;  /* 0 <= day   < 32 */
    unsigned int month  : 4;  /* 0 <= month < 16 */
    unsigned int year   : 11; /* 0 <= year  < 2048 */
};
```

Figure 13.1 illustrates the example above.

Figure 13.1 Data Alignment in Bit Fields

Other compilers may not use the same storage techniques.

13.1.6 Processor Arithmetic Mode

Two types of arithmetic are common on digital computers: one's-complement arithmetic and two's-complement arithmetic. Some programs assume that all target computers perform two's-complement arithmetic. If you take advantage of the fact that a given operation causes a particular bit pattern to be set on either a one's-complement or two's-complement computer, your program will not be portable. For example, two's-complement machines represent the eight-bit integer value −1 as a binary 11111111. A one's-complement machine represents the same decimal value (−1) as 11111110. Some programmers assume that −1 will fill a byte or a word with ones, and use it to construct a mask template that they later shift. This will not work correctly on one's-complement machines, but the error will not surface until the least-significant bit is used.

In two's-complement arithmetic, there is only one value that represents zero. In one's-complement arithmetic, there is a value for zero and a value for negative zero. Use the C relational operators to handle this anomaly correctly; if you write code that deliberately circumvents the C relational operators, tests for zero or **NULL** may not operate correctly.

Microsoft C Specific

Microsoft C produces code only for the Intel 80*x*86 processors, which all perform two's-complement arithmetic.

13.1.7 Pointers

One of the most powerful but potentially dangerous features of the C language is its use of indirect addressing through pointers. Bugs introduced by misusing pointers can be difficult to detect and isolate because the error often corrupts memory unpredictably.

Casting Pointers

Be sure you do not make nonportable assumptions when casting pointers to different types.

```
/* Nonportable coercion */
char c[4];
long *lp;

lp = (long *)c;
*lp = 0x12345678L;
```

This code is nonportable because using a cast to change an array of **char** to a pointer of type **long** assumes a particular byte-ordering scheme. This is discussed in greater detail in Section 13.1.3, "Byte Order in a Word."

Pointer Size

A pointer can be assigned (or cast) to any integer type large enough to hold it, but the size of the integer type depends on the machine and the implementation. (In fact, it can even depend on the memory model.) Therefore, you cannot assume:

```
sizeof( char * ) == sizeof( int )
```

To determine the size of any unmodified data pointer, use

```
sizeof( void * )
```

the size of a generic data pointer.

Pointer Subtraction

Code that assumes that pointer subtraction yields an **int** value is nonportable. Pointer subtraction yields a result of type **ptrdiff_t** (defined in STDDEF.H). Portable code must always use variables of type **ptrdiff_t** for storing the result of pointer subtraction.

The Null Pointer

In most implementations, **NULL** is defined as 0. In Microsoft C, it is defined as
((void *)0). Because code pointers and data pointers are often different
sizes, using 0 for the null pointer for both can lead to nonportability. The difference in size between code pointers and data pointers will cause problems for
functions that expect pointer arguments longer than an **int**. To avoid these problems, use the null pointer, as defined in the include file STDDEF.H; use prototypes; or explicitly cast **NULL** to the correct data type. Here is a portable way to
use the null pointer:

```
/* Portable use of the NULL pointer */
main()
{
    func1( (char *)NULL );
    func2( (void *(*)())NULL );
}

void func1( char * c )
{
}

void func2( void *(* func)() )
{
}
```

The invocations of func1 and func2 explicitly cast **NULL** to the correct
size. In the case of func1, **NULL** is cast to type **char ***; in the case of func2,
it is cast to a pointer to a function that returns type **void**.

Microsoft C Specific

Subtraction of pointers to huge arrays that have more than 32,767 elements may
yield a **long** result. The **_huge** keyword is implementation-defined by Microsoft
C and is not portable. Here is how to subtract pointers to huge arrays:

```
char _huge *a;
char _huge *b;
long        d;
.
.
.
d = (long)( a - b );
```

In Microsoft C, the memory model selected and the special keywords **_near**, **_far**, and **_huge** can change the size of a pointer. The Microsoft memory models and extended keywords are nonportable, but you should be aware of their effects.

Sizes of generic pointers and default pointer sizes are shown in Tables 13.2 and 13.3, respectively.

Table 13.2   Size of Generic Pointers

Declaration	Name	Size
void _near *	Generic near pointer	16 bits
void _far *	Generic far pointer	32 bits
void _huge *	Generic huge pointer	32 bits

Table 13.3   Default Pointer Sizes

Memory Model	Code Pointer Size	Data Pointer Size
Tiny	16 bits	16 bits
Small	16 bits	16 bits
Medium	32 bits	16 bits
Compact	16 bits	32 bits
Large	32 bits	32 bits
Huge	32 bits	32 bits

13.1.8 Address Space

The amount of available memory and the address space on systems varies, depending on many factors outside your control. A program designed with portability in mind should handle insufficient-memory situations. To ensure that your program handles these situations, you should always check the error return from any of the dynamic memory allocation routines, such as **malloc**, **calloc**, **strdup**, and **realloc**.

These situations occur not only because of a lack of installed memory but also because too many other applications are using memory. For example,

- Installed resident software can cause your program to fail. In DOS, these programs are usually device drivers or terminate-and-stay-resident (TSR) utilities.

- An event or combination of events in a multitasking operating system such as OS/2 or XENIX can cause your program to fail. These failures are complex and difficult to predict. Here is an example: the user has installed a daemon to "pop up" every so often and check the system status. The user is running your application along with enough other large applications to cause a critical shortage of memory. When the daemon pops up, your program may fail on a memory allocation request.

- An application running under Windows can use an extraordinary amount of the global heap and not return it to the free pool. This type of behavior will cause Windows to deny a **GlobalAlloc** request.

13.1.9 Character Set

The C language does not define the character set used in an implementation. This means that any programs that assume the character set to be ASCII are nonportable.

The only restrictions on the character set are these:

- No character in the implementation's character set may be larger than the size of type **char**.

- Each character in the set must be represented as a positive value by type **char**, whether it is treated as signed or unsigned. So, in the case of the ASCII character set and an eight-bit **char**, the maximum value is 127 (128 is a negative number when stored in a **char** variable).

Character Classification

The standard C run-time support contains a complete set of character-classification macros and functions. These functions are defined in the CTYPE.H file and are guaranteed to be portable:

isalnum	isdigit	isprint	isupper
isalpha	isgraph	ispunct	isxdigit
iscntrl	islower	isspace	

The following code fragment is not portable to implementations that do not use the ASCII character set:

```
/* Nonportable */
if( c >= 'A' && c <= 'Z' )
    /* uppercase alphabetic */
```

Instead, consider using this:

```
/* Portable */
if( isalpha(c) && isupper(c) )
    /* uppercase alphabetic */
```

The first example above is nonportable, because it assumes that uppercase A is represented by a smaller value than uppercase Z, and that no lowercase characters fall between the values of A and Z. The second example is portable, because it uses the character classification functions to perform the tests.

In a portable program, you should not perform any comparison on variables of type **char** except strict equality (==). You cannot assume the character set follows an increasing sequence—that may not be true on a different machine.

Case Translation

Translation of characters from upper- to lowercase or from lower- to uppercase is called "case translation." The following example shows a coding technique for case translation not portable to implementations using a non-ASCII character set.

```
#define make_upper(c) ((c)&0xcf)
#define make_lower(c) ((c)|0x20)
```

This code takes advantage of the fact that you can map uppercase to lowercase simply by changing the state of bit 6. It is extremely efficient but nonportable. To write portable code, use the case-translation macros **toupper** and **tolower** (defined in CTYPE.H).

13.2 Assumptions about the Compiler

Different compilers translate C source code into object code in different ways. The ANSI draft standard for the C programming language defines how many of these translations must be done; others are implementation-defined.

This section describes assumptions about how the compiler translates your C code, which can make your programs nonportable. For a complete description of how Microsoft C handles implementation-defined operations, see Appendix C, "Implementation-Defined Behavior."

13.2.1 Sign Extension

"Sign extension" is the propagation of the sign bit to fill unoccupied space when promoting to a more-significant type or when performing bitwise right-shift operations.

Promotion from Shorter Types

Integral promotions from shorter types occur when you make an assignment, perform arithmetic, perform a comparison, or perform an explicit cast.

The behavior of integral promotion is well defined, except for type **char**. The implementation defines whether type **char** is treated as signed or unsigned. The code fragment below is an example of promotion as a result of assignment:

```
char c1 = -3;
int  i1;

i1 = c1;
```

In this example, the expected result of the assignment statement is that i1 will be set to –3. If the implementation defines type **char** as unsigned, however, sign extension will not occur, and i1 will be 253 (on a two's-complement machine).

Promotion can also occur as a result of a comparison of different types:

```
char c;

if( c == 0x80 )
    .
    .
    .
```

This comparison will never evaluate as true on an implementation that sign-extends **char** types but treats hexadecimal constants as unsigned. Use a character constant of the form **'\x80'**, or explicitly cast the constant to type **char** to perform the comparison correctly.

The following comparison, which is an example of promotion as a result of a cast, is also nonportable:

```
char c;
unsigned int u;

if( u == (unsigned)c )
```

There are two problems with this code:

- The **char** type may be treated as signed or unsigned, depending on the implementation.

- If the **char** type is treated as signed, it can be converted to **unsigned** in two different ways: the **char** value may first be sign-extended to **int**, then converted to **unsigned**; or the **char** may be converted to **unsigned char**, then sign-extended to **int** length.

It is always safe to compare a **signed int** with a **char** constant because C requires all character constants to be positive.

Variables of type **char** are promoted to type **int** when passed as arguments to a function. This will cause sign extension on some machines. Consider the following code:

```
char c = 128;

printf( "%d\n", c );
```

Microsoft C Specific

Microsoft C allows you to treat type **char** as signed or unsigned. By default, a **char** is considered signed, but if you change the default **char** type using the /J compiler option, you can treat it as unsigned.

Bitwise Right-Shift Operations

Positive or unsigned integral types (**char**, **short**, **int**, and **long**) yield positive or zero values after a right bitwise shift (>>) operation. For example,

```
(char)120 >> 4
```

yields 7,

```
(unsigned char)240 >> 8
```

yields 0,

```
(int)500 >> 8
```

yields 1, and

```
(unsigned int)65535 >> 4
```

yields 4,095.

Negative-signed integral types yield implementation-defined values after a bitwise right-shift operation. This means that you must know whether you want to do a signed or unsigned shift, then code accordingly.

If you don't know how the implementation performs, you may get unexpected results. For example, `(signed char)0x80 >> 3` yields 0xf0 if the implementation performs sign extension on right bitwise shifts. If the implementation does not perform the sign extension, the result is 0x10.

You can use right shifts to speed up division when the divisor can be represented by powers of 2 and the dividend is positive. To maintain portability, you should use the division operator.

To perform an unsigned shift, explicitly cast the data to an unsigned type. To perform a shift that extends the sign bit, use the division operator as follows: divide by 2^n, where n is the number of bits you want to shift.

13.2.2 Length and Case of Identifiers

Some implementations do not support long identifiers. Some allow only 6 characters, while others allow as many as 32. They may report each identifier that exceeds the maximum length or truncate identifiers to a given length. Truncation causes serious problems, especially if you have a number of similarly named variables within the scope of a block of code, such as the following:

```
double acct_receivable_30_days;
double acct_receivable_60_days;
double acct_receivable_90_days;
double current_interest_rate;

acct_receivable_30_days *= current_interest_rate;
```

If your target system retains only six significant characters, you will have to rename all your `acct_receivable` variables.

Case sensitivity also affects portability. C is usually a case-sensitive language. That is, `CalculateInterest` is not considered the same identifier as `calculateinterest`. Some systems are not case sensitive, however, so to write portable code, differentiate your identifiers by something other than case.

These problems with identifiers can occur in two locations: the compiler and the linker or loader. Even if the compiler can handle long and case-differentiated identifiers, if the linker or loader cannot, you can get duplicate definitions or other unexpected errors.

Microsoft C Specific

The Microsoft C compiler issues the /NOIGNORECASE command to the Microsoft Segmented-Executable Linker (LINK), specifically instructing it to consider the case of identifiers.

13.2.3 Register Variables

The number and type of register variables in a function depend on the implementation. You can declare more variables as **register** than the number of physical registers the implementation uses. In such a case, the compiler treats the excess register variables as **automatic**.

Since the types that qualify for **register** class differ among implementations, invalid **register** declarations are treated as **automatic**.

If you declare variables as **register** to optimize performance, declare them in decreasing order of importance to ensure that the compiler allocates a register to the most important variables.

Microsoft C Specific

The compiler ignores **register** declarations if you select the global register allocation optimization. You can select global register allocation as follows:

Environment	Selection
CL command line	Specify either the /Oe or /Ox option.
PWB	Select the Global Register Allocation option in the Debug Build Options or Release Build Options dialog boxes.
pragma	Use the **optimize** pragma with the **e** parameter.

13.2.4 Functions with a Variable Number of Arguments

Functions that accept a variable number of arguments are not portable. Although both the ANSI Standard and *The C Programming Language* specify how to write these functions and how they behave, differences still exist among compiler implementors about how to use variable argument lists.

Many UNIX® systems support a standard that differs from the ANSI Standard for variable arguments. Although this may change, it currently presents a portability concern.

Microsoft C run-time libraries and macros allow you to use whichever version of variable argument support you expect to be most portable for your application.

13.2.5 Evaluation Order

The C language does not guarantee the evaluation order of most expressions. Avoid writing constructs that depend on evaluation within an expression to proceed in a particular manner. For example,

```
i = 0;
func( i++, i++ );
.
.
.
func( int a, int b )
{
```

A compiler could evaluate this code fragment and pass 0 as a and 1 as b. It could also pass 1 as a and 0 as b and conform equally with the standards.

The C language does guarantee that an expression will be completely evaluated at any given "sequence point." A sequence point is a point in the syntax of the language at which all side effects of an expression or series of expressions have been completed.

These are the sequence points in the C language:

1. The semicolon (;) statement separator

2. The call to a function after the arguments have been evaluated

3. The end of the first operand of one of the following:

   - Logical AND (**&&**)

   - Logical OR (**||**)

   - Conditional (**?**)

   - Comma separator (**,**) when used to separate statements or in expressions; the comma separator is not a sequence point when it is used between variables in declaration statements or between parameters in a function invocation

4. The end of a full expression, such as

- An initializer

- The expression in an expression statement (for example, any expression inside parentheses)

- The controlling expression of a **while** or **do** statement

- Any of the three expressions of a **for** statement

- The expression in a **return** statement

13.2.6 Function and Macro Arguments with Side Effects

Run-time support functions can be implemented either as functions or as macros. Avoid including expressions with side effects inside function invocations unless you are sure the function will not be implemented as a macro. Here is an illustration of how an argument with side effects can cause problems:

```
#define limit_number(a) ((a>1000)?1000:(a))

a = limit_number( a++ );
```

If $a \leq 1000$, it is incremented once. If $a > 1000$, it is incremented twice, which is probably not the intended behavior.

A macro can be used safely with an argument that has side effects if it evaluates its parameter only once. You can determine whether a macro is safe only by inspecting the code.

A common example of a run-time support function that is often implemented as a macro is **toupper**. You will find your program's behavior confusing if you use the following code:

```
char c;

c = toupper( getc() );
```

If `toupper` is implemented as a function, `getc` will be called only once, and its return value will be translated to uppercase. However, if `toupper` is implemented as a macro, `getc` will be called once or twice, depending on whether `c` is upper- or lowercase. Consider the following macro example:

```
#define toupper(c) ( (islower(c)) ? _toupper(c) : (c) )
```

If you include the **toupper** macro in your code, the preprocessor expands it as follows:

```
/* What you wrote */
c = toupper( getc() );

/* Macro expansion */
ch = (islower( (getc()) ) ? _toupper( getc() ) : (getc()) );
```

The expansion of the macro shows that the argument to `toupper` will always be called twice: once to determine if the character is lowercase and the next time to perform case translation (if necessary). In the example, this double evaluation calls the **getc** function twice. Because `getc` is a function whose side effect is to read a character from the standard input device, the example requests two characters from standard input.

13.2.7 *Environment Differences*

Many programs perform some file I/O. When writing these programs for portability, consider the following:

- Do not hard-code file or path names. Use constants you define either in a header file or at the beginning of the program.

- Do not assume the use of any particular file system. For example, the UNIX-model, hierarchical file system is prevalent on small computers. On larger systems, the file system often follows a different model.

- Do not assume a particular display size (number of rows and columns).

- Do not assume that display attributes exist. Some environments do not support such attributes as color, underlined text, blinking text, highlighted text, inverse text, protected text, or dim text.

13.3 *Portability of Data Files*

Data files are rarely portable across different CPUs. Structures, unions, and arrays have varying internal layout and alignment requirements on different machines. In addition, byte ordering within words and actual word length may vary.

The best way to achieve data-file portability is to write and read data files as one-dimensional character arrays. This procedure prevents alignment and padding problems if the data are written and read as characters. The only portability problem you are likely to encounter if you follow this course is a conflict in character sets; many computers have character-set conversion utilities.

13.4 *Portability Concerns Specific to Microsoft C*

Microsoft C offers extensions that let you take advantage of the full capabilities of the computer. These extensions are not portable to other compilers or environments. The following list shows keywords specific to Microsoft C:

_asm	_far	_interrupt	_saveregs
_based	_fastcall	near	_segment
cdecl	fortran	_near	_segname
_cdecl	_fortran	_loadds	
_export	huge	pascal	
far	_huge	_pascal	

The *Microsoft C Reference* contains compatibility information for every function in the run-time library. Any function or macro that does not have the ANSI box marked may not be portable to other compilers or computer systems.

13.5 *Microsoft C Byte Ordering*

Tables 13.4 and 13.5 summarize Microsoft C byte ordering for **short** and **long** types, respectively. In these tables, the least-significant byte of the data item is b0; the next byte is denoted by b1, and so on.

Since byte ordering is machine specific, any program that uses this byte ordering will not be portable.

Table 13.4   Byte Ordering for Short Types

CPU	Byte Order
8086	b0 b1
80286	b0 b1
PDP-11®	b0 b1
VAX-11®	b0 b1
M68000	b1 b0
Z8000®	b1 b0

Table 13.5   Byte Ordering for Long Types

CPU	Byte Order
8086	b0 b1 b2 b3
80286	b0 b1 b2 b3
PDP-11	b2 b3 b0 b1
VAX-11	b0 b1 b2 b3
M68000	b3 b2 b1 b0
Z8000	b3 b2 b1 b0

PART 4

OS/2 Support

CHAPTERS

OS/2 Support

The Microsoft C Professional Development System provides
support for OS/2 development.

Chapter 14 explains many of the general issues of OS/2 development, including accessing the OS/2 system functions, creating
module-definition files, and using the OS/2-specific features of
utilities such as the linker and BIND. Chapter 15 focuses on how
to create a multithread application, including information about
C run-time library support, potential problem areas, and how to
use CodeView to debug multithread applications. Chapter 16
concentrates on the creation of dynamic-link libraries, including
C run-time library support, application program interface with
DLLs, and debugging DLLs with CodeView.

Building OS/2 Applications

Using Microsoft C 6.0, you can create applications for OS/2. This chapter explains features in the compiler and the utilities that

- Call the OS/2 operating system directly from C functions

- Perform multitasking within your program by starting multiple execution paths known as "threads"

- Create dynamic-link libraries that can be used by multiple applications

- Work in either OS/2 or DOS to create programs for both environments

- Develop "dual-mode" applications that will run under both OS/2 and DOS from a single executable program file

This chapter contains information about accessing the OS/2 Applications Program Interface (API) from your C programs. It also discusses compile options that affect applications you develop for OS/2, module-definition files and import libraries, linker options specific to developing OS/2 applications, and using the BIND utility to create dual-mode applications.

Chapters 15 and 16, "Creating Multithread OS/2 Applications" and "Dynamic-Linking with OS/2," contain detailed information about how Microsoft C supports these advanced OS/2 features.

14.1 The OS/2 Applications Program Interface

The entire set of OS/2 system calls is known as the OS/2 API. You need to access the OS/2 API for the low-level functions provided by the operating system, such as

- Requests for information about the display

- Requests to display information

- Requests for information from the pointing device (mouse)

- Requests for information from the keyboard

- Requests for blocks of memory

- Requests for disk actions, including reading and writing

You can call all of the OS/2 system services directly from programs written in C. Under DOS, the API operates at a lower level, requiring programs to set up hardware registers and generate a software interrupt to access the system services. Under OS/2, programs use function calls to access the operating system services.

Sections 14.1.1–14.1.3 describe the calling conventions and precautions you must observe when accessing OS/2 API functions.

14.1.1 Calling the OS/2 API

Your program must declare calls to the OS/2 API with both the **_far** and **_pascal** keywords. Adding the **_pascal** keyword to the function declaration ensures that the FORTRAN/Pascal calling convention is used. The **_far** keyword directs the compiler to generate an intersegment call instruction. A sample declaration for the OS/2 API function **DosExit** follows:

```
void _far _pascal DosExit( unsigned int, unsigned int );
```

You must be sure that all pointers passed to OS/2 API functions are far pointers, even if you are writing a program using the small or medium memory models. This process can be simplified if you include the OS2.H header file.

OS/2 API function calls are far and must use the FORTRAN/ Pascal calling convention.

OS/2 API functions use the FORTRAN/Pascal language calling convention. They expect arguments to be pushed onto the stack in left-to-right order, with the last argument in the list pushed onto the stack last. OS/2 API functions remove their arguments from the stack before returning to the caller. Standard C functions push their arguments from right to left, with the first argument being the last one pushed.

All OS/2 API functions return 0 if the operation is successful. They return an error code if the operation fails.

14.1.2 Including the OS/2 Header Files

You do not have to construct your own API declarations if you use the OS2.H header file. It is the first file of a set of header files that supply function prototypes for every OS/2 API call and definitions of special OS/2 structures, data types, and constants.

The API function prototypes define all functions as far procedures with the FORTRAN/Pascal calling convention. They also take care of casting all near pointers to far pointers and other similar type coercions.

Define a constant before including OS2.H.

When you include OS2.H, the most commonly used data types and macros are automatically defined. To minimize compile time for the C preprocessor, other definitions are grouped by function. They are included only if your source file defines the appropriate constant before including OS2.H. The following list shows how these manifest constants affect functions from the OS/2 API:

Constant	Effect
INCL_BASE	All error constants, kernel, keyboard, video, and mouse definitions (same as **INCL_DOS** + **INCL_SUB** + **INCL_DOSERRORS**)
INCL_DOS	All kernel system definitions
INCL_DOSERRORS	All error constants
INCL_KBD	All keyboard definitions
INCL_MOU	All mouse definitions
INCL_SUB	All keyboard, video, and mouse definitions (same as **INCL_KBD** + **INCL_VIO** + **INCL_MOU**)
INCL_VIO	All video-display definitions
INCL_WIN	Basic set of Presentation Manager definitions

The header files have additional constants that let you include smaller subsets or functions not defined in the standard sets.

The statement #define INCL_DOS affects the functions defined. The program in the example below calls the OS/2 kernel to request a nonshareable, nondiscardable memory segment for an 8K buffer. The **INCL_DOS** constant in the #**define** statement instructs the C preprocessor to include all of the kernel function definitions. The function prototype for **DosAllocSeg** declares the first and third arguments as **USHORT** (unsigned short integers). The second argument is a far pointer to the OS/2 data type **SEL**, which is used for segment selectors.

```
#define  INCL_DOS
#include <os2.h>

VOID GetMemorySegment()
{
    SEL    selector;

    if ( DosAllocSeg( 8192, &selector, 0 ) )
        puts( "Allocation failed\n" );
    else
        puts( "Successful allocation\n" );
}
```

The function call in the example works correctly even in a small or medium memory model program where the selector variable is a **near data** type. All three arguments are coerced by the function prototype to the proper types, regardless of the memory model used.

14.1.3 Creating Dual-Mode Programs as Family Applications

The OS/2 API has a subset of system functions that have direct DOS equivalents. This subset is known as the "Family Applications Program Interface" (Family API). Programs that use only the Family API can be run under DOS and the OS/2 compatibility box, as well as under OS/2.

You can build a single executable file for use under both OS/2 and DOS.

By creating a Family API application, you can distribute the same executable file to both OS/2 and DOS users. The Microsoft C compiler, linker, and object module librarian are examples of family applications. The benefit of having a single executable file is offset by a few disadvantages:

- The executable file is larger, because it includes a special loader and OS/2 API-simulator routines for running in DOS mode.

- In real mode, the application loads more slowly than a program created specifically for either OS/2 or DOS. There is no performance penalty in loading or running in OS/2 protected mode.

- When running in real mode, the program cannot use advanced OS/2 features such as multiple threads or system calls that are not part of the Family API. If you take special precautions (described in Section 14.5, "The BIND Utility"), the program can take advantage of these features when running in OS/2 protected mode.

Follow the same steps to build both family and protected-mode applications but add an extra step at the end to create the Family API program. This step links functions from the dynamic-link libraries directly into a stand-alone executable file that can run in both real and protected mode.

Restrictions on Family Applications

Programs that use the Family API are subject to certain restrictions:

- They cannot overcommit memory; they must fit into the DOS 640K environment.

- They cannot use advanced OS/2 features, such as threads and semaphores, that do not have DOS counterparts.

- They must restrict their use of some calls to the defined common subset. For example, some of the file-mode options for the **DosOpen** function are not available in real mode.

Family API Functions

The system calls that make up Family API are listed below. The calls marked with an asterisk (*) have different options or behavior, depending on whether they are running in real mode or protected mode. The *Microsoft OS/2 Programmer's Reference* explains the functions and the differences between their real- and protected-mode implementations.

DosAllocHuge*	DosHoldSignal*	DosSubSet
DosAllocSeg*	DosInsMessage*	DosWrite
DosBeep	DosMkDir	KbdCharIn*
DosBufReset	DosMove	KbdFlushBuffer*
DosCaseMap*	DosNewSize	KbdGetStatus*
DosChdir	DosOpen*	KbdPeek*
DosChgFilePtr	DosPutMessage*	KbdSetStatus*
DosCLIAccess	DosQCurDir	KbdStringIn*
DosClose	DosQCurDisk	VioGetBuf
DosCreateCSAlias*	DosQFHandState	VioGetConfig
DosDelete	DosQFileInfo	VioGetCurPos
DosDevConfig	DosQFileMode	VioGetCurType
DosDevIOCtl*	DosQFSInfo	VioGetMode
DosDupHandle	DosQHandType	VioGetPhysBuf
DosErrClass	DosQVerify	VioReadCellStr
DosError*	DosRead*	VioReadCharStr
DosExecPgm*	DosReallocHuge*	VioScrLock*
DosExit*	DosReallocSeg*	VioScrollDn
DosFileLocks	DosRmDir	VioScrollLf
DosFindClose	DosSelectDisk	VioScrollRt
DosFindFirst	DosSetCp	VioScrollUp
DosFindNext*	DosSetDateTime	VioScrUnLock
DosFreeSeg*	DosSetFHandState*	VioSetCurPos
DosGetCollate*	DosSetFileInfo	VioSetCurType
DosGetCp	DosSetFileMode	VioSetMode
DosGetCtryInfo*	DosSetFSInfo	VioShowBuf
DosGetDateTime	DosSetSigHandler*	VioWrtCellStr
DosGetDBSCEv*	DosSetVec*	VioWrtCharStr
DosGetEnv	DosSetVerify	VioWrtCharStrAtt
DosGetHugeShift	DosSizeSeg	VioWrtNAttr
DosGetMachineMode	DosSleep	VioWrtNCell
DosGetMessage*	DosSubAlloc	VioWrtNChar
DosGetVersion	DosSubFree	VioWrtTTy

14.2 Compile Options for the CL Command

This section describes the compile options you must specify in the Programmer's WorkBench or on the CL command line to designate a program's target environment (OS/2, DOS, or both). It also introduces options you should use with certain types of OS/2 applications, such as multithread programs, dynamic-link libraries, and programs calling C function dynamic-link libraries. For an in-depth discussion of topics that affect multithread processes and dynamic-link libraries, see Chapter 15, "Creating Multithread OS/2 Applications," and Chapter 16, "Dynamic-Linking with OS/2."

14.2.1 The Link Mode Options (/Lp, /Lr, and /Lc)

The /L*x* options (/Lp, /Lr, and /Lc) provide the flexibility of programming for both OS/2 and DOS in either environment. Regardless of the host operating system, you can build applications for either target operating system. You do not have to switch to the target system to build the program.

The /Lp option produces an OS/2 protected-mode program; the /Lr option creates a DOS real-mode program. /Lc is a synonym for /Lr.

To use these options, the mode-specific combined libraries must be installed. Unless you choose a default operating environment, each mode-specific library has the letter P or R at the end of its base name. For example, the protected-mode small memory model library with the emulator floating-point option is named SLIBCEP.LIB. The corresponding real-mode library is named SLIBCER.LIB. The default name, however, is SLIBCE.LIB.

Installing and Using the Microsoft C Professional Development System describes how to create mode-specific libraries with the SETUP program. It also explains how to establish a default target environment by renaming libraries. A default environment is useful if you work mainly in one mode (OS/2 or DOS) but sometimes write programs for the other mode. When you set up OS/2 as the default mode, SLIBCEP.LIB, for example, becomes SLIBCE.LIB.

Don't use /Lx options unless you have mode-specific libraries.

When you use the /L*x* options, you instruct the compiler to override the default library name in the object module's library search record and to substitute the mode-specific combined library name. The compiler also generates a link response file with the /NODEFAULTLIBRARYSEARCH (/NOD) linker option to override the default library. See Section 14.4, "Link Command-Line Options," for more information about the /NOD option.

Do not use the /Lp option to specify protected mode when OS/2 is the default environment. If you do this, the compiler uses the name of the mode-specific library (e.g., SLIBCEP.LIB). Because SETUP renamed the library to SLIBCE.LIB to create a default environment, the library search fails. This caution also applies to specifying /Lr when you have installed DOS as the default environment.

If you invoke the linker in a separate step from the compilation, you must specify the /NOD link option.

NOTE *There is a special library, LLIBCMT, for building multithread OS/2 applications. Another special library, LLIBCDLL, supports multithread dynamic-link libraries. If you use LLIBCMT or LLIBCDLL, you must use one of the library selection options described in Section 14.2.3 instead of /Lp.*

14.2.2 Creating Bound Programs Option (/Fb)

The /Fb option allows you to compile, link, and bind an application in one step. Binding an executable file creates a Family API program that can run under both OS/2 and DOS.

When you use /Fb, the compiler invokes the BIND utility program immediately after the link step. You can also execute BIND directly (as described in Section 14.5, "The BIND Utility"). You must have the API.LIB and OS2.LIB files in the path specified by the LIB environment variable or in your current working directory.

The syntax for the /Fb option is

/Fb[[*bound-exe*]]

You can specify a separate name for a bound-executable file.

The optional *bound-exe* parameter specifies the name of the bound program. It must directly follow the /Fb option, without intervening spaces. The *bound-exe* name can be a file specification, a drive name, or a directory specification. If you specify a file name without an extension, the compiler appends the .EXE extension to the name. If you give a directory specification for *bound-exe*, the name must end with a backslash (\ ) so the compiler can distinguish it from an ordinary file name. If you do not supply a name, BIND uses the name of the unbound program and overwrites it.

When creating both bound and protected-mode versions with different names, consider this example:

```
CL /Lp /Fbsampleb sample.c
```

The protected-mode executable file that this command creates is called SAMPLE.EXE; the bound-executable file is called SAMPLEB.EXE.

You may need to run BIND as a separate step instead of using the /Fb option.

The /Fb option works only if you are doing a single-step compile and link. If the CL command line includes the /c (compile without link) option, the compiler ignores the /Fb option. If you use /c, you must run the BIND utility as a separate step of the program build.

If your program includes calls to API functions that are not in the FAPI subset, you must use the /n option of the BIND utility, described in Section 14.5, to build the dual-mode executable file. If you need to use the /n BIND option, you cannot compile with /Fb. You must compile without linking by using the /c option at the compile stage; then link the program and run the BIND utility with the /n option.

14.2.3 Library Selection Options (/MT, /ML, /MD, /Zl)

Special libraries are provided for building OS/2 multithread applications and dynamic-link libraries. You must not use these libraries with any other C run-time library.

Special libraries must be the only C run-time libraries linked with your program.

If you use one of these special libraries, apply one of the library selection options (/ML, /MD, or /MT) to tell the compiler to replace the default library name in the object file with the name of the special library. This ensures that the linker does not bring in code from the default libraries. If you do not specify one of the options when compiling, you must link with the /NOD option to prevent search of a default library, such as SLIBCE.LIB.

If you fail to include any of these options, the linker searches the default library and may select the wrong version of a library function. It might, for example, select the single thread version of the **printf** function for a multithread program that has more than one thread calling **printf**.

Because the /Lp option (see Section 14.2.1, "The Link Mode Options") instructs the compiler to specify the default protected-mode libraries rather than the special multithread or DLL-specific libraries, do not use it with /Zl or /Mx.

Multithread Library Option (/MT)

When you specify the /MT option, the compiler embeds the LLIBCMT.LIB library name in the object file. Chapter 15, "Creating Multithread OS/2 Applications," explains how to build multithread applications using LLIBCMT.LIB. The /MT option also has the effect of combining these command-line options:

/ALw /FPi /G2 /D MT

C Run-Time Library for Building DLLs (/ML)

Use the /ML option to specify that you are building a dynamic-link library that calls functions in LLIBCDLL.LIB, the C run-time library for dynamic-link libraries. The library name is embedded in the object file. The /ML option also has the effect of combining these command-line options:

/ALw /FPa /G2 /D MT

C Run-Time Library for DLLs (/MD)

Use the /MD option to create a dynamic-link library of C run-time routines. With this option, the object file does not have any library search records. The /MD option has the effect of combining these command-line options:

/ALw /FPi /G2 /DDLL /D MT

Chapter 16, "Dynamic Linking with OS/2," describes the process of building and using dynamic-link libraries with LLIBCDLL.LIB.

Suppress Default Library Option (/Zl)

Use the /Zl option when you want to suppress selection of a default library. It tells the compiler not to place the default library name in the object file.

You can specify libraries and additional LINK options on the CL command line.

You can specify link options or the names of libraries on the CL command line with the /LINK option. You can also give the library name, with its .LIB extension, before the /LINK option. Each command below selects the multithread C run-time library:

```
CL /Zl myprog.c llibcmt.lib

CL /Zl myprog.c /link llibcmt
```

If you compile with the /c (compile without link) option, your link command must include the library name:

```
LINK myprog, myprog.exe, myprog.map, llibcmt.lib, myprog.def
```

14.2.4 Memory-Model Options (/Ax)

You must select the memory model appropriate to your application. For protected-mode applications, the large model provides the most convenient interface with the special libraries. It provides the additional benefit of placing code and data into multiple segments, allowing OS/2 to swap parts of the program to disk efficiently.

Use the large memory model with LLIBCMT (/AL and /MT).

The multithread run-time C library, LLIBCMT.LIB, is a large-model library. All library function calls must be far calls. In addition, all pointers passed to functions in the library must be far pointers. If you do not compile with the /AL option, you use must use the keyword **_far** when declaring pointers. Variables can be declared either near or far as long as they are either passed by value or cast to a far address.

If you want to call **fopen** for example, you must use code such as the following:

```
FILE _far * fp;
fp = fopen( ... );
```

NOTE *If you are using the compact, large, or huge memory model, data pointers are far by default, so you do not need to explicitly specify **_far**.*

Because each thread has its own stack, you have to compile in an SS != DS model.

Multithread applications require that each thread have its own stack. As a result, you cannot safely assume that the stack segment is in the default data group (DGROUP). That means that the stack segment can be different from the data segment (SS != DS).

To specify that you have selected an SS != DS model, you must use the /Au or /Aw option. The /MT option is a shorthand way of specifying this combination of options to the compiler:

/ALw /FPi /G2 /D MT

The /MT option also causes the compiler to place a library search record for LLIBCMT in the object file.

14.3 *Module-Definition Files and Import Libraries*

A module-definition file tells the linker about the characteristics of an application or dynamic-link library. It describes names, segments, memory requirements, and import and export definitions. Export definitions make functions in the OS/2 dynamic-link libraries (DLLs) available to other programs. Each export definition specifies a function name. A program using these functions must have import definitions in order to find each dynamic-link function. Each import definition specifies a function name and the name of the dynamic-link library where the function resides.

The IMPLIB utility generates a library of import definitions that can be examined during the link. For imported functions, the import library can be used in place of a module-definition file.

Module-definition files are optional for most OS/2 programs. Two types of programs must use them:

- Dynamic-link libraries
- Programs with I/O privileges

Each module-definition file contains one or more module statements defining attributes of the executable program. The statements and their associated attributes are listed below:

Statement	Attribute
CODE	Gives default attributes for code segments
DATA	Gives default attributes for data segments
DESCRIPTION	Describes the module in one line
EXETYPE	Identifies the operating system
EXPORTS	Defines exported functions
HEAPSIZE	Specifies local heap size, in bytes
IMPORTS	Defines imported functions
LIBRARY	Names a dynamic-link library
NAME	Names an application
OLD	Preserves import information from a previous version of the library
PROTMODE	Specifies that the module runs only in OS/2 protected mode
REALMODE	Relaxes some restrictions that the linker imposes for protected-mode programs
SEGMENTS	Gives attributes for specific segments
STACKSIZE	Specifies local stack size, in bytes
STUB	Adds a DOS 3.x executable file to the beginning of the module, usually to terminate the program when run in real mode

In addition to the keywords listed above, each statement includes one or more fields to complete the attribute description. All keywords must be entered in uppercase. You can include comments in the module-definition file by beginning the line with a semicolon (;). For a complete list of the keywords and their meaning, see on-line help for information about module-definition files.

14.3.1 Adding a Module-Definition File to the LINK Command

The module-definition file name is the last field of the link command:

LINK *objects* [[,[[*exe*]]]] [[, [[*map*]]]] [[, [[*lib*]]]] [[, [[*def*]]]] [[;]]

This example uses the default libraries:

```
LINK sample, sample.exe, sample.map,,sample.def
```

When you use a module-definition file, you must use the /c option on the CL command line and link in a separate step. If you are linking without a module-definition file, you can use a semicolon after your last entry to suppress LINK's prompt for the module-definition file name and other missing parameters.

The segmented-executable linker is the only LINK program that recognizes module-definition files. Since it is backwards compatible, it should be the only linker in your path. The QuickC linker does not process these files.

The following sections illustrate ways to use module-definition files. On-line help describes all of the commands and options available.

14.3.2 Creating Dynamic-Link Libraries (DLLs)

You can build your own dynamic-link libraries. A simple module-definition file for such a library with one public function is shown below:

```
LIBRARY Mylib INITINSTANCE

DATA MULTIPLE

EXPORTS
        MyProc
```

You can use the same module-definition file you used to create the dynamic-link library as input to the IMPLIB utility. IMPLIB generates a library file with a .LIB extension for use by applications calling your dynamic-link routines. Section 14.3.5 describes the IMPLIB program. Chapter 16, "Dynamic Linking with OS/2," explains how to build a dynamic-link library.

The **LIBRARY** statement tells the linker that this is a dynamic-link library rather than an application. (Applications use the **NAME** statement instead of the **LIBRARY** statement.)

The **EXPORTS** statement gives the name of the public function.

You can designate exported functions in a C source file.

The C language keyword **_export** is an alternative to the **EXPORTS** statement. When **_export** appears in a function declaration or definition, the compiler puts the function and its parameter size in the object module's export record. Functions with the **_export** keyword that are not listed in the module-definition file cannot have input/output privileges or alias names.

Using generic library names is dangerous.

Since OS/2 systems have many dynamic-link libraries installed, try to pick a name that uniquely identifies your library. If you choose a generic name, such as CRT.DLL or WINDOWS.DLL, you run the risk of having your library overwritten by someone else's dynamic-link library with the same name.

14.3.3 Creating Programs with I/O Privileges

OS/2 programs that must access hardware directly can designate a code segment with input/output privileges. This segment can then perform a limited set of I/O instructions but cannot make any calls to dynamic-link libraries.

You cannot use the C run-time library functions **inp** and **outp** for input and output. Their use is limited to real-mode programs. You can, however, use in-line assembler code in your C source program to access a port.

The sample module-definition file below shows two segments for a program:

```
NAME          IOPROG

EXETYPE       OS/2

SEGMENTS
    _IOSEG    IOPL
    _TEXT     NOIOPL

EXPORTS
    CharIn    4
    CharOut   4
```

The first code segment contains the I/O portion of the program and has the **IOPL** keyword. The second segment is designated **NOIOPL** (the default).

The EXPORT statement for IOPL functions must include parameter size.

The **EXPORTS** section names two functions in the **IOPL** segment that can be called by procedures outside the segment. It also specifies the size of the function's parameters. Procedures with I/O privileges must specify the number of words needed for their parameters.

NOTE *Unless the user has specified IOPL=YES in the CONFIG.SYS file, the program will not load.*

14.3.4 *Creating Presentation Manager Applications*

The Presentation Manager calls window and dialog procedures inside a Presentation Manager application. The sample module-definition file below exports these procedures and gives the linker additional instructions for building the program. Module-definition files are optional for Presentation Manager applications. They can be used to control the way different segments of the program are loaded.

```
NAME          PMSAMPLE    WINDOWAPI

EXETYPE       OS/2
STACKSIZE     4096

SEGMENTS
    _INIT       PRELOAD
    _HELP       LOADONCALL
    _TEXT       LOADONCALL
```

In the preceding example, the **NAME** statement identifies the program as an application named PMSAMPLE. The **WINDOWAPI** keyword tells the linker to mark the executable file as a Presentation Manager application. Only programs marked as windows applications or windows-compatible applications can share the Presentation Manager screen group.

The **EXETYPE** statement tells the linker to build a program that runs only in protected mode and to produce the optimal executable file for OS/2.

The **STACKSIZE** statement allocates 4096 bytes of local stack space. This is the minimum stack size recommended for Presentation Manager programs.

You can reduce run-time memory requirements. The **SEGMENTS** statement controls the way code and data segments are handled. By default, segments are not brought into physical memory until needed. The **PRELOAD** keyword in the example tells the system loader to load the _INIT segment when the program starts. The _TEXT and _HELP segments are loaded on demand. You can use the compiler's /NT option to generate your own segment names, such as _INIT and _HELP. Separate segments are useful for code that is executed infrequently, such as a help subsystem. This reduces the amount of run-time memory required for your application, since each segment will be loaded when and if there is a request for it.

14.3.5 *Creating Import Libraries with the IMPLIB Utility*

Applications that call dynamic-link library functions must use import definitions that specify the location of each dynamic-link function. The definitions consist of a function name and the name of the dynamic-link library file where it resides.

Although the application can use a module-definition file to create the import definitions, it is easier to use import libraries built by the IMPLIB utility.

IMPLIB creates an import library in the form of a file with a .LIB extension, which is read by the linker. At link time, the .LIB file is specified in the LINK command line, along with other libraries.

IMPLIB accepts two types of sources:

- The module-definition file used to create the dynamic-link library

- The dynamic-link library itself

The IMPLIB command has the syntax:

IMPLIB [[/c]]*libfile deffile* [[*deffile* ...]]

or

IMPLIB [[/c]]*libfile dynlib* [[*dynlib* ...]]

The /c option directs IMPLIB to be case sensitive. By default, it is case insensitive.

The *libfile* field names the new import library file. The *deffile* or *dynlib* fields name the input files, which are dynamic-link library or module-definition files.

The following example creates the import library file named MYLIB.LIB from the MYLIB.DLL dynamic-link library:

```
IMPLIB mylib.lib mylib.dll
```

For more information about import libraries and IMPLIB, consult on-line help.

14.4 Link Command-Line Options

This section describes command-line options that control various aspects of the linker and the circumstances in which you will need to use them.

/NODEFAULTLIBRARYSEARCH (/NOD)

If you did not compile with /MT, /MD, or /ML, suppress default library searching.

The /NODEFAULTLIBRARYSEARCH option prevents the linker from searching any library specified in an object file. When you specify this option, you should also specify the name of the library to be linked. The minimum abbreviation for this option is /NOD.

If you are using the multithread library, LLIBCMT, or the dynamic-link library, LLIBCDLL, you should use this option. Use it with dynamic-link libraries built with LLIBCDLL. This is mandatory if you did not compile with the /Zl, /MT, or /ML options.

You can select a specific library by appending the library name to the /NOD option, as in

```
/NOD:LLIBCMT.LIB
```

/NOEXTENDEDDICTSEARCH (/NOE)

The /NOEXTENDEDDICTSEARCH option prevents the linker from searching the extended dictionary, which is an internal list of symbol locations maintained by the linker. You need to use this option if a library symbol (such as **_setargv**, **_binmode**, or **_varstck**) is redefined and you receive error L2044 from the linker. The minimum abbreviation for this option is /NOE.

/NOIGNORECASE (/NOI)

The /NOIGNORECASE option preserves case sensitivity. By default, LINK maps all names to uppercase characters. Because many C function names are a mix of upper- and lowercase letters, it is important to use this option. The compile option /Zc causes any name declared with the **_pascal** keyword to be treated without regard to case at the source level. The minimum abbreviation is /NOI.

/PMTYPE

The /PMTYPE option is an alternative to specifying Presentation Manager compatibility with the **NAME** statement of a module-definition file. Use the following syntax:

/PMTYPE:*type*

Type must be one of the following:

Type	Effect
PM	The application is an OS/2 Presentation Manager application using the Presentation Manager API and running in the Presentation Manager screen group. This type corresponds to specifying **WINDOWAPI** in the **NAME** statement of a module-definition file.
VIO	The application is compatible with the OS/2 Presentation Manager and can run in a window or in a separate screen group. This type corresponds to specifying **WINDOWCOMPAT** in the **NAME** statement of a module-definition file.
NOVIO	The application is not compatible with the OS/2 Presentation Manager. It must run in a separate screen group. This type corresponds to specifying **NOTWINDOWCOMPAT** in the **NAME** statement of a module-definition file.

14.5 The BIND Utility

The BIND utility converts a protected-mode program into a program that runs in both OS/2 and DOS environments. It replaces Family API calls to dynamic-link library functions with DOS emulator routines from the API.LIB library. (See Section 14.1.3, "Creating Dual-Mode Programs as Family Applications," for a list of Family API calls.) BIND produces a stand-alone program file that can run under

- OS/2 protected mode

- OS/2 real mode

- DOS 2.x and DOS 3.x

BIND is an alternative to the C compiler's /Fb option described in Section 14.2.2, "Creating Bound Programs Option." You must use BIND instead of the /Fb option when you compile with the /c (compile without link) option or when your program includes functions that operate only in protected mode.

You can include functions in a bound application that are not members of the Family API.

To include functions available only in protected mode, you must run the BIND utility with the /n option. Your run-time code must call the Family API function **DosGetMachineMode** to determine whether it is running in real or protected mode. When your program executes in real mode, it will be aborted if it tries to call a function available only in protected mode.

You might choose to design your application so it executes different sections of code, depending on the machine mode. For example, the application may need to keep track of the passage of elapsed time or to detect time-outs. In real mode, you might use polling or timing loops or perhaps intercept the timer interrupts. In protected mode, you should use the OS/2 semaphore and timer services, such as **DosSetSem** and **DosTimerAsync**, instead.

Invoke BIND with the following syntax:

BIND *infile* [[*implibs*]] [[*linklibs*]] [[/o *outfile*]] [[/n @*file*]] [[/n *names*]] [[/m *mapfile*]]

The /n option provides a way to include protected-mode functions. It has two formats:

- A list of one or more names, separated by spaces.

- The name of a file, preceded by the at (@) sign. The file should consist of a list of functions, one name per line.

The /o option specifies a name for the bound-executable file. If it is not present, the name of the input file is used.

The /m option causes a link map to be generated for the real-mode version of the executable file.

To bind a program named TIMER that uses **DosTimerAsync** to manage time-outs when running in protected mode, invoke BIND as follows:

```
BIND TIMER /n DosTimerAsync
```

For more information about BIND and other command-line options, consult on-line help.

Creating Multithread OS/2 Applications

Microsoft C, version 6.0, provides support for creating multithread applications under OS/2. You should consider using more than one thread if your application needs to manage multiple activities, such as simultaneous keyboard and mouse input. One thread can process keyboard input while a second thread filters mouse activities. A third thread could update the display screen based on data from the mouse and keyboard threads. At the same time, other threads can access disk files or get data from a communications port.

This chapter explains the features in C 6.0 that support the creation of multithread programs. It also describes some important ways in which programming for OS/2 is different than programming for DOS.

15.1 Multithread Programs

OS/2 performs the scheduling and allocation of real hardware resources to multiple programs, or "processes." It does not actually schedule the processes themselves; it schedules threads belonging to the processes.

A thread is basically a path of execution through a program. It is also the smallest unit of execution that OS/2 schedules. A thread consists of a stack, the state of the CPU registers, and an entry in the execution list of the system scheduler. Each thread shares all of the process's resources.

A process consists of one or more threads and the code, data, and other resources of a program in memory. Typical program resources are open files, semaphores, and dynamically allocated memory. A program executes when the system scheduler gives one of its threads execution control. The scheduler determines which threads should run and when they should run. Threads of lower priority may have to wait while higher priority threads complete their tasks.

Threads operate independently and are unaware of other threads.

All threads in a process operate independently of one another. Unless you take special steps to make them visible to each other, each thread executes while completely unaware of the existence of other threads in a process. Threads sharing common resources, however, must coordinate their work by using flags, semaphores or some other method of interprocess communication. See Section 15.3, "Writing a Multithread Program," for more information about synchronizing threads.

15.1.1 Library Support

All shared functions in a multithread program must be re-entrant.

If one thread is suspended by the OS/2 scheduler while executing the **printf** function, one of the program's other threads might start executing. If the second thread also calls **printf**, data might be corrupted. To avoid this, access to static data used by the function must be restricted to one thread at a time. This process of restricting access to certain data is called serialization.

You do not need to serialize access to stack-based (automatic) variables because each thread has a different stack. Therefore, a function that uses only automatic (stack) variables is re-entrant. The standard C run-time libraries, such as SLIBCE, have a limited number of re-entrant functions. A multithread program needing to use C run-time library functions that are normally not re-entrant should be built with the multithread library LLIBCMT.LIB.

The Multithread C Library LLIBCMT.LIB

The support library LLIBCMT.LIB is a re-entrant large-model library for creating multithread programs.

A multithread program linked with LLIBCMT.LIB can use any memory model.

All calls to library functions must use the large-model calling interface (far code pointers, far calls, and far data pointers). When your application calls functions in this library,

- All library calls must be far calls.

- All library calls must use the C calling convention; programs compiled using the /Gr (fastcall calling convention) or /Gc (Pascal calling convention) options must use the standard include files for the run-time library functions they call.

- All data and code pointers must be far pointers.

- Variables passed to library functions must either be passed by value or cast to a far address.

- Your main function must be declared far if you are compiling with the small or compact memory models.

You do not need to explicitly declare far pointers if you are using the compact, large, or huge memory models, since these models use far pointers as default. For the large and huge memory models, the function calls are also far by default.

A small-model program calling a library function such as **isupper**, for example, must use declarations like the following:

```
int _far _cdecl isupper( int _c );
```

Programs built with LLIBCMT.LIB are entirely self-contained.

Programs built with LLIBCMT.LIB do not share C run-time library code or data with any dynamic-link libraries they call. Chapter 16 explains how to build DLLs and how to share code and data between processes.

Alternatives to LLIBCMT.LIB

If you choose to build a multithread program without using LLIBCMT.LIB, you must do the following:

- Use the standard C libraries and limit library calls to the set of re-entrant functions.

- Use the OS/2 API thread management functions, such as **DosCreateThread**.

- Provide your own synchronization for functions that are not re-entrant by using OS/2 services such as semaphores and the **DosEnterCritSec** and **DosExitCritSec** functions.

The C run-time library functions listed below are re-entrant and can be used in multithread programs linked with the standard libraries.

abs	memccpy	strcat	strnset
atoi	memchr	strchr	strrchr
atol	memcmp	strcmp	strrev
bsearch	memcpy	strcmpi	strset
chdir	memicmp	strcpy	strstr
getpid	memmove	stricmp	strupr
halloc	memset	strlen	swab
hfree	mkdir	strlwr	tolower
itoa	movedata	strncat	toupper
labs	putch	strncmp	
lfind	rmdir	strncpy	
lsearch	segread	strnicmp	

WARNING *The multithread library LLIBCMT.LIB includes the* **_beginthread** *and* **_endthread** *functions. The* **_beginthread** *function performs initialization without which many C run-time functions will fail. You must use* **_beginthread** *instead of* **DosCreateThread** *in C programs built with LLIBCMT.LIB if you intend to call C run-time functions.*

The Multithread Library Compile Option (/MT)

The /MT option for the CL command is the best way to build a multithread program with LLIBCMT.LIB. The /MT option embeds the LLIBCMT library name in the object file. Using the /MT option automatically specifies the /ALw /FPi /G2 /D MT options. The following list describes what these options do.

Switch	Effect
/ALw	Use the large memory model with separate stack segment; do not reload the DS register as part of the entry sequence for every function
/FPi	Generate in-line floating-point instructions and select the emulator math package
/G2	Use the 80286 processor instruction set
/D MT	Use the multithread version of the include files

These options can be combined with other options to specify different memory models and different relationships between the data segment and the stack. You can override the /G2 and /FPi options by specifying a different option later on the command line. The following example shows how to override the floating-point package option:

```
CL /MT /FPa /Lp PROG.C
```

NOTE *You cannot replace the /MT option with /ALw /FPi /G2. You must use /MT to generate multithread programs.*

15.1.2 Include Files

The Microsoft C 6.0 include files contain conditional sections for multithread applications using LLIBCMT.LIB. To compile your application with the appropriate definitions, you can

- Compile with the /MT option described in Section 15.1.1, "Library Support."

- Define the symbolic constant **MT** in your source file or on the command line with the /D option.

Always use the standard include files. Standard include files declare C run-time library functions as they are implemented in the libraries. If you used the Maximum Optimization (/Ox) or Register Calling Convention (/Gr) option, the compiler assumes that all functions should be called using the register calling convention. The run-time library functions were compiled using either the C or the FORTRAN/Pascal calling convention, and the declarations in the standard include files tell the compiler to generate correct external references to these functions.

See Section 15.4, "Compiling and Linking," for examples of how to use the **MT** constant.

15.1.3 C Run-Time Library Functions for Thread Control

All OS/2 programs have at least one thread. Any thread can create additional threads. A thread can complete its work very quickly and then terminate, or it can stay active for the life of the program.

The LLIBCMT and LLIBCDLL C run-time libraries provide two functions for thread creation and termination: the **_beginthread** and **_endthread** functions. They also declare the global variable **_threadid**, which contains the address of an application's current thread identifier.

The **_beginthread** function creates a new thread and returns a thread identifier if the operation is successful. The thread will terminate automatically if it completes execution, or it can terminate itself with a call to **_endthread**.

The global variable **_threadid** holds the address of the identifier of the current thread. It is defined in the STDDEF.H file as shown below:

```
/* define pointer to thread id value */
extern int far * _threadid;
```

WARNING *If you are going to call C run-time routines from a program built with LLIBCMT.LIB, you must start your threads with the* **_beginthread** *function. Do not use the OS/2 functions* **DosExit** *and* **DosCreateThread***. Using* **DosSuspendThread** *can lead to a deadlock condition when more than one thread is blocked waiting for the suspended thread to complete its access to a C run-time data structure.*

The **_beginthread** and **_endthread** functions are described in detail below. Section 15.2 illustrates their use in a sample multithread program.

The _beginthread Function

All threads in a process can execute concurrently.

The **_beginthread** function creates a new thread. A thread shares the code and data segments of a process with other threads in the process but has its own unique register values, stack space, and current instruction address. The system gives CPU time to each thread, so that all threads in a process can execute concurrently. You can find a complete description of **_beginthread** and its arguments in on-line help.

The **_beginthread** function is similar to the **DosCreateThread** function in the OS/2 API with these differences:

- The **_beginthread** function lets you pass arguments to the thread.

- The stack address points to the bottom of the stack. It is the address of the start of an array or of the start of a block of dynamically allocated memory. When you use the **DosCreateThread** call, the stack address points to the top of the stack.

- If you specify **NULL** for the stack address, **_beginthread** manages allocation and deallocation of the thread stack for you. This option is advantageous because it is difficult for your program to determine when a thread has terminated, so you cannot know when to deallocate the thread stack. However, **_beginthread** maintains enough information to know when a thread has terminated and deallocates the thread's stack the next time its thread ID is used.

The **_beginthread** function returns the thread ID number of the new thread if successful or –1 if there was an error. Errors include specifying an odd-address stack or an odd- or zero-length stack (which is different than passing **NULL** for the stack address) or trying to create too many threads. The multithread library, LLIBCMT.LIB, supports the maximum number of threads allowed by OS/2.

The _endthread Function

The **_endthread** function terminates a thread created by **_beginthread**. Threads terminate automatically when they complete. The **_endthread** function is useful for conditional termination from within a thread. A thread dedicated to communications processing, for example, can quit if it is unable to get control of the communications port. You can find a complete description of **_endthread** in on-line help.

15.2 Sample Multithread C Program

BOUNCE.C is a sample multithread program that creates a new thread each time the letter 'a' or 'A' is entered at the keyboard. Each thread bounces a "happy face" of a different color around the screen. Up to 32 threads can be created. The program's normal termination occurs when 'q' or 'Q' is entered. It will also terminate if it receives the CTRL+C or CTRL+BREAK signals. See Section 15.4, "Compiling and Linking," for details on compiling and linking BOUNCE.C.

```
/*  Bounce - Creates a new thread each time the letter 'a'is typed.
 *  Each thread bounces a happy face of a different color around the screen.
 *  All threads are terminated when the letter 'q' is entered or when
 *  the CTRL+C/CTRL+BREAK signals are received.
 *
 *  This program requires the multithread library. For example, compile
 *  with the following command line:
 *      CL /MT BOUNCE.C
 */

#define INCL_NOCOMMON                       /* Use only what we need */
#define INCL_NOPM                           /* Don't need PM */
#define INCL_DOSPROCESS                     /* DosBeep and DosSleep */
#define INCL_DOSSEMAPHORES                  /* OS/2 semaphore functions */
#define INCL_DOSSIGNALS                     /* OS/2 signal functions */
#define INCL_VIO
#define INCL_KBD
#include <os2.h>
#include <stdlib.h>
#include <string.h>
#include <stdio.h>
#include <process.h>

#define STACK_SIZE   4096
#define MAX_THREADS  32

void main( void );                          /* Thread 1: main */
void KbdThread( void );                      /* Thread 2: keyboard input */
void BounceProc( char * MyID );             /* Threads 3 to n: display */
void VioClrScr( void );                     /* Screen clear */
void ShutDown( void );                      /* Program shutdown */
void VioWrtCStr( char *pchString,           /* Write string to display */
                unsigned usRow, unsigned usColumn );
void pascal far SigHandler( unsigned SigArg,/* Signal handler */
                unsigned SigNum );
                                            /* Screen clear macro */
#define VioClrScr() VioScrollDn( 0, 0, 50, 80, 50, BlankCell, 0 )
```

```c
struct tagCoords                                /* Display coordinates */
{
    int xLoc;
    int yLoc;
    int xInc;
    int yInc;
};

unsigned long  RunFlag = 0;                     /* "Keep Running" semaphore */
unsigned long  ScreenLock = 0;                  /* Screen update semaphore  */

char BlankCell[2] = { 0x20, 0x07 };
VIOMODEINFO vmi = { sizeof( VIOMODEINFO ) };/* Mode information */

PFNSIGHANDLER PrevHandler;                      /* for SetSigHandler call */
unsigned int  PrevAction;                       /* for SetSigHandler call */

void main()                                     /* Thread One */
{
    /* Get display screen's text row and column sizes & clear the screen.*/
    VioGetMode( &vmi, 0 );
    VioClrScr();
    VioWrtCStr( "Threads running: 00.  Press 'a' to start another thread",
                vmi.row - 1, 0 );

    /* Set the "we are running" semaphore. */
    DosSemSet( &RunFlag );

    /* Start keyboard thread. Let _beginthread allocate memory
     *  for the thread's stack.
     */
    _beginthread( KbdThread, NULL, STACK_SIZE, NULL );

    /* Install signal handler for CTRL+BREAK & CRTL+C. */
    DosSetSigHandler( (PFNSIGHANDLER)SigHandler, &PrevHandler, &PrevAction,
                      SIGA_ACCEPT, SIG_CTRLC );

    /* Wait for "running" semaphore to clear (from signal or 'q' key). */
    DosSemWait( &RunFlag, SEM_INDEFINITE_WAIT );

    _endthread();               /* Kill all threads */
}
```

```
void pascal far SigHandler( unsigned int SigArg, unsigned int SigNum )
{
    static char BreakMsg[] = "Signal Termination";

    ShutDown();
    VioWrtCStr( BreakMsg, vmi.row - 1, 0 );
    /* Restore original signal handler for CTRL+BREAK & CRTL+C. */
    DosSetSigHandler( (PFNSIGHANDLER)PrevHandler, &PrevHandler, &PrevAction,
                      PrevAction, SIG_CTRLC );
}
void ShutDown( void )                          /* Clean up display when done */
{
    /* Lock out screen updates from BounceProc & clear "running" semaphore */
    DosSemWait( &ScreenLock, SEM_INDEFINITE_WAIT );
    DosSemSet( &ScreenLock );
    VioClrScr();
    DosSemClear( &RunFlag );
}

void KbdThread( void )                          /* Thread Two: keyboard */
{
    KBDKEYINFO   KeyInfo;                       /* for KbdCharIn call */
    char         ThreadNr = 0;
    char         NThreadMsg[4];

    do
    {
        /* Block this thread by waiting for keyboard input. */

        KbdCharIn( &KeyInfo, IO_WAIT, 0 );
        if( tolower( KeyInfo.chChar ) == 'a' && ThreadNr < MAX_THREADS)
        {
            ThreadNr++;
            _beginthread( BounceProc, NULL, STACK_SIZE, &ThreadNr );
            VioWrtCharStr( NThreadMsg, sprintf( NThreadMsg, "%02d", ThreadNr ),
                           vmi.row - 1, 17, 0 );
        }
    } while( tolower( KeyInfo.chChar ) != 'q' );

    ShutDown();
}

/* getrandom returns a random number between min and max, which must be in
 * integer range.
 */
#define getrandom( min, max ) ((rand() % (int)(((max) + 1) - (min))) + (min))
```

```
void BounceProc( char * MyID )                          /* Threads Three to n */
{
    int       xOld, yOld;
    char      MyCell[2];
    char      CurrentCell[2];
    int       CellLen = 2;
    struct tagCoords Coords;

  /* Generate update increments and initial display coordinates. */
    srand( (unsigned) *MyID * 3 );
    Coords.xLoc = getrandom( 0, vmi.col - 1 );
    Coords.yLoc = getrandom( 0, vmi.row - 1 );
    Coords.xInc = getrandom( -3, 3 );
    Coords.yInc = getrandom( -3, 3 );

    /* Set up "happy face" & generate color attribute from thread number.*/
    if( *MyID > 16)
        MyCell[0] = 0x01;          /* outline face */
    else
        MyCell[0] = 0x02;          /* solid face */
    MyCell[1] =  *MyID & 0x0F;     /* force black background */

    for( ;; )
    {
        /* Wait for display to be available, then lock it. */
        DosSemWait( &ScreenLock, SEM_INDEFINITE_WAIT );
        DosSemSet( &ScreenLock );

        /* If we still occupy the old screen position, blank it out. */
        VioReadCellStr( CurrentCell, &CellLen, yOld, xOld, 0 );
        if ( CurrentCell[0] == MyCell[0] && CurrentCell[1] == MyCell[1] )
            VioWrtCellStr( BlankCell, CellLen, yOld, xOld, 0 );

        /* Draw new face, then clear screen lock */
        VioWrtCellStr( MyCell, CellLen, Coords.yLoc, Coords.xLoc, 0 );
        DosSemClear( &ScreenLock );

        /* Increment the coordinates for next placement of the block. */
        xOld = Coords.xLoc;
        yOld = Coords.yLoc;
        Coords.xLoc += Coords.xInc;
        Coords.yLoc += Coords.yInc;
```

```
                    /* If we are about to go off the screen, reverse direction */
                    if( Coords.xLoc < 0 || Coords.xLoc >= vmi.col )
                    {
                        Coords.xInc = -Coords.xInc;
                        DosBeep( 400, 50 );
                    }
                    if( Coords.yLoc < 0 || Coords.yLoc >= vmi.row )
                    {
                        Coords.yInc = -Coords.yInc;
                        DosBeep( 600, 50 );
                    }

                    /* Sleep to slow down screen update rate */
                    DosSleep( 75L );
                }
            }

            void VioWrtCStr( char *pchString, unsigned usRow, unsigned usColumn )
            {
                VioWrtCharStr( pchString, strlen( pchString ), usRow, usColumn, 0 );
            }
```

15.3 *Writing a Multithread Program*

When you write a program with multiple threads, you must coordinate their behavior and use of the program's resources. You must also make sure that each thread receives its own stack.

Sharing Common Resources

Each thread has its own stack and its own copy of the CPU registers. Other resources, such as files, static data, and heap memory, are shared by all threads in the process. Threads using these common resources must coordinate their work. OS/2 provides semaphores and the **DosEnterCritSec** and **DosExitCritSec** system services for synchronizing resources.

Your program must provide for resource conflicts.

When multiple threads are accessing static data, your program must provide for possible resource conflicts. Consider a program where one thread updates a static data structure containing *x,y* coordinates for items to be displayed by another thread. If the update thread alters the *x* coordinate and is preempted before it can change the *y* coordinate, the display thread may be scheduled before the *y* coordinate is updated. The item would be displayed at the wrong location. You can avoid this type of problem by using semaphores to control access to the structure.

Using semaphores is a way of communicating among threads or processes that are executing asynchronously of one another. This communication is usually used to coordinate the activities of multiple threads or processes, typically by controlling access to a shared resource by "locking" and "unlocking" the resource. To solve the *x,y* coordinate update problem described above, the update thread would set a semaphore indicating that the data structure is in use before performing the update. It would then clear the semaphore when both coordinates had been processed. The display thread must wait for the semaphore to be clear before updating the display. This process of waiting for a semaphore is often called "blocking" on a semaphore because the process is blocked and cannot continue until the semaphore clears.

RAM semaphores are faster than system semaphores.

OS/2 supports two types of semaphores: system and RAM semaphores. You must use a system semaphore if more than one process needs to access the semaphore. You can use the much faster RAM semaphores if their use is confined to the threads within a process.

The BOUNCE.C program in Section 15.2 uses a RAM semaphore named `ScreenLock` to coordinate screen updates. Each time one of the display threads is ready to write to the screen, it calls **DosSemWait** with a pointer to `ScreenLock` and constant **SEM_INDEFINITE_WAIT** to indicate that the **DosSemWait** call should block on the semaphore and not time out. If the `ScreenLock` semaphore is clear, the wait function returns immediately. Otherwise, the thread blocks until the semaphore clears. When the thread receives control again, it calls **DosSemSet** to set the `ScreenLock` semaphore so other threads cannot interfere with the display. When the thread completes the display update, it releases the semaphore by calling **DosSemClear**.

The `ShutDown` routine in BOUNCE.C is called from both the keyboard thread and the signal handler. The routine uses the `ScreenLock` semaphore to make sure other threads do not write to the screen after the screen has been cleared.

Screen displays and static data are only two of the resources requiring careful management. For example, your program may have multiple threads accessing the same file. Since another thread may have moved the file pointer, each thread must reset the file pointer before reading or writing. In addition, each thread must make sure that it is not preempted between the time it positions the pointer and the time it accesses the file. These threads should use a semaphore to coordinate access to the file by bracketing each file access with **DosSemRequest** and **DosSemClear** calls. The following code fragment illustrates this technique:

```
HSEM     hsemIOSem;

DosSemRequest( hsemIOSem, SEM_INDEFINITE_WAIT );
fseek( fp, desired_position, 0L );
fwrite( data, sizeof( data ), 1, fp );
DosSemClear( hsemIOSem );
```

Thread Stacks

Stack checking is performed for each thread.

All of an application's default stack space is allocated to the first thread of execution, which is known as thread 1. As a result, you must allocate memory to provide a separate stack for each additional thread your program needs. You must do this before creating the thread. Stack checking, if enabled, is performed for each thread. The keyboard thread in BOUNCE.C calls the **malloc** function each time the user wants to start a new display thread. If the allocation is successful, the **_beginthread** function is called. The first argument in the **_beginthread** call is a pointer to the **BounceProc** function, which will execute the threads. The last argument is an ID number that is passed to **BounceProc**. **BounceProc** uses the ID number to seed the random number generator and to select the thread's color attribute and display character.

Threads that make calls to the C run-time library or to the OS/2 API must allow sufficient stack space for the library and API functions they call. The C **printf** function requires more than 500 bytes of stack space, and you should have 2K of stack space available when calling OS/2 API routines. To be safe, allocate at least 4K for each thread's stack.

Use as little static data as possible.

Since each thread has its own stack, you can avoid potential collisions over data items by using as little static data as possible. Design your program to use automatic stack variables for all data that can be private to a thread. The only global variables in the BOUNCE.C program are either RAM semaphores or variables that never change once they are initialized.

Signal Handling

Signals are events that interrupt the normal flow of your program's execution. They are similar to hardware interrupts, but they come from the operating system or other programs and occur asynchronously. If you do not provide your own routines, OS/2 will take the default action for each signal, such as cancelling your program when the user enters CTRL+BREAK. You can install your own signal handler with the OS/2 API function **DosSetSigHandler**.

WARNING   *The C run-time function signal is not supported in the multithread library LLIBCMT.LIB.*

When a signal occurs, OS/2 always suspends thread 1 and gives control to the signal handler, if installed. As a result, thread 1 must not be executing C run-time library code when the signal handler gets control or a potential deadlock condition can occur. In addition, the signal handler must not call C run-time library functions. Consider the following sequence of events:

1. Thread 2 is executing **printf** when the user interrupts it by pressing CTRL+C. The program has designated a CTRL+C signal handler, so OS/2 immediately transfers control to the signal handler in thread 1.

2. The signal handler in thread 1 tries to execute the statement:

   ```
   printf( "^C: Do you want to quit?" );
   ```

3. The **printf** call in thread 2 has already locked output to the console, so thread 1's **printf** must wait for release of that lock.

4. The thread 2 **printf** function never regains control because the signal handler must complete before other processing can continue. As a result, it is never able to release the lock on console output.

If a situation like this happens, the program will wait indefinitely for resolution of the two mutually exclusive conditions.

A multithread C program can process signals if it adheres to the following restrictions:

- Thread 1 must be dedicated to signal handling and must not call the C run-time library once it identifies the signal handler to OS/2 using the API function **DosSetSigHandler**. When the signal handler gets control, it should set a semaphore or flag so other threads in the program can determine that the signal has occurred and is being processed.

- The other threads in the process must check the status of semaphores set by thread 1 and respond accordingly.

The BOUNCE.C sample program waits until thread 2, the keyboard handler, starts before installing the signal handler. It then dedicates thread 1 to signal handling by having the thread wait for a semaphore. Thread 1 blocks until either the keyboard thread or the signal handler clears the semaphore. It then calls **_endthread** to terminate the process, including all the other threads.

15.4 Compiling and Linking

The steps for compiling and linking the multithread program BOUNCE.C are given below:

1. Ensure that the files LLIBCMT.LIB and OS2.LIB are in the directory specified in your LIB environment variable.

   The file LLIBCMT.LIB takes the place of the regular C run-time library files. The file OS2.LIB provides support for OS/2 system calls made in the program, such as **KbdCharIn**.

2. Compile and link the program with the CL command-line option /MT.

   The /Lp option instructs the compiler to create a protected-mode application. The /MT option implies the large memory model with a separate stack segment (/ALw). The multithread library functions have their own data segment but use the caller's stack. This option also sets the library search record to LLIBCMT.LIB and sets the **MT** symbolic constant for the multithread versions of the include files. The /link GRTEXTP option instructs the linker to search GRTEXTP.LIB, the character-graphics library for protected mode.

   To compile and link in a single step, use this CL command line:

   ```
   CL /Lp /MT BOUNCE.C /link grtextp
   ```

   For separate compile and link steps, you invoke the compiler and the linker with this code:

   ```
   CL /c /Lp /MT BOUNCE.C
   LINK BOUNCE;
   ```

3. If you choose not to use the /MT option, you must take these steps:

   - Ensure that the special multithread include file support is enabled.
   - Use the /Aw option. This is required because the functions in LLIBCMT.LIB have their own data segment but use the caller's stack. The /Aw option specifies a segment setup of SS not equal to DS with DS not reloaded on function entry.
   - Make sure that only far pointers are passed to library functions.
   - Make sure that all variables are either passed by value or cast to a far address (the large memory model).
   - Specify the multithread library and suppress default library selection.

The multithread include files are used when you define the symbolic constant **MT**. You can do this with the CL command line option /D MT or within the C source file before any include statements, as shown below:

```
#define MT
#include <stdlib.h>
```

To compile and link in a single step with the default libraries suppressed, this is the complete CL command line:

```
CL /Lp /ALw /Zl /D MT BOUNCE.C /link LLIBCMT+OS2
```

To perform a two-step compile and link with the default libraries suppressed in the link step, use these commands:

```
CL /c /Lp /ALw /D MT BOUNCE.C
LINK /NOD BOUNCE,,,LLIBCMT+OS2;
```

4. Run the program under OS/2.

15.5 *Avoiding Problem Areas*

There are several problems you can encounter in creating, linking, or executing a multithread C program. Some of the more common ones are described here.

Problem	Probable Cause
LINK searches for mLIBC *f*.LIB.	If you omit the /NOD option from the LINK command, LINK searches for the default library. The default library should not be used with multithread programs. The /NOD option tells the computer not to search the default libraries. This problem can also be avoided by compiling with the /Zl option, which suppresses default library search records in the object files.
You get error SYS1943. A program caused a protection violation.	Many OS/2 programming errors cause protection violations. A common cause of protection violations is the indirect assignment of data to null pointers. This results in your program trying to access memory that does not "belong" to it, so a protection violation is issued. Protection violations also occur if your program gets a memory buffer from the operating system and then tries to read or write past the end of the

buffer. Another cause of this error is failing to specify the condition "SS is not equal to DS" in the CL command invocation. Specify the correct conditions with the /ALw memory model option.

An easy way to detect the cause of a protection violation is to compile your program with CodeView information, then run it in CodeView. When the protection fault occurs, OS/2 will transfer control to CodeView, and the cursor will be positioned on the line that caused the problem. See Chapter 9, "Debugging C Programs with CodeView," for more information about the CodeView debugger.

Your program generates numerous compile and link errors.	If you attempt to compile and link a multithread program without defining the symbolic constant **MT**, many of the definitions required for the multithread library will be missing. Define **MT** on the CL command line with /MT or /D MT, or use `#define MT` in your program.

You can eliminate many potential problems by setting the compiler's warning level to one of its highest values and heeding the warning messages. By using the /W3 or /W4 warning level options, you can detect unintentional data conversions, missing function prototypes, and use of non-ANSI features.

15.6 Using the Protected-Mode CodeView Debugger

The protected-mode version of CodeView (CVP) has special commands for debugging multiple processes and threads. It adds Thread and Process items to the standard Run Menu. Your CONFIG.SYS file must specify IOPL=YES for protected-mode CodeView to run.

To enable multiple process debugging, invoke CodeView with the /O (offspring) option. Selecting the Process item from the Run Menu brings up a list box of child processes associated with the parent process. You choose the process to be debugged by selecting it with the list box. The Process item will be grey (unselectable) if you did not specify the /O option. The /O option applies only to debugging multiple processes. You do not need to use it to debug multiple threads.

Selecting the Thread item from the Run Menu produces a list box showing the status of each thread associated with the current process. You can use the list box to designate a different current thread or to change a thread's status. There are equivalent keyboard commands for each option.

15.6.1 Compiling with the /Zi Option

The compiler option /Zi causes the compiler to include symbolic information and line numbers in the object file for debugging with CodeView. If you run LINK in a separate step, you must invoke it with the /CODEVIEW option, which can be abbreviated as /CO. To compile and link the sample program BOUNCE.C in a single step, enter this code:

```
CL /MT /Zi BOUNCE.C
```

The following commands are for a two-step compile and link:

```
CL /c /MT /Zi BOUNCE.C

link /CO BOUNCE;
```

15.6.2 Prompt for Thread Number

When you debug a protected-mode program with CodeView, the command prompt is preceded by a three-digit number indicating the current thread. Thread 1 is always the current thread when you start a program. The prompt appears as

```
001>
```

15.6.3 Thread Commands

Protected-mode CodeView (CVP) has special commands to control the execution of threads. The CodeView Thread commands are accessed using the Thread command from the Run menu. Dialog commands for thread control start with the tilde character (~). Thread commands specify which thread(s) the command applies to, followed by the command. The syntax of the dialog version of the Thread command is

~[[*specifier*[[*command*]]]]

Entering the tilde character by itself displays the status of all threads. Enter the tilde and a specifier to see the status of particular threads. Legal values for the specifier field are listed below:

Specifier	Function
(blank)	Displays the status of all threads
#	Specifies the last thread that executed
.	Specifies the current thread

| * | Specifies all threads |
| n | Specifies the number of an existing thread |

The optional command field controls the way specified threads are executed. If it is omitted, status is displayed, but thread activity is not affected. Thread commands are summarized below, followed by examples. For more information about command execution and about how other threads in the process may be affected, consult on-line help.

Command	**Function**
(blank)	Display status
BP	Set a breakpoint (used with the normal Breakpoint Set command syntax)
E	Execute in slow motion
F	Freeze the thread(s)
G	Pass control to a thread
P	Execute a program step
S	Select specified thread as the current thread
T	Trace a thread
U	Unfreeze thread(s)

Controlling a Thread Being Debugged

If your program has multiple threads using the same functions, you may want to monitor the behavior of one particular thread. The standard Breakpoint Set command will affect every thread. The thread Breakpoint Set command lets you limit the breakpoint to one or more threads. The sample program BOUNCE.C has multiple threads executing the function **BounceProc**. This function erases the symbol at the thread's current screen position, writes it to a new location, computes the display coordinates to be used the next time the thread receives control, and then sleeps to slow down the rate at which the display is updated.

Since thread-specific breakpoints can only be set for threads that are already running, you can set a breakpoint that will be executed after the target thread starts. In BOUNCE.C, the source line in thread 2 that tests each character received from the keyboard is a good location for such a breakpoint (line 113). Since thread 2 is not active when the program begins, you must first set a breakpoint in thread 1 after it has started thread 2 (line 73). The first breakpoint can be set by conventional methods or by using the thread breakpoint command:

```
001>~1BP .73
```

Once you have reached the first breakpoint, you can set the keyboard test breakpoint for thread 2:

```
001>~2BP .113
```

The BOUNCE.C program starts a new thread each time the letter 'a' is typed. ('A' is also accepted.) Once you have started the desired number of threads, you can trigger the thread 2 breakpoint without starting a new thread by pressing another key, such as the space bar. When you reach the breakpoint in thread 2, you can set breakpoints for the other threads. To set a breakpoint in thread 3's **BounceProc** function immediately after it has updated the screen (source line 168), enter this code:

```
001>~3BP .168
```

When this breakpoint is reached, the CodeView prompt will reflect the current thread number:

```
003>
```

You can then set other breakpoints for the thread, execute it in slow motion without any other threads running in the background, or enter other CodeView commands, such as Breakpoint Clear.

Freezing and Unfreezing Threads

Frozen threads do not execute.
It can be useful to freeze one or more threads so they don't interfere with execution of a thread you are debugging. In the BOUNCE.C program, for example, you can monitor the path of a single bouncing ball by freezing all but one of the bounce threads. Frozen threads will not be scheduled for execution.

If you have a large number of threads running, you can freeze all of them in a single command and then unfreeze the threads you want to monitor. Unfrozen threads continue to operate normally and will execute any breakpoints they encounter. The following example freezes all threads, enables threads 1 and 4, and then checks the status of all threads:

```
001>~*F
001>~1U
001>~4U
001>~
```

If thread 1 is waiting for a semaphore when the status command is invoked, the report shows the following:

```
001 Blocked
002 Frozen
003 Frozen
004 Runnable
```

Switching to a Particular Thread

The **S** (select) and **E** (execute) variations of the Thread command can be used to switch the current thread. However, when another thread causes the program to stop by hitting a breakpoint, the debugger will select the thread that encountered the breakpoint as the current thread.

If you include **~.S** in the breakpoint command, CodeView stops the thread that encounters the breakpoint, then immediately switches back to the current thread. The following example selects thread 4, sets a breakpoint at line 168 in thread 3, and switches to thread 4 when the breakpoint is hit:

```
001>~4S
001>~3BP .168 "~.S"
001>G
```

15.6.4 Screen Groups Used by CodeView

Only one CodeView session at a time is supported in protected mode. You cannot run multiple copies in concurrent screen groups.

The View Output Screen command (\ ) works differently in protected mode and in real mode. In protected mode, your application's output will be displayed for three seconds. The display will then revert to the CodeView display. To view the output window for a longer period, specify a different delay interval, measured in seconds, as follows:

```
\10
```

Dynamic Linking with OS/2

An OS/2 dynamic-link library (DLL) is an executable file containing functions that are available to other programs. In a statically linked program, you link the program with all its component functions when you build the executable file. In a dynamically linked program, the program-build step does not link all of the code. Instead, OS/2 links calls to functions in dynamic-link libraries at program load time or while the program is running. The DLL code and data become part of the address space of each program, even when the DLL is being accessed by several application programs.

This chapter describes how to build your own dynamic-link libraries and how to build programs that use them.

16.1 Overview of Dynamic Linking

Dynamic linking is the process of resolving external calls when a program runs, instead of at link time. It offers several benefits:

- Multiple programs can use the same dynamic-link library simultaneously. Since only one copy of the DLL is in memory, there are fewer demands for physical memory and swap space.

- Updates to dynamic-link libraries do not affect the programs that use them, since the only connection between DLLs and application programs is the function-calling sequence.

- Application programs require less disk space and memory, since their executable program files contain the names of DLL functions but not the code for the functions.

- Dynamic-link libraries can call other dynamic-link libraries.

- DLLs can extend the OS/2 operating system to provide new or improved system services. This is possible because most of OS/2 consists of a set of dynamic-link libraries.

16.1.1 Load-Time and Run-Time Linking

Dynamic linking can take place both at program load time and while the program is running. A program can call functions in more than one DLL and combine both load-time and run-time linking.

For load-time dynamic linking, build a program that calls DLL functions by name.

The linker creates special records containing the name of each DLL subroutine and the name of its DLL file. It does not put any DLL code into the program's executable file. At load time, OS/2 dynamically links the program and its DLLs. It brings the program and the DLLs into memory and updates the program's DLL calls with the address of each DLL routine. If a DLL is already in memory, it is not reloaded.

With run-time dynamic linking, the program creates the DLL file name and sub-routine names during execution. The program then passes these names to OS/2 so the operating system can load the dynamic-link library.

An example of a run-time dynamic link is an extension to the Programmer's WorkBench (PWB). PWB has no information about which extensions it needs until it reads the initialization file, TOOLS.INI. PWB then sends requests to OS/2 to demand-load the DLLs that it needs.

16.1.2 Application Programs and DLLs

With static linking, all library code is bound into the executable program when you link the program. If the library changes, all programs using the library must be relinked. With the exception of some Microsoft Windows programs, all DOS programs use static linking.

Updates to parts of a program are easier to deliver using DLLs.

You can create loosely coupled applications and DLLs and modify the DLLs without relinking the program. For example, if your product has an underlying database access mechanism, you can package the database access routines into a DLL. You can then ship improvements or changes to the database code in a new dynamic-link library. The executable files for the program do not have to be re-linked or redistributed.

The programs calling a DLL are known as the DLL's "clients."

16.1.3 DLLs and Microsoft C Run-Time Libraries

You can construct three types of dynamic-link libraries with the Microsoft C Professional Development System. All of them can be multithreaded; they can support more than one client at a time. There are three types:

- A stand-alone dynamic-link library that includes both your routines and code for the Microsoft C run-time library functions used by your DLL. This type of DLL is self-contained and completely independent of the programs that call it.

- A dynamic-link library that does not use any functions from the Microsoft C run-time library. This type of DLL is also self-contained.

- A private dynamic-link library that consists only of selected functions from the Microsoft C run-time library. This DLL is usually specific to one program or a closely tied group of programs. Application programs and dynamic-link libraries using this DLL do not contain any code for the C run-time library functions.

The following sections provide more information about the differences between the various types of DLLs.

Stand-Alone Dynamic-Link Libraries

Stand-alone DLLs include C run-time functions. If you want to call C run-time library functions in your DLL, you can include the functions you need. These run-time functions are statically linked in the DLL and the DLL does not rely on the client or any other DLL for run-time support.

Figure 16.1 illustrates the relationships between this type of DLL, an application program, and C run-time library functions. Both the application program and the dynamic-link library have their own copies of functions from the C run-time library. This ensures that

- The DLL always has access to the C run-time library routines it needs.

- The DLL is not dependent on the calling application for any support code.

- The programs using the DLL do not depend on the DLL for C run-time library functions.

Section 16.3.1, "DLLs with Static C Run-Time Library Functions," describes the steps involved in creating this type of dynamic-link library using the special library LLIBCDLL.LIB.

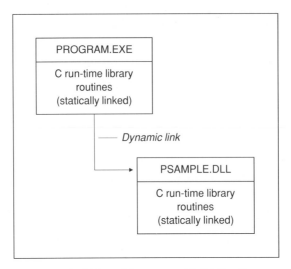

**Figure 16.1 DLL and Program with Statically
Linked C Run-Time Functions**

DLLs without C Run-Time Library Functions

You can write a dynamic-link library in C without calling any functions from the C run-time library. Section 16.3.2, "DLLs without C Run-Time Library Functions," shows how to set up this type of DLL. These DLLs contain only your code and require no run-time library support; they make no calls to run-time library functions.

Private C Run-Time DLLs

You can create a custom C run-time DLL.

A C run-time DLL can be shared by multiple programs and their DLLs. You generate the C run-time DLL in two steps. The first builds a module-definition file with a list of the C run-time library functions needed by your application and its DLLs; the second step links the module-definition file with the special library CDLLOBJS.LIB to create a C run-time DLL.

The executable files for programs and DLLs linked with a customized C run-time DLL do not contain any code for the C run-time library functions. Figure 16.2 shows the relationships of the components.

A private C run-time DLL must be closely tied to its programs and associated DLLs.

Processes and DLLs that share a private run-time DLL share environment strings and global C run-time data (for example, file pointers for buffered I/O and memory allocated with the **malloc** function). Therefore, the program and the DLLs must cooperate on the use of this data.

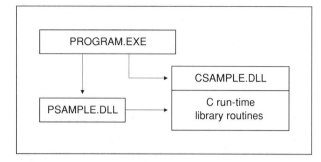

Figure 16.2 Program and DLL Calling C Run-Time DLL

A closely tied structure is suitable for a complex application consisting of a set of application programs that act as front-end processors to several DLLs. A word processor, for example, might support one user interface for beginners, another for intermediate users, and a third for expert users. The different user interfaces could be implemented in three separate executable program files. All three programs would share the DLLs that do most of the real work.

Section 16.3.3, "Programs and DLLs with a C Run-Time DLL," describes the procedures for building a C run-time library DLL and its associated programs and dynamic-link libraries.

16.2 Designing and Writing DLLs

Before you write a DLL, you must determine some of the DLL's requirements. You need to know

- Floating-point math requirements

- Special initialization requirements such as allocation of buffers or registration of special termination routines

- Termination requirements such as clearing semaphores or releasing allocated memory

- Re-entrancy requirements; if the DLL is to be called by more than one process, it must be re-entrant

This section explains how to design a DLL to take these requirements into account.

16.2.1 Floating-Point Math Requirements

Stand-alone DLLs built with the LLIBCDLL library are independent of the programs calling them. They are "black boxes" that must operate without knowing anything about their client programs and without interfering with their clients.

One area of potential conflict for stand-alone DLLs is control of the 80x87 math coprocessor. For a DLL to use the 80x87 coprocessor or the emulator floating-point library, the DLL and all of its client programs must agree on which process is going to handle floating-point exceptions and on which process is going to handle emulation if the machine does not have a coprocessor.

Floating-point emulation is not possible with a genuinely independent DLL. A stand-alone DLL must use the alternate math library, which ignores the math coprocessor chip. The alternate math library provides the fastest processing available without a coprocessor, but results are not as accurate as those produced by the emulator floating-point library. Because the constraint applies only to the DLL and not to applications, clients of a stand-alone DLL can use any floating-point model. Since the DLL uses the alternate math library, it does not conflict with clients over control of the math coprocessor.

In contrast, DLLs and programs using a private C run-time DLL are tightly coupled. This means that the floating-point math option is known when the program is built. Because these programs and DLLs all use the same C run-time functions (unlike the stand-alone DLL and its clients, which may incorporate different C run-time libraries), no contention can arise over control of the math coprocessor. The same floating-point math library is used for the entire application.

The only way to use a math coprocessor within a DLL is with a private C run-time DLL.

A private C run-time DLL uses the CDLLOBJS library and the emulator floating-point package. The emulator uses the 80x87 math coprocessor if one is installed; otherwise, it emulates the coprocessor. Floating-point emulation produces the most accurate results. There is no conflict over use of the coprocessor, since the C run-time DLL performs all floating-point math. The programs and DLLs calling the C run-time DLL do not have any C run-time library code of their own.

16.2.2 Initialization and Termination Requirements

When you design a DLL, you must decide if it has special initialization or termination requirements. If the DLL needs to initialize variables or allocate memory buffers when it starts, it needs custom start-up procedures. If the DLL acquires system resources for a client program, the resources must be released when the program completes its processing.

Initialization

All DLLs built with the Microsoft C run-time libraries must use per-process initialization to set up the C run-time data. Per-process initialization (also known as instance initialization) means that OS/2 calls the DLL's initialization code each time it loads a program linked with the DLL. For most DLLs, the default initialization routine is sufficient, and you do not need to take any other measures.

If your DLL has special requirements, you must provide additional start-up processing.

The C run-time library initialization function is called each time a new client is attached to the DLL. To override the default initialization, you must link your DLL with one of the following object modules, which are provided with the Microsoft C Professional Development System:

File Name	Description
DLLINIT.OBJ	Initialization module for DLLs built with LLIBCDLL.LIB and using C run-time library code
CRTDLL_I.OBJ	Initialization module for DLLs using a C run-time DLL built with CDLLOBJS.LIB (replaces CRTDLL.OBJ)

In addition, you must declare an entry point for your own DLL initialization function. Your function, or the application program calling your DLL, must initialize the C run-time data by calling the library function **C_INIT** before any other C run-time library functions are called.

The prototype for **C_INIT** is

```
void _far _pascal C_INIT( void );
```

Designate your initialization function as the DLL's starting point.

To have your custom function recognized as the DLL's default initialization routine, it must be the starting point for the DLL. This requires an assembly language file with an **END** statement naming your function. The sample file, SETENTRY.ASM, in the following example shows the minimum assembler code required for specifying a C language function named **SampleInit** as the DLL's entry point.

```
; SETENTRY.ASM
extrn _SampleInit:FAR          ;name of C start-up routine
end   _SampleInit
```

The following example, SAMPLE.C, shows a simple custom initialization routine that maintains a count of how many clients it is currently serving. Since this example overrides the default dynamic-link library initialization, it must return a nonzero status code to OS/2 to show a successful start-up. If a DLL initialization function returns a status of 0, OS/2 will not load the program using the DLL.

```
/*                      SAMPLE.C                    */
void _far _pascal C_INIT( void );
int  UserCount = 0;

int _export _loadds SampleInit()
{
    UserCount++;          /* increment number of users  */
    C_INIT();             /* initialize C run-time data */
    return( 1 );          /* indicate successful start  */
}

/* code for other DLL functions belongs here */
```

All DLLs must be linked with a module-definition file that contains a **LIBRARY** statement, such as the following:

```
LIBRARY SAMPLE INITINSTANCE
```

The following commands will create object files from the sample files and link them with DLLINIT.OBJ to make a stand-alone dynamic-link library named SAMPLE.DLL. The /ML compile option, explained in Section 16.2.6, "Compile Options for Dynamic-Link Libraries," sets the library search record to LLIBCDLL.LIB.

```
MASM /Mx SETENTRY;
CL /c /Gs /ML SAMPLE.C
LINK /NOE DLLINIT+SETENTRY+SAMPLE,SAMPLE.DLL,,,SAMPLE.DEF;
```

WARNING   *For DLLs linked with Microsoft C run-time libraries, the **LIBRARY** statement in the DLL's module-definition file must specify **INITINSTANCE** in the initialization field. If you omit this, the initialization routine is called only when the DLL is loaded into memory for the first client program, and the DLL will not function properly if it is called by additional programs.*

Termination

You may have to clean up before terminating.

You may need to know when an application using your DLL is finished. If your DLL has created buffers, semaphores, or other resources for a particular application, they must be released when the application terminates.

You can have an initialization routine in your DLL that calls the OS/2 API function **DosExitList** to register one or more exit subroutines for your DLL. OS/2 will call the exit routines when the client program finishes. The exit functions should free any resources your DLL acquired for the client program.

DLLs built with LLIBCDLL.LIB have a default termination routine.

The start-up routine for dynamic-link libraries built with the LLIBCDLL library calls **DosExitList** with a pointer to a default termination function. To replace the default processing with your own function, link the module DLLTERM.OBJ into the DLL. This suppresses the call to **DosExitList**. During initialization, your DLL must register its own routine by calling **DosExitList** unless you are sure the termination routine will be called explicitly. The termination processing must include a call to the library function **C_TERM**.

The prototype for **C_TERM** is

```
void _far _pascal C_TERM( void );
```

There is no equivalent to DLLTERM.OBJ and **C_TERM** for DLLs using a private C run-time DLL built with the CDLLOBJS library. If special cleanup processing is required, these DLLs must provide their own termination function. The function is registered during initialization by calling either the C run-time library function **atexit** or the OS/2 API function **DosExitList**.

Any DLL that calls DosExitList should also have a termination function.

DLLs that set exit lists must provide termination functions that can be called by clients when they no longer need the DLL. If a program attaches itself to the DLL at run-time (using **DosLoadModule**), it cannot disconnect from the DLL as long as the exit list points to a function in the dynamic-link library. The DLL's termination function can perform any necessary cleanup and call **DosExitList** to remove itself from the exit list.

NOTE   There is no special termination procedure for DLLs build with CDLLOBJS.LIB because the C run-time termination code is called by the **exit** or **_exit** functions. If the process is terminated by a critical error or **DosExit**, C run-time termination does not occur.

16.2.3 Making the DLL Re-Entrant

Re-entrant code is code that can be shared by multiple programs in a multitasking environment. DLLs that may be used by more than one program must be re-entrant. To do this, they must isolate each client program's data and resources. File handles belonging to one client, for example, must not be used for other clients. Re-entrancy also means that the DLL cannot allow itself to be switched to a different thread while it is performing certain operations.

Global Versus Instance Data

A dynamic-link library can have separate data segments for each program that calls it.

Separate data segments are known as "instance" data. With instance data segments, the DLL does not have to keep track of which resources belong to each client. OS/2 assigns a different data segment to each process calling the DLL, even though the selectors are the same.

A dynamic-link library can also have a global data segment used for internal purposes or to support all of the programs using its services.

A DLL providing time and date conversions might, for example, keep the current date in a global storage area. The same DLL might provide functions to compute elapsed time, such as the number of minutes between two clock readings. If static variables are used by the elapsed time functions, they should be in instance data segments, since the OS/2 scheduler might preempt the function and schedule another thread that calls the same function with different arguments before it has completed the first caller's task.

Data sharing is controlled by **DATA** and **SEGMENTS** statements in a dynamic-link library's module-definition file. By default, a DLL's automatic data segment (the local stack and heap) is shared by all processes calling the DLL. You can specify a unique automatic data segment for each client process by specifying **DATA MULTIPLE**.

WARNING   *DLLs built with the LLIBCDLL or CDLLOBJS C run-time libraries must use* **DATA MULTIPLE** *in the module-definition file.*

You can use SEGMENTS to specify attributes on a segment-by-segment basis.

Using the **SEGMENTS** statement allows you to have both global and per-process (instance) data in the same DLL. The C run-time data segment must be per-process. The following is an example of a C program fragment and module-definition file that implement both instance and global data:

```
/* Define static data in the shared segment SHR_SEG */
int _based(_segname("SHR_SEG")) intvar;
char _based(_segname("SHR_SEG")) charvar;
```

In the module-definition file, define all data segments as nonshareable, then override that default for SHR_SEG as follows:

```
DATA MULTIPLE NONSHARED
SEGMENTS
    SHR_SEG      CLASS    'FAR_DATA'   SHARED
```

Global data segments are created when OS/2 brings the dynamic-link library into memory for its first client process. All of the processes calling the DLL share the same global variables.

Serializing Nonatomic References

An atomic operation is an operation that can be completed in one machine language instruction. When writing a re-entrant procedure (in a multithread program or in a DLL), you must ensure that changes to static or global data are not preempted by the OS/2 scheduler before the update is complete. To prevent this, you must explicitly serialize nonatomic references to static or global data. The following code example is safe from preemption, because incrementing an integer requires only one machine instruction:

```
int int_var;
_export _loadds void _far _pascal dynlink_proc( void )
{
    int_var++;
}
```

The following variation on the same function is not safe because incrementing a **long** variable is not atomic; it requires two machine instructions. Between incrementing the least-significant word and the most-significant word, another thread could gain control of the processor. If that thread executes code in your DLL that uses long_var, that data would be in an indeterminate state.

```
long long_var;
_export _loadds void _far _pascal dynlink_proc( void )
{
    long_var++;
}
```

Critical Code Sections

A critical code section is a section of code that manipulates a resource (such as the long variable in the previous example) while blocking all other threads. When your program enters a critical section, it cannot be preempted until it performs a **DosExitCritSec** or until a signal is received. You don't usually just alter the value of a variable; you alter it and then use it later. In this case, you must isolate the smallest group of operations that must occur without interruption. You define these sections with the **DosEnterCritSec** and **DosExitCritSec** OS/2 API functions, as in the following example:

```
_export _loadds void _far _pascal dynlink_proc( void )
{   static int_var;

    DosEnterCritSec();
    int_var += 7;
    SetLeftCorner( int_var, int_var );
    DosExitCritSec();

    /* Code that does not reference int_var */
}
```

Keep your critical sections as short as possible.

While in a critical section, all other threads in the process are blocked from execution. Writing extremely long critical sections can make your program inefficient and can degrade system performance.

Although other threads are blocked from execution by **DosEnterCritSec** and **DosExitCritSec**, these functions do not block signal handling.

Note that static variables in DLLs are protected from interference from other processes if they are in an instance data segment designated as **MULTIPLE** in the **DATA** statement of the DLL's module-definition file. Memory is "owned" by a process and, unless specifically allocated as shareable, cannot be altered by any other process.

16.2.4 Signal Handling

The C library function **signal** is not supported for multithread programs or for DLLs. If you need to process signals, use the OS/2 API signal functions, such as **DosSetSigHandler**.

See Chapter 15, "Creating Multithread OS/2 Applications," for more information about signal handling in OS/2 programs.

16.2.5 Using Microsoft C Keywords

The **_export** and **_loadds** keywords simplify writing DLLs. They are used to define or declare functions or pointers to functions. In the DLL, an exported function with a single argument might be defined as

```
int _export _loadds sample( int )
```

The _export Keyword

All DLL functions that will be called from outside the library must be exported.

The **_export** keyword gives a function the export attribute. Stack checking must be disabled for exported entry points. You can use the /Gs compile option or the **check_stack** pragma to accomplish this.

Using the **_export** keyword is an alternative to declaring the name of the function in the **EXPORTS** section of a module-definition file. It assigns certain default attributes: no I/O privilege, shared data, load on demand, and no alias name. If the defaults are not acceptable, you must specify the proper attributes in the module-definition file.

Not all functions in a DLL are for external use. A DLL can have any number of utility subroutines supporting the work of the exported functions. Functions that are private to the DLL should not have the **_export** keyword.

The _loadds Keyword

At entry to a DLL, the DS (data segment) register points to the calling program's data segment. To access the DLL's data, the DS register has to be loaded with the DLL's segment selector. The **_loadds** keyword causes the compiler to add prolog and epilog code to the function. The prolog code initializes the DS register to point to the function's data group. The epilog code restores the caller's DS register when the function terminates.

Since loading the DS register is a high overhead operation, you should limit the use of **_loadds** to the exported functions in your DLL.

WARNING *Do not use the **_loadds** keyword in a function definition if the function uses only stack variables. If you specify **_loadds** in a DLL that does not have any static data, the linker will issue a segment fix-up error.*

16.2.6 Compile Options for Dynamic-Link Libraries

Dynamic-link libraries must be compiled with specific options that control linking, memory models, and library selection.

Compile without Linking (/c)

You must use the /c option to build your DLL in separate compile and link steps. This is necessary because the DLL must be linked with a module-definition file specifying that the output file is a dynamic-link library. (The compiler does not pass module-definition file names to the linker.) The /c option is automatically specified in the makefile generated by the Programmer's WorkBench.

Large Memory Model with Separate Stack (/ALw)

The /ALw option instructs the compiler to use the large memory model with a separate stack segment. Because all DLLs use the caller's stack, you must use /Aw or /Au. The /Aw option sets up separate stack and data segments but does not cause the DS register to be reloaded at the entry to each function. This allows you to call private functions (functions that you do not export) without incurring the overhead of loading the DS register. Functions that you do export must also be declared using the **_loadds** keyword, described above, which sets up the proper DS register handling. If you use the /Au option, the DS register will be reloaded on entry to every function, which can cause the function calls in your DLLs to execute more slowly.

All DLL functions are reached using far calls. Pointers passed to and from the DLL must be far pointers.

Remove Stack Probes (/Gs)

Since the DLL uses the caller's stack, you should usually use the /Gs option to disable stack checking within the DLL.

Specify 80286 Code (/G2)

Use the /G2 option to designate code generation for the 80286 processor instruction set, since OS/2 runs only on 80286 and higher model processors.

Link C Run-Time into Stand-Alone DLL (/ML)

Use the /ML option to build a stand-alone dynamic-link library that includes static code for C run-time library functions. This option has the same effect as using the /ALw, /FPa, /G2, and /D MT options. It changes the library search record to LLIBCDLL.LIB. See Section 16.3.1, "DLLs with Static C Run-Time Library Functions" for more information about these options.

Link Executable or DLL with C Run-Time DLL (/MD)

Use the /MD option to build an executable file or a dynamic-link library that calls a C run-time DLL. This option has the same effect as using the /ALw, /FPi, /G2, /D DLL, and /D MT options. It inhibits library search records. See Section 16.3.3, "Programs and DLLs with a C Run-Time DLL," for more information about these options.

Suppress Default Library Selection (/Zl)

If you do not compile with the /MD or /ML options described above, compile with the /Zl option or use the /NOD option when you link in order to inhibit searches for default libraries.

16.3 Building DLLs with Microsoft C

Building a DLL for OS/2 is like building an executable program file.

To build a DLL, compile and link the dynamic-link library like any other executable file, but add a module-definition file. This module-definition file tells the linker that the output is a dynamic-link library.

When you build applications that use a dynamic-link library, you must tell the linker where to find the library's dynamically linked functions. You use import libraries and module-definition files for this purpose.

16.3.1 DLLs with Static C Run-Time Library Functions

The LLIBCDLL library is used to create stand-alone DLLs. The library functions are re-entrant and can be called by multiple threads within a program as well as by multiple programs. The code for the stand-alone DLL's C run-time library functions is contained within the DLL. Programs that call stand-alone DLLs have their own run-time library code.

Building the DLL

The files required to build a stand-alone DLL with the LLIBCDLL library are listed below:

File Name	Description
OS2.LIB	OS/2 kernel import library
LLIBCDLL.LIB	Large-model multithread C run-time library for DLLs
DLLINIT.OBJ	Optional initialization module for DLLs requiring custom initialization
DLLTERM.OBJ	Optional termination module for DLLs requiring custom exit processing
userdll.C	Source code for the DLL you create
userdll.DEF	Module-definition file for the DLL you create

The module JUSTIFY.C, below, is an example of source code for a simple dynamic-link library. The **RightJustify** routine calls the **strlen** function from the C run-time library and right-justifies a caller's buffer. The function definition includes the **_export** keyword. The **_loadds** keyword is omitted, since this function does not need any static data. If it did, you would need to specify **_loadds**.

For simplicity, JUSTIFY.C below shows a DLL with a single function. In actual practice, you would usually package a group of similar utilities into one DLL.

```
/* JUSTIFY.C -- Sample Dynamic-Link Library */

#include <string.h>

/* Right justifies the string in TargetBuff to TargetSize
 * and inserts necessary number of FillChars on the left.
 */
```

```
#pragma stack_check(off)

int _export RightJustify( char *TargetBuff, int TargetSize,
                                char FillChar)
{
    char *s, *d;
    s = TargetBuff + strlen( TargetBuff );
    d = TargetBuff + TargetSize;
    while ( s = TargetBuff )
        *d-- = *s--;
    while ( d = TargetBuff )
        *d-- = FillChar;

    return( 0 );
}
```

The steps for creating a stand-alone dynamic-link library with JUSTIFY.C are given below. The DLL in the example is named JUSTLIB1.DLL.

1. Compile with the /ML Option.

   Compile the source file without linking. Dynamic-link libraries linked with LLIBCDLL must be compiled with specific options.

   Use the /ML option to set the library search record to LLIBCDLL.LIB and to indicate that C run-time code is to be included in the DLL. When you use /ML, the following options take effect:

Option	Effect
/ALw	Use large memory model with separate stack segment
/G2	Use 80286 processor instruction set
/D MT	Use the multithread version of the include files
/FPa	Generate floating-point calls and select the alternate math library

   The /G2 and the /ALw options can be overridden.

   You should also use the /Gs option to suppress stack checking and the /c option to compile without linking. The complete command to compile the sample file JUSTIFY.C is

   ```
   CL /ML /Gs /c JUSTIFY.C
   ```

2. Create a module-definition file.

Create a module-definition file, JUSTLIB1.DEF, which includes the following lines:

```
LIBRARY JUSTLIB1 INITINSTANCE
DATA MULTIPLE
```

The **LIBRARY** statement identifies the executable file, JUSTLIB1.DLL, as a dynamic-link library. DLLs linked with the LLIBCDLL library must specify **INITINSTANCE** in the initialization field. You could add an **EXPORTS** statement for the **RightJustify** function in JUSTIFY.C, but it is optional since the **_export** keyword was used in the source code.

See Chapter 14, "Building OS/2 Applications," for more information about module-definition files.

3. Link with LLIBCDLL.LIB.

Ensure that the file LLIBCDLL.LIB, which takes the place of the regular C run-time library, is available.

Create JUSTLIB1.DLL with a command such as

```
LINK justify,justlibl.dll,,,justlibl.def/NOI
```

WARNING   *When you link with LLIBCDLL, you cannot have any other C run-time libraries in the link.*

---

4. Create an import library.

Applications that call DLLs use import libraries to identify DLL functions to the linker. The following example uses JUSTLIB1.DLL and the IMPLIB utility to create an import library named JUSTLIB1.LIB.

```
IMPLIB justlibl.lib justlibl.dll
```

For more information about import libraries, see Chapter 14, "Building OS/2 Applications."

Building Programs that Call the DLL

To link a dynamic-link library with an application, you must have one of the following:

- A module-definition file with an **IMPORTS** statement for each DLL function called by your program

- An import library created from the DLL itself or from a module-definition file

All calls to DLLs must be far calls; all pointers passed must be far data pointers. If you do not compile with the large memory model option (/AL), you must cast the DLL function calls and pointers yourself.

The sample file below, TESTJUST.C, is compiled and linked into a small-model program named SAMPLE1.EXE. TESTJUST.C includes a function prototype that declares **RightJustify** as a far function expecting a far pointer as its first argument. Because of the prototype, the compiler will generate a far call to **RightJustify** and coerce the pointer argument to the proper value.

```
/* TESTJUST.C. Call sample DLL library */

#include <stdio.h>
#include <string.h>

/* DLL function prototype */

int _far RightJustify( char _far *, int, char );

void main( void )
{
    char buff[12];

    strcpy( buff, "ABCD" );

    /* Right justify to 8 characters and zero fill. */
    RightJustify( buff, 8, '0' );
    printf( "Result: %s\n", buff );
}
```

You need several files to link an application with a stand-alone DLL:

File Name	Description
userdll.LIB	Import library file for the DLL
userapp.DEF	Optional module-definition file for your application that contains an **IMPORTS** statement for each DLL function called (required if not using an import library)
OS2.LIB	Optional import library file for the OS/2 kernel (required if your application calls the kernel directly or via a C run-time library function)
userapp.OBJ	Object module(s) for your application
*m*LIBC*f*P.LIB	Regular C run-time library for protected mode, where *m* indicates memory model (S, C, M, L) and *f* indicates math package (A, E, 7)

The following command lines illustrate how TESTJUST.C can be compiled and linked with the standard libraries, plus the sample dynamic-link library, JUSTLIB1.DLL. The example uses the small memory model library and the JUSTLIB1.LIB import library created from JUSTLIB1.DLL to create SAMPLE1.EXE.

```
CL /AS /G2 /c TESTJUST.C
LINK TESTJUST,SAMPLE1.EXE,,JUSTLIB1;
```

Make sure that the JUSTLIB1.DLL file is in a directory on your LIBPATH before executing SAMPLE1.EXE.

16.3.2 DLLs without C Run-Time Library Functions

Building a DLL that does not call any of the C run-time library functions is similar to creating a stand-alone DLL.

To use the JUSTIFY.C sample program shown in Section 16.3.1, "DLLs with Static C Run-Time Library Functions," without calling C run-time functions, one change must be made. You must remove the call to the C run-time library function **strlen**. The **strlen** function was used in the sample program to calculate a pointer to the end of the caller's buffer. Remove the following line in the program JUSTIFY.C:

```
s = TargetBuff + strlen( TargetBuff );
```

Replace the line above with the following code fragment, which does the same thing without calling **strlen**:

```
s = TargetBuff;
while ( *s )
    s++;
```

After making this change, you can use the following commands to create a DLL named JUSTLIB2.DLL and its import library:

```
CL /c /ALw /G2s /Z1 JUSTIFY.C
LINK JUSTIFY,JUSTLIB2.DLL,,,JUSTLIB2.DEF/NOI
IMPLIB JUSTLIB2.LIB JUSTLIB2.DLL
```

Note that object modules compiled with releases of Microsoft C prior to Version 6.0 refer to the C run-time library variable **_acrtused**. C 6.0 defines this variable if the **main** function is present. This causes the linker to automatically add the C run-time start-up module to the DLL. To suppress the start-up module, your source file must include a line defining **_acrtused** as follows:

```
int _acrtused = 0;
```

This is required only if you do not use a C run-time library and if the link includes object modules built with earlier versions of the compiler.

16.3.3 Programs and DLLs with a C Run-Time DLL

The CDLLOBJS.LIB and CDLLOBJS.DEF files are the foundation for building a DLL that consists only of C run-time library functions. The application programs and optional dynamic-link libraries linked with this DLL do not contain any C run-time library code.

You create an application to use the C run-time DLL in either two or three phases, depending on whether or not the application has additional DLLs:

- Build a C run-time DLL.

- Build any optional DLLs that use the C run-time DLL.

- Compile and link the application.

The examples in this section use the JUSTIFY.C and TESTJUST.C source files shown in Section 16.3.1, "DLLs with Static C Run-Time Library Functions."

Building a C Run-Time DLL

The C run-time DLL is derived from the CDLLOBJS.LIB and CDLLOBJS.DEF files provided with the Microsoft C Professional Development System. The CDLLOBJS.DEF file includes export definitions for all of the C run-time library functions.

The steps for creating a C run-time DLL are given below. The C run-time DLL in the example is named CEXAMPLE.DLL.

1. Create a module-definition file.

   You can use CDLLOBJS.DEF as the basis for your own module-definition file by copying and editing it. This allows you to create a customized DLL that contains only the functions your application requires. If you use the CDLLOBJS.DEF file without modification, every program that links to your C run-time DLL will get the entire C run-time library.

The following examples create the sample file CEXAMPLE.DEF to define the custom dynamic link library CEXAMPLE.DLL. The CEXAMPLE.DEF file, shown below, exports the three C run-time library functions called from JUSTIFY.C and TESTJUST.C. It also exports functions required by the C run-time library start-up modules.

```
LIBRARY CEXAMPLE INITINSTANCE
DESCRIPTION 'Sample Dynamic-link C Run-Time Library'
DATA MULTIPLE
PROTMODE
EXPORTS
        _printf
        _strlen
        _strcpy
        __CRT_INIT
        __aFchkstk
        _exit
```

2. Create the C run-time DLL.

   The files for creating a C run-time DLL are listed below:

File Name	Description
OS2.LIB	Import library for the OS/2 kernel
CDLLOBJS.LIB	Dynamic link C run-time library
CRTLIB.OBJ	Start-up code for C run-time DLL
yourclib.DEF	Module-definition file specifying C run-time library functions for the DLL

   The command to create the sample CEXAMPLE.DLL file is

```
LINK /NOD /NOE /NOI crtlib.obj,cexample.dll,,cdllobjs+os2,cexample.def
```

3. Create an import library.

You need to create a library file of import definitions that can be used by programs that will be linked with your custom DLL. This is a two-step process. The first phase uses the module-definition file and the IMPLIB utility to create an interim version of the library, as in this example:

```
IMPLIB cexample.lib cexample.def
```

Note that the IMPLIB utility accepts either a module-definition file or a DLL as input.

The second step uses the LIB utility to append the file CDLLSUPP.LIB to the import library. You must append CDLLSUPP.LIB because it contains some routines that cannot be dynamically linked. The LIB utility requires the full path name for CDLLSUPP.LIB. If it is in a directory named C:\LIB, the command to complete the library build for CEXAMPLE.LIB is

```
LIB CEXAMPLE.LIB+C:\LIB\CDLLSUPP.LIB;
```

When you have finished building the custom DLL, be sure to copy it to a directory specified in the **LIBPATH** statement of the CONFIG.SYS file.

Building an Application-Specific DLL

You must compile a DLL that calls a C run-time DLL with specific options and link it with the C run-time DLL's import library. The steps for building an application-specific DLL named JUSTLIB3.DLL are given below.

1. Compile with the /MD option.

The easiest way to be sure you choose the proper options is to use the /MD switch, which indicates that the DLL will be used with a C run-time DLL. When you use /MD, library search records are suppressed and the following options are in effect:

Option	Effect
/ALw	Use large memory model with separate stack segment
/G2	Use 80286 processor instruction set
/D MT	Use the multithread version of the include files
/D DLL	Use a C run-time dynamic-link library
/FPi	Generate in-line floating-point instructions and select the emulator math package

The /G2 and /ALw options can be overridden. The FPi option can be replaced with /FPi87 or /FPc, but not with /FPa. See Chapter 4, "Controlling Floating-Point Math Operations," for more information about compatible floating-point options.

You should also use the /c option to compile without linking. The command line to compile the sample file JUSTIFY.C is

```
CL /MD /c JUSTIFY.C
```

2. Create a module-definition file.

   Create a module-definition file named JUSTLIB3.DEF that includes the following line:

```
LIBRARY JUSTLIB3 INITINSTANCE
```

3. Link the DLL with the C run-time and OS/2 import libraries.

   To create a DLL that will call a C run-time DLL, the following files must be linked together:

File Name	Description
OS2.LIB	Import library for the OS/2 kernel
yourclib.LIB	Import library for your C run-time DLL
CRTDLL.OBJ	Start-up code for DLLs using a C run-time DLL
CRTDLL_I.OBJ	Optional initialization module for DLLs requiring custom initialization (replaces CRTDLL.OBJ)
yourdll.OBJ	Object file for your DLL
yourdll.DEF	Module-definition file for your DLL

The command for linking these files to create JUSTLIB3.DLL is

```
LINK justify+crtdll,justlib3.dll,,cexample+os2,justlib3.def
```

4. Create an import library.

   Use JUSTLIB3.DLL and the IMPLIB utility to create an import library file, JUSTLIB3.LIB, for use by applications calling JUSTLIB3.DLL:

```
IMPLIB JUSTLIB3.LIB JUSTLIB3.DLL
```

   Remember to copy JUSTLIB3.DLL to a directory named in the **LIBPATH** statement in the CONFIG.SYS file.

Using C Run-Time and Application-Specific DLLs

Application programs using a C run-time DLL, such as the sample program CEXAMPLE.DLL (described earilier in this section), must define the symbolic constants **MT** and **DLL**. These constants cause the compiler to use the multi-thread and DLL sections of the include files. You can define the constants in your source code or with the compiler's /D command-line option. Since the C run-time DLL uses the large memory model, your program must either use the same model or declare all C run-time functions and pointers passed to them as **_far**. If you use the standard include files for the C run-time functions in your program, all these declarations are made for you.

The following files are required to link an application that calls a C run-time DLL:

File Name	Description
OS2.LIB	Import library for the OS/2 kernel
yourclib.LIB	Import library for your C run-time DLL
yourdll.LIB	Import library for each optional application DLL
CRTEXE.OBJ	Start-up code for executable files calling a C run-time DLL
yourapp.OBJ	Object file(s) for your application
yourapp.DEF	Optional module-definition file for your application

The following commands compile and link the TESTJUST.C file from Section 16.3.1 for use with the dynamic-link libraries CEXAMPLE.DLL and JUSTLIB3.DLL. The link command uses the /NOD option to suppress selection of the standard large-model library. The result is a program named SAMPLE2.EXE.

```
CL /AL /D MT /D DLL /G2 /c TESTJUST.C
LINK /NOD TESTJUST+CRTEXE,SAMPLE2.EXE,,CEXAMPLE+OS2+JUSTLIB3;
```

16.3.4 Using CodeView to Debug Dynamic-Link Libraries

The protected-mode version of CodeView (CVP) supports debugging of dynamic-link libraries. The /L option lets you name one or more DLLs to be debugged with your application.

To enable full symbolic debugging, use the CodeView options /Zi when compiling and /CO when linking. Do this for both the DLL to be debugged and for the program that calls the DLL.

The syntax for the /L CodeView option is

/L *file*

At least one space must separate /L from the file name(s). You can enter multiple DLL names. To debug the JUSTLIB3.DLL dynamic-link library and the SAMPLE2.EXE program discussed in the previous section, use this command line:

```
CVP /L JUSTLIB3.DLL SAMPLE2.EXE
```

Use the CodeView Trace command (F8) to enter and view DLL code.

A simple way to use CodeView is to place a breakpoint at the instruction that calls the DLL function you want to debug. When you reach the breakpoint, press F8 to execute the current source line. CodeView will then display the DLL function's source code, allowing you to set additional breakpoints and enter other CodeView commands.

Appendixes

Appendix A
Using Exit Codes

When C programs terminate, they return values to the process that started them. These values are called "exit codes." The process that starts a C program can be either an operating system, such as DOS or OS/2, or another program. The process that starts the C program is referred to as the "parent process"; the program started is referred to as the "child process." The parent process can interpret return values as an error code sent to the operating system or use those return values as a form of interprocess communication (communication between two separate processes).

A.1 The exit Function

The **exit** function terminates execution of your C program and returns an exit code (an integer value) to the parent process. The parent process can be the operating system or another program, depending on how the child process was executed. Note that a C program always returns an integer, regardless of how you declare the **main** function.

Most programs use exit codes to communicate errors to the parent process; these are called "error codes." By convention, programs return zero if they complete normally and a nonzero value if they are exiting because of an error. This error code (the nonzero value) can then be used by the operating system to control the execution of other programs (for example, from inside a batch file).

The Microsoft C compiler is a good example of a program that returns an exit code. It returns 0 if no errors occur in your compile and a positive value if an error occurs during compilation.

The following program attempts to open a file for reading. If the file cannot be opened, **exit** returns 1 to the calling program. Therefore, 1 and 0 are both exit codes.

```
#include <stdio.h>

int main(void)
{
    FILE * fp;

    if( !(fp = fopen( filename, "rb" )) )
    {
        printf("Error %d: Could not open file\n", errno);
        exit(1);
    }

    do_file_access(fp);
}
```

In the preceding example, the exit code is unpredictable because the **exit** function is not used. The value actually returned to the parent process (or to the operating system shell) is whatever happens to be in the AX register when the program terminates—in this case, whatever `do_file_access` returned.

A.2 *Testing Exit Codes from Command and Batch Files*

Using the IF ERRORLEVEL command, you can test to see if a program has executed successfully by checking its exit code. The IF ERRORLEVEL command is an OS/2 command file or DOS batch file command that tests the exit code of the most recently executed program.

IF ERRORLEVEL can help you organize program execution. For example, you can define program execution to be dependent on the successful exit code testing of earlier programs by IF ERRORLEVEL. You can also use the value of the exit code to branch to different commands in a batch or command file.

When placed in a batch or command file, the following commands will execute REPORTS.EXE only if FILEMNG.EXE does not return an error:

```
echo Running file manager....
FILEMNG.EXE
IF NOT ERRORLEVEL 1 REPORTS.EXE
```

Despite the name `ERRORLEVEL`, the exit code does not always denote an error. You can define error codes to communicate any information useful to you.

Refer to the *Microsoft Operating System/2 User's Guide* or the *Microsoft MS-DOS User's Guide and User's Reference* for more information about the IF ERRORLEVEL command.

A.3 Accessing Exit Codes from Other Programs

When you use any of the **spawn** family of functions to run a program as the child of another program, the return value of **spawn** is the exit code of the function. The following code performs the same function as the batch file in Section A.2:

```
void main( void )
{
    if( !spawnl( P_WAIT, "filemng.exe", "filemng.exe",
            NULL ) )
        spawnl( P_WAIT, "reports.exe", "reports.exe",
            NULL );
}
```

The program `reports.exe` is executed only if the program `filemng.exe` terminates with an exit code of 0.

The following code uses the exit code as part of a simple menu system:

```
void main(void)
{
    int option;
    int menu_num = 0;  /* Initialize for first execution */

    while( (option = spawnl( P_WAIT, "menu.exe",
                        "menu.exe", menu_num, NULL )) )
    {
        switch( option )
        {
            case 1 :
                menu_num = spawnl( P_WAIT, "program1.exe",
                            "program1.exe", NULL );
                break;
            case 2 :
                menu_num = spawnl( P_WAIT, "program2.exe",
                            "program2.exe", NULL );
                break;
            case 3 :
                menu_num = spawnl( P_WAIT, "program3.exe",
                            "program3.exe", NULL );
                break;
            default:        /* Guard against a bad option */
                break;
        }
    }
}
```

The preceding example demonstrates how you could have a program, `menu.exe`, that solicits input from a menu of choices. This input is interpreted and passed back to the main program in the form of an exit code. (The **spawnl** function returns the value of the child process's exit code.) This exit code value is stored in `option`, which is used as a selector variable in a switch statement.

Based on the value returned from `menu.exe`, the main program executes `program1.exe`, `program2.exe`, or `program3.exe`. Finally, `menu_num`, the exit code of the program selected, is used as a parameter to the next execution of `menu.exe`.

Appendix B
Differences between C Versions 5.1 and 6.0

This appendix describes the differences between versions 5.1 and 6.0 of Microsoft C, including additions, deletions, and changes. Some of the changes are required by the American National Standards Institute (ANSI) draft standard for the C programming language. Other changes improve or augment the existing capabilities of the compiler.

Many of the changes will have no effect on code that was written and compiled with previous versions of Microsoft C. In some cases, however, you may have to modify or correct existing code before compiling with version 6.0.

B.1 Modifications for ANSI Compatibility

A number of changes have been made to the compiler to support the ANSI draft standard. These include new features (Section B.1.1) and changes (Sections B.1.2 – B.1.8).

B.1.1 ANSI-Mandated New Features

The following ANSI-mandated features are new to version 6.0:

- The semantics for **volatile** have been implemented.

- Both **long** and **unsigned long** values are allowed in switch expressions and case constants.

- The compiler supports **unsigned long** decimal constants. It is now possible to initialize **unsigned long** variables with values larger than **MAX_LONG** using decimal (rather than hexadecimal or octal) constants.

- Bit fields are permitted in unions.

- The address-of operator (**&**) works correctly on arrays and functions.

- Storage classes or types (or both) are now required on variable declarations. The compiler previously assumed that untyped variables (such as `a;`) were integers. This declaration now generates a warning.

- The LOCALE.H header file is new to version 6.0. It declares functions and structures for describing conventions that vary from one country to the next, such as the currency symbol and the way calendar dates are printed.

B.1.2 Integer Promotion Rules

The ANSI draft standard requires a change in the evaluation of some expressions that mix signed and unsigned integers. Earlier versions of the compiler attempted to preserve an expression's unsigned nature as much as possible. Version 6.0 attempts to preserve the expression's value.

In version 5.1, an **unsigned char** promotes to an **unsigned int**; an **unsigned int** promotes to an **unsigned long**.

In version 6.0, an **unsigned char** promotes to a **signed int**; an **unsigned int** promotes to a **signed long**.

For example,

```
main()
{
  long int li = -256L;
  test( li );
}

test( long li)
{
  if( li < 0xffff )
     puts( "C 6.0 does a signed compare" );
  else puts( "C 5.1 does an unsigned compare" );
}
```

B.1.3 Defining NULL as a Pointer

The constant **NULL** is now defined as `((void *)0)`. Previous versions of Microsoft C defined **NULL** as 0x0000 in small and medium models and 0x00000000L in compact and large models.

B.1.4 Shift Operators

Shift operators now give a result that is of the same type as the left side. For example,

```
short si;
long li;
si = 0x0001;
li = si << 16L;
```

The compiler previously yielded a result that was the size of the largest of the two values. In the example above, the short value would be automatically cast to a long because 16L is long. The value assigned to `li` would be 0x00010000L in Microsoft C 5.1.

To adhere to the ANSI draft standard, Microsoft C 6.0 maintains the size of the left operand. The variable `si` has 16 bits. Shifting left 16 times produces a value of 0, which is then assigned to `li`.

B.1.5 Pointers to Typedefs

The rules for handling pointers to typedefs have changed subtly. For example, C 5.1 interprets

```
typedef int far f_int;
f_int *fp_i;
```

as being equivalent to

```
int *far fp_i;
```

which means `fp_i` is a distant pointer to an integer. The address of `fp_i` contains 32 bits. The size of the integer's address is indeterminate.

C 6.0 interprets it as

```
int far *fp_i;
```

This means `fp_i` is a far pointer to an integer. The address of the integer contains 32 bits. The size of the address of `fp_i` is indeterminate.

This affects typedefs containing **_near**, **_far**, **_based**, and other modifiers. Although these are Microsoft-specific keywords, their new behavior is consistent with what the ANSI draft standard requires for the **const** and **volatile** keywords.

B.1.6 Identifying Nonstandard Keywords

The following modifiers are specific to Microsoft C; they are not described in the ANSI draft standard. To identify these implementation-defined keywords as non-ANSI, an initial underscore has been added.

C 5.1 Keyword	C 6.0 Keyword
far	_far
huge	_huge
near	_near
cdecl	_cdecl
fortran	_fortran
interrupt	_interrupt
pascal	_pascal

The compiler still accepts the obsolescent versions of these keywords, unless the /Za option is used.

B.1.7 Trigraphs

To maintain compatibility with and portability to other systems, Microsoft C 6.0 supports the following trigraphs:

Trigraph	Character
??=	#
??(	[
??/	\
??)	]
??'	^
??<	{
??!	|
??>	}
??–	~

B.1.8 ANSI Nonconformance

This section lists the areas where Microsoft C 6.0 does not conform to the ANSI draft standard.

- Microsoft C does not support multibyte characters, wide-character and string constants, and the related library functions and types.

- Microsoft C contains some name-space violations in the language (extended keywords, such as **near** and **far**) and in the library (non-ANSI macros and types in header files and extended library function names, such as **read** and **write**).

B.2 New Keywords and Functions

This section describes keywords and functions that did not exist in previous versions of Microsoft C. Details about how to use these features can be found elsewhere in the documentation.

B.2.1 In-Line Assembler

The new **_asm** keyword allows you to mix assembly instructions with C source code. This feature includes the **_emit** function, which lets you enter arbitrary values into the code stream.

See Chapter 3, "Using the In-Line Assembler."

B.2.2 Based Pointers and Objects

A based pointer is a special, compact form of pointer. It is always represented as a short offset. The address represented by such a pointer is calculated by adding the based pointer to its base. The base must be supplied each time the pointer is dereferenced, either explicitly using a special operator or implicitly by associating the base value with the pointer when it is declared. The base can be a far pointer, a near pointer, or a new type that represents a segment.

Based pointers and objects are declared using the new keyword, **_based**.

Segment Types

The new type specifier, **_segment**, specifies a segment.

Any pointer or address can be cast to **_segment**. If the operand is a near pointer, the result is the current value of the data segment register (DS). If the operand is a far pointer, the result is the segment part of the far pointer.

Segment Names

Segment names are declared using the built-in function **_segname**. The compiler recognizes four predefined segment names: **_CODE**, **_CONST**, **_DATA**, and **_STACK**.

Each segment name represents a constant of type **_segment**.

Base Operator

The base operator (**:>**) associates a base expression (usually a segment) with a based pointer, to form a far pointer value. For example,

```
0x0F01:>0x0015
```

combines the segment 0x0F01 with the offset 0x0015 to form the effective address 0x0F025. The base operator's precedence falls between ( ) and [ ].

Casting Based Pointers

A based pointer can be cast to a pointer, a long integer, a short integer, or another based pointer. When a based pointer is converted to a far pointer, a long integer, a near pointer, or another based pointer having a different base expression, it is first normalized to a far pointer (including adding the offset in the base, if present, to the based pointer); then any additional conversions are applied.

Operations on Based Pointers

Based pointers, for the purpose of arithmetic and dereferencing, are treated as semantically equivalent to far pointers. When a based pointer mixes with another integral type (**int**, **long**, near pointer, far pointer, or based pointer), implicit casting is done. In some cases, the compiler can optimize these references and treat the pointer as an offset.

The value of 0 is treated specially, as it is for near and far pointers. No conversions are applied to the constant 0 because it is assumed to be a null pointer.

See Chapter 2, "Managing Memory."

B.2.3 Based Heap Allocation Support

The functions listed below provide support for allocating, expanding, and freeing memory for based heaps, which dynamically allocate memory for based items. The functions are prototyped in the MALLOC.H include file.

_bcalloc	_bheapchk	_bmalloc
_bexpand	_bheapmin	_bmsize
_bfree	_bheapseg	_brealloc
_bfreeseg	_bheapset	
_bheapadd	_bheapwalk	

See Chapter 2, "Managing Memory."

B.2.4 Releasing Unused Heap Memory

The following routines release unused heap memory by shortening data segments. MALLOC.H contains the function prototypes.

_fheapmin

_heapmin

_nheapmin

B.2.5 Making Static Data Available to the Heap

The **_heapadd** function is new. It allows the user to make unused static data available to the heap.

B.2.6 Long Doubles

Microsoft C version 5.1 treated **double** and **long double** as syntactically different types that were semantically equal. Both types were stored in memory as 64-bit quantities. For purposes of type-checking, **long double** and **double** have always been different types.

Because the 80x87 family of math coprocessors supports an 80-bit floating-point type, Microsoft C version 6.0 stores **long double** variables in the 80x87 10-byte (80-bit) form.

Certain functions have been modified to handle the **long double** type. The **printf** and **scanf** family of functions supports **long double** values with the trailing **l**. The library contains new versions of the transcendental functions as well as intrinsic forms that accept **long double** arguments.

B.2.7 Long Double Functions

All the functions below are defined in the standard include file MATH.H. They return **long double** values and results and error codes analogous to the double versions.

acosl	expl	_matherrl
asinl	fabsl	modfl
atanl	floorl	powl
atan2l	fmodl	sinl
_atold	frexpl	sinhl
cabsl	hypotl	sqrtl
ceill	ldexpl	tanl
cosl	logl	tanhl
coshl	log10l	

B.2.8 Model-Independent String and Memory Functions

The following functions make it easier to write mixed-model programs by providing model-independent (large model) forms for most of the standard string and memory functions. These functions can be called from any point in any program, no matter which memory model has been selected. These functions take only far pointers as arguments. Thus, any data item, near or far, in any combination, can be handled.

The names of these functions are the same as the model-dependent forms, except they include an **_f** prefix. For example, **_fstrlen** is the model-independent version of the **strlen** function.

The functions listed below are defined in the standard include file STRING.H.

Memory Functions

_fmemccpy	_fmemcpy
_fmemchr	_fmemmove
_fmemcmp	_fmemset
_fmemicmp	

String Functions

_fstrcat	_fstrlwr	_fstrrchr
_fstrchr	_fstrncat	_fstrrev
_fstrcmp	_fstrncmp	_fstrset
_fstricmp	_fstrnicmp	_fstrspn
_fstrcpy	_fstrncpy	_fstrstr
_fstrcspn	_fstrnset	_fstrtok
_fstrlen	_fstrpbrk	_fstrupr

String Duplication Functions

_fstrdup

_nstrdup

B.2.9 Mixed-Model Memory Allocation Support

The following functions are based on **realloc**, **calloc**, and **expand**, but they affect only near memory or far memory. MALLOC.H contains the function prototypes.

_fcalloc	_ncalloc
_fexpand	_nexpand
_frealloc	_nrealloc

B.2.10 The _fastcall Attribute (/Gr Option)

Individual function prototypes can be declared with the new attribute **_fastcall**.

The /Gr option enables the fastcall function-calling convention for all functions that are not explicitly prototyped with the **_cdecl**, **_pascal**, or **_fortran** attributes. Using /Gr on the command line causes each function in the module to compile as **_fastcall** unless the function is declared with a conflicting attribute, or the name of the function is **main**.

When you use the /Gr option, all functions are assumed to use the **_fastcall** convention. As a result, to use any run-time library functions, you must either include the standard include files or explicitly prototype the function you want to call.

A fastcall function receives up to three 16-bit arguments, passed in registers rather than on the stack. Arguments are passed in the AX, BX, and DX registers. This may change in future versions of the compiler.

The argument types and their potential register assignments are

Argument	Registers
character (3)	AL, DL, BL
short integer (3)	AX, DX, BX
near pointer (3)	BX, AX, DX
long integer (1)	DX:AX
far pointer (1)	ES:BX

If the registers for a particular class have already been used, or if an argument is not one of the five types listed above, it is pushed on the stack as usual. An argument list of types **long**, **float**, **short** would pass the **long** in DX:AX, push the **float**, and pass the **short** in BX.

The treatment of character arguments depends further on prototypes. If there is no prototype, the argument is promoted to **short** and the rules for short integers apply. Only if the argument is prototyped as a **char** do the character rules apply.

The **_fastcall** convention is not compatible with any of the following attributes: **_interrupt**, **_saveregs**, **_export**, **_cdecl**, **_fortran**, or **_pascal**.

See Chapter 1, "Optimizing C Programs."

B.2.11 Drive and Directory Functions

Several new functions make it easier to get and set the current drive and the current directory. The prototypes for the following routines are in DIRECT.H:

_chdrive

_fullpath

_getdrive

_getdcwd

B.2.12 Text Output Functions for OS/2

Several text-mode screen functions have been added to Microsoft C 6.0 for OS/2. With the exception of the new **_scrolltextwindow** function, they are identical to what is defined in real mode, except for any references to behavior in graphics modes. The following routines are located in GRTEXT.LIB, and the prototypes are in GRAPH.H:

_clearscreen	**_getvideoconfig**	**_settextrows**
_displaycursor	**_outtext**	**_settextwindow**
_getbkcolor	**_setbkcolor**	**_setvideomode**
_gettextcolor	**_settextcolor**	**_setvideomoderows**
_gettextcursor	**_settextcursor**	**_scrolltextwindow**
_gettextposition	**_settextposition**	**_wrapon**

See Part 4 of this manual, "OS/2 Support."

B.3 New Features

The features described in Sections B.3.1–B.3.10 are new to version 6.0.

B.3.1 Strings and Macros

The compiler now allows longer string literals (up to 4K) and longer macro expansions (up to 6K).

B.3.2 CL Options

The following options are new to Microsoft C 6.0:

Option	Action
/AT	Compiles in tiny model (.COM files).
/Fr[[*filename*]]	Outputs source browser information file.
/FR[[*filename*]]	Outputs extended source browser information file.
/Gd	Forces **_cdecl** calling conventions.
/Gr	Enables register (**_fastcall**) function-calling conventions.
/MA*masmoption*	Supports invocation of the assembler using the CL driver. All MASM-supported options are accepted. In addition, the compiler recognizes file names with .ASM suffixes and passes them directly to MASM.
/MD	Uses C run-time as DLL option. Defaults to /ALw /FPi /G2 /DDLL /DMT and inhibits library search records.
/ML	Links C run-time as part of a dynamic-link library (DLL). Defaults to /ALw /FPa /G2 /DMT and changes library search record to LLIBCDLL.LIB.
/MT	Enables multithread option. Defaults to /ALw /FPi /G2 /DMT and changes library search record to LLIBCMT.LIB.
/Oe	Enables global register allocation.
/Og	Enables global optimizations and global common subexpressions (CSEs).
/Ox	Is now equivalent to /Ocegilt /Gs. Note that this implies that maximum optimization includes the **_fastcall** function-calling convention.

/Oz	Enables aggressive optimizations.
/Ta *name*	Specifies that *name* is to be treated as an assembler input file.
/W4	Turns on extra warning level which supports more detailed (LINT-like) warnings and recognition of ANSI violations.
/WX	Causes warnings to be treated as errors. If a warning occurs, the .OBJ file is not created.

B.3.3 *Tiny Memory Model (.COM Files)*

Microsoft C 6.0 now supports the tiny memory model, which produces .COM rather than .EXE files (for DOS only).

The /AT option selects the tiny model. This forces the linker to use options /NOE and /TINY. Within the linker, /TINY turns on /FARCALLTRANSLATION to help eliminate far segment relocations. If you link your own .OBJ files, link with CRTCOM.OBJ.

B.3.4 *The Optimize Pragma*

The **optimize** pragma turns optimizing options on or off:

#pragma optimize(" *<optimization switch list>*** ",{off | on})**

where *<optimization switch list>* can be an empty list or one or more of the following: a, c, e, g, l, w, n, p, t, and z. For example,

```
#pragma optimize("lp",on) /* equivalent to /Olp */
#pragma optimize("",off)  /* turns off all optimization */
#pragma optimize("",on)   /* restores default settings */
```

See Chapter 1, "Optimizing C Programs."

B.3.5 *Nameless Structures and Unions*

Both **struct** and **union** declarations can now be specified without a declarator when they are members of another structure or union.

A nameless union would look like this:

```
struct str
{
   int a,b;
   union            /* unnamed union */
   {
      char c[4];
      long l;
      float f;
   };
   char c_array[10];
} my_str;
.

.

.
my_str.l == 0L;
```

A nameless structure would look like this:

```
struct s1
{
   int a,b,c;
};

struct s2
{
   float y;
   struct s1;
   char str[10];
} *p_s2;
.

.

.

p_s2->b = 100;
```

B.3.6 Unsized Arrays as the Last Member of a Structure

The compiler now allows an unsized or zero-sized array as the last member of a structure. The declaration of such a structure would look like this:

```
struct var_length
{
   <set of declarations>;
   <type> array[];
};
```

Unsized arrays can appear only as the last member of a structure. Structures containing unsized array declarations can be nested within other structures as long as no further members are declared in any enclosing structures. Arrays of such structures are not allowed.

The **sizeof** operator, when applied to a variable of this type or to the type itself, assumes 0 for the size of the array.

B.3.7 Improved Warnings

A new warning level four (CL option /W4) has been added for the following warnings:

- Detection of unused global variables

- Expressions without side effects

- Nonportable (non-ANSI) constructs

- Local variable referenced before being initialized

- Undefined or implementation-defined constructs

B.3.8 Macros

The number of macros definable with /D options has increased from 20 to 30.

B.3.9 Improved Multithread Support in OS/2

The number of OS/2 threads supported at run time has increased from 32 to the operating system limit. Three new options aid development of multithread applications and dynamic-link libraries:

1. /MT for building multithread programs. It implies /ALw /FPi /G2 /D MT, and changes the library search record emitted in the object file to reference LLIBCMT.

2. /ML for building a DLL that uses the C run-time library. It implies /ALw /FPa /G2 /D MT, and changes the library search record emitted in the object file to reference LLIBCDLL.

3. /MD for building .EXE files and DLLs that share a C run-time DLL. It implies /ALw /FPi /G2 /DDLL /D MT, and no library search records are emitted in the object file.

B.3.10 Pipe Support in OS/2

Microsoft C 6.0 supports pipes as part of the file I/O system. The functions listed below are defined in the standard include file IO.H:

_pipe

_popen

_pclose

B.4 Differences in Code Generation

This section lists ways in which the executable files produced by Microsoft C 6.0 may differ from the files produced by previous versions of the compiler.

B.4.1 Speed and Space Improvements

Executable files are smaller and faster.

B.4.2 Code Quality

Microsoft C 6.0 generates improved local code in default optimization cases and, under full optimization, supports global (function level) register allocation and common subexpressions (CSEs), loop optimizations, parameter passing through registers, and generation of in-line code for certain intrinsic functions.

B.4.3 Floating-Point Code Generation

In Microsoft C 6.0, the /FPi87 option suppresses the fixups previously used for emulation. Pure coprocessor instructions are now emitted. This makes object files smaller and speeds up linking, in addition to making in-line assembly easier to use.

In version 5.1, /FPi and /FPi87 generated the same code; the only difference was the library. In C 6.0, the two options generate different code. It is no longer possible to force /FPi87 to act like /FPi. If you use /FPi87, the math coprocessor must be in the computer on which the program is running.

Note that if you use /FPi87 you must link with mLIB7, not mLIBCE.

B.4.4 Intrinsic Functions

The intrinsic function optimization option (/Oi) causes the compiler to generate in-line code for the following functions:

abs	_lrotl	_rotl
_disable	_lrotr	_rotr
_enable	memcmp	strcat
fabs	memcpy	strcmp
inp	memset	strcpy
inpw	outp	strlen
labs	outpw	strset

The compiler does not generate in-line code for the following functions, although it will modify the calling convention to pass the arguments on the floating-point chip:

acos	pow	coshl
asin	sin	expl
atan	sinh	floorl
atan2	sqrt	fmodl
ceil	tan	logl
cos	tanh	log10l
cosh	acosl	powl
exp	asinl	sinl
floor	atanl	sinhl
fmod	atan2l	sqrtl
log	ceill	tanl
log10	cosl	tanhl

B.5 Changes and Deletions

The changes and deletions listed in this section have a high probability of affecting existing programs.

B.5.1 Deleted Features

The **data_seg** pragma has been deleted.

The memory management routine **sbrk** has been deleted.

The compiler and tools do not run under DOS 2.1. The run-time files produced by the compiler and linker will continue to run under DOS 2.1.

B.5.2 Evaluation of Real Expressions

Real expressions inside parentheses are now evaluated according to the semantics of the parentheses. For example, in the expression

```
((r1 / r2) * r3)
```

the division is performed before the multiplication. Previous versions of the compiler might have reordered the operations.

B.5.3 Default Optimizations

Version 6.0 performs more extensive optimizations than version 5.1. This implies that code that had aliasing but worked with the /Oa option in 5.1 might not work with version 6.0 and /Oa. Also, because of the improved optimizations, the /Od option should be used to turn off all optimizing before you begin debugging with CodeView.

B.5.4 Sign Extension of char Arguments

Previous versions of Microsoft C would sign-extend **char** arguments to **int** size before passing them to a second function. Version 6.0 does not extend the sign if the function is prototyped and the prototype includes a **char** argument. The most-significant byte is considered undefined.

B.5.5 *Conditional Compilation and Signed Values*

Version 5.1 of Microsoft C treated conditional compilation expressions as **signed long** values. Version 6.0 evaluates these expressions using the same rules as expressions in C. For example,

```
#if 0xFFFFFFFFL > 1UL
.
.
.
#endif
```

The expression evaluates to be true. It was evaluated as false in version 5.1.

B.5.6 *The const and volatile Qualifiers*

The **const** and **volatile** qualifiers must be placed after the type they qualify. The declaration

```
int (const *p);
```

is now treated as a syntax error. Previous versions of the compiler would accept such a construction.

The following declarations are legal:

```
int const *p_ci;    /* pointer to constant int */
int const (*p_ci);  /* pointer to constant int */
int *const cp_i;    /* constant pointer to int */
int (*const cp_i);  /* constant pointer to int */
```

B.5.7 *Memory Allocation*

The **_fmalloc** function attempts to allocate far memory. It previously called **_nmalloc** if far memory was not available. Now it returns a null pointer if far memory isn't available, even if near memory is available.

B.5.8 *Memory Used by Command-Line Arguments*

Previous versions of the compiler placed the command-line argument strings and environment strings in the near heap. Now they are allocated though **malloc**, which means that they will be in far memory in compact and large models.

B.5.9 *Format Specifiers in printf*

The **printf** format specifier modifiers **N**, **F**, **h**, and **l** have changed.

The specifier **%Np** is a synonym for **%hp**, but the latter is preferred. Likewise, **%Fp** is a synonym for **%lp**.

For **scanf**, **N** and **F** refer to the distance to the object being read in; that is, whether the pointer itself is allocated near or far. The modifiers **h** and **l** refer to the size of the object (16-bit near pointer or 32-bit far pointer). In these examples,

```
scanf("%Nlp", n_fp);
scanf("%Fhp", f_np);
```

the first line reads in an address that resides in near memory (N) but holds a 32-bit far pointer variable (lp). The second line reads in a near pointer value (hp) into a pointer variable that resides in far memory (F).

B.5.10 *Functions that Return Float Values*

In Microsoft C 5.1, a prototype or definition such as

```
float funcname();
```

was interpreted as

```
double funcname()
```

Version 6.0 interprets it as

```
float
```

Appendix C
Implementation-Defined Behavior

The American National Standards Institute (ANSI) Standard for the C programming language contains an appendix called "Portability Issues." The ANSI appendix lists areas of the C language that ANSI leaves open to each particular implementation. This appendix describes how Microsoft C handles these implementation-defined areas of the C language.

This appendix follows the same order as the ANSI Standard appendix. Each item covered includes references to the ANSI chapter and section that explains the implementation-defined behavior.

NOTE *This appendix describes the U.S. English-language version of the C compiler only. Foreign-language implementations of Microsoft C may differ slightly.*

C.1 Translation

C.1.1 Diagnostics

How a diagnostic is identified (§2.1.1.3)

Microsoft C produces error messages in the form:

filename(*line-number*) **:** *diagnostic* **C***number message*

where *filename* is the name of the source file in which the error was encountered; *line-number* is the line number at which the compiler detected the error; *diagnostic* is either "error" or "warning"; *number* is a unique four-digit number (preceded by a **C**) that identifies the error or warning; *message* is an explanatory message.

C.2 Environment

C.2.1 Arguments to main

The semantics of the arguments to main (§2.1.2.2)

In Microsoft C, the function called at program start-up is called **main**. There is no prototype declared for **main**, and it can be defined with zero, two, or three parameters:

```
int main( void )
int main( int argc, char *argv[] )
int main( int argc, char *argv[], char *envp[] )
```

The third line above, where **main** accepts three parameters, is a Microsoft extension to the ANSI Standard. The third parameter, **envp**, is an array of pointers to environment variables. The **envp** array is terminated by a null pointer. See on-line help for more information about **main** and **envp**.

The variable **argc** never holds a negative value.

The array of strings ends with **argv[argc]**, which contains a null pointer.

All elements of the **argv** array are pointers to strings.

A program invoked with no command-line arguments will receive a value of one for **argc**, as the name of the executable file is placed in **argv[0]**. (In DOS versions prior to 3.0, the executable file name is not available. The letter "C" is placed in **argv[0]**.) Strings pointed to by **argv[1]** through **argv[argc – 1]** represent program parameters.

The parameters **argc** and **argv** are modifiable and retain their last-stored values between program start-up and program termination.

C.2.2 Interactive Devices

What constitutes an interactive device (§2.1.2.3)

Microsoft C defines the keyboard and the display as interactive devices.

C.3 Identifiers

C.3.1 Significant Characters without External Linkage

The number of significant characters without external linkage (§3.1.2)

Identifiers are significant to 31 characters. The compiler does not restrict the number of characters you can use in an identifier; it simply ignores any characters beyond the limit.

C.3.2 Significant Characters with External Linkage

The number of significant characters with external linkage (§3.1.2)

Identifiers declared **extern** in programs compiled with Microsoft C are significant to 31 characters. You can modify this default to a smaller number using the /H (restrict length of external names) option. See on-line help for more information on the syntax of the /H option.

C.3.3 Upper- and Lowercase

Whether case distinctions are significant (§3.1.2)

Microsoft C treats identifiers within a compilation unit as case sensitive. Externally linked identifiers may or may not be case sensitive, depending on whether you use /NOIGNORECASE option when you invoke the linker. The default for the linker is to ignore case, making externally linked identifiers case insensitive.

Thus, symbols in source files are sensitive to case. By default, symbols in object files are not.

Two CL command-line options affect case sensitivity:

1. The /Gc (generate Pascal-style function calls) command-line option converts all external identifiers (including function names) to uppercase.

   The **_pascal** declarator performs the same operation on a function-by-function basis.

2. The /Zc (compile case insensitive) converts all identifiers (excluding function names) to uppercase.

C.4 Characters

C.4.1 The ASCII Character Set

Members of source and execution character sets (§2.2.1)

The source character set is the set of legal characters that can appear in source files. For Microsoft C, the source character set is the standard ASCII character set. Figure C.1 contains an ASCII table.

WARNING *Because keyboard and console drivers can remap the character set, programs intended for international distribution should check the country code.*

C.4.2 Multibyte Characters

Shift states for multibyte characters (§2.2.1)

Multibyte characters are used by some implementations to represent foreign-language characters not represented in the base character set. Microsoft C 6.0 does not support multibyte characters.

C.4.3 Bits per Character

Number of bits in a character (§2.2.4.2)

The number of bits in a character is represented by the manifest constant **CHAR_BIT**. The LIMITS.H file defines **CHAR_BIT** as 8.

C.4.4 Character Sets

Mapping members of the source character set (§3.1.3.4)

The source character set and execution character set include the ANSI ASCII characters listed in Table C.1. Escape sequences are also shown in Table C.1.

Table C.1

Escape Sequence	Character	ASCII Value
\a	Alert/bell	7
\b	Backspace	8
\f	Form feed	12
\n	Newline	10
\r	Carriage return	13
\t	Horizontal tab	9
\v	Vertical tab	11
\"	Double quotation	34
\'	Single quotation	39
\\	Backslash	92

C.4.5 Unrepresented Character Constants

The value of an integer character constant that contains a character or escape sequence not represented in the basic execution character set or the extended character set for a wide character constant (§3.1.3.4)

Microsoft C does not support wide characters.

C.4.6 Wide Characters

The value of an integer character constant that contains more than one character or a wide character constant that contains more than one multibyte character (§3.1.3.4)

Microsoft C does not support wide characters or multibyte characters.

C.4.7 Converting Multibyte Characters

The current locale used to convert multibyte characters into corresponding wide characters (codes) for a wide character constant (3.1.3.4)

Microsoft C does not support multibyte characters.

Ctrl	Dec	Hex	Char	Code
^@	0	00		NUL
^A	1	01		SOH
^B	2	02		STX
^C	3	03		ETX
^D	4	04		EOT
^E	5	05		ENQ
^F	6	06		ACK
^G	7	07		BEL
^H	8	08		BS
^I	9	09		HT
^J	10	0A		LF
^K	11	0B		VT
^L	12	0C		FF
^M	13	0D		CR
^N	14	0E		SO
^O	15	0F		SI
^P	16	10		DLE
^Q	17	11		DC1
^R	18	12		DC2
^S	19	13		DC3
^T	20	14		DC4
^U	21	15		NAK
^V	22	16		SYN
^W	23	17		ETB
^X	24	18		CAN
^Y	25	19		EM
^Z	26	1A		SUB
^[	27	1B		ESC
^\	28	1C		FS
^]	29	1D		GS
^^	30	1E		RS
^_	31	1F		US

Dec	Hex	Char
32	20	
33	21	!
34	22	"
35	23	#
36	24	$
37	25	%
38	26	&
39	27	'
40	28	(
41	29	)
42	2A	*
43	2B	+
44	2C	,
45	2D	-
46	2E	.
47	2F	/
48	30	0
49	31	1
50	32	2
51	33	3
52	34	4
53	35	5
54	36	6
55	37	7
56	38	8
57	39	9
58	3A	:
59	3B	;
60	3C	<
61	3D	=
62	3E	>
63	3F	?

Dec	Hex	Char
64	40	@
65	41	A
66	42	B
67	43	C
68	44	D
69	45	E
70	46	F
71	47	G
72	48	H
73	49	I
74	4A	J
75	4B	K
76	4C	L
77	4D	M
78	4E	N
79	4F	O
80	50	P
81	51	Q
82	52	R
83	53	S
84	54	T
85	55	U
86	56	V
87	57	W
88	58	X
89	59	Y
90	5A	Z
91	5B	[
92	5C	\
93	5D	]
94	5E	^
95	5F	_

Dec	Hex	Char
96	60	`
97	61	a
98	62	b
99	63	c
100	64	d
101	65	e
102	66	f
103	67	g
104	68	h
105	69	i
106	6A	j
107	6B	k
108	6C	l
109	6D	m
110	6E	n
111	6F	o
112	70	p
113	71	q
114	72	r
115	73	s
116	74	t
117	75	u
118	76	v
119	77	w
120	78	x
121	79	y
122	7A	z
123	7B	{
124	7C		
125	7D	}
126	7E	~
127	7F	Δ[†]

† ASCII code 127 has the code DEL. Under DOS, this code has the same effect as ASCII 8 (BS). The DEL code can be generated by the CTRL + BKSP key combination.

Figure C.1   ASCII Character Set

Dec	Hex	Char
128	80	Ç
129	81	ü
130	82	é
131	83	â
132	84	ä
133	85	à
134	86	å
135	87	ç
136	88	ê
137	89	ë
138	8A	è
139	8B	ï
140	8C	î
141	8D	ì
142	8E	Ä
143	8F	Å
144	90	É
145	91	æ
146	92	Æ
147	93	ô
148	94	ö
149	95	ò
150	96	û
151	97	ù
152	98	ÿ
153	99	Ö
154	9A	Ü
155	9B	¢
156	9C	£
157	9D	¥
158	9E	₧
159	9F	ƒ

Dec	Hex	Char
160	A0	á
161	A1	í
162	A2	ó
163	A3	ú
164	A4	ñ
165	A5	Ñ
166	A6	ª
167	A7	º
168	A8	¿
169	A9	⌐
170	AA	¬
171	AB	½
172	AC	¼
173	AD	¡
174	AE	«
175	AF	»
176	B0	░
177	B1	▒
178	B2	▓
179	B3	│
180	B4	┤
181	B5	╡
182	B6	╢
183	B7	╖
184	B8	╕
185	B9	╣
186	BA	║
187	BB	╗
188	BC	╝
189	BD	╜
190	BE	╛
191	BF	┐

Dec	Hex	Char
192	C0	└
193	C1	┴
194	C2	┬
195	C3	├
196	C4	─
197	C5	┼
198	C6	╞
199	C7	╟
200	C8	╚
201	C9	╔
202	CA	╩
203	CB	╦
204	CC	╠
205	CD	═
206	CE	╬
207	CF	╧
208	D0	╨
209	D1	╤
210	D2	╥
211	D3	╙
212	D4	╘
213	D5	╒
214	D6	╓
215	D7	╫
216	D8	╪
217	D9	┘
218	DA	┌
219	DB	█
220	DC	▄
221	DD	▌
222	DE	▐
223	DF	▀

Dec	Hex	Char
224	E0	α
225	E1	β
226	E2	Γ
227	E3	π
228	E4	Σ
229	E5	σ
230	E6	µ
231	E7	τ
232	E8	Φ
233	E9	Θ
234	EA	Ω
235	EB	δ
236	EC	∞
237	ED	φ
238	EE	ε
239	EF	∩
240	F0	≡
241	F1	±
242	F2	≥
243	F3	≤
244	F4	⌠
245	F5	⌡
246	F6	÷
247	F7	≈
248	F8	°
249	F9	∙
250	FA	·
251	FB	√
252	FC	ⁿ
253	FD	²
254	FE	■
255	FF	

C.4.8 Range of char Values

Whether a "plain" char has the same range of values as a signed char or an unsigned char (§3.2.1.1)

All character values range from 0x00 to 0xFF, signed or unsigned. If a **char** is not explicitly marked as **signed** or **unsigned**, it defaults to the **signed** type.

The CL option /J changes the default from **signed** to **unsigned**.

C.5 Integers

C.5.1 Range of Integer Values

The representations and sets of values of the various types of integers (§3.1.2.5)

Short integers contain 16 bits (two bytes). Long integers contain 32 bits (four bytes). Signed integers are represented in two's-complement form. The most-significant bit holds the sign: 1 for negative, 0 for positive and zero. The values are listed below:

Type	Minimum and Maximum
unsigned short	0 to 65535
signed short	–32768 to 32767
unsigned long	0 to 4294967295
signed long	–2147483648 to 2147483647

C.5.2 Demotion of Integers

The result of converting an integer to a shorter signed integer, or the result of converting an unsigned integer to a signed integer of equal length, if the value cannot be represented (§3.2.1.2)

When a **long** integer is cast to a **short**, or a **short** is cast to a **char**, the least-significant bytes are retained.

For example, this line

```
short x = (short)0x12345678L;
```

assigns the value 0x5678 to x, and this line

```
char y = (char)0x1234;
```

assigns the value 0x34 to y.

When signed variables are converted to unsigned and vice versa, the bit patterns remain the same. For example, casting –2 (0xFE) to an unsigned value yields 254 (also 0xFE).

C.5.3 Signed Bitwise Operations

The results of bitwise operations on signed integers (§3.3)

Bitwise operations on signed integers work the same as bitwise operations on unsigned integers. For example, `-16 & 99` can be expressed in binary as

```
  11111111  11110000
& 00000000  01100011
  -----------------
  00000000  01100000
```

The result of the bitwise AND is 96.

C.5.4 Remainders

The sign of the remainder on integer division (§3.3.5)

The sign of the remainder is the same as the sign of the dividend. For example,

```
 50 / -6 == -8
 50 % -6 ==  2
-50 /  6 == -8
-50 %  6 == -2
```

C.5.5 Right Shifts

The result of a right shift of a negative-value signed integral type (§3.3.7)

Shifting a negative value to the right yields half the absolute value, rounded down. For example, –253 (binary 11111111 00000011) shifted right one bit produces –127 (binary 11111111 10000001). A *positive* 253 shifts right to produce +126.

Right shifts preserve the sign bit. When a signed integer shifts right, the most-significant bit remains set. When an unsigned integer shifts right, the most-significant bit is cleared. Thus, if 0xF000 is signed, a right shift produces 0xF800. If 0xF000 is unsigned, the result is 0x7800.

Shifting a positive number right sixteen times produces 0x0000. Shifting a negative number right sixteen times produces 0xFFFF.

C.6 Floating-Point Math

C.6.1 Values

The representations and sets of values of the various types of floating-point numbers (§3.1.2.5)

The **float** type contains 32 bits: 1 for the sign, 8 for the exponent, and 23 for the mantissa. Its range is +/– 3.4E38 with at least 7 digits of precision.

The **double** type contains 64 bits: 1 for the sign, 11 for the exponent, and 52 for the mantissa. Its range is +/– 1.7E308 with at least 15 digits of precision.

The **long double** type is new to Version 6.0 of Microsoft C. It contains 80 bits: 1 for the sign, 15 for the exponent, and 64 for the mantissa. Its range is +/– 1.2E4932 with at least 17 digits of precision.

C.6.2 Casting Integers to Floating-Point Values

The direction of truncation when an integral number is converted to a floating-point number that cannot exactly represent the original value (§3.2.1.3)

When an integral number is cast to a floating-point value that cannot exactly represent the value, the value is rounded (up or down) to the nearest suitable value.

For example, casting an **unsigned long** (with 32 bits of precision) to a **float** (whose mantissa has 23 bits of precision) rounds the number to the nearest multiple of 256. The **long** values 4294966913 – 4294967167 are all rounded to the **float** value 4294967040.

C.6.3 Truncation of Floating-Point Values

The direction of truncation or rounding when a floating-point number is converted to a narrower floating-point number (§3.2.1.4)

When an underflow occurs, the value of a floating-point variable is rounded down to zero. An overflow causes a run-time math error.

C.7 Arrays and Pointers

C.7.1 Largest Array Size

The type of integer required to hold the maximum size of an array—that is, the size of size_t (§3.3.3.4, 4.1.1)

The **size_t** typedef is an **unsigned short**, with the range 0x0000 to 0xFFFF. Huge arrays can exceed this limit if they contain more than 65,535 elements. Arithmetic operations on huge arrays should therefore cast **size_t** and the results of an arithmetic operations on pointers to **unsigned long**.

C.7.2 Casting Pointers

The result of casting a pointer to an integer or vice versa (§3.3.4)

Near pointers are the same size as short integers; casting near to short (or short to near) has no immediate effect on the value.

Far pointers and huge pointers are the same size as long integers. Casting far/huge to long (or long to far/huge) has no immediate effect on the value.

When a near pointer is cast to a long, the 16-bit value is "normalized," which means the segment (usually DS) and offset are combined to produce a 32-bit memory location.

When a far or huge pointer is cast to a short, the long value is truncated to a short.

The compiler normalizes based pointers when necessary, unless the based pointer is a constant zero, in which case it is assumed to be a null pointer. See Chapter 13, "Writing Portable Programs," for more information about based pointers.

C.7.3 Pointer Subtraction

The type of integer required to hold the difference between two pointers to elements of the same array, ptrdiff_t (§3.3.6, 4.1.1)

A **ptrdiff_t** is a signed integer in the range –32768 to 32767, with one exception. Because huge pointers can address more than 64K of memory, subtracting one huge pointer from another can yield a result that is a long integer. The result of subtracting two huge pointers should be cast to a long.

The compiler normalizes based pointers when necessary. In most cases, based pointers are treated as far pointers.

C.8 Registers

C.8.1 Availability of Registers

The extent to which objects can actually be placed in registers by use of the register storage-class specifier (§3.5.1)

Two registers, SI and DI, are available in Microsoft C. Register variables with a type that has 16 bits may be allocated in these registers.

C.9 Structures, Unions, Enumerations, and Bit Fields

C.9.1 Improper Access to a Union

A member of a union object is accessed using a member of a different type (§3.3.2.3)

If a union of two types is declared and one value is stored, but the union is accessed with the other type, the results are unreliable.

For example, a union of **float** and **int** is declared. A **float** value is stored, but the program later accesses the value as an **int**. In such a situation, the value would depend on the internal storage of **float** values. The integer value would not be reliable.

C.9.2 Sign of Bit Fields

Whether a "plain" int field is treated as a signed int bit field or as an unsigned int bit field (§3.5.2.1)

Bit fields can be signed or unsigned. Plain bit fields are treated as signed.

C.9.3 Storage of Bit Fields

The order of allocation of bit fields within an int (§3.5.2.1)

Bit fields are allocated within a 16-bit integer from least-significant to most-significant bit. In the following code,

```
struct mybitfields
{
    unsigned a : 4;
    unsigned b : 5;
    unsigned c : 7;
} test;

void main( void )
{
    test.a = 2;
    test.b = 31;
    test.c = 0;
}
```

the bits would be arranged as follows:

```
00000001 11110010
cccccccb bbbbaaaa
```

Since the 80*x*86 processors store the low byte of integer values before the high byte, the integer 0x01F2 above would be stored in physical memory as 0xF2 followed by 0x01.

C.9.4 Alignment of Bit Fields

Whether a bit field can straddle a storage-unit boundary (§3.5.2.1)

Bit fields default to size **short**, which can cross a byte boundary (see Section C.9.3 above) but not a 16-bit boundary. If the size and location of a bit field would cause it to overflow the current integer, the field is moved to the beginning of the next available integer.

If a bit field is declared as a **long**, it can hold up to 32 bits.

In either case, an individual field cannot cross a 16- or 32-bit boundary.

C.9.5 The enum Type

The integer type chosen to represent the values of an enumeration type (§3.5.2.2)

A variable declared as **enum** is a signed short integer.

C.10 Qualifiers

C.10.1 Access to Volatile Objects

What constitutes an access to an object that has volatile-qualified type (§3.5.3)

Any reference to a volatile-qualified type is an access.

C.11 Declarators

C.11.1 Maximum Number

The maximum number of declarators that can modify an arithmetic, structure, or union type (§3.5.4)

Microsoft C does not limit the number of declarators. The number is limited only by available memory.

C.12 Statements

C.12.1 Limits on Switch Statements

The maximum number of case values in a switch statement (§3.6.4.2)

Microsoft C does not limit the number of **case** values in a **switch** statement. The number is limited only by available memory.

C.13 Preprocessing Directives

C.13.1 Character Constants and Conditional Inclusion

Whether the value of a single-character character constant in a constant expression that controls conditional inclusion matches the value of the same character constant in the execution character set. Whether such a character constant can have a negative value (§3.8.1)

The character set used in preprocessor statements is the same as the execution character set. The preprocessor recognizes negative character values.

C.13.2 Including Bracketed File Names

The method for locating includable source files (§3.8.2)

The preprocessor first searches the directories specified by the CL option /I. If the /I option is not present or if it fails, the preprocessor uses the INCLUDE environment variable to find any include files within angle brackets. If more than one directory appears as part of the /I option or within the INCLUDE variable, the preprocessor searches them in the order they appear.

For example, the command

```
CL /ID:\MSC\INCLUDE MYPROG.C
```

causes the preprocessor to search the directory D:\MSC\INCLUDE for include files such as STDIO.H.

The commands

```
SET INCLUDE = D:\MSC\INCLUDE
CL MYPROG.C
```

have a similar effect.

If both sets of searches fail, a fatal error is generated.

C.13.3 Including Quoted File Names

The support for quoted names for includable source files (§3.8.2)

If the file name is fully specified, with a path that includes a colon (for example, F:\C6\SPECIAL\INCL\ORANGE.H), the preprocessor follows the path.

If the file name is not fully specified, the preprocessor searches the directory of the file that included it. If the file is not found there, the preprocessor searches the parent directory, the parent's parent, and so on, terminating with the root directory.

If the include file is not found in any of those directories, the rules for bracketed file names apply.

C.13.4 Character Sequences

The mapping of source file character sequences (§3.8.2)

Preprocessor statements use the same character set as source file statements with the exception that escape sequences are not supported.

Thus, to specify a path for an include file, use only one backslash:

```
#include "path1\path2\myfile"
```

Within source code, two backslashes are necessary:

```
fil = fopen( "path1\\path2\\myfile", "rt" );
```

C.13.5 Pragmas

The behavior on each recognized #pragma directive (§3.8.6)

The following pragmas are defined in the *Microsoft C Reference*:

#pragma alloc_text	#pragma optimize
#pragma check_pointer	#pragma pack
#pragma check_stack	#pragma page
#pragma comment	#pragma pagesize
#pragma function	#pragma same_seg
#pragma intrinsic	#pragma skip
#pragma linesize	#pragma subtitle
#pragma loop_opt	#pragma title
#pragma message	

C.13.6 Default Date and Time

The definitions for _DATE_ and _TIME_ when, respectively, the date and time of translation are not available (§3.8.8)

When a hardware clock is not accessible, the default values for _DATE_ and _TIME_ are Friday, May 3, 1957 and 5:00 PM.

C.14 Library Functions

C.14.1 NULL Macro

The null pointer constant to which the macro NULL expands (§4.1.5)

Several include files define the NULL macro as `((void *)0)`.

C.14.2 Diagnostic Printed by the assert Function

The diagnostic printed by and the termination behavior of the assert function (§4.2)

The **assert** function prints a diagnostic message and calls the abort routine if the expression is false (0). The diagnostic message has the form

Assertion failed: [*expression*], file [*filename*], line [*linenumber*]

where *filename* is the name of the source file and *linenumber* is the line number of the assertion that failed in the source file. No action is taken if *expression* is true (nonzero).

C.14.3 Character Testing

The sets of characters tested for by the isalnum, isalpha, iscntrl, islower, isprint, and isupper functions (§4.3.1)

Function	Tests For
isalnum	Characters 0–9, A–Z, a–z ASCII 48–57, 65–90, 97–122
isalpha	Characters A–Z, a–z ASCII 65–90, 97–122
iscntrl	ASCII 0–31, 127
islower	Characters a–z ASCII 97–122
isprint	Characters A–Z, a–z, 0–9, punctuation, space ASCII 32–126
isupper	Characters A–Z ASCII 65–90

C.14.4 Domain Errors

The values returned by the mathematics functions on domain errors (§4.5.1)

The ERRNO.H file defines the domain error constant EDOM as 33.

C.14.5 Underflow of Floating-Point Values

Whether the mathematics functions set the integer expression errno to the value of the macro ERANGE on underflow range errors (§4.5.1)

A floating-point underflow does not set the expression **errno** to ERANGE. When a value approaches zero and eventually underflows, the value is set to zero.

C.14.6 The fmod Function

Whether a domain error occurs or zero is returned when the fmod function has a second argument of zero (§4.5.6.4)

When the **fmod** function has a second argument of zero, the function returns zero.

C.14.7 The signal Function

The set of signals for the signal function (§4.7.1.1)

The first argument passed to **signal** must be one of the symbolic constants listed below. The constants are defined in SIGNAL.H. Also listed is the operating mode support for each signal.

Signal Argument	Description
SIGABRT	Abnormal termination (real and protected mode).
SIGBREAK	CTRL+BREAK signal. Terminates the calling program (protected mode only).
SIGFPE	Floating-point error, such as overflow, division by zero, or invalid operation. Terminates the calling program (real and protected mode).
SIGILL	Illegal instruction. Terminates the calling program (protected mode only).
SIGINT	CTRL+C interrupt. Issues INT 23H (real and protected mode).

SIGSEGV   Illegal storage access. Not generated by DOS or OS/2, but supported for ANSI compatibility. Terminates the calling program (real and protected mode).

SIGTERM   Termination request sent to the program. Not generated by DOS or OS/2, but supported for ANSI compatibility. Terminates the calling program (real and protected mode).

SIGUSR1   OS/2 process flag A (protected mode only).

SIGUSR2   OS/2 process flag B (protected mode only).

SIGUSR3   OS/2 process flag C (protected mode only).

C.14.8 Default Signals

If the equivalent of signal (sig, SIG_DFL) is not executed prior to the call of a signal handler, the blocking of the signal that is performed (§4.7.1.1)

Signals are set to their default status when a program begins running.

C.14.9 The SIGILL Signal

Whether the default handling is reset if the SIGILL signal is received by a handler specified to the signal function (§4.7.1.1)

The SIGILL signal applies to OS/2 applications only. When SIGILL is received, the signal handling is not reset to the default SIG_DFL.

C.14.10 Terminating Newline Characters

Whether the last line of a text stream requires a terminating newline character (§4.9.2)

Stream functions recognize either newline or end-of-file as the terminating character for a line.

C.14.11 Blank Lines

Whether space characters that are written out to a text stream immediately before a newline character appear when read in (§4.9.2)

Space characters are preserved.

C.14.12 Null Characters

The number of null characters that can be appended to data written to a binary stream (§4.9.2)

Any number of null characters can be appended to a binary stream.

C.14.13 File Position in Append Mode

Whether the file position indicator of an append mode stream is initially positioned at the beginning or end of the file (§4.9.3)

When a file is opened in append mode, the file position indicator initially points to the end of the file.

C.14.14 Truncation of Text Files

Whether a write on a text stream causes the associated file to be truncated beyond that point (§4.9.3)

Writing to a text stream does not truncate the file beyond that point.

C.14.15 File Buffering

The characteristics of file buffering (§4.9.3)

Disk files accessed through standard I/O functions are fully buffered. By default, the buffer holds 512 bytes. Some of the low-level DOS and BIOS functions (all of which are non-ANSI) are unbuffered.

C.14.16 Zero-Length Files

Whether a zero-length file actually exists (§4.9.3)

Files with a length of zero are permitted.

C.14.17 File Names

The rules for composing valid file names (§4.9.3)

A file specification can include an optional drive letter (always followed by a colon), a series of optional directory names (separated by backslashes), and a file name.

File names and directory names can contain up to eight characters followed by a period and a three-character extension. Case is ignored. The wild-card characters * and ? are not permitted within the name or extension.

C.14.18 File Access Limits

Whether the same file can be open multiple times (§4.9.3)

Opening a file that is already open is not permitted.

C.14.19 Deleting Open Files

The effect of the remove function on an open file (§4.9.4.1)

The **remove** function deletes a file, even if the file is open.

C.14.20 Renaming with a Name that Exists

The effect if a file with the new name exists prior to a call to the rename function (§4.9.4.2)

If you attempt to rename a file using a name that exists, the **rename** function fails and returns an error code.

C.14.21 Printing Pointer Values

The output for %p conversion in the fprintf function (§4.9.6.1)

Microsoft C supports three types of pointer conversions: **%p** (a pointer), **%lp** (a 32-bit far pointer), and **%hp** (a 16-bit near pointer).

The **fprintf** function produces hexadecimal values of the form *XXXX* (an offset) for near pointers or *XXXX:XXXX* (a segment plus an offset, separated by a colon) for far pointers. The output for **%p** depends on the memory model in use.

C.14.22 Reading Pointer Values

The input for %p conversion in the fscanf function (§4.9.6.2)

When the **%p** format character is specified, the **fscanf** function converts pointers from hexadecimal ASCII values into the correct address.

C.14.23 Reading Ranges

The interpretation of a dash (–) character that is neither the first nor the last character in the scanlist for % [conversion in the fscanf function (§4.9.6.2)

The following line

```
fscanf( fileptr, "%[A-Z]", strptr );
```

reads any number of characters in the range A–Z into the string to which strptr points.

C.14.24 File Position Errors

The value to which the macro errno is set by the fgetpos or ftell function on failure (§4.9.9.1, 4.9.9.4)

When **fgetpos** or **ftell** fails, **errno** is set to the manifest constant **EINVAL** if the position is invalid or **EBADF** if the file number is bad. The constants are defined in ERRNO.H.

C.14.25 *Messages Generated by the perror Function*

The messages generated by the perror function (§4.9.10.4)

The **perror** function generates these messages:

```
0   Error 0
1
2   No such file or directory
3
4
5
6
7   Arg list too long
8   Exec format error
9   Bad file number
10
11
12  Not enough core
13  Permission denied
14
15
16
17  File exists
18  Cross-device link
19
20
21
22  Invalid argument
23
24  Too many open files
25
26
27
28  No space left on device
29
30
31
32
33  Math argument
34  Result too large
35
36  Resource deadlock would occur
```

C.14.26 *Allocating Zero Memory*

The behavior of the calloc, malloc, or realloc function if the size requested is zero (§4.10.3)

The **calloc**, **malloc**, and **realloc** functions accept zero as an argument. No actual memory is allocated, but the memory size can be modified later by **realloc**.

C.14.27 The abort Function

The behavior of the abort function with regard to open and temporary files (§4.10.4.1)

The **abort** function does not close files that are open or temporary. It does not flush stream buffers.

C.14.28 The atexit Function

The status returned by the atexit function if the value of the argument is other than zero, EXIT_SUCCESS, or EXIT_FAILURE (§4.10.4.3r)

The **atexit** function returns zero if successful, or a nonzero value if unsuccessful.

C.14.29 Environment Names

The set of environment names and the method for altering the environment list used by the getenv function (§4.10.4.4)

The set of environment names is unlimited.

To change environment variables from within a C program, call the **putenv** function. To change environment variables from the DOS command line, use the SET command (for example, SET LIB = D:\LIBS).

Environment variables exist only as long as their host copy of DOS is running. For example, the line

```
system( "SET LIB = D:\LIBS" );
```

would run a copy of DOS, set the environment variable LIB, and return to the C program, exiting the secondary copy of DOS. Exiting that copy of DOS removes the temporary environment variable LIB.

Likewise, changes made by the **putenv** function last only until the program ends.

C.14.30 The system Function

The contents and mode of execution of the string by the system function (§4.10.4.5)

The **system** function executes an internal DOS or OS/2 command, or an EXE, COM, or BAT file from within a C program rather than from the command line.

It examines the COMSPEC environment variable to find the command interpreter, which is typically COMMAND.COM in DOS or CMD.EXE in OS/2. The **system** function then passes the argument string to the command interpreter.

C.14.31 *The strerror Function*

The contents of the error message strings returned by the strerror function (§4.11.6.2)

The **strerror** function generates these messages:

```
0    Error 0
1
2    No such file or directory
3
4
5
6
7    Arg list too long
8    Exec format error
9    Bad file number
10
11
12   Not enough core
13   Permission denied
14
15
16
17   File exists
18   Cross-device link
19
20
21
22   Invalid argument
23
24   Too many open files
25
26
27
28   No space left on device
29
30
31
32
33   Math argument
34   Result too large
35
36   Resource deadlock would occur
```

C.14.32 The Time Zone

The local time zone and Daylight Saving Time (§4.12.1)

The local time zone is Pacific Standard Time. Microsoft C supports Daylight Saving Time.

C.14.33 The clock Function

The era for the clock function (§4.12.2.1)

The **clock** function's era begins (with a value of 0) when the C program starts to execute. It returns times measured in 1/1000th seconds.

Index

I

MICROSOFT PRODUCT ASSISTANCE REQUEST

Microsoft Product Support Services - Phone (206) 454-2030

Instructions

When you need assistance with a Microsoft product, call our Product Support Services group at (206) 454-2030. So that we can answer your question as quickly as possible, please gather all information that applies to your problem. Note or print out any on-screen messages you get when the problem occurs. Have your manual and product disks close at hand and have all the information requested on this form available when you call.

Diagnosing a Problem

So that we can assist you more effectively, please be prepared to answer the following questions regarding your problem, your software, and your hardware.

1. Can you reproduce the problem?
   ❏ yes   ❏ no

2. Does the problem occur with another copy of the original disk of your Microsoft Software?
   ❏ yes   ❏ no

3. Does the problem occur with another system (if available)?
   ❏ yes   ❏ no

4. If you were running other windowing or memory-resident software at the same time, does the problem also occur when you don't use the other software?
   ❏ yes   ❏ no

Product

_____

Product name

_____   _____

Version Number   Registration Number

Software
Operating System

_____

Name/Version number

Windowing Environment

If you were running Microsoft Windows or another windowing environment, give name and number of windowing software:

_____

CD ROM Software

_____

Name/Version number

Other Software

Name/Version number of any other software you were running when problem occurred, including memory-resident software (such as keyboard enhancers or print spoolers):

_____

_____

Hardware

So that we can assist you more effectively, please be prepared to answer the following questions regarding your problem, your software, and your hardware.

Computer

_____   _____
Manufacturer/model   Total memory

Floppy-disk drives
Number: ❏ 1 ❏ 2 ❏ Other
Size: ❏ 3 1/2" ❏ 5 1/4"
Number of Sides: ❏ 1 ❏ 2
Density: ❏ Single ❏ Double ❏ Quad
Capacity:
5 1/4": ❏ 160K ❏ 360K ❏ 1.2 megabytes
3 1/2": ❏ 360K ❏ 400K ❏ 720K ❏ 800K
           ❏ 1.4 megabytes

System Memory

_____   _____
Manufacturer/model   Total memory
(If using DOS, you can run CHKDSK to determine the amount of memory available. If using Apple Macintosh Finder, select "About The Finder..." from the Apple menu to determine the amount of memory available.)

Peripherals
Hard Disk

_____   _____
Manufacturer/model   Capacity(megabyte)

Printer/Plotter

_____
Manufacturer/model

❏ Serial   ❏ Parallel

Printer peripherals, such as font cartridges, downloadable fonts, sheet feeders:

_____

_____

Mouse
Microsoft Mouse: ❏ Bus ❏ Serial ❏ InPort™
❏ Other

_____
Manufacturer/model

Boards
❏ Add-on RAM board

_____
Manufacturer/model

❏ Graphics-adapter board

_____
Manufacturer/model

❏ Other boards installed

_____
Manufacturer/model

Modem

_____
Manufacturer/model

CD ROM Player

_____
Manufacturer/model

Version of Microsoft MS-DOS® CD ROM Extensions:

_____

Network
Is your system part of a network? ❏ Yes ❏ No

_____
Manufacturer/model

What hardware and software does your network use?

_____

_____

_____